THE UPPER ROOM

Disciplines

2017

CANOEING THE MOUNTHIN

UPPER
ROOM BOOKS®
NASHVILLE

AN OUTLINE FOR SMALL-GROUP USE OF DISCIPLINES

Here is a simple plan for a one-hour, weekly group meeting based on reading *Disciplines*. One person may act as convener every week, or the role can rotate among group members. You may want to light a white Christ candle each week to signal the beginning of your time together.

OPENING

Convener: Let us come into the presence of God.

Others: Lord Jesus Christ, thank you for being with us. Let us hear your word to us as we speak to one another.

SCRIPTURE

Convener reads the scripture suggested for that day in *Disciplines*. After a one- or two-minute silence, convener asks: What did you hear God saying to you in this passage? What response does this call for? (Group members respond in turn or as led.)

REFLECTION

- What scripture passage(s) and meditation(s) from this week was (were) particularly meaningful for you? Why? (Group members respond in turn or as led.)
- What actions were you nudged to take in response to the week's meditations? (Group members respond in turn or as led.)
- Where were you challenged in your discipleship this week? How did you respond to the challenge? (Group members respond in turn or as led.)

PRAYING TOGETHER

Convener says: Based on today's discussion, what people and situations do you want us to pray for now and in the coming week? Convener or other volunteer then prays about the concerns named.

DEPARTING

Convener says: Let us go in peace to serve God and our neighbors in all that we do.

Adapted from *The Upper Room* daily devotional guide, January–February 2001. © 2000 The Upper Room. Used by permission.

CONTENTS

An Outline for Small-Group Use of *Disciplines* 3

Foreword 11
Shawn Bakker

January 1 13
The Lord Provides
Danny Wright

January 2–8 15
Sensing the Sacred in a New Year
Whitney R. Simpson

January 9–15 23
Called to Faithful Service
Cynthia B. Astle

January 16–22 31
No Need to Fear
Alina Kanaski

January 23–29 39
Who Are We Becoming in Christ?
Harriett Jane Olson

January 30–February 5 47
Walking in the Light
W. Robert Abstein

February 6–12 55
Saying Yes to Life
Abby Thornton Hailey

February 13–19 63
Meditations on Holiness
Jason E. Vickers

February 20–26 71
Mountaintop Experiences
Paul Wesley Chilcote

February 27–March 5 79
Living into Lent
Roberta Bondi

March 6–12 87
Walking by Faith, Not by Sight
Dan R. Dick

March 13–19 95
Not Again!
Sharon G. Austin

March 20–26 103
Seeing, Feeling, Acting
Larry J. Peacock

March 27–April 2 111
Seeing with the Eyes of God
Deirdre Good

April 3–9 119
God's Unfailing Love
Barry Sloan

April 10–16 127
Not What We Expected
Emily Anderson

April 17–23 135
Life in Light of the Resurrection
Deborah van Deusen Hunsinger

April 24–30 143
Lord and Messiah
Matthew Croasmun

May 1–7 151
Led by the Divine Shepherd
Diane Luton Blum

May 8–14 159
Who Are Those Guys?
Bradford Bosworth

May 15–21 167
Following Christ in All Circumstances
Judy Wooldridge

May 22–28 175
In the Power of the Spirit
Joyce Hollyday

May 29– June 4 183
The Coming of the Holy Spirit
Bronson C. Davis

June 5–11 191
Grace for God's Community
Elaine Eberhart

June 12–18 199
Self-Emptying Power
Niall McKay

June 19–25 207
Intimacy, Promise, and Threat
Sharonne Price

June 26–July 2 215
Hard Conversations
Brian McCaffrey

July 3–9 223
Trust in God's Leading
Marysol Diaz

July 10–16 231
The Promise and Work of God's Word
John Adcox

July 17–23 239
Unexpected Grace
Elmer Lavastida Alfonso

July 24–30 247
Treasures from God
Chris Folmsbee

July 31–August 6 255
Seeking God's Presence
Emily M. Akin

August 7–13 263
Faith through Discomfort
Dan Wunderlich

August 14–20 271
Reconciling Love
Karla Kincannon

August 21–27 279
Courageous Faith through Obedience
Bo Prosser

August 28–September 3 287
The Challenge in the Call
Gennifer Benjamin Brooks

September 4–10 295
Searching the Scriptures
Mark H. Stephenson

September 11–17 303
The Ever-Present God
Regina Franklin-Basye

September 18–24 311
Presence and Provision
Hakyoung Cho Kim

September 25—October 1 321
Fearlessly Faithful
Terry Shillington

October 2–8 329
God's Grace in Life's Disorder
Thomas Edward Frank

October 9–15 337
Supplicate, Sing, and See
Wen-Ling Lai

October 16–22 345
Show Me Your Ways
Arthur McClanahan

October 23–29 353
Redeem the Time
Pat Handlson

October 30–November 5 361
The Word at Work in You
Will Willimon

November 6–12 369
Listen to the Teachings
George Hovaness Donigian

November 13–19 377
Multiplying Mercy in Many Forms
Donna Claycomb Sokol

November 20–26 385
The God Who Searches for Us
Joe E. Pennel Jr.

November 27–December 3 393

Longing for Hope

Ginger E. Gaines-Cirelli

December 4–10. 401

Faithful Wilderness Waiting

Frank Rogers Jr.

December 11–17. 409

The Shape of Advent Joy

Beth Ludlum

December 18–24. 417

Imagine!

Stephen Bauman

December 25–31. 425

Love Is Born

Becca Stevens and Don Welch

The Revised Common Lectionary for 2017 433

A Guide to Daily Prayer 439

FOREWORD

My four-year-old daughter, Savannah, has been struggling to stop sucking her thumb. She began the habit while she was in utero. It has been with her, quite literally, since her beginning. So it is no wonder to me that despite her working hard for over six months to create new patterns of behavior, she returns to her old ways seemingly without thinking. Whenever an environmental cue triggers her need for comfort, she reflexively turns to her thumb and sucks it until a different cue calls her attention to it. It is as though something deep within her overrules any conscious choice she has in the matter. I have often wondered whether the practice was encoded in her very being. And I recently learned that many cognitive scientists would agree that my rather rough analogy is not too far from the truth.

In the 1990s, scientists affiliated with the Brain and Cognitive Sciences department at the Massachusetts Institute of Technology discovered that a small mass of tissue buried deep in the center of the brain plays a key role in habit formation. Known as the basal ganglia, this ancient set of brain structures converts sequences of action into cognitive patterns. As we go about our days, our basal ganglia assemble individual actions into chunks of memory that we can recall later with little to no effort. This process of cognitive storage allows our brain to conserve energy. As we think less and less about basic behaviors—such as the discrete actions involved in walking, talking, or eating—we can devote more mental energy to the higher-order tasks that drive human and technological development. Habits free us to engage the world more fully.

This is the logic of *The Upper Room Disciplines.* As we read, study, and pray with others each day, we can gain freedom to devote ourselves more fully to steady growth in love of God and neighbor. Our repeated listening for the divine and the deepest desires of our neighbors can empower us to discern God's work in this noisy world. Our disciplined study of Christian scripture can help us find our place in God's creative goodness. And all this should come naturally to us, created as we are in the image of God. But life has a way of alienating us from our sacred roots.

As an ordained clergywoman and the executive publisher of The Upper Room, I have often felt compelled to encourage people to follow Paul's admonition to the Thessalonians: "Pray without ceasing" (5:17). As a mother of three young children and a wife employed full-time, however, I have often wondered at the same time whether such a goal defies reason. I have made commitments to my family, friends, and colleagues that I cannot abandon in order to devote myself solely to prayer. I have not been called to the ordered life of a cloistered monastic. Nonetheless, my experience with Savannah has taught me that I *can* attain a life of unceasing prayer. I simply must work each day to awaken what was encoded in my very being before I was born.

At its root, Christian spiritual formation is the lifelong process by which the Holy Spirit reveals the image of Christ hidden within each of us. A disciplined search for God frees us to manifest the Holy Spirit's proclamation of what all humans have known since their beginnings: God has created us for love. May we each find a time and a place to habituate God's presence. Let us practice love in the company of God and, together, transform the world.

—SHAWN BAKKER
Executive Publisher, Upper Room Ministries

The Lord Provides

JANUARY 1, 2017 • DANNY WRIGHT

SCRIPTURE OVERVIEW: The scriptures that mark the new year offer a panorama of perspectives, from Ecclesiastes as a poetic musing on how life is measured out in seasons, to the vision in Revelation of what we commonly consider the end of time itself. Psalm 8 asks what the role is for humans in God's magnificent creation, and Matthew 25 gives us a sobering criterion for how that role might be judged. At the core of all these scriptures is a strong sense of God's presence, a loving steadfastness in which we can rest. [With only one day given, the writer has chosen to write on the Ecclesiastes passage; the other texts are listed in the readings at the back of the book.]

QUESTIONS AND SUGGESTIONS FOR REFLECTION

• Read Ecclesiastes 3:1-13. How will you celebrate this new year? What practices will you consider taking up in order to participate fully in God's future?

Associate minister, New Paradigm Christian Church, Broadripple area of Indianapolis, Indiana

NEW YEAR'S DAY

The time has come again, as old has gone and new has arrived. Some of us pray that this year will not be like the last, remembering only the pains, struggles, and losses of what often seemed, at best, the meaningless march of one incessant second after another. Some of us anticipate the new as our hearts beat to the sound of a different drum that guarantees a fresh melody that will forever change our symphony of existence.

This new day of promise offers sacred space that beckons us to leave the celebrations, forgo anxieties, and simply rest in the thought that God has made everything beautiful and appropriate in its time. Life is, has, and will be experienced somewhere in the range of this list of fourteen pairs of opposites in Ecclesiastes 3 that briefly define the totality of human experience.

The Teacher reminds us that God has placed eternity in our hearts. Therefore, we realize that what we see is not all there is. We search for purpose and reason, yet find ourselves unable to grasp it all. The advice we receive for moving forward in these coming seconds, minutes, and hours that will too quickly become days, months, and another year is this: rejoice and do good. We are to eat and drink and find pleasure in our work because that is God's gift to us.

We often make it too complicated. We have been blessed to "rejoice always, pray without ceasing, give thanks in all circumstances" (1 Thess. 5:16-18), while letting our good works point others to the God who meets us on every pole and every point in between. Our God is in the business of creating beauty.

May we rejoice, do good, and recognize the beauty regardless of our place on the continuum of existence.

Sensing the Sacred in a New Year

JANUARY 2–8, 2017 • WHITNEY R. SIMPSON

SCRIPTURE OVERVIEW: Many will read the Isaiah text and identify the servant with Jesus, the one God enables to do the work of justice and transformation. The psalm announces the glory of God, a king powerful over the turbulence of nature and whose voice is a transcendent revelation. Matthew's story of Jesus' baptism joins the themes of servant and king. The baptism inaugurates Jesus' ministry in which he proclaims God's righteousness. Peter's speech in Acts reminds us that Jesus' baptism carries with it the promise of baptism in the Spirit.

QUESTIONS AND SUGGESTIONS FOR REFLECTION

- Read Isaiah 42:1-9. In this new year, what promises of God do you want to breathe in?
- Read Psalm 29. When the storms of life rage, how do you listen for God's promptings?
- Read Acts 10:34-43. To whom do you need to proclaim the promises of Jesus Christ?
- Read Matthew 3:13-17. How does your understanding of your own baptism encourage you to live as an obedient child of God?

Retreat leader, spiritual director, and Holy Yoga instructor; pursued professional certification in Spiritual Formation at Garrett-Evangelical Theological Seminary

The start of a new year provides an opportunity for new beginnings—new calendar pages, new food plans, new exercise routines, new budgeting goals. Many of us embrace a fairly common practice of realigning goals at the start of each year. We may need a reset to promote positive change, but it does not take a crisp calendar page or the latest food plan to receive new life, a fresh beginning. Each breath reminds us of the new life God offers.

Breathing is the only autonomous body system that we can control. While our breathing will continue without controlled effort, we can consciously change *how* we breathe. Take a deep breath right now. Pause your reading, and breathe deeply and fully. Breathe deep into your lungs, allowing your chest to expand; then exhale fully. Repeat this for five breaths.

In verse 5 we can translate the Hebrew word for breath as "life" or "spirit." Stop and breathe in again. As you inhale, imagine that you are breathing in God's Spirit, filling your lungs to capacity with God's gracious gift of life.

Verses 5-7 remind us that God grants breath for a purpose: to bring justice—"a light to the nations, to open the eyes that are blind, to bring out the prisoners from the dungeon. . . ." Breath/life/spirit comes with an intentionality. How will you engage each breath as an opportunity to live for your Creator this year?

God extends glory and blessing and promises new things. Breathe in those promises for yourself. What "new things" does God declare to you as you slow down and pay attention to your own breath of life? Recognizing the sacredness of each breath, breathe more deeply in the days to come—live with purpose the life of unique servanthood to which God calls you.

Breath of Life, open me to the new things you long to foster through my life as your servant this year. May I make the most of each breath. Amen.

God longs to offer us peace, but we must listen. Pause for a moment and listen. What do you hear? If scripture included sound effects, the voice of the Lord in this passage might sound like a raging thunderstorm. Think of a time when you physically found yourself amid a thundering storm. Now consider a time in your life when circumstances led you through what felt like a never-ending storm.

Just as in an outdoor storm, we often have no idea when the thunderous times of life may come or when they will pass on by. During the stormy seasons in my own life, I have difficulty sensing what is taking place beyond the lightning and thunder. In those times, I sometimes find it hard to hear what God desires that I hear, even if it is loud and clear.

The majestic and powerful voice of God in this psalm calls the people to praise. But how do we praise God in a storm of breaking cedars and flames of fire? Amid the whirling oaks and the bare forest, how do we offer our praise? The Common English Bible translates verse 2 in this way, "Bow down to the LORD in holy splendor!"

Many scriptures address the matter of prayer postures, here by bowing down. Maybe you have bowed your head or brought your hands to prayer posture at your heart. Today I invite you to find a safe space and physically bow down to the Lord with your entire body. Yes, bow on your knees in your living room, office, bedroom, or even your closet floor. Offer your entire body in prayer, worshiping your Creator. Then listen. God's voice offers strength and blessing. With each exhalation, let the noise of the world fall away. Then you may join those in God's temple as they cry, "Glory!"

Lord, may I praise you with my whole being. In both quiet and stormy times, may I receive your sacred gifts of strength and peace. Amen.

Leading others to listen with their bodies by using the tools of spiritual direction and yoga has given me the opportunity to work with individuals of various religious backgrounds, ages, shapes, and sizes. Each of our stories and our bodies offers varying degrees of flexibility. One factor that causes persons to hesitate when exploring the body/spirit relationship comes in their perception of their physical ability. Fortunately, a life with Christ has nothing to do with our physical abilities or lack thereof.

In today's reading, Peter speaks to the Gentiles, proclaiming the good news of Jesus Christ to Cornelius, his family, and friends. Peter, an unlikely messenger, delivers a message that Cornelius and his household fully embrace. Peter tells them of Jesus' baptism by John and Jesus' ministry of healing in Judea and Jerusalem. Though put to death, Jesus is raised to life on the third day. Peter preaches the amazing testimony that everyone who believes in Christ receives forgiveness. God's accessibility hinges on accepting the miracle of transformed lives—not on faith background, social status, geographical location, gender, ethnicity—and especially not on an ability to touch our toes. Peter proclaimed the miracle of a life in Christ to the Gentiles; we hear that miracle proclaimed today.

Later verses in this passage allow us to witness the descent of the Spirit on Cornelius and conclude with a water baptism. As we look toward the celebration of our Lord's baptism, we affirm that Jesus' baptism leads us to the miracle of a life in Christ. Do you believe Peter's message for your life today? Christ is for you. In what ways is he your "Lord of all"?

Lord of all, thank you for the baptism and resurrection of Jesus, which allows me to live a life focusing on your promises rather than on my own abilities. Amen.

Paul is privy to a secret! And while the secret has been around for time eternal, only within the present age has the secret been made known; "it has now been revealed to [Christ's] holy apostles and prophets by the Spirit." The Gentiles and Jews are fellow heirs in the promise of Jesus Christ—all one body.

Paul, though "the very least of all the saints," proclaims the meaning of God's mystery. He conveys to the Gentiles the amazing abundance of God's grace and affirms God's eternal purpose in bringing all people to Christ. The mystery breaks free, moving from darkness to light for the world as Paul proclaims that we are *all* heirs—members of the body of Christ and recipients of the promises of Jesus Christ.

As people of God, we acknowledge Jesus as the revelation of God and the answer for our hurting world. How can we proclaim this good news and share it with those who may need to hear? It starts within us, just as it started within Paul. This year, consider how you will shine the truth of Christ's promise as light in the dark places.

Find a dimly lit place, and light a candle. Watch the flame begin to spread light in the darkness. Invite your entire being into receiving the gift of God's revelation for all, Jesus. Watch the flame flicker; listen to the wick burn; smell the wax or match; and breathe in the promise of the light that *you* are part of the body of Christ. You are called to proclaim this mystery. This year choose to shine; be bold; be confident.

Creator, give me boldness and confidence to shine your light for all the world to see. May I sense the sacredness of the life of servanthood to which I am called and participate in the mission to make your wisdom known in the world. Amen.

EPIPHANY

Epiphany concludes the Christmas season on the Christian calendar. The word *epiphany* means to "show" or "reveal." As the magi brought gifts revealing and celebrating Jesus, the season of Epiphany reminds us of our sacred role in revealing Christ to the world.

The star shone bright, revealing the way for the wise ones. We also require light to see where we are, where we have been, and where we are headed.

The glow of God's glory illumines Israel, the light to the nations. The thick darkness will come, but God's glory will appear. Notice that God's glory in verses 1 and 2 "bookend" the darkness, overcome the darkness. And we then recall the words of John 1:5, "The light shines in the darkness, and the darkness did not overcome it." We as God's servants reflect the glow of God's glory to a world in need of light.

This week you have used your breath, ears, and eyes. Now will you engage your imagination for a moment? Envision God's light shining over you. Now picture that light radiating from you into the world. God called Israel to arise and shine. With that shining came prosperity—the wealth of other nations. From that prosperity the people brought gold and frankincense in praise of God, just as the wise ones offered the gifts of gold, frankincense, and myrrh in homage to the Christ child.

How do you reflect God's glory? What light can you offer the world in your praise of God? Francis of Assisi wrote, "All the darkness in the world cannot extinguish the light of a single candle." Each light matters.

Lord Jesus, thank you for being a light in our world. Show me today the ways in which I may share your light with others, revealing you to the world as the magi did so long ago. Amen.

We can hear the majesty of God's voice no matter the volume, but we must be willing to listen. During one of the loudest, most stressful, and chaotic moments of my life (while in an MRI machine undergoing a medical test on my brain), I heard the clearest whisper of a prayer and offered it back to God as a request. The whisper was not audible, but I made no mistake about whose voice it was. I still wonder if I heard the voice clearly that day because of my crisis or because nothing else distracted me. I could not escape the small space or loud noise of the machine in which I lay. Thankfully, God came through loud and clear, speaking a prayer I have clung to for a decade.

Psalm 29 opens with God's thundering, majestic, and powerful voice. It closes by inviting us to receive the gift of God's strength and peace (which may be easier at some times than others). Amid the noise and crisis in my own life, I cried out, acknowledging my need for God's strength and the gift of peace. God gave me this prayer: "Jesus, give me peace." I muttered those words in the form of a breath prayer on the scariest day of my then just thirty-one years. That prayer became synchronized with my breath, inhaling the name of Jesus and exhaling my request for peace in that dark, loud—yet sacred—space.

This psalm invites us as servants to acknowledge God's voice. No matter the circumstance or volume, our Lord longs to bless us with strength and peace. Slow down long enough to sense the sacred wherever you find yourself. God's prayer to me has become one I turn to often. May you breathe it in and receive the gift of God's strength and peace in this new year.

Inhale: Jesus,
Exhale: Give me peace.

BAPTISM OF THE LORD

Has anyone ever told you they are proud of you? My parents did a good job of modeling this behavior over the years. Even now in my adulthood they tell me how proud they are of my parenting skills, professional work, desire to give back, and willingness to grow as the person God created me to be. They are proud of me and tell me not for my ego but because I am their daughter and they love me.

Jesus receives heavenly confirmation after his baptism by John. Jesus has come from Galilee and requests that John baptize him. John hesitates, believing he is unworthy of this act. Yet Jesus convinces John. As Jesus comes up from the water, a voice from heaven speaks, the clouds part, and the Spirit descends on him from above. Unlike Mark and John, in Matthew's Gospel, all who are gathered hear the heavenly voice. And we who read this text listen in as well. Jesus is God's chosen and obedient son, baptized by John to fulfill all righteousness. The heavenly voice reminds us of our own naming and commissioning to obedience in our life with Christ.

Isaiah 42:1, which we read earlier in our week's reflections, connects to our Gospel reading today as a prophecy, "Here is my servant, whom I uphold, my chosen, in whom my soul delights; I have put my spirit upon him; he will bring forth justice to the nations." We as Christians affirm the fulfillment of Hebrew scriptures through God's sending of the Son.

Whether or not your earthly parents verbalized their pride, God offers new life in Christ and chooses us to live as obedient daughters and sons. May we revel in the knowledge that we are those in whom God's soul delights.

Thank you, Holy Spirit, for allowing me to hear you and be made new in you today. May I live out a life of obedience in Christ. Amen.

Called to Faithful Service

JANUARY 9–15, 2017 • CYNTHIA B. ASTLE

SCRIPTURE OVERVIEW: The theme of God's calling all believers to a life of ministry runs through all four of this week's scripture passages. We discover that God's call always requires a response! The Isaiah passage, one of the Servant Songs that points to Jesus, reminds us that God is the one who pursues and calls. The psalmist exemplifies the call to give witness when God shows up and is found to be faithful. In the opening of his letter to the church in Corinth, Paul reminds us of his own calling and then goes on to emphasize that all are called by God and set apart for ministry. And in John's Gospel, we receive an example of testifying to God's presence in our lives and the important calling of bringing others to Jesus.

QUESTIONS AND SUGGESTIONS FOR REFLECTION

- Read Isaiah 49:1-7. How has God taken the initiative to work in your life and call you to faith? What mission has God given you?
- Read Psalm 40:1-11. List the ways that God has been faithful to you in showing up and answering your prayers. How have you given witness to God's faithfulness?
- Read 1 Corinthians 1:1-9. What gifts has God given you to fulfill your calling to ministry?
- Read John 1:29-42. How might you cultivate the discipline of "mindfulness" in your spiritual life?

Member of St. Stephen United Methodist Church; a certified spiritual director; member of the Order of Saint Luke, an ecumenical monastic association

Allof us know what it's like not to be chosen. From our childhood days when we're chosen last or not at all for school yard games, a sense of inadequacy haunts us for failing to meet some human standard. Even when we succeed, that nagging internal voice tells us we aren't worthy.

Often when challenges confront us, we can remember only those times we've faltered or failed in life. By relying on our own abilities, we delude ourselves that we're unable to accomplish something extraordinary. But God knows better, and waits to reassure us.

This passage begins with testimony of a servant who seems to be Israel: "You are my servant, Israel, in whom I will be glorified," even while bearing a message from God to Israel (in verse 6). These verses confront the lie of unworthiness. Stunned by the knowledge that God has charged him with an urgent task—calling Israel back into relationship with God—the servant laments that his earthly experiences haven't prepared him for such an exalted charge. Yet, at some point he comes to the realization that only his identity in God matters, an identity that provides strength far beyond his human skills.

Today's passage reminds us that God sees us as spiritual beings. As such, we live most fully when we anchor ourselves in God. Who we are in God matters far more than anything we may achieve on our own. God empowers us with abilities to face life's challenges with strength, courage, and confidence.

We are God's chosen before we realize it! "The Lord called [us] before [we were] born." Having been hidden away like a sharp sword or polished arrow, we step forth to proclaim God's glory to the world.

O Holy One, grant me the wisdom to see myself as you see me—chosen. May I anchor myself in you so that my life reflects your glory. Amen.

Put yourself in the servant's place. First, God tells you that you have been chosen to lead the nation of Israel back to righteous living. Then God says you're not only to guide Israel but that your efforts and example will bring enlightenment to the whole world. How would you react?

Like many of us, the servant at first sees himself as unworthy of the great task God has set out for him. Then he realizes that his feelings of inadequacy aren't merely a falsely modest response. False modesty denies God's power to redeem human failings and to transform those failings into holiness. This "impostor sense" borders on sin because it separates us from our authentic identities as spiritual beings rooted in the Creator.

Once the servant embraces this enlightenment, God expands the holy task. To our contemporary eyes, God seems like a coach who urges an athlete on to greater feats. Thus the servant will guide not only Israel back to God; he will serve as "a light to the nations" so that all who encounter him or his story will turn toward God themselves.

In ancient texts, the word *salvation* carries a much broader, more inclusive meaning than merely the assurance of eternal life. In God's economy, salvation embraces all the spiritual and physical health and wholeness that makes human life a joyous, satisfying experience.

In verse 7, God speaks, confirming that the willingness of others to hear and affirm the words of the servant depends solely on God's faithfulness and choosing of the servant. Only God's choosing of him endows the lowly servant with significance. Each of us has a holy task to perform in God's quest for human salvation; we are chosen and empowered for that purpose.

O Holy One, grant me the urgent desire to learn your will for my life, and give me the faith to pursue what you have chosen for me. Amen.

The psalmist waits patiently. Then God acts on the psalmist's behalf: God inclines, hears, draws up, and sets feet on rock. The psalmist's response is one of joy. Wouldn't we be joyful at being chosen by God, being the object of God's attention? We like to feign an "aw, shucks" reaction to being singled out for some special task. False modesty compels us to deny the joy in being chosen. We may think it's unseemly to rejoice at our selection, but this reaction damages our relationship with God.

Denying the joy that comes from living day by day with God is a temptation we face. We tend to focus on the "shall nots" of our faith and to wallow in self-pity because we fail to live up to high standards. And we too often look down on those who can't contain their unabashed joy at knowing God.

The world tells us that happiness depends upon riches or fame. The psalmist says that joy gushes forth from loving relationships with God and one another. God gives the psalmist a "new song" that bears witness to the working of God in the psalmist's life. As a result of the psalmist's witness, "many will see and fear, and put their trust in the LORD."

God's chosen can be joyous even in the midst of sadness or oppression. Our joy does not depend upon our circumstances, for we live *beyond* our surroundings. God secures our steps and puts a "new song" in our mouths.

Considering the atmosphere of fear and hatred that has overshadowed our world in the early twenty-first century, perhaps our joyful testimony to the work of God in our lives is what the world most needs. We bear witness to an incomparable God whose wondrous deeds and thoughts toward us are manifold. What joy!

Exalted God, make me a channel of your joy to a fearful, worried world. Amen.

God acts, and the psalmist moves from exaltation to action. His happiness has given him insight and energy to become a witness for God to all he meets. Look at the words the psalmist uses to describe his experience of God's support: *deliverance, saving help, faithfulness,* and *salvation.* These words provide a sharp contrast with ideas about things and experiences that supposedly bring us happiness. The contrast gives us clues to the true nature of joy.

For example, the world tells us we *earn* our pleasures in the same way that some construed their burnt offerings and animal sacrifices as a way to gain favor with God. The psalmist affirms that he has made no sacrifice or offering; instead, God's law resides within his heart.

The world's pleasures can leave us uncomfortably stupefied or aching with emptiness. We may eat too much food, drink too many intoxicating beverages, or spend beyond our means. Even when we think we have it all, we may view our supposed sources of happiness with discouragement or despair.

The psalmist has discovered that friendship with God brings the kind of wholesome, fulfilling life that the Creator intends for us all. His joy at this insight fuels the psalmist's motivation to share his experience of God with others. The psalmist eagerly tells "the great congregation" how his relationship with God has changed his life for the better. He tells us that the joyful experience of God's saving mercy and grace isn't something we can keep to ourselves. With unrestrained lips, we tell others "the glad news of deliverance": God's steadfast love, faithfulness, and mercy will keep us safe forever.

Day by day, O God, may I tell those around me of my delight in living close to you. Amen.

God often chooses "unworthy" people to fulfill holy tasks. Moses killed an Egyptian. A younger son in a minor Hebrew clan, Gideon lacked any social status. One of only four women mentioned in Jesus' ancestral lineage, Rahab was a prostitute. As a Pharisee, Paul persecuted the early Christians. It confounds our human sense of righteousness that God deliberately calls flawed people for sacred work!

In today's scripture, notice how frequently some form of the word *called* appears. Paul describes himself as "called to be an apostle of Christ Jesus." He identifies the members of the church at Corinth as "those who are sanctified in Christ Jesus, called to be saints." We may wonder what kind of people these Corinthian saints were. Did they dress in rags or fine clothes? Did they give a little to the church, or did they put in all they had? Did they seek front seats to pray sanctimoniously before the crowd, or did they stand in the back and plead for God's mercy?

In all likelihood, the church at Corinth held a mixture of all these kinds of people and more. Since scholars believe this letter to have been written within thirty years of Jesus' death, the church there probably looked a lot like the people with whom Jesus spent time.

So how does such a diverse and "flawed" group of people carry out their holy task? Paul affirms that these saints "are not lacking in any spiritual gift." The cohesive nature of this community of saints hinges on their being called to a vocation as Christians. God calls the unflawed and the flawed, the saints and the sinners into "the fellowship of . . . Jesus Christ our Lord." May we affirm our calling, for holy tasks await.

Jesus, son of David, be merciful to me, a sinner. May I live as your saint, available to serve your holy purposes. Amen.

John the Baptist's ascetic practices of self-discipline and prayer distinguish him as one who sought union with God. His intimacy with God leads to his discernment of being chosen for a holy task: to prepare the way for "a man who ranks ahead of me because he was before me."

In the Fourth Gospel, Jesus' baptism—with its descent of the Spirit on Jesus—identifies Jesus as the one for whom John has waited. In this Gospel, we read of no kinship with Jesus or foreknowledge of Jesus by John. Twice in this passage John states, "I myself did not know him."

So John steps onto the stage as narrator to report the account of Jesus' baptism and its significance: "I myself have seen and have testified that this is the Son of God." We cannot overemphasize the importance of John's testimony. By the time Jesus begins his public ministry, John has many followers. He has become well known because of his fervent preaching of repentance for sin. Furthermore, John gives people a way to move closer to God through a baptism that combined symbolic cleansing from sin with anointing for holy living.

Thus when Jesus appears, John carries great spiritual authority with the people. His acknowledgment and endorsement of Jesus as the Lamb of God carries a lot of weight with his own followers and the general community. As we see in the next verses, John's testimony intrigues two of his disciples enough that they follow Jesus and study with him for the day.

Like John, we too can testify publicly to what we know about Jesus. We need not know the results; we simply rest assured that God will use it for good.

O Holy Mystery, give me vision to see you at work in the world and the courage to proclaim your presence. Amen.

Imagine yourself to be Andrew. Already a follower of John the Baptist, you pay close attention when your spiritual master, John, proclaims Jesus to be the Lamb of God. You and a companion follow Jesus, who invites you to "come and see" who he is. Convinced that Jesus really is the Messiah, you lose no time in bringing your brother Simon to meet him. Before you can formally introduce them, Jesus looks at your brother and gives him a new name! Andrew and his companions must have felt awestruck at this encounter. And to think it all happened because Andrew paid attention!

In spiritual direction, we call this kind of attention "mindfulness." It's a spiritual discipline that means paying attention to God's presence in a profound way. To cultivate mindfulness, we give our attention first to God. We develop a heightened state of focus in which our senses become attuned to the energy, the "aliveness" of God's marvelous creation that includes us.

Mindfulness can be considered the opposite of today's penchant for multitasking. Instead of trying to do many things all at once (often poorly), mindfulness calls us to focus first on who we are—spiritual beings in union with God. It's the contemporary expression of Jesus' invitation to "come and see." Through mindfulness, we "come" into God's presence through meditation; we "see" with our inner being; and then we take our awareness and our witness into the world.

Practiced with discipline, mindfulness enables us to respond to spiritual promptings as quickly as Andrew did when Jesus extended the invitation to know him better. Choosing mindfulness brings us closer to God and gives us the ability to seize our daily opportunities to invite someone to "come and see" what Jesus is like.

Holy God, keep me mindful of you every day, so that like Andrew I may invite others to "come and see." Amen.

No Need to Fear

JANUARY 16–22, 2017 • ALINA KANASKI

SCRIPTURE OVERVIEW: The image of light figures in three of the texts. Light not only illumines but brings a changed situation. The psalmist's confession links light with salvation. The Gospel lesson expresses deliverance in terms of the nearness of God's reign, which overcomes diseases and distortions. Light permits well-being. Light is the mode of God's presence.

QUESTIONS AND SUGGESTIONS FOR REFLECTION

- Read Isaiah 9:1-4. When has God called you out of the darkness of an old habit, a familiar circumstance, into the light of new opportunity for ministry?
- Read Psalm 27:1, 4-9. Do you feel more comfortable talking with God about your joys or your pains? Is there need for more openness in either?
- Read 1 Corinthians 1:10-18. In your faith community, when have members found themselves at odds over priorities of no eternal value?
- Read Matthew 4:12-23. Put yourself into the story. What do you hear, see, feel, or smell? How have you answered the call of Jesus?

Recent seminary graduate still waiting for God to tell her what to do next

God is like light, like a stronghold. Light, by its very nature, drives away the darkness and shows what has been hidden; it can do no less. A stronghold could be a place with thick walls and tiny windows perched somewhere inaccessible. Its nature is to be a place of safety, and that will not change. In just that way the psalmist knows God's nature; he acknowledges it as a nature that offers salvation and help, love and glory. God's salvation and ability to rescue from despair remains constant. God's nature will not change and cannot be defeated, whereas the sun's light will one day fade, and the protection of a stronghold can be destroyed or breached.

God's nature offers us reason for hope. Knowing God's qualities gives reason for hope. God loves us; God offers us salvation and presence. The psalmist boldly proclaims these facts by naming God *light*, *salvation*, and *stronghold*. He longs for God's presence in his life, desires to orient his life around worship and prayer: "to behold the beauty of the LORD." The author's passion for the Temple, the center of religion and devotion, makes known his commitment to the Lord.

The psalmist's experiences of God's past faithfulness result in his praise of God. God hides him in times of trouble, conceals him in God's tent, sets the psalmist high on a rock. Such knowledge of God comes not from memorized words and phrases but from experience. God comforts the psalmist, driving him to praise and dedication. It gives him confidence as he struggles through life's trials.

When has God come into your life situation like a light, a stronghold? How do you experience God's salvation? What one thing would you ask of the Lord?

Help us to know you more fully, O God, every day. Amen.

TUESDAY, JANUARY 17 ～ *Read Psalm 27:1, 4-9*

The states of confidence and doubt are jarringly juxtaposed in this psalm. How can the psalmist go from praise to impassioned pleas for a glimpse of God's help? How often do we go from the spiritual high of Sunday morning to forgetfulness the rest of the week? the joy of devotional time to stress about life? Knowing God's nature, knowing God loves us and offers us salvation, doesn't mean we feel no emotions. We still grieve, still doubt, still feel anger or abandonment or sorrow while having faith in God.

So often we feel guilty for these feelings. *Shouldn't my faith sustain me?* The psalmist has not the least bit of guilt. He moves from confidence to despair without transition. He seems unaffected by the shift of declaring his faith and then stating his problems with equal confidence. He isn't afraid to be honest with God.

Sometimes I lack the psalmist's courage; I find myself trying to be "good enough," with super faith, no doubts, and definitely no problems. Then I don't have to face my sins or my uncomfortable emotions. The psalmist gives me hope. He doesn't fear expressing his feelings to God—the good and the bad. He's willing to explore those emotions with God, to pour them out and wrestle with them.

We need not fear either. We can explore our deepest emotions and secrets, our ugliness and beauty and joy and pain with our God: God the light, shining into our darkness; God the refuge, protecting us when we can't bear the pain of truth any longer; and, most of all, God our salvation, reaching out to us with love and concern whether we're confident or terrified, faithful or straying.

What parts of yourself are you afraid to talk with God about? Why?

They leave everything. That's what strikes me. Peter and Andrew, James and John leave behind everything they've ever known—the boats and nets they employ to make a living, their families. They leave all behind at the words of Jesus: "Follow me." They seemingly give no thought, no deliberation, no time for reflection. They go "immediately," leave everything they've known "immediately." What special quality does Jesus radiate that they immediately abandon all else?

I've never felt such a conviction, one that seizes me and leads to immediate action. I deliberate and prepare and worry. The knowledge of who God is, my light and salvation and stronghold and so much more, gets me there eventually; but I'm not the spontaneous type. I'm not sure I'd ever drop everything on a moment's notice. And that makes me afraid—afraid that I'm doing something wrong, afraid I'm missing something, afraid that I let fear keep me from God's plan for me.

"Do not be afraid," God's messengers so often tell God's people. But I do fear. I often fall into the trap of believing that I am not the "right" kind of Christian—but Jesus died for me so I am good enough because he is good enough. He called working-class people from their boats. They left their nets and followed.

I also tend to let my fear paint pictures of everything that could go wrong, forgetting that God is bigger than any possible difficulty. I allow my fear to dictate my action rather than God.

Lack of conviction and fear of action! If we can respond readily to God's call, we can release our fear of missing out, leave behind our nets, and follow into a future of promise. God is calling. Will we listen?

Lord, give us the courage to fight our fear and listen to your voice today. Amen.

Paul understands his primary call to be that of proclamation. Paul's conversion came in a flash of light, with Jesus himself speaking to Paul. The story involved visions, blindness, and healing. (Read Acts 9.) Most of us do not experience God's call on our lives in quite so flashy a way. Rather, it comes in the quiet of prayer, a whisper of thought, the suggestion of a friend, a passion that flowers over years. There is nothing dramatic about the times of doubt and struggle, redefinition and prayer. Many of us need finally to realize: "Oh! That is what God is telling me to do!" Few experience anything as certain as God telling us what to do.

The uncertainty is frightening. The places God sends us and what we're asked to do can frighten us. The act of trusting God and stepping out in faith is scary. *Why would God want that? What is God thinking?*

Paul reminds the Corinthians that the wisdom of fancy speech and status represents the world's wisdom. The cross of Christ makes no sense when analyzed logically or when we employ the code of the survival of the fittest. God's nature is love and mercy, goodness and wisdom. Acting from love doesn't always make sense. Allowing the Son to die for others doesn't make sense. Yet, the Corinthians, who find themselves in conflict with one another, by their very division empty the cross of its power.

What God asks of us doesn't always make sense. But God is trustworthy. However frightening God's call may seem, we are being saved by "the power of God."

God, may I face my fears and pursue your calling, knowing your power is at work in me. Amen.

No Need to Fear

Light has come into the darkness. Hope has come into hopelessness. Healing has come to sickness—all through Jesus Christ. Jesus calls Simon and Andrew, James and John in this moment, but he calls all people to repent—those in first-century Galilee and those across time. He calls you to repent; he calls me to repent. And why this call to repentance? Because "the kingdom of heaven has come near."

The idea of repentance makes me uncomfortable. It requires me to face myself. Repentance demands that I look at my own life and see the dark places that need the light of God's grace. Letting the light in—acknowledging my sins and failings—brings pain. *Can't you just leave that little habit alone, God? Must you address that issue now?* The nearness of the kingdom of heaven asks us for a change of direction, a change of behavior. The kingdom of heaven demands obedience, a readiness to follow. It's a hard place to be. God calls and asks for response.

However, we are in good hands. We are in the hands of a healer. Jesus begins his ministry by speaking the truth and calling disciples, but he also begins by healing. He heals all those who come to him with illnesses. Jesus heals physical sicknesses and also soul sicknesses. He roots out our greed and lies, our obsessions and selfishness. He reaches out to us saying, "Follow me." By following in obedience, we find a better way, a difficult way—but one that brings joy and peace.

All we have to do is follow.

Jesus, the light of the nearness of the kingdom shines on my path. May I choose to follow and obey. Amen.

What drives us to split into groups, to drive others away because of differences real or imagined? Why do we wall ourselves off to other points of view except that of "our" group? I'm not sure it's a comfort to know that we're not alone in this tendency, to remember that since the early years, Christians have been splitting into groups and walling one another off.

Belonging to a group affords security, a sense of safety and inclusion. There are so many things to fear, and so many shapes fear can take: fear of being alone, fear of what is different, fear of being wrong, fear of having to change. When you belong to a group, you can face threats together.

Paul has heard of quarrels among members of the Corinthian church. People are identifying with different leaders: Paul, Apollos, Cephas. He calls the Corinthians back to their primary allegiance by asking, "Has Christ been divided? Was Paul crucified for you?" Of course not; their overarching allegiance is to Christ—Christ who was crucified, Christ in whose name they were baptized. It is Christ's name with which Paul opens his letter to them: "Now I appeal to you . . . by the name of our Lord Jesus Christ."

The church is meant to be a group of love—united in Christ across races, nations, denominations, genders, and classes. What is the church if not the family of God brought together by God's love? So often we allow competing claims and commitments to get in the way of what brings us together. We are all unique, created in the image of God, yet unified in our faith in Jesus who is our salvation and the light of the world.

God, show us the way to unity in you and bring us together. Amen.

This joyful pronouncement promises a time to come when all will rejoice before God, when oppression and war will end, when the anguish of darkness shall cease. God has promised us good, good things.

God comes, bringing light. Isaiah contrasts the former time of contempt with the latter time of glory. The coming of light creates new possibilities: "You have multiplied the nation, you have increased its joy."

Jesus fulfills Isaiah's prophecy by ministering in Galilee. Jesus, the light of God, walked through Galilee, healing and teaching and calling people to God. Jesus brought the kingdom of heaven to earth and offered it to everyone he met. He began the work of healing and the destruction of evil and the bringing of good, good things that God has promised. And Jesus continues that work; he still offers us the kingdom of God.

Jesus started it: the end of death and pain and oppression and hunger, but the work is incomplete. That's why we still suffer from war and grief and oppression and fear and all those other things that we pray God will take away.

Yet we, like the Israelites, "rejoice . . . as with joy at the harvest," for God keeps promises, roots out oppression, shines light in every dark place. It's God's nature. The promise of the future good, good things fills us with determination to keep bringing God's light to the world, one ray at a time. We have seen a great light. God is bringing good, good things.

God, thank you for bringing light to our darkness. May we rejoice. Amen.

Who Are We Becoming in Christ?

JANUARY 23–29, 2017 • HARRIETT JANE OLSON

SCRIPTURE OVERVIEW: The four texts for this Sunday join in warning the people of God that they should not be confused or intimidated by appearances or by how the larger society values this or that. A faithful hearing and responsiveness to the God of the Bible may not fare so well or look so good in terms of the world's standards of judgment. But what is required and blessed is a community ordered according to the covenantal commitments, shaped by God's gracious promises, and attuned to what Paul called the "foolishness" and "weakness" of God.

QUESTIONS AND SUGGESTIONS FOR REFLECTION

- Read Micah 6:1-8. When have you sensed God's anguish over human injustice?
- Read Psalm 15. Where do you need to speak truth from the heart, do what is right, be without blame, or be reconciled?
- Read 1 Corinthians 1:18-31. How have my limited expectations of how God works caused me to miss God's action in my life or the lives of others?
- Read Matthew 5:1-12. Which of the Beatitudes do you feel most blessed by? Which best describes your life of faith?

General Secretary of United Methodist Women, New York, New York

The scripture texts assigned for this week seem to contain a lot of lists. Some describe what is good, and some note what is not good. If you are a list person, you might be tempted to turn any one of these passages into a sort of holy checklist of "to-do" items. Commentators warn us against doing this. Rather than lists, these are a series of descriptions pointing to how the beloved community acts. They are not lists of qualifications for belonging. As today's reading points out—the work of God in Christ Jesus is what qualifies those who are being saved.

That being said, it is tempting to read these as a list. I have a love-hate relationship with lists. I make them to help me remember various things; sometimes I even follow them. When I check over a list, I gain a sense of accomplishment from what I've completed and I may be prompted to act on some remaining items. So far, so good. However if a list (or in this case, a description) turns into an indictment for the uncompleted work and stops me from pressing on, it is not helpful. At all.

This week we will be looking for descriptions of who we are becoming in Christ, as faithful followers and as a community. We will find some things that need attention, and we will find some areas in which we can see and claim God's work. As we study and reflect let us keep in mind that it is God who invites us on the journey and it is God who qualifies us, not our wisdom or our own efforts.

Paul lists the criteria God has used for this qualification: "God chose what is foolish in the world to shame the wise; God chose what is weak in the world to shame the strong; God chose what is low and despised in the world . . . so that no one might boast in the presence of God."

As I am being saved, O Lord, teach me again to rely on Christ.
Give me a new vision of your completed work of salvation. May
I respond anew to your amazing, self-giving love. Amen.

In these verses that lead up to one of the most oft-cited passages from Micah, the prophet lets the people of Israel know that God is lodging a complaint against them. God calls upon creation to sit in judgment—from the high places of the earth (the hills and mountains) to its foundations. Creation listens while God challenges and laments.

The charges against the people offer a narrative of redemption. God has redeemed the people from slavery and sent them leaders and prophets. When foreign rulers tried to use the prophet Balaam to turn God's power against the people, Israel actually received blessing through God's own word.

What an amazing message! God's deep care and concern for the people results in God's taking repeated action to call them into relationship. God also enlists creation to call them back from ways that undermine the essence of who they were created to be. God continues to call them, as God called Abram, to be a blessing to the nations.

Hearing the actions taken by the Holy One of Israel confirms one aspect of divine character: God persistently works to reclaim the people God has called.

As people created in God's image and claimed by God through baptism, we could well ask ourselves: What testimony would God offer about the times God has reached out to gather me in—as an individual and within a community of faith? In the narrative from Micah, God asserts that these acts matter, that they are part of a relationship, and that they set the context in which a faithful people are empowered and expected to live lovingly and justly. God's lament urges Israel to remember God's acts so that they can live as people of the covenant.

May we remember the many times you have called us into relationship, O Lord, and may our lives reflect our own commitment and love in response. Amen.

Who Are We Becoming in Christ?   41

After hearing God's brief against the people in verses 1-5, in this passage we hear Micah's own words. The prophet seems to repeat a list of questions posed to him. Can I appease God by some ritual action? What is the proper posture? How large an offering must I make? The questions become more and more extreme until the prophet bursts out with his familiar answer about what God requires.

Making a grand gesture has a certain appeal. In lieu of living out our commitments on a daily basis, a gesture could assert our belief that we are in right relationship. An extravagant offering might be a bid for reconciliation on our own terms. But extravagant religious observance will not excuse us from changing our hearts and lives. We are to move beyond attempts to confine our relationship with God to "religious matters," with how to come before the Lord, as if our whole lives were not lived before God.

The prophet's brief list of God's requirements for how to act is one of the most powerfully succinct statements in all of scripture: "to do justice, and to love kindness, and to walk humbly with your God." Doing justice requires that we speak up, that we change our own actions, and that we call others into just ways of relating as well. We know what the Lord requires of us, but applying this knowledge and loving mercy in the big and small actions that make up our everyday lives requires a changed heart and patterns and practices that focus on the well-being of the whole community. Nothing excuses us from engaging in the work for racial justice, for gender justice, for fair treatment of workers, for care of the environment, and for the many actions required to make our communities more loving and just.

Sharpen our hearing, O Lord, to your witness. Move us to prayer; move us to action. May we live as your beloved children by doing justice, loving mercy, and walking humbly with you. Amen.

Who Are We Becoming in Christ?

Many people speak, blog, and tweet about their spiritual practice. They may hail movement or stillness, meditations or mantras, knowing your own heart or serving others as practices to help us know God and to sense God's presence. Folks also make a variety of assertions about which beliefs demonstrate that people *are* or *are not* close to God. We may wonder, *Who really does dwell with God?* The psalmist lists the criteria: 1) those who walk blamelessly 2) those who do what is right 3) those who speak the truth from their heart 4) those who do no evil to their friends.

Instead of focusing on matters of spiritual practice or belief, the psalmist refers us to daily living to find evidence of people who are close to God. These people allow God's own character to shape them. Blameless, they do what is right in speech, in allegiances, and in business.

The description of abiding with God comforts and encourages us as we attempt to live loving, just, full-hearted, and humble lives. However, if we believed this passage meant that *only* the blameless would sojourn with God, I suspect we would find that thought troubling. The attributes listed in this psalm do not represent a list of qualifications for entry, for who then would God welcome? These verses describe the life to which we are called and in which God enables us to walk.

The psalm begins with an image of blessing—dwelling with God—and ends with a promise. We who are being saved, who are living lives that lift up and reflect God's own character, shall not be moved. We shall dwell and abide close to God. Even when living in the way that God desires takes us into new patterns that challenge our own practices and beliefs, we need not fear that we will ever be moved from God's presence.

Gracious God, may our study of your character help us to live lives that reflect you, strengthened in the knowledge that we abide with you through your grace. Amen.

Who Are We Becoming in Christ?

FRIDAY, JANUARY 27 ～ *Read 1 Corinthians 1:18-31*

We often hear it said that "seeing is believing," but "believing is seeing" can also be true. Our expectations and beliefs shape what we see or perceive. Paul notes that the work of God in Christ did not meet the expectations or beliefs of either the Greeks or the Jews. Similarly, you and I risk missing the wisdom and power of God at work because of our expectations.

Our experience shapes our expectations. The Jews, who Paul says are looking for signs, are a people whose story is replete with signs: manna, pillars of cloud and fire, a staff that becomes a snake. The people observed many signs that they cited as evidence of God's presence. The same is true of wisdom. While Paul mentions it as a preoccupation of the Greeks, we also consider the wisdom of Deborah, Solomon, Daniel, or Jesus as signs of God's presence.

Signs and wisdom may indeed demonstrate God's presence, but seeking them may become "worldly"—relying on signs rather than the movement of the Spirit, which they signify. We must learn to tell the difference.

Godly wisdom and godly signs surprise and confound normal worldly expectations. They are not restricted to the credentialed; they don't manifest at expected times and places; and they often do not depend on sophistication and training. Think about the lay preachers of early Methodism, the laypeople who have served at the heart of the mission movement.

Paul cites the life, death, and resurrection of Christ as the greatest evidence of unexpected power and wisdom. Institutions and credentials are all well and good, but we must also steep ourselves in the "foolishness" of God and expect to see the Spirit at work in new places.

Startle and shape me, O God, by the signs and the wisdom of the Spirit at work all around me. Amen.

Jesus goes up the mountain to teach. The writer of Matthew's Gospel addresses a Jewish audience for whom Moses' teaching from Mount Sinai loomed large in both geography and self-understanding. Commentators suggest that Matthew places this interaction on the mountain in order to make this very connection. Matthew's report of Jesus' message makes a claim about Jesus' authority and his prophetic role in salvation history.

Micah's description of salvation history directly refers to Moses, as well as to Aaron and Miriam. The inclusion of Miriam is unique to Micah, as is his claim that she, like her brothers, was sent by God. The Hebrew Bible records pieces of her story: Her mother sends her to protect the baby Moses. She is a prophet and leads in worship. She is punished with a skin disease and isolation when she and Aaron play politics; she dies in the desert and is buried there.

Both Matthew and Micah curate the narrative of God's power in action. They claim that God is at work in the world through these particular people. Making these sorts of claims is risky. Miriam, like Moses or Aaron, did not perfectly follow God's call. Jesus doesn't claim to be a new Moses—not abolishing the law but fulfilling it—and overt comparisons would surely have inflamed the religious leaders.

However, being a disciple, just like being a prophet, involves seeing the work of God and making some risky claims. We claim that God is still at work. We claim that God works in and through people in this time in history. We claim that God speaks through unlikely people, men and women. We claim that we can receive new understandings that express and fulfill the message God has been telling since the world began.

Inspire us, O God, as disciples and prophets, to see how you call people today, and give us wisdom and courage to keep telling of your work of salvation in and through us. Amen.

Who Are We Becoming in Christ?

The Beatitudes are a prophetic utterance. They claim and proclaim God's favor in places and for people for whom it is not yet apparent. They point the disciples and us to the culmination of God's work—the new creation, when the blessing will be apparent to all. They also claim that the blessing is now—blessed are you, *now*, not just in the time to come.

The disciples come to Jesus as he withdraws on the mountain, away from the crowds. We overhear his instruction. Jesus directs this message to the people who already follow him, those who have heard him preaching and seen him healing throughout Galilee. Jesus attempts to shift their gaze from the crowds and the action to the characteristics of the community that he desires to call forth.

Again, as with other lists in our readings this week, the Beatitudes are not a checklist of the present yearnings and struggles that entitle the listeners to eventual blessing. Nor are they an inventory of the kinds of people who will gain entrance to God's kingdom. Further, this pronouncement of blessing is not a charm against trouble, not a signal or a promise of temporal well-being, nor is it a reason to accept the suffering of ourselves and others passively. Rather, Jesus casts the vision of "kindom" values on which we must act.

We need not forget that we are blessed. Even when we experience the limits of our own faithfulness and desperately yearn for righteousness, we are blessed. Even when others resist and disparage us, we are blessed. Even when our work for justice seems fruitless and endless, we are blessed. We are blessed, and because we are blessed, we are called to live our yes to those values now.

Gracious God, kindle in me such confidence in your present blessing that I will be able to walk in your way today. Amen.

Walking in the Light

JANUARY 30–FEBRUARY 5, 2017 • W. ROBERT ABSTEIN

SCRIPTURE OVERVIEW: Living genuinely out of a deep inner sense of connectedness to the Trinity (God, Jesus, and the Holy Spirit) is a common theme for this week's texts. By living out of this spiritual center, we match our actions with our words and avoid the judgment the prophet Isaiah casts upon the people of Israel. Psalm 112 is a hymn of praise for the blessings God brings upon those who revere and follow. In Paul's letter to the Corinthians, he urges them to move beyond their flirtation with wisdom and to go to the deeper regions of the Spirit, the source of true wisdom. And, finally, Jesus, in his Sermon on the Mount, calls his listeners to move beyond the mere words of the law to the deep meaning and intent of the law.

QUESTIONS AND SUGGESTIONS FOR REFLECTION

• Read Isaiah 58:1-12. When have you felt strengthened by God for a particular task? How did your light "break forth like the dawn"?

• Read Psalm 112:1-10. Where have you been a light to those struggling in the shadows?

• Read 1 Corinthians 2:1-16. When have you faced unimaginable circumstances and had no words to speak? How did God's wisdom help you in those times?

• Read Matthew 5:13-20. How do you fulfill God's intended purpose for you as salt and light to the world?

Served the Episcopal Church for fifty years and recently completed a third interim; now serving as a supply priest for the Diocese of Tennessee

The Creation story in Genesis reveals God first creating light that enlightens an earth bathed in darkness. God speaks light into being. Many understand this first light of Creation as the enlightening Spirit that God showers on creation. The enlightening Spirit enables us to know the unknowable God.

God calls Isaiah to bear that light to the nations (42:6). He will speak the word about God's displeasure and reveal God's call to everyone to live in right relationship with God. Part of Isaiah's call comes in examining the ways Israel practices its faith: the religious festivals and fasts and personal piety. The people pay only lip service to God while turning a blind eye to the pain and suffering of the least, the lost, and the lonely.

The fast of God's choosing involves rolling up spiritual sleeves and working to right wrongs perpetuated by unjust laws, unfair labor practices. A faithful fast creates safety nets for those unable to perform their labor. The light that shines through the faithful, Isaiah says, brings a willingness to unloose bonds, to undo thongs of the yoke. Healing comes both to those liberated and to those who practice their faith in this manner. They gain a sense of security knowing that God's light is the source of their strength.

We see so many instances today of the powers of darkness that enslave people: wages that do not provide enough for minimal support, inadequate health care for the poor, the growing gap between the rich and the poor, and governments unable to provide the basics of good education and safety. Only as faithful followers of God speak up and advocate for those who have no voice will their light "break forth like the dawn."

Lord, give us, we pray, your enlightening Spirit that we may lift our hands and hearts to respond to those in need. Amen.

TUESDAY, JANUARY 31 ~ *Read Psalm 112*

In some parts of the world, Christians practice evangelism by sending a young Christian couple to a village to live and work. The couple begins their family and lives faithfully day after day at home, in the village, and at work. Only when others begin to question this family's peace and joy does the couple share the light of Christ that fills their hearts and minds. They do not attempt to coerce but to share the story that brought them to faith.

I once heard it said that we may be the only Bible someone else will ever read. The psalmist writes, "Happy are those who fear the LORD, who greatly delight in his commandments." Notice the correlation between happiness and doing justice. The righteous do not fear; they move forward with steady hearts, giving freely to the poor. Their happiness goes beyond mere smiles to a sense of wholeness and fulfillment. It does not mean a life without troubles; rather, an understanding that God does not create the troubles but gives us the strength to live through them. Those who walk with this kind of faith draw others to them.

Walking in God's commandments enables us to "rise in the darkness as a light for the upright; they are gracious, merciful, and righteous." We too can be the light for others by reflecting on God's commandments to love God with our heart, mind, and spirit and to love our neighbors as ourselves.

We may ask ourselves these questions as we continue our journey in faith: Where have we been a light to others struggling in life's shadows? Where have we failed to love those closest to us? Our examination of our lives today may open new possibilities for spiritual renewal as we live out our Christian commitment.

Lord, help us to live so that others may see your light within us and be drawn to you. Amen.

Walking in the Light   49

Paul proclaims "God's wisdom, secret and hidden." The light of Christ that blinded him on the road to Damascus has filled his heart and mind. Freed from his blindness, he receives strength through the Spirit to follow Christ through hardships, dangers, and abuse.

Paul contrasts God's wisdom with human wisdom. Rather than "lofty words or [human] wisdom," he preaches Christ crucified. This stumbling block in the gospel brings persons to faith not as a result of human wisdom but through "the power of God." The focus of Paul's preaching and teaching reveals the creative power that brought order from chaos and lightened the darkness at the beginning of time. It is not revealed through elegant preaching but by the witness and faith of persons so filled with light that those who encounter them discover their lives changed.

As a pastor I have found myself in situations that made me feel completely inadequate given the magnitude of the pain and suffering involved: a young child choking to death in the arms of his mother, the suicide of a young college student, or the deaths of a husband and only child in a boating accident. I have walked into tragedies not knowing what to say or do. The lofty words of my human wisdom cannot fill the void.

In those circumstances, I must, with Paul, rely on my faith in the Spirit to speak God's wisdom to those experiencing such unimaginable loss. We in our weakness and fear can allow the power of God to work in us. Only then may we adequately share the gospel of Christ with others. Only then may we be truly present to those who are in need ofcomfort, love, and support.

Lord, may we speak and proclaim Christ crucified out of your wisdom and power. Amen.

Many years ago I studied Anglican spirituality at Canterbury Cathedral in England. The first night the dean of that church introduced participants to the program with a candlelight pilgrimage through the cathedral. At times the only sounds were our footsteps. Our candles gave off a surprising amount of light in that cavernous edifice.

We were given time in the catacombs for prayer and meditation. I reflected then on the light from those candles. We could see one another clearly in what would have been total darkness. That is what the light of Christ does within us: It allows us to see others and to realize they are our brothers and sisters even in the darkest of times.

Jesus drew on the common experiences of people when teaching them about the love of God. He could use a single mustard seed to describe how the kingdom of God grows, or a farmer sowing seeds in an unplowed field to describe how the Word spreads and is received. Jesus uses a lighted candle that brings light to those inside the home to encourage the disciples to be a light to the world. Just as a single candle can bring light to a whole room, a single voice in a dark world can bring the light of hope.

Unlike salt, which can lose its capacity to provide flavor, the light shines brightly; rather than being hidden, we place it on a lampstand, and it shines on all within its range. Jesus calls the disciples to shine forth—not for their own benefit but to the glory of God. We manifest through our hands and hearts the light that brightens our souls. Often, the simplest acts bring others the greatest hope.

God of light, open our eyes to see those in need as our sisters and brothers. Give us willing hearts and hands to touch those as you have touched us. Amen.

Walking in the Light

In many of his letters, Paul enumerates a list of the gifts the Holy Spirit bestows on those who follow Christ. His concern for the churches he founded and supported through prayer and letters of encouragement was that their members understand this profound truth: All have received gifts by the Spirit for building up the body of Christ, the church.

When I became the rector of a fairly large church, I responded to the congregants' call for a "strong leader" with endless participation in all the committees and activities of the church. Eighteen months later I was in the hospital with a stomach condition. My doctor, a friend, said, "I have watched you since you came to us. I can tell you what is wrong with you clinically but actually you have a belly full of church!"

My doctor was right. I lay there exhausted believing I had to do everything because I was the leader. That night in the hospital I reread Corinthians on the meaning of the body of Christ. God reminded me that all members have been gifted by the Spirit. My job involved empowering my church members to use their gifts for the health of the whole community of faith.

We who follow Christ have been given the Spirit of God through our baptism. Our faith and wisdom comes through that avenue. Through spiritual discernment, we employ the mind of Christ. We begin to walk in a path made bright by God's gift of light. We know things only dimly, as Paul says, in this life. There will come a time when we shall see God in all of God's fullness. Each of us has gifts to use for the very purpose we were called to follow from the beginning.

Grant us, Lord, the wisdom to understand the gifts you have given us and the courage to use them for your sake and to your glory. Amen.

I heard a story about Mother Teresa when she was beginning her ministry to the poor and dying in Calcutta, India. She had taken a plate of food to a woman who was trying to keep herself and her family alive. The woman thanked her for the food and quickly scraped half of it into a pot. Then she started for the door, at which point Mother Teresa asked where she was going. The woman told her that her neighbor was also hungry.

Isaiah pleads for the people to call upon the Lord and begin to show compassion for others by unburdening them; by no longer articulating harsh thoughts; through acts of charity like feeding the hungry, clothing the naked, and relieving some of the suffering that surrounds them. Then not only will those they help experience relief, but those acting in a compassionate manner will begin to experience life in a new and different way. They will become bearers of light instead of adding to the gloom around them.

Isaiah also reminds us that if we call upon the Lord, the Lord will answer, "Here I am." It is hard sometimes to navigate this life of faith. But we can often overthink it and struggle by making impossible demands on ourselves. In essence this is not rocket science. It is about reaching out and making others the center of our concern.

To live our faith daily is the goal of the faithful. Through acts as simple as those to which Isaiah calls his people, we act out of love for God. And as we reach out to others in care, we shall find ourselves renewed. The Lord will satisfy our needs, strengthening our bones to be about our chosen work. Then we will become repairers of the breach, restorers of streets.

Show us your pathway, Lord, that we who follow might become bearers of light so that others can journey in your footsteps. Amen.

Today's passage helps us understand qualities of discipleship and puts forth two images for Christian community: salt and light. Salt is an amazing ingredient that flavors and preserves. Yet, when "salt has lost its taste, how can its saltiness be restored?" The history of humanity is strewn with examples of our many failures to live as God would have us live. In many situations, we have lost our flavor, our saltiness.

Jesus moves on to mention light. The sole purpose of a lamp is to give light. A person does not light a lamp and then hide it. He called his disciples to be points of light much like a city, which cannot be hidden if it sits on a hilltop. They are to shine not to bring attention to themselves but to "give glory to your Father in heaven."

Jesus goes on to say, "I have come not to abolish [the law] but to fulfill [it]." Jesus expands the disciples' understanding of God's commandments: The disciples hear Jesus' call to love their enemies, to forgive those who sin against them, to turn the other cheek when rebuked or insulted. Love is the light that came into the world through him. In these verses the disciples are to be salt and light. They are to maintain their flavor and tastiness in order to flavor the world with the gospel. And they become light bearers to the nations.

When we follow Christ we also bear his light . . . we bear the Light that came into the world: "The true light, which enlightens everyone, was coming into the world" (John 1:9). We too become like a beacon on a hill so that others can find their way in this often darkened world.

Lord, help us to see ourselves as you see us: your gifted children called for service in the world. Amen.

Saying Yes to Life

FEBRUARY 6–12, 2017 • ABBY THORNTON HAILEY

SCRIPTURE OVERVIEW: How are Christians to understand and relate to the Jewish law? The text from Deuteronomy confronts Israel with a sharp choice: Follow the commandments of Yahweh or bow to the gods of the Canaanites. Choosing the law means choosing a way of life. Psalm 119 praises the Torah as God's gift bestowed on Israel to be the authentic guide as to how life should be lived. Jesus becomes the authoritative interpreter of the Torah, the one who pushes beyond external behavior to a consistency between disposition and deed. Christians are invited by the text to be different and become what Paul describes as "spiritual people."

QUESTIONS AND SUGGESTIONS FOR REFLECTION

- Read Deuteronomy 30:15-20. How do you go about choosing between the call of God and the call of the idols that surround you?
- Read Psalm 119:1-8. How has keeping God's commandments been a joyful experience in your life?
- Read 1 Corinthians 3:1-9. What do you consider to be the "milk" of the gospel versus the "solid food" of the gospel?
- Read Matthew 5:21-37. Which of the "But I say to you" teachings of Jesus surprise you the most? Why?

Ordained Baptist minister; pastor of Broadneck Baptist Church, Annapolis, Maryland; curriculum writer and editor for Baptist, Mennonite, Church of the Brethren, and United Methodist publishers

For generations in Egypt, a small but growing group called the Hebrews lived in slavery, brutally oppressed by the powerful Pharaoh. Their circumstances changed when God led them out of Egypt to a mountain called Sinai. There, God taught them how to live as free people, giving them two tablets naming ten ways to live in right relationship with God and others. God hoped that when these people came to establish a land of their own, they would embody a different way than the one modeled by their Egyptian oppressors.

Now these liberated people stand on the edge of the Promised Land. After their wandering in the desert, God invites a new generation to reaffirm God's way. Recognizing that new temptations lie ahead, their leader, Moses, begs them to commit heart, soul, and body to a vibrant relationship with God and one another. "Choose life," Moses says—a challenge that means far more than continuing to breathe in and breathe out. It means saying yes to God's vision for human thriving. It means deciding to live in a new way.

Moses knows such a choice will be harder than ever when the people enter a life of relative comfort, finally settled in their own land. They may find themselves, for the first time, stronger than others. How will they use their newfound power? Again and again, they must choose the new way God has laid out before them rather than the oppressive ways they have known in the past.

Today what does it look like to say yes to life as God intends? How is God calling you to live out an alternate vision for human thriving, an approach that differs from the oppressive, hierarchical ways of the world around you?

God, you continue to set before us life and prosperity, death and adversity. Help us choose the way that leads to life not just for ourselves but for all your beloved children. Amen.

Saying Yes to Life

We live in a culture that celebrates choice. We have a vast number of options for what airline to fly, what cell phone carrier to use, what side we'd like with our combo meal. In a recent interview, the chairman of Starbucks noted that on the typical Starbucks menu there are over eighty-two thousand possible drink combinations. We can find it overwhelming to consider the number of options we negotiate and choose between on a daily basis!

The Israelites had never known a life of choice. While enslaved, they obeyed Pharaoh's demands if they wanted to live. In the wilderness, they depended on God's provision for their daily needs in order to survive. The Promised Land, however, offers new options. They will no longer need manna and quail sent from heaven in a land flowing with milk and honey. The gods of the Canaanites might prove tempting choices when they want a divinity a little more controllable than one who answers only to the cryptic name, "I AM WHO I AM" (Exod. 3:14).

For Moses, however, the choice is stark: The people can choose life or death, prosperity or adversity. Choosing to follow God's commands, to live by God's ways of love, is to choose long life, thriving in the land, and flourishing of community. Choosing to listen, instead, to the call of the idols of their new neighbors is a clear-cut choice to perish; they will not last long as a community without the ways laid out by the God who has brought them together.

What choices do you face today? What will it look like if you choose the life God desires for you in each decision?

God, many choices confront me every day. When it comes to setting the course for my life, help me choose the things that say yes to your way of being in this world. Amen.

Saying Yes to Life   57

Matthew's Gospel portrays Jesus as the new Moses, bringing God's law and leading God's people into freedom. Nowhere is the parallel more apparent than in the readings for the next two days from the Gospel of Matthew. Jesus expands upon three of the Ten Commandments intended to lead God's people into a new way of life: Do not murder; do not commit adultery; do not bear false witness.

If you read Jesus' words in this section and feel overwhelmed, you are not alone! Imagine if a pastor stood up before the offering and said, "Wait, before you give your gifts, go reconcile with anyone who has something against you." Our churches would go bankrupt! Imagine if you could be taken to court just for insulting someone. The litigation would never end!

But what is Jesus actually saying? Apparently, Jesus believes that carrying anger around, insulting others, and devaluing brothers and sisters by calling them names can have consequences as grave as murder. The word translated "anger" describes not an outburst or fleeting moment of losing it but rather a sense of seething, underlying rage that takes root as we continue feeding it. Nurturing such attitudes, Jesus says, will land us in "the hell of fire." Words and even thoughts can be as deadly as the sticks and stones that break others' bones.

So how do we say yes to God's new way of life when it comes to the command not to murder? For Jesus, it means engaging the hard work of reconciliation as much as the more visible act of physical restraint. It means transforming our inner lives as much as our external deeds. How would our society differ if we chose such a way of life?

God, help me not to stop at external restraint but to deal with the attitudes that strip life away from within so that I may love in a way that is life-giving and abundant. Amen.

As Jesus continues expanding on the law of Moses as a way of life, a little cultural background is in order. Jesus' society and culture defined adultery as the male of a community being dishonored by another man having sexual relations with his wife. The law focused on the man's suffering, with little regard for the well-being of the woman. Jesus declares that faithfulness and respect need to run deeper, upholding the honor of men *and* women in a truly life-giving manner. Women must not be possessions or objects casually cast out at the whims of the man.

The same was true in matters of divorce. In Jesus' time, a man could divorce his wife without turning to the courts; he simply needed to make the decision in the presence of witnesses and then give her a certificate. His words and actions would leave her bereft of any security. A community where people are disregarded and discarded, Jesus says, does not reflect divine intent for God's people.

The same went for swearing oaths. The law stated that persons must stand by their words if they had promised God they would do so. But Jesus challenges his hearers to honor *every* word they speak. If we cannot trust our neighbors to speak with integrity to one another in all times and places, how can our communities experience true life? Jesus sees God's community as one where people speak in a transparent and trustworthy way, keeping community relationships intact because individuals refuse to break trust for their own gain.

Can you imagine it—a life where we honor every individual as one truly blessed and beloved by God? How can we start disentangling ourselves from the cords of death and find the living way Jesus so passionately presents in the Sermon on the Mount—and in the sermon he lived with his life?

God, help me honor those around me by saying yes to living truthfully and with integrity, not objectifying others but regarding each as your precious child. Amen.

Saying Yes to Life

The time has come for the Corinthians to grow up. This early church had received the gospel from Paul when he spent more than a year and a half teaching them about life in Christ (Acts 18:11). While there, Paul says in today's reading, "I fed you with milk, not solid food, for you were not ready for solid food."

Now, though the church is older, its members still eat applesauce and mushed-up bananas, metaphorically speaking. They continue to live in childish ways, obsessing over the same things that divided them before they became the body of Christ. They quarrel over which human leader they will follow—Paul or Apollos, another teacher who has come among them.

Paul asks, Why are you still stuck on this kids' stuff? Life doesn't grow out of such division. Life as God intends comes from a collaborative effort—Paul planting, Apollos watering, God giving the growth. Saying yes to new life in Christ involves living in a cooperative community, a community undivided by petty allegiances. Paul models this maturity through his respect of Apollos as a fellow worker whose good desires for the community are the same as his own, even if they manifest differently.

Even today churches split over seemingly small issues, from allegiances to human leaders to the color of the carpet or the presence of video screens in the sanctuary. We divide as a wider society over political viewpoints, nationalistic commitments, socioeconomic differences, and power struggles. Grow up! Paul says to us as well. Focus on the things that matter, that are essential to life—the common purpose we share in growing in God's ways. Then we'll truly thrive.

God, help me leave infants' milk behind and drink deeply of the things that bring life. Amen.

One of the first things you likely learned—before you even went to school—was your alphabet. My infant son and I read book after book together that teach this building block of language in fun, engaging ways: "A is for Athletic Aardvark . . . B is for Belly-flopping Buffalo . . . C is for Cavorting Catfish . . . " Even if my child's current vocabulary only includes cooing and drooling, I figure it's never too early to start working on these foundations that will shape his ability to communicate and understand the world.

The psalmist thought similarly. Multiple Psalms—9; 10; 25; 34; 37; 111; 112; and 145—are acrostic in form, with each line starting with the next letter of the Hebrew alphabet. Psalm 119 is the mother of all acrostic psalms; not only does each section start with a different letter of the Hebrew alphabet, but every line in each stanza starts with that same letter. So verses 1-8 start with the letter *aleph*, verses 9-16 begin with *beth*, and so on—all the way to verses 167–76, where scripture's longest chapter concludes with eight verses beginning with *taw*.

Why write in this way? Perhaps for the same reason we read alphabet books to children: We want them to internalize and remember what's foundational to their functioning. If they don't get this one aspect right, everything else will be much harder! For the writer of Psalm 119, that one aspect is God's statutes, God's ways. The law is the blood that animates life, which shapes the ability to communicate and understand the world. It is the building block for all that they know and are.

Think about what your life would be like if you did not know the basic letters of your language. How would your life be similarly disoriented without God's teaching?

God, when I need direction, return me to the building blocks laid out in your word, knowing I will find life there. Amen.

If hearts are not on your mind this week, perhaps they should be! We are days away from that annual holiday of conversation hearts, heart doilies, and hearts poured out in love. In the United States, we also observe American Heart Month. With heart disease the leading cause of death nationally, campaigns this month encourage people to take steps toward improved heart health by exercising, eating well, and ceasing smoking.

What makes a heart healthy and happy? The psalmist has very different ideas than those just named. The heart, in ancient Hebrew thought, was not an organ that pumped to keep us alive, nor was it a sentimental symbol. The heart served not only as the location of emotion but of persons' entire personality, intellect, desire, and will—everything that makes us who we are. The heart was the seat of those intangibles that make us human, encapsulating what makes us tick—the dynamic forces that make us unique individuals. The heart served as the center of all that we have been, are, and will be.

How does the knowledge above inform how you hear the psalmist's declaration that it is those who seek God with their whole heart who are happy? The secret to a happy, healthy heart—a self fully alive and on a life-giving course—comes from centering our core being on the law of the Lord. The observance of God's decrees, statutes, commandments, ordinances, and precepts shapes the deepest part of who we are and who we become. How happy and healthy is your heart today?

God, help me follow you with my whole heart—not just to feel love toward you or think loving thoughts about you but to live in a way that shows I center my whole being on your desires for our world. Amen.

Meditations on Holiness

FEBRUARY 13–19, 2017 • JASON E. VICKERS

SCRIPTURE OVERVIEW: These texts evidence relentless concern with the moral requirements that belong to life with the God of the Bible. They assume the foundation of covenantal law in God's rescuing acts. That foundation is implicit in undergirding these several treatments of God's commands. The psalmist is aware that the commands of God constitute a radical counter-obedience. The text from Leviticus brings us to the core claims of covenantal law. The rule of the God of Israel leads directly to focus on the neighbor. The neighbor is not just an inconvenience or an intrusion but is the stuff of moral awareness. Paul's admonitions to the Corinthian Christians state the bold claim that Jesus Christ is the central focus of every Christian's commitment. The Gospel reading invites the community to reflect on, imagine, and devise extra measures of neighbor love that reflect the character of God.

QUESTIONS AND SUGGESTIONS FOR REFLECTION

- Read Leviticus 19:1-2, 9-18. What would be some signs that you are attaining the holiness God desires?
- Read Psalm 119:33-40. The writer states that "Jesus did not come to abolish the law but to perfect it." How did/does Jesus do that?
- Read 1 Corinthians 3:10-11, 16-23. Consider how these two statements relate to your life: "We do not have to be morally perfect before God will dwell within us" and "We can be morally impure *after* God comes to dwell with us."
- Read Matthew 5:38-48. What instances in your life show that you "reject the call for retaliation or revenge in favor of the higher calling of forgiveness"?

Professor of Theology and Memphis Site Coordinator, Asbury Theological Seminary

Just two verses long, today's passage contains one of the most daunting commands in all of scripture: You shall be holy! It is one thing to say that we shall be morally good and loving because God is good and loving. We can handle that. Basic goodness and a loving disposition seem like attainable goals. By contrast, the command to be holy because God is holy makes us nervous. It sounds too lofty a goal. Yet God commands that very quality. So we face a dilemma: Either God has given us a command that we cannot live up to, or we are capable of being holy. Which is it?

To answer this question, we begin by noticing that we are not told to be *God*. God says we will be *holy*. Whatever being holy entails, it doesn't mean being God. God and holiness are related, but they are not the same thing.

When it comes to God, holiness denotes two dynamics simultaneously. First, holiness denotes the absolute difference between God and creation. Put simply, we are never to confuse God with any part of creation, and we are not to desire or otherwise approach any aspect of creation as though it were God. Second, holiness also denotes God's drawing near to God's good creation. So while we do not confuse God with creation, God condescends to dwell within creation.

When God commands us to be holy, God does not suggest that we cease being part of God's good creation. We become holy when, with the help of the Holy Spirit, we open our hearts and lives to the indwelling presence of God. We are capable of holiness because God freely chooses to dwell within us. God's presence in our lives produces the fruit of goodness and love.

Holy God, I celebrate the fact that you not only made the world but that you are present within the world. In this moment, I welcome you into my heart and life. I long to know your presence and to be transformed by it. Amen.

God is altogether different than creation. God transcends creation; God is holy! Today's passage unfolds in a series of paired verses, each of which begins with a command or law that governs our relations with one another and then concludes with a rationale for that command or law. In each case, the rationale is the same. We are to live by these laws because we are not God. The repetition of "I am the LORD" reminds us that God is the source of all of creation. Therefore, we walk humbly and treat our neighbor with loving-kindness. We take our place within creation with humility and gratitude. The whole of creation is a gift freely given; it need not have been.

Because we are not the source of creation, we constitute our relationship to creation on freedom. Because we have freely received the good gifts of creation, we share those gifts freely with our neighbors. Thus we do not reap to the corners of our fields or glean every grape from our vineyard. Rather, we leave some of the harvest for the poor. Put simply, we do not hoard the gifts of creation for ourselves.

While the command not to reap and glean to the corners of the fields or vineyards seems to speak to an agrarian context, the principle that it represents has broad application. All our resources, including our money, time, homes, and food ultimately come from God. Whatever we may have done to procure our resources, we did not create them. Before they were our possessions, they were gifts from God. When we forget this fact, we run the risk of idolatry. By contrast, when we remember and celebrate the sheer giftedness of creation by sharing our resources with others, we are set free to enjoy that which exceeds creation—the beauty and splendor of God's holiness.

Holy God, we give you thanks this day for the gift of creation in all of its splendor. Help us to walk humbly with you and to welcome and care for all those we meet along the way. Amen.

While God's holiness reminds us that God is altogether unlike creation, it also denotes the ways in which God draws near to creation in order to bring healing and renewal. When we speak of holy Eucharist or holy ground or the holy mountain of God, we affirm that God draws near to us in all these places. Our God is incomparable! God chooses to draw near to creation in order to bring healing and renewal.

One way God draws near comes through the provision of God's law. Too often, we Christians view the law in a negative way. We draw false contrasts between the law and the gospel, forgetting that Jesus did not come to abolish the law but to perfect it. (See Matthew 5:17.)

In today's reading, the psalmist speaks of delighting in the law of the Lord. The law, we are told, is life-giving. It brings renewal and healing to human life. Rather than fear or resent God's law, we celebrate it and long for it. When we do, the law of the Lord has the power to revive us and make us whole.

If we do not get all warm and fuzzy over the idea of longing for the law of God, then it is most likely because we fail to recall that God's law is an instance of God's holiness. The law of the Lord goes far beyond a static or abstract set of rules that we must follow. The law represents God's life-giving presence and power in our midst. Indeed, we would do well to think of God's law in the same way we think of the sacraments. When we meditate on the law of the Lord, we draw near to the One who draws near to us in order to heal and to save us!

Gracious Lord, help us to delight in your law and not to fear it. May we long to encounter your healing presence in the law just as we long to encounter you in the meal that bears your name. Through your word and sacrament alike, revive us, O Lord! Amen.

In today's passage, the apostle Paul insists that Jesus Christ is the only foundation for the Christian faith and the Christian life. This fits beautifully with the theme of God's holiness that we have been developing over the last few days. In ages past, we have seen God draw near to creation on mountaintops, in burning bushes, in the altar of the tabernacle, and in the word of the Lord that comes through the mouths of prophets. But in Jesus Christ, we have seen God draw near in the most unthinkable of ways, becoming incarnate in human flesh and thereby subject to all that befalls creation, including suffering and death.

It really is mind-boggling that the One who utterly transcends creation would freely accept all the limitations of creaturely life in order to heal and renew the world. But this is precisely what we learn about God in the coming of Jesus Christ; namely, that God will stop at nothing to bring about the healing and renewal of God's good creation. Moreover, we learn that, with respect to God's holiness, Jesus' coming ultimately trumps radical otherness. Indeed, whatever else we think we know about God, because of Jesus Christ we now know that God has determined always to be drawing near to creation, which is to say, to be coming toward us.

When we say that Jesus Christ is the foundation of our faith, we do not simply bear witness to a coming that has already taken place. We also anticipate a coming that has yet to take place. We look forward in faith and hope to the second coming of our Lord. But there is more. We believe that in the power of the Holy Spirit, the risen Lord draws near to us even now. He draws near in a thousand places and a thousand ways.

Holy God, when we meditate on the coming of your Son, Jesus Christ, we are overwhelmed. Help us, O God, to draw near to you even as you draw near to us this day in the presence and power of the Holy Spirit. Amen.

The divine decree, "You will be holy," is first and foremost about God coming to dwell within us. Our goodness comes because God dwells within us and not the other way around.

Paul confirms the thought that God's holiness takes place within us. Paul and his companions have built a building on the foundation of Jesus Christ. They have built a community, a group of people who live as Christ-followers. Just as the glory of God dwelt in the Temple in ancient Israel, it now dwells within us—the Christian community! Our very bodies are temples of the Holy Spirit. And just as the priests had to keep the Temple free from contamination, Paul instructs us that we must do the same with our bodies. It is one thing to say that we do not have to be morally perfect before God will dwell within us. It is another thing entirely to say that we can be morally impure *after* God comes to dwell within us. The former statement is true; the latter is false. God's holiness purifies whatever space it enters, driving out all that is impure or unholy.

The major takeaway is clear: In affirming God's presence within us, we do not neglect our bodies. Christianity is not a disembodied form of religion. On the contrary, God's presence raises the stakes considerably with regard to our bodies.

The care of the community demands that we not deceive ourselves about our own wisdom, nor do we boast. Both qualities can destroy the temple of community. "All things are [ours], . . . all belong to [us], and [we] belong to Christ, and Christ belongs to God." We all live within God's presence.

Holy God, it is a fearful and wonderful thing to know that you dwell within us. Purify our hearts, O God, and help us to be more mindful of our bodies. Amen.

Because God's holiness dwells within us, we walk in the way of the Lord. We do not have to achieve moral perfection before God's holiness will indwell our hearts, but we do strive for perfection after the fact. God's purifying presence will not leave us as we are.

All this sounds good until we read today's passage and discover God's actual expectations. God does not call us to a life of ordinary good manners or being held in high regard in our churches and civic communities. When God's holiness invades our lives, we become sons and daughters of God. And just as earthly parents and guardians expect their children to live in ways that reflect their commitments and values, God expects us to live in ways that represent divine commitments and values.

So what are those commitments and values? What, precisely, does God expect from us? We know that God in Jesus Christ will stop at nothing to bring life, healing, and renewal to God's good creation.

Today's passage suggests that God expects the same from us. Empowered by the indwelling presence of the Holy Spirit, we take the necessary steps to bring life and healing and renewal to all those with whom we have contact, including our enemies and those who would do us harm. Indeed, this passage presses us to reject the demand for retaliation or revenge in favor of the higher calling of forgiveness—a tall order to be sure. But with God's help, Christians will undertake this higher calling.

Gracious Lord, your call to perfection overwhelms us. On our own, we are not capable of living in the way that you call us to live. But we know that we are not alone. With the help of the Holy Spirit, we know that we can love as you love, that we can extend grace and mercy and loving-kindness to all people. Even so, come, Holy Spirit. Amen.

Today we come full circle, ending our meditations on holiness where we began—namely, with God's declaration that we will be holy. The call to holiness can feel intimidating, even terrifying. None of us feels up to the task. And yet we dare not ignore the call. God doesn't say we will strive for holiness but most likely come up short. Rather, God declares that we will be holy as God is holy.

In some sense we rightly feel intimidated by the call to holiness. On our own, we simply aren't capable of the life God envisions for us. We aren't capable of sharing our resources with friends and strangers alike. We aren't capable of taking deep delight in God's laws. We aren't capable of loving our neighbors and enemies the way Christ does. We aren't capable of showing grace and mercy to everyone we meet, regardless of how they treat us.

The good news is that the call to holiness is first and foremost a promise that God will do for us and in us what we cannot do for ourselves. Apart from the indwelling presence and power of God, we will languish spiritually, falling well short of the lives God intended us to lead. But when God draws near, that which we would otherwise deem impossible becomes possible, including our holiness and perfection in Christ Jesus

Finally, while God's presence makes our holiness and perfection possible, we must also do our part. We must remember the sabbath and keep it holy. We must desire and honor God's law. We must participate in the means of grace whereby God draws near to God's good creation. And we can accomplish all this because the Holy Spirit accompanies us every step of the way, fostering the desire for God and the things of God in the innermost recesses of our hearts.

Holy God, have your way with us and in us so that we may be your holy people, transmitting your holiness everywhere we go. Amen.

Mountaintop Experiences

FEBRUARY 20–26, 2017 • PAUL WESLEY CHILCOTE

SCRIPTURE OVERVIEW: In deep deference and careful obedience, Moses enters the zone of God's glory, which certifies Moses' authority. Psalm 99 praises the kingship of Yahweh, while bringing to mind the human agents of God's rule who facilitate Yahweh's conversation with the people. The Gospel lesson, like Exodus 24, characterizes what is not fully seen or clearly heard. Jesus is taken up into the zone of God's glory and so is filled with transcendent authority. Speech about glory points to the assignment of new authority. The epistle reading asserts the authority of the true teachers of the church who rightly present and interpret the scriptural tradition.

QUESTIONS AND SUGGESTIONS FOR REFLECTION

- Read Exodus 24:12-18. When did you last experience a life-altering encounter with God?
- Read Psalm 99. Have you ever felt that if God really knew you, you would be hopeless? What changed your mind?
- Read 2 Peter 1:16-21. For the epistle writer, the Transfiguration event focuses more on hearing than on seeing. How do you listen for God's words?
- Read Matthew 17:1-9. What dark places have you seen brightened by Christ's presence—through you or others?

Academic Dean; Professor of Historical Theology and Wesleyan Studies, Ashland Theological Seminary in Ohio

On May 29, 1993, I made my first climb up Mount Chiremba above Old Mutare in Zimbabwe. Just about a hundred years earlier Joseph Crane Hartzell, the newly elected bishop for Africa, stood atop this mountain and received a vision from God. He saw young people running to this place from all directions with books in their hands, eager to learn. As a founding faculty member of Africa University, I figured I owed it to him to attempt that climb in order to see what he had seen.

It was a perfect day to ascend the mountain. Our guide, who knew the mountain well, safely directed the climbers upward. About halfway up we took a break to rest. We sat in silence and absorbed all the sounds and sights below. We could hear the babies crying at the orphanage off to the right. Students were singing and clapping in the chapel almost directly below. Shadows of clouds glided across the hillsides several miles away to the south with the Africa University construction site at their base. Everything around us seemed alive. The panorama from the summit was breathtaking. I could see why Bishop Hartzell received a vision there as he knelt in prayer. He had a mountaintop experience, and we did too.

This week we shall explore several important mountaintop experiences recorded in scripture. Experiences like these offer us new perspectives. Mountains always draw our attention upward and remind us of God's presence. But they also provide a view of all that lies below. Moses had such an experience atop Mount Sinai. He met God there and received a vision that included instruction about how to live. Perhaps you will meet God on your own mountain this week.

Lord, we long to come up the mountain to spend time with you. Help us to find that sacred space in our lives to dwell in your presence. Amen.

The term *majestic* comes to mind whenever we think about mountains, those towering features of the earth's landscape that are both beautiful and mysterious. Whether it is Everest or Kilimanjaro, Ararat or Arenal, Fuji or the Matterhorn, we are drawn to the mountains because of their height, their glory, their majesty—reminders of the glory, grandeur, and majesty of God.

When my family lived in Africa, we went on safari in hopes of seeing Kilimanjaro. Clouds almost always shrouded the mountain. This fact added to the mysterious quality of the mountain. Over the course of several days the mountain only revealed its full glory on one day for a brief period of time. The mountain, like God, is seldom fully visible, and this hiddenness amplifies the mystery. God, like these great mountains, fascinates us but repels us at the same time. Something overwhelms us when we encounter these mountains or meet the one, true God.

The account of Moses' mountaintop experience includes many symbolic references. The cloud—God's presence—covers the mountain for six days. But on the seventh day—a symbol of completion—God calls to Moses. A blazing fire crowns the mountain's summit. For forty days and nights—a traditional period of testing—Moses dwells on the mountain. Joshua, the representative of the next generation, and the elders who serve as leaders of the people accompany Moses only so far. Then God summons; Moses enters the cloud and waits in silence.

Sometimes we feel that God is distant and inaccessible, or the waiting becomes unbearable. But Moses emerges from his time in God's presence filled with wonder, transformed and empowered to be a true child of God.

Holy God, sometimes we feel like you are shrouded in a cloud like a great mountain. In those moments, give us courage to move into the cloud and abide in your presence. Amen.

Mountaintop Experiences   73

Earthquakes occur in the Holy Land. When the psalmist sings "let the peoples tremble" and "the earth quake," he is reflecting on a familiar experience. He uses this image to underscore a quality of the nature and power of God. To put it simply, God shakes things up.

The trembling and the quaking associated with God's actions revolve around God's love of justice and righteousness. God will continue to quake and shake to bring all things into proper alignment with justice. In a baccalaureate address in August 1967, Martin Luther King Jr. reframed the words of Theodore Parker when King observed, "The arc of the moral universe is long, but it bends toward justice."

I will never forget meeting Desmond Tutu at the World Methodist Conference of 1986 in Nairobi, Kenya. He had been invited to the event because of his role in helping to bring down the injustice of the apartheid system in South Africa. It would be eight long years before apartheid fell, but Tutu felt confident of its demise. I can still see him standing at the podium, waving his Bible over his head and declaring boldly, "Apartheid is dead! Apartheid is dead." He knew that even in the midst of the struggle, injustice would not prevail in God's universe.

God is exalted in Zion. God oversees all matters from the heights of that holy hill. God looks upon our world filled with injustice, malice, and strife, and works all day for good. God continues to shake. God continues to quake. In the end, God's justice will triumph over racism, xenophobia, discrimination, and fear. God will establish the beloved community.

God of justice and righteousness, we long for peace and reconciliation. Shake our world with the power of your love and establish your beloved community of peace. Amen.

These verses mention three of Israel's noted intercessors: Moses, Aaron, and Samuel. They cried out, and God answered! Our God of justice hears the cries of the needy and acknowledges the plight of the people. Verse 7 recounts the giving of the Ten Commandments—a gracious response from a gracious God. Justice and righteousness characterize God's holiness and so do mercy and forgiveness. God looks upon the world not only in judgment but with grace and love.

We often worry that if God really knew us, we would be without hope. Fully exposed before God's divine majesty, we would be lost indeed. But because God loves us and forgives us, while we are yet sinners, we magnify God's holy name and prostrate ourselves at God's holy mountain!

Charles Wesley had a profound understanding of this God of justice and mercy. His hymns reveal a divine love that descends into our hearts from above with healing in its wings. One of his Redemption Hymns (1747) contains this poignant stanza:

Weary of this war within,
Weary of this endless strife,
Weary of ourselves and sin,
Weary of a wretched life;
Fain we would on thee rely,
Cast on thee our sin and care,
To thy arms of mercy fly,
Find our lasting quiet there.

When we abide in Christ, God frees us from the burden of feeling we can never do enough to please God, others, or ourselves. The holy God before whom we bow writes forgiveness on our hearts.

Forgiving God, we come to you weary and seeking rest from all those forces that deplete our lives. Help us to rest secure in the promise that you are a God who forgives. Amen.

The reading from Second Peter anticipates the story of the Transfiguration that we will celebrate this coming Sunday. Peter alludes to that event by quoting God's statement concerning Jesus, "This is my Son, my Beloved, with whom I am well pleased." We have heard these words spoken about Jesus before in reference to his baptism. After Jesus came up out of the water, a voice from heaven spoke these very words. Jesus' baptism and the Transfiguration proclaim his true and glorious identity.

Central to this text, however, is the apostle's claim to have been an eyewitness of Jesus' majesty. Can any of us possibly imagine the visible splendor of his divine majesty? In talking with his students on one occasion, Martin Luther described the way we should tremble when we stand before an earthly ruler; all the more when we stand before the Lord of lords and King of kings. The experience on the mountain must have overwhelmed Jesus' inner circle of disciples. Little wonder that the language pouring onto the page in Peter's account includes terms like *honor, glory, power* and *coming*.

This reading reminds us that the God of glory whom we honor is the One who comes. God came in the person of Jesus who died, was raised, and will come again. Without question, the "power and coming" of Jesus here refer directly to the coming of the "Son of Man" about which Matthew wrote (24:30). The power is that of the risen Christ, whose power will be demonstrated ultimately in his return. The Transfiguration not only provides a backward glance through its connection to Jesus' baptism; it turns our attention to the future and the coming of Jesus Christ in final victory.

God of honor, glory, and power, we look forward to your coming in final victory and that time when we will fall down before you and worship you, for you are our God. Amen.

Biblical prophets are less interested in predicting the future as in declaring the word of God. Elijah, who engaged in dialogue with Jesus and Moses on the Mount of Transfiguration, embodies the true prophetic spirit. He symbolized the essence of prophecy, bringing to visibility those things that often remain hidden. The continuing text from Second Peter, therefore, links the prophetic word with light, whether a lamp shining in a dark place or the morning star rising in our hearts. Prophets open our eyes so that we can see.

Perhaps Peter alludes here to John the Baptist, described in John's Gospel as "a burning and shining lamp" (5:35). He had illuminated and made straight the path for the Messiah. But the apostle quickly shifts to a different image. The verb translated "dawns" literally describes the light that pierces the horizon at sunrise. Peter draws the attention of the reader from an external, objective source of light to an immediate and interior radiance— the light of Christ shining in the human heart. This spiritual and prophetic light enables us to find God in unexpected places. It turns the world upside down.

A group of Christian peacemakers were nearly killed in a car accident in the first days of "Shock and Awe" during the Iraq War in 2003. They were rescued, however, by Iraqi Muslims who took them to a clinic in Rutba, offered them sanctuary, and cared for their needs. Those sheltered saw Christ in the faces of their Muslim brothers and sisters, and it changed their world forever. As Peter testifies, only the Spirit of God reveals such things to our hearts and minds.

Surprising God, open our eyes that we may see you in the face of all whom we meet this day. Amen.

TRANSFIGURATION SUNDAY

Today we celebrate the event of the Transfiguration—an event of central importance in Jesus' life, as well as the lives of his three intimate companions. The event looks backward and forward, focusing our attention on the past, on earlier events in the life of Jesus and, indeed, on the central acts of God among the Hebrew people. At the same time, it points to the future, to the fulfillment of God's redemptive purpose in Jesus Christ and the mission in which we all participate.

Consider the central figures of the scene: Moses, the prototype of the Messiah, the great deliverer, the embodiment of the Law, and Elijah, the forerunner of the Messiah, the greatest of the prophets, whose name itself means "the Lord is my God." The Transfiguration reveals and confirms that Jesus is the Messiah, the fulfillment of both the Law and the Prophets. In Luke's Gospel, this mountaintop experience immediately follows the account of Peter's confession where the apostle boldly proclaims Jesus as the "Messiah of God" (9:20)

The Messiah approved by God on the mountaintop is the One through whom God now acts in the dark valleys of life. The way of Jesus is not a detached glory; it is a glory relevant and active in the most sordid of human situations. Through his actions, Jesus shines all the more clearly as he illumines the dark spaces in which people live. He gets his hands dirty in the world of everyday life and transforms it by his presence. The way of Jesus is to be pierced by the hatred and cruelty of those he came to save and to go on loving. You and I are called to nothing less!

Christ, whose glory fills the skies, Christ, the true, the only light. . . . More and more thyself display, shining to the perfect day. Amen. ("Christ, Whose Glory Fills the Skies," UMH, no. 173)

Living into Lent

FEBRUARY 27–MARCH 5, 2017 • ROBERTA BONDI

SCRIPTURE OVERVIEW: The texts for Ash Wednesday are all ominous in nature, pointing forward to the redemptive power of God's grace. Lent is a time when Christians reflect on their mortality and sin, as well as on the creative and re-creative power of God. The original parents of humanity could not resist the seduction of the serpent, but that narrative stands beside the story of Jesus' lonely and painful resistance to the power of Satan. In Romans, the "one man's obedience" by which "the many will be made righteous" is the quality that endures. The Joel passage is an alarm bell in the darkness of the night. Those who are caught in this terrible moment cannot hope to save themselves, for they are powerless to do anything on their own behalf. They are powerless to do anything, that is, except to repent and to open themselves to God's intervening mercy.

QUESTIONS AND SUGGESTIONS FOR REFLECTION

- Read Genesis 2:15-17; 3:1-7. What choices have you made that put you outside God's intention for your life?
- Read Psalm 32. Are there unconfessed wrongdoings in your life that need God's forgiveness? Will this Lent be a time when you can find the freedom forgiveness brings?
- Read Romans 5:12-19. Have you experienced a relationship that has died? How has God renewed that time in your life?
- Read Matthew 4:1-11. What has tempted you to set faith aside and to trust only in yourself? How did that work out?

Professor Emerita, Candler School of Theology, Emory University

This week we enter Lent, a time of preparation in the early church for those being baptized at Easter. On Easter those being baptized learn that though caught in the death and sin of the human condition, they will enter the waters of death symbolically with Jesus and rise with him into a new creation. Sin and death will no longer have a stranglehold on them.

Today's passage tells part of the story about how our first parents, Adam and Eve, and we as human beings got into the broken world we live in now. In the beginning, nothing existed on the earth—no plants or animals or human beings.

Then, one day, God decided to create our world and made human beings from the dust and God's breath. God places the first two human beings in a wonderful garden filled with plants and animals and trees bearing fruit to eat. God gives them oversight of this lovely place. Then God issues a command: Do not eat of the tree of the knowledge of good and evil because it will bring death.

Of course, the first people are unable to resist. Why do they disobey and eat? One ancient writer says they are greedy. Others say they want to be like God or that they are curious. I suspect that they wanted to have everything—just as we do in our consumer culture. Though they don't literally die when they give in, this "consumerism" is surely one thing that ultimately kills them. Thus, the first parents move from a life of goodness intended by God into a life of choosing something "other." Our choices can likewise move us outside God's well-ordered and blessed intention for our well-being into a place just outside God's desiring.

Our God, in the weeks that are to come, help us remember how death, literally or figuratively, follows when we are enticed to confuse what we crave for what we need. Amen.

Adam and Eve do not passively listen to the snake's temptation. It is clear from Eve's response to him that she has been thinking about this all along. The snake says, "Did God say, 'You shall not eat from any tree in the garden'?" Eve answers by enlarging and elaborating on the original simple command, adding that they were also told where the tree was and that they were not even to touch it, or they would die.

The snake tells them they won't die. He hints that the God who has provided them up to this point with everything they need now holds out on them to keep them from becoming like God. Perhaps their thinking that God has secret motives is their ultimate temptation.

Sure enough, Adam and Eve eat the fruit and don't die. The great knowledge God has been holding back from them, however, seemingly turns out to be no more than to notice that they are naked and to feel shamed by it. Rather than preparing a confession to God about their action, they sew some makeshift clothes to hide in.

When God comes to find them in the garden, the man does not take responsibility for his own actions. He blames Eve, and even God's own self for giving him Eve. Eve, meanwhile, plans to blame the snake. The result of all this blaming signifies more than symbolic death. All human relations, divine relations, and relations with the animals are forever broken as we humans fail to take responsibility for our actions and, instead, try to save ourselves by turning against one another.

If only this story had no relevance to us now! But this broken human state is what we will seek to recognize during Lent with the promise of a coming Easter.

Dear God, help us to realize that, whatever we may suspect, you want only what is best for our well-being. Amen.

ASH WEDNESDAY

Psalm 51 has been the psalm for the first day of Lent, Ash Wednesday, since the church's beginnings. It is a prayer of deep repentance, when we find ourselves able to do what Adam and Eve would not. We ask not only for mercy, which we know we already have, but also for a cleansing of the effects of our sins in God's eyes. We know we have been transgressors and sinners since our very beginnings, but we ask God for clean hearts, for new spirits, and for the joy of being restored to God. To receive this, the psalmist tells us, we can forget our extravagant sacrifices and showy worship practices. God desires only one thing: broken and contrite hearts from which God will never turn away.

But how does this psalm speak to our hearts today? Few of us perceive ourselves to be quite so full of the individual sin described in Psalm 51 that we can't bear it. Are we really so guilty from the moment of our conception?

But remember that our primary identity is as members of the human race—not individuals. We are all linked together, after all, to make one human body. This means that wherever children go hungry, wherever war rages, wherever genocides and other atrocities occur, wherever the earth is polluted, and the poor are oppressed, we accept responsibility for a collective state of sin. We are responsible simply by virtue of our being human from the day of our birth.

How do we bear this painful knowledge of our human identity? Psalm 51 tells us to ask for forgiveness, God's truth, wisdom in our secret hearts, and the restoration of God's joy for which we were all created.

Loving God, may we acknowledge the extent of our sin so that we may ask for forgiveness and restoration. Amen.

Understanding today's passage depends on remembering our single humanity. Adam and Eve, standing in for us all, chose not just sin but death itself. Our problem ever since is not that we sin but that in the broadest sense of the term, we die. Our bodies die; our relationships die; crops die; the very earth is dying. Sin and death, then, make up the human race's fundamental condition. Paul tells us that Jesus Christ came to repair that condition for us all.

Symbolically, Adam and Eve chose death for the human race. God has now given us Christ as our new Founder. But the parallel with Adam and Eve is not an exact one. Sin and death result from the bad choice of our first parents. Our new life in Jesus Christ, the second Adam, however, does not come about by anything we do ourselves but strictly from God's gift of grace.

The interesting aspect to note is that the actions and choices of both Adam and Jesus affect everyone. In Adam and Eve we are all sinners who die. In Jesus Christ we are all freed from the necessity of sin, made right with God (justified), and given the promise of eternal life. Just as we are all included in Adam and Eve, now we are all, as Christians, incorporated into the second Adam in the new creation. Paul says we become part of the second Adam, the new collective humanity, through baptism, for which Lent prepares us.

We seldom think of ourselves as anything other than individuals who live in a larger society. The pattern of thought in which we first identify ourselves as part of humanity are unfamiliar in our time. We have done great damage to one another in our failure to recognize that truth. Lent provides a good time to ponder how we are to live as part of the human race!

Loving God, may we understand and follow what Paul is talking about: our intimate relationship to all human beings first, and second, our relationship to one another in Christ. Amen.

Jesus begins his ministry with a forty-day fast in the wilderness, paralleling the Israelites' forty years in the wilderness after their rescue from slavery in Egypt. They faced many trials in the wilderness. They found themselves tested by God, and they barely passed. God miraculously provided for their care. Nevertheless, while Moses busied himself on Sinai with receiving the Ten Commandments, at the foot of the mountain the Israelites busily made a golden god to worship.

In the Bible many stories of new beginnings include God's testing of the people and the leaders to determine their commitment. Adam and Eve failed outright when they ate from the forbidden tree. God tested Abraham, the father of the Jewish people, by commanding him to sacrifice Isaac, his son of the promise. So it does not surprise us to find that Jesus, who will serve as our new head, also faced testing in the wilderness.

Temptation and testing point to the same hard reality of life. In the Lord's Prayer, Jesus himself tells his disciples to ask God not to lead them into temptation or to put them to the test. The events of Jesus' life and death tested their faith.

From Jesus' temptations, we gain key information about the kind of messiah Jesus would be and whether or not we can trust him. Our understanding of that relationship provides support in our own times of temptation.

All these stories—about Adam and Eve, Abraham, Jesus' disciples—teach us that when we fail our inevitable tests and give in to our temptations, God does not abandon us. After failing in the desert, the people of Israel still entered their new land. Upon leaving the Garden, Adam and Eve received God's care. And in spite of our failures, God loves us still.

Loving God, we know that giving in to our temptations does not mean you abandon us. Amen.

At the end of Jesus' forty-day fast in the wilderness, he is starving. So not surprisingly, the devil's first temptation invites Jesus to turn stones into bread—not only for food but to prove that he is the Son of God by performing a miracle. Miraculous food figures in two other places in the Bible. The first comes in Eden. After God gives our ancestors everything to eat, they want more. The second arises in the story of the Israelites' forty years in the wilderness during which God miraculously supplied bread and quail.

Both of these stories involve testing God. If Adam and Eve eat the forbidden fruit, will God really let them die? If the Israelites want more than manna will God really supply them with something else, like quail? Will God live up to God's word?

This background sets the context of Jesus' temptations. If you are really the Son of God, says Satan, find out if God will turn these stones into bread. His second temptation is to hurl himself off the top of the temple to prove he is the Son of God by having God rescue him. Jesus states the following in reply, "Do not put the Lord your God to the test." Jesus' third temptation does not test God—only Jesus. If Jesus will worship Satan, Satan will give him the whole world. Jesus resists, quoting scripture, "Worship the Lord your God, and serve only him."

In resisting temptation, Jesus models faithful discipleship. When he shouts, "Away with you, Satan!" He exercises an inner power that even the devil obeys. Jesus refuses to let himself be trapped into proving himself and forgetting his primary focus. We can find ourselves tested in similar ways. Standing strong, we may find ourselves being waited on by angels.

Loving God, help us to recognize where we too are being tested. Save us by your grace. Amen.

FIRST SUNDAY IN LENT

Today's psalm calls us to confess our wrongdoings to God lest these unconfessed wrongdoings eat us up from the inside out. The psalmist says when he failed to confess, he experienced consequences in his body. He lost weight, groaned all day, and felt his physical strength depleted.

Adam and Eve's deceitful refusal to admit their wrongdoing leads to a story that ends badly. They irreparably damage their relationship to each other, to God, and to their world.

The psalmist's story has a happier ending when he goes ahead and admits his wrongdoing to God. Having done so, he finds himself in a new reality. Living without deceit, he knows God has forgiven him. Inside himself, he resides in a new place surrounded with "glad cries of deliverance" and "steadfast love."

Notice that God does not punish the characters in either story. Their punishment comes as the inevitable result of their refusal to admit what they have done. I fear that our destruction of the planet and our refusal to take responsibility for that destruction implies that our modern story will end as unhappily as did Adam and Eve's. We may still lose everything on the planet that makes our lives good through our refusal to acknowledge our destructive actions and to change our behavior.

But this does not need to be the end of our story. Lent offers a time for repentance. The promise of Easter that follows is new life no longer governed by death if only we give up our individual and collective stubbornness. We must take responsibility for the devastating things we've done and are doing even now. God will instruct and teach us the way we should go. Then we shall shout for joy.

Loving God, help us to stop blaming others and take responsibility for what we do so that we may truly celebrate the coming Easter. Amen.

Walking by Faith, Not by Sight

MARCH 6–12, 2017 • DAN R. DICK

SCRIPTURE OVERVIEW: Faith in God and deliverance by God are themes that dominate these scriptures. Abraham casts aside all baser loyalties and in daring fashion entrusts life and well-being to God's care. Abraham follows God's initiatives into new realms of loyalty and purpose. Paul reminds us that while Abraham models good works, his righteousness results from his faith. Nicodemus models an Abraham who has yet to leave Ur of the Chaldees. Nicodemus's comprehension of God's initiatives is shallow and sterile. The psalm for this day greets with joy God's invitation to renewal.

QUESTIONS AND SUGGESTIONS FOR REFLECTION

- Read Genesis 12:1-4a. How is God calling you to leave behind the familiar for some new opportunity?
- Read Psalm 121. What aspect of this psalm draws your attention? What offers you comfort and hope? To whom do you turn for help?
- Read Romans 4:1-5, 13-17. What distinction do you draw between your doing great things *for* God and God's doing great things *through* you?
- Read John 3:1-17. What experience does the phrase *born again* bring to your mind? Does it foster positive notions? In what ways do you evidence your baptism in the Spirit?

Assistant to the Bishop, Wisconsin Annual Conference of The United Methodist Church

This psalm gave my Grandmother Dortie great confidence and comfort. She could recite it by heart, and it empowered her to cope with everything life threw at her. Through desperate times on her farm, the loss of her husband, recovery from accidents, illness, loss of loved ones, she lifted her eyes to the hills and patiently waited for help to come from God.

My grandmother was never alone a day in her life. God was her constant, faithful companion. She never doubted God's presence, never once questioned God's love. She took the good and the bad in stride because in all things she believed—no, she *knew*—that God was with her.

How does a person develop such a deep and abiding trust and confidence? What moves a person from belief to a faith of certainty and peace? My grandmother employed a simple yet transformative process for developing her strong faith. It is not unique, profound, or unusual. She committed to four practices that worked together to build an indestructible faith: prayer, reading the Bible, praising God, and loving neighbor.

I do not remember a day when my grandmother did not take time for prayer. Nor can I recall one day passing where she did not read and reflect on scripture. For every blessing, she offered thanks to God, and for every setback, she asked what she could learn from the experience. And I have never known one other person who did so much for so many as a basic daily practice. She fed the hungry, housed the visitor, welcomed the stranger, and visited the sick.

My grandmother lived a hard but fulfilling life. She never cursed the difficulties; she always praised the blessing. Few people have ever known more joy, comfort, security, or hope than my grandmother, Dortie.

Lord, be with me in prayer, speak to me through your word, and remind me to do for others. Amen.

Years ago I attended two churches in the same community. One congregation had about 3,000 members, while the other boasted just over 300. Both congregations were having celebrations of their ministries. When I attended the larger of the two churches, the lead pastor proudly proclaimed, "Let us celebrate together all the good and wonderful work we are doing for God!" The lay leader of the smaller church framed it a little differently. She said, "Friends, let us celebrate together all the amazing things that God is doing through us!"

There is a significant difference between what we do *for* God and what God does *through* us. Both may have multiple benefits and make a positive impact, but they illustrate for us the difference between justification through works and justification by faith. Doing good work for God is great. We honor God by taking actions that we believe please God. But we express a completely different level of faith when we surrender our own will to allow God to use us as God wills.

It is impossible to judge Abraham and other fathers and mothers of the faith from Hebrew scriptures by works. So much of what they did lies beyond our comprehension. Moses, Abraham and Sarah, Isaac, and David, for example, undertook challenges that make absolutely no sense apart from faith. Opposing Pharaoh, leaving home and country, wrestling with angels, taking on giants—these actions display foolishness and recklessness apart from a deep and abiding faith. The works are nothing more or less than expressions of the core beliefs and trust of the individuals. By and through such faith we are justified before God. What we do does not validate our belief; what we believe allows God to do in us that which most needs doing.

Gracious God, may I remember that I can do little for you that will make a great difference; but working through me, you can do things that can change the world. Amen.

Go from your country. . . . " In our postmodern, transitory, global community, this command doesn't seem like such a big deal. Social media and instantaneous communication make it possible never to be out of contact with family and loved ones.

But for Abram this command sounds incredible. The crucial values of Abram's day and culture were bloodline, place, family, and name. Most people never traveled more than forty or fifty miles from the place of their birth. Possessing land and having many children conferred great honor and prestige. Age evidenced wisdom and worth among the people who knew one another best. Older members of well-established families would sacrifice everything if they chose to leave home.

Even God's promises to make Abram's name great and his lineage a large nation sound risky and irrational. People earned honor and prestige over a lifetime—neither easily given or transferred. At the basic level, God asks Abram to risk everything with little assurance of success or security.

Amazingly, Abram obeys. And in his obedience, Abram illustrates three central aspects of our belief system: faith, trust, and hope. From a rational, modern, count-the-cost mentality, what Abram chooses to do makes no sense whatsoever. He risks everything on a promise. His faith in God is complete. The trust he displays falls nothing short of miraculous. To believe in God's promises means committing his own life and the life of his progeny through all generations to an unrealized vision. This course of action requires a hope for the future and a firm belief that the good of God's people is a higher value than any personal and individual risk he will take.

O Lord, work within me to increase my faith, my trust, and my hope. With Abram as my teacher, help me live with courage the convictions of my heart. May I be obedient to your will, O God, that I may bless others as I have been blessed. Amen.

The apostle Peter provides a good example of how easily people of faith miss the point. We sometimes get so caught up in the pageantry and excitement that we lose sight of the significance of the moment. Weddings are a fine example of this. Blessing the union of a couple's love can easily get lost in the costumes, the decorations, the stage directions, the music, and the emotions. Many couples spend much more time (and money) planning the reception than they do the service.

Were the Transfiguration story to take place today, I can almost hear Peter burst into modern marketing jargon. "We gotta set up booths! One for Moses, one for Elijah, and one for you! People will come from all over just to see where you three got together. We can sell programs. We can sell T-shirts, coffee mugs, refrigerator magnets, and bobble-heads! We need a logo! We need to brand this!" Peter wants to spread the miracle and share the awe, but why did Jesus want Peter, James, and John to witness this event?

We have no idea what Elijah, Moses, and Jesus talked about. But the three disciples witness the Law, the Prophets, and the Word combined and connected. They hear the voice of God confirming Jesus as the beloved Son. In the hard days to come, these three pillars of the early church will possess an indelible and unforgettable assurance of Jesus as the Son of God.

Jesus often instructed the disciples not to go overboard with stories of miracles and supernatural power. True faith stays strong in the absence of miracles, not just in their presence. The truth of Jesus the Christ is valid in the quiet and calm times, not just when the miracles take place.

Help us to walk by faith and not by sight, O Lord. Teach us to trust you, merciful God, so that when miracles occur, they don't surprise us but in fact reinforce what we already know. Amen.

For this reason it depends on faith, in order that the promise may rest on grace." Reflect on these words. This simple sentence offers a critical truth. We can do nothing to earn God's grace. We can do nothing to deserve God's grace. We can do nothing to force God's grace. The grace of God—unconditional love, acceptance and forgiveness—is a gift in the purest sense of the word. God offers grace to all; our only response is acceptance or rejection.

Human beings spend an inordinate amount of time in worry and anxiety. Are we good enough? Are we worthy? Are we too broken and corrupted? What all is wrong with us? How in the world can a holy God want to have anything to do with us? Theologians have built entire theological frameworks on the notion of our fallen, dirty, and shameful human nature. Some Christian communities spend much more time deciding who doesn't belong and who isn't acceptable rather than who needs the love, grace, and mercy of God.

Most of us are baptized into the faith as babies, with representatives accepting the faith on our behalf. Some of us choose this faith for ourselves. But through baptism, we are made acceptable to God and to one another in the fellowship. We acknowledge the free gift of God's grace and promise to live it before one another.

This understanding lies at the heart of incarnational theology: We are made one with Christ, one with each other, and one in service to all the world. We become the body of Christ together. The question is never "who belongs and who doesn't," but "where does each one fit in?" As we become one in heart, mind, and spirit, God makes us who God needs us to be.

Make us one, Lord, make us one. Help us to accept one another as you accept us, that we may be sources of acceptance, welcome, love, and forgiveness to everyone we meet. Amen.

Christians live in two worlds. We dwell in an earthly realm where we experience life through our five senses and interact with things reasonable, rational, ordinary, and necessary. We are all part of the natural world governed by physical laws and moral agreements. This is the world into which we are born.

But Jesus awakens us to a second reality and shares with Nicodemus that to experience this second reality fully we must be "born from above." That phrase, sometimes translated as "born again," elicits a variety of reactions, but at its basic level it clarifies that life is more than what we experience in the physical realm. It acknowledges a spiritual reality that requires a spiritual birth. Our baptism with water consecrates us to God, and we accept the grace and love that God freely gives. Our baptism with the Spirit deepens the covenant, and we give ourselves completely to God and to discerning and doing God's will. "Born of the Spirit" means we will develop and use our spiritual gifts for the greater good, and the evidence of the infilling of God's Spirit comes through our being more loving, more joyful. We are peacemakers; we are patient, generous, faithful, kind, gentle; and we exercise exemplary self-control.

We live by different rules and model different priorities. The common good is a higher priority than having our own way. We use our time for building relationship with God through prayer, reflection on scripture, and worship, while building relationships in Christian community through faith sharing, accountability, and Christian service. We become new people in Jesus Christ, and we bear witness to the transforming power of the Holy Spirit.

Come Holy Spirit, work within me. Use my gifts to serve others, and produce within me spiritual fruit of kindness, love, joy, and generosity. Allow others to know your love and grace through me, O Lord. Amen.

SECOND SUNDAY IN LENT

John 3:16 expresses an overwhelming love: "God so loved the world that he gave his only Son, so that everyone who believes in him may not perish but may have eternal life." The sheer gift of grace through this miraculous sacrifice is our eternal life. Yet, the line that follows is just as important and just as powerful. "Indeed, God did not send the Son into the world to condemn the world, but in order that the world might be saved through him."

We can more accurately translate the word *world* in verses 16 and 17 as "cosmos," "created order," or "system of reality." God's love is an inclusive and accepting love, unconditional and universal. God so loves the *whole* world and everyone in it that God sent Jesus so all might be saved.

Do some reject this gift? Certainly. Do some people remain ignorant of this great love? Without doubt. But we do not decide who receives this love and who does not. God is love. The very nature of God is grace. Being a Christian doesn't make us better than anyone else, just more fortunate and blessed. And we are blessed to be a blessing. We have received this great love. We have been touched by this amazing grace. We who know God and have been transformed by God's Spirit are charged with sharing this good news, this gospel, with everyone we meet.

Many aspects of life are uncertain. In this life we may lose or squander our possessions or virtues, and we may have items taken from us. But the one certainty, the one thing we can count on never to lose, is the love of God in Jesus Christ.

Gracious God, teach me to love as you love. Help me to sacrifice for the good of others and to be prepared to share your love and grace with the people I meet. Empower me by your Spirit to bless others as I have been so richly blessed by you. Amen.

Not Again!

MARCH 13–19, 2017 • SHARON G. AUSTIN

SCRIPTURE OVERVIEW: All the readings affirm God's benevolent care of those who place their well-being in God's hands. While imperishable, God's love can be frustrated by human pride and faithlessness. Water is an important symbol of God's sustaining grace. In Exodus 17 the Israelites' dependence on water becomes a statement about their dependence on God. The manner in which they obtain their water stands as commentary on human pride and arrogance. The psalm recounts this episode as a means of warning the people against the kind of obstinacy that impedes grace. John 4 focuses on the full actualization of God's love in Jesus Christ through the "living water." Paul speaks of God's love being "poured into our hearts," a grace that comes in the death and life of Jesus Christ.

QUESTIONS AND SUGGESTIONS FOR REFLECTION

- Read Exodus 17:1-7. When have you complained to God about a situation, only to discover God had already begun to forge a way through?
- Read Psalm 95. How does weekly worship allow you to hear God's voice? How do you testify to God's goodness?
- Read Romans 5:1-11. Reflect on a time when your suffering produced endurance and ultimately character.
- Read John 4:5-42. How do the words of Paul to Timothy about a worker "who correctly handles the word of truth" serve as a bridge between the "truth hurts" and the "truth will set you free"?

————————

Director of Connectional Ministries, Florida Annual Conference, The United Methodist Church

You've got to be kidding! We're often amazed to read the ongoing saga of faith and doubt that Exodus chronicles in the story of the Israelites and their quest to enter the Promised Land. Today's scripture follows the thirsty Israelites, ten plagues and one harrowing escape through water later! Moses must have wondered what it would take to ensure the people's faith in the living God who had delivered them from their Egyptian oppressors and then cared for them in the desert wilderness. To us it appears that God, with Moses as divine instrument, performs one miracle after another. This situation actually reflects a crisis in leadership—a lack of trust in Moses and in God. How dare the Israelites grumble, question, and make demands?

If we honestly reflect on our own situations, we realize that much of our frustration with the Israelites stems from our private, possibly sheepish, admissions about our own questions and demands of God. We, like the Israelites, have repeatedly experienced God's undeserved blessings throughout our lives. I acknowledge many such blessings that have emerged in my life: timing of challenges and resolutions synced; a way opened in the midst of circumstances that at the time appeared to have no resolution.

My own wilderness experiences and God's providential care have resulted in an undeniable pattern of goodness in my life. Yet, I sometimes allow an amnesia of grace to affect my testimony adversely. Pain, disillusionment, and fear exist. Struggles and hardships can seem more real than joy. But through it all, our faithful, loving, and powerful God cares and provides for us.

Dear God, bless me with a memory and a conviction of your presence and deliverance in my life that is stronger than the memories of my anxieties. I can tell the story today because your power is real in my life. Amen.

When the Israelites leave Egypt, the dream of promise shines brightly in their minds. They confuse potential promise with pie-in-the-sky promise.

Moses, a reluctant leader, also serves at times as an exasperated messenger. The Israelites in the desert push for and insist that their physical needs be met. As the leader, Moses actively engages in moving the people-mass and facilitates the meeting of their needs. He positions himself to make daily decisions, hear daily complaints, and receive pushback. Scripture does not single out individuals as the source of complaint. These complaints surface from "the people."

"The people" voice their concerns and complaints to their leader in soft-spoken words as well as shouts. They sidle up to the leader and speak confidentially; they also elbow and butt their way in, interrupting while the speaker converses with others. While Moses doesn't receive suggestions and complaints by snail mail, e-mail, Twitter, and Facebook, we can assume that he receives them continuously. A leader leads in every season and under every circumstance.

The people's voiced concerns imply that they judge God's presence or absence by the meeting of their demands: "Is the Lord among us or not?" God, the leader behind the leader, chooses to take action by providing water from an unlikely source. This God who makes a way out of no way provides water from a rock. Yahweh sustains life and once again commands the trust of the Israelites. They will live to quarrel and test the Lord and the Lord's servant Moses another day.

Lord, we can only lead if you lead us all. Give your leaders strength to endure. Help every leader remember what it is like to follow. Amen.

The psalmist calls us to praise the Lord with joyful noise and songs of praise, to worship the Lord as Creator and King. Then he evokes a pastoral setting: "We are the people of his pasture, and the sheep of his hand." The psalmist looks to God for help, guidance, and instruction. He trusts in God's steadfast love and care. Such a God deserves obedience.

To be captured by the spirit and action of the Lord is nothing short of awesome! The expanse of the Lord's majesty, creative prowess, and perfection boggles the mind. God fashioned us and knows us better than we know ourselves. We cannot make wise choices without the Lord's help. All the options belong to the Lord, who led the Israelites in the wilderness and leads them at the time of this psalm's writing. The psalmist goes on to recall a time of self-gratification in the desert, a time when the people failed to trust that God the shepherd would provide—the M & M (Meribah and Massah) incident. But wait. We praise and worship the Lord with all we have. We testify to the goodness of God with all that is within us. Meribah and Massah did occur and they still do—even among the chosen people. No one is exempt.

Meribah and Massah—a moment the Israelites would have preferred to forget. "For forty years I loathed that generation, the Lord says." The Israelites, who have come so close to the promise, remain so very far away. Despite the people's hardened hearts, God remains faithful. Only obedience to God's covenants and decrees keeps the psalmist on the paths of steadfast love and faithfulness.

Holy God, we are not worthy to come into your presence. We have been faithless children; the more you give the more we expect. May the memory of history deliver us from our sense of entitlement. Amen.

Not Again!

God's covenant with Abraham has been reformed in this credo, "justified by faith." Paul writes and teaches and reminds us of the mighty acts of a God who loves us, courts us, and receives us, even before we respond in like fashion.

Paul invites collective ownership and embrace of the new covenant that the Lord has forged through his Son, Jesus Christ. See what God has done! We boast in response to this word. Paul instructs us to boast in hope, in suffering, and in God. Paul does not promote suffering as a good thing; he acknowledges, however, that suffering produces endurance, which produces character, which produces hope. "And hope does not disappoint us." We live in a confident hope. We have been justified; we have peace; we gain access; we boast in the hope. We have a relationship with God that takes our willful intent and our best unrealized intentions into account.

We have received the unmerited favor of God. The season of Lent calls us to deep introspection for all that we are and are not. Contrite before God, we hold tightly to the gift of our faith. We acknowledge both the pardon and the assurance of God's love.

How does this gift provide an opportunity to consider those places in our lives where we feel stuck? Consider those occasions and circumstances that threatened to pull us down. Just when we thought all hope was lost, a way was made. We can move forward, maybe slowly, even falteringly, but we can make it. The health diagnosis, the child for whom we have been praying, the perilous marriage in which we have been so invested—all have been given new life. We will survive! "Hope does not disappoint us."

How much more should we rejoice and boast in the God of our salvation!

O Holy Way-maker, you commit to our well-being with a resounding Yes! May we always hear your yes and respond with our yes! Amen.

When people have experienced a windfall (not always in the form of money), we may describe their experience as a real rags-to-riches story. It usually depicts a one-hundred-eighty-degree shift in their circumstances, representing a significant increase.

Imagine, if you will, the full impact of the literal truth of having nothing and then gaining everything. This is an understatement of God's gift of forgiveness, We had nothing and were nothing, yet God's greatest gift was given to us while we lived in this state of being. We brought nothing to the table; God brought the entire meal. Paul wants us to understand the greatness of the gift. He points out the enormity of God's gift, even if sin had not been our issue. How much more, then, is it a gift of unbelievable proportions, given our low estate.

God's love and grace are magnanimous, deep and wide, and all-encompassing. The gift is amazing in its sacrificial nature, its perfection, the intended recipients, and its perpetual nature. We could not have acquired it on our own, and we have not earned it. It is as if Paul says that when we are at our worst, God is at God's best! God saves the ungodly and assures the godly of their salvation. We boast only in what God has done for us!

Who among us can fathom extending love on that basis, much less receiving it? Yes, when we are at our most unlovable, God loves us all the more. What God has done for the entire world (all people for all time), God has done for you and me!

Now that's a real nothing-to-everything story!

Lord, thank you for your all-or-nothing love. In you, we have everything. Amen.

One reading of this well-known story would claim that it defies convention. A man, a Jew, in open conversation with a woman who is a Samaritan sets up an unheard-of scene. It would be easy to say that the story's novelty comes solely in the fact that Jesus speaks to a Samaritan woman in public. Yet scholars also point to the fact that it is unusual for a woman to come to the well and draw water during the hottest portion of the day.

If Jesus had instead held a conversation with this woman in a private place under dark of night as he had met with Nicodemus, the story when heard would have led to a scandalous buzz. How does the Gospel writer describe this daylight, public conversation?

Jesus extends the grace of hearing and responding to the truth of this woman's life without recoil, and instead of passing judgment, passes her fresh, living water. Some might hold to the adage, "the truth hurts." Others might hold to the adage, "the truth will set you free."

If interviewed, is it possible that the Samaritan woman would acknowledge that both were true? She, unlike Nicodemus, evidences some understanding as Jesus speaks of the new life available to her. This is the longest recorded conversation with Jesus contained in the Bible. The woman opens up as they speak: her personal life, her spiritual life. And then she goes to bear witness: "He told me everything I have ever done." And many come to believe.

We, like this woman, may discover that our admission of truth's painful reality can free us. Hers is not simply the story of an open conversation with Jesus but of a life being opened to Jesus.

Lord Jesus, shine the light of your compassion and forgiveness in my life. May I thirst no more. Amen.

THIRD SUNDAY IN LENT

My reading of the Gospel accounts of Jesus and the disciples sometimes surprises me that the *disciples* were surprised. *After all*, I think, *they were with Jesus.*

The scripture lesson today provides yet another account in which they respond to the surface story and miss the deeper meaning. The disciples have apparently gone to a neighboring town to buy food when Jesus and the Samaritan woman meet each other. As unusual as this encounter is by the social and religious standards of the day, the disciples return to find them together. While astonished, they offer no comment—not a question, a rebuke, nothing. They almost appear to be the stereotype of the parent who thinks every problem can be solved with a good meal, as they offer Jesus something to eat.

Jesus' response to their offer to eat is met by words they do not understand. Jesus' source of life is a bread far beyond what they offer. As he tells them: "My food is to do the will of him who sent me and to complete his work."

Jesus had engaged in an exchange of far greater depth with the woman of Samaria, which he now extends to his disciples. Their agenda is mealtime and, left to their own devices, they would have missed the opportunity to understand the deep work of the kingdom in which Jesus is engaged and in which they, by virtue of being his followers, are also to be be engaged. It doesn't take many trees to block the forest. Sometimes it just takes one. But he summons them to the fields that are "ripe for harvesting."

Only our openness to understanding the deeper meanings of Jesus' conversations with us will allow us to reap and help Jesus "complete his work."

Jesus, help me to disengage my preoccupations and listen. You are a loving teacher; may I become your willing pupil. Amen.

Seeing, Feeling, Acting

MARCH 20–26, 2017 • LARRY J. PEACOCK

SCRIPTURE OVERVIEW: First Samuel 16 reminds us of the bold risk that Yahweh took in the anointing of this young and unheralded shepherd. If 1 Samuel 16 causes us to wonder about the adequacy of all human shepherds, Psalm 23 reassures us that one Shepherd never fails. The New Testament passages consider the tension between light and darkness as a metaphor for the conflict between good and evil. In Ephesians 5, the struggle has already been resolved but takes seriously the continuing problem of sin. By means of the love and presence of Jesus Christ, even the power of evil cannot withstand the light. Then John 9 emphasizes the power of Christ as a bringer of light in the story of the man born blind.

QUESTIONS AND SUGGESTIONS FOR REFLECTION

- Read 1 Samuel 16:1-13. How often do you allow external appearances to affect your decisions? In what ways are you learning to look on the heart?
- Read Psalm 23. When do you take time for yourself by slowing your pace, breathing deeply, and allowing God to restore your soul? How might this become a daily habit?
- Read Ephesians 5:8-14. How do you discover what pleases God? How does your living reflect your discovery?
- Read John 9:1-41. When have you experienced a "healing" that brought you back into community—either at home, work, or faith setting?

United Methodist minister, retreat leader, and spiritual director recently retired and now living in Portland, Oregon

Fear can hold us back. We sometimes think our only response to fear is to fight or take flight, but I think we can also remain immobilized, frozen and stuck, incapable of action. God tells Samuel that it's time for a change, time for a new king. And Samuel is to pick one of Jesse's sons. Samuel neither fights nor flees, but he raises a good objection: "Saul will kill me."

Sometimes when I struggle with a concern, my spiritual director will ask me, "What is the worst that could happen?" Samuel knows the worst, and he wants no part of this kingly transition. Yet Samuel learns, as we all do, that our worst fear pales in comparison to what God can do. God has a plan. Under the pretext of worship, Samuel will check out the sons of Jesse. Then God will open the envelope and announce the surprising winner.

Upon arrival, Samuel meets some compatriots in fear. The leaders of Bethlehem are cautious and nervous. Wrong political allegiances can be tragic and deadly. No one wants to be on the bad side of the king or God's prophet. But Samuel comes in peace and on a mission. He has moved past his fear toward God's plan.

Knowing the worst that can happen can free us. We may lose money or popularity, we may be demoted or fired, we may lose friends or family; but moving ahead with God's guidance is crucial. Knowing God is with us we can willingly speak the truth with love, choose what is right over what is expedient, say no to shady deals or tempting schemes. With God, we discover surprising and new possibilities.

Amazing God, move me from fear to trust, from frozen to flowing, from stuck to motion. Move me to do your will, one step at a time. Amen.

"You can't judge a book by its cover." This wise and familiar expression is true not only of books but also of people, according to the words God whispers to the prophet Samuel. Good looks, expensive haircuts, tanned and tall are not the hallmarks of God's leaders. God looks at the heart, not outward appearances.

In 1936, Adolph Hitler gathered the best-looking, most talented Germans to show the world the superiority of his race and clan. Jesse Owens, a black American, did not fit Hitler's bias, but the Olympian challenged and changed such a narrow and wrong perception by winning four gold medals in the summer Olympics.

Jesse parades seven good-looking sons before Samuel but God chooses the youngest who is not even invited to the show. David is tending the flock. As we know from several sources, he also happens to be good with stones in a sling, making music with the lyre, composing songs about nature and sheep. God looks on the heart, and David, despite some errors and yielding to temptation in his reign, remains the strongest and best-known leader in Jewish history.

Can we develop a way to see the heart of another? Can we slow down our judgments based on external observations? Perhaps if we listen deeply before we rush to speak. Perhaps if we don't pay attention to name brands or skin color. Perhaps if we see the grace of God in every person we meet and take a moment to ask God to bless our every encounter. Perhaps if we know that God looks at our heart with infinite wisdom and compassion and calls us to love and serve with our unique gifts.

God of surprises and wisdom, teach me a holy way of seeing.
Help me notice your goodness and blessing in everyone. Open
my eyes to see creativity waiting to flourish, leadership waiting
to be developed, and self-assurance ready to blossom. Amen.

Seeing, Feeling, Acting   105

Shepherds spend lots of time outside, and this familiar and popular psalm attributed to David invites us to the healing landscape of green meadows, flowing rivers, and tree-shaded paths. Such places offer renewal and restoration, and needs are cared for.

I remember a time of discernment around a possible vocational shift. I spent many Saturday mornings walking along smooth, shaded trails that eventually led over a rocky path to a hidden pool that only turned into a stream in wet seasons. There, with my journal, I would reflect on current ministry, notice the changes in my "still waters," and listen for nudges of a new call. I experienced the nurture of nature, the soothing sounds of water, the envelopment of peace. I trusted that I was being led on the right paths.

Today, many people focus their attention on screens of all sizes and spend less time outside. Long work hours and many obligations keep people from enjoying the outdoors. Vacations become destinations to air-conditioned resorts or spent in fancy recreational vehicles complete with satellite hookups. Some writers say we have an illness, a nature deficit that no pill and no amount of watching a nature show can make up. Researchers have discovered that walking in meadows or among trees can lower stress and improve blood pressure.

The first verses of the psalm invite us to slow down, feel the grass under our feet, and watch the river. They bid us rest and breathe deeply, receive the good tidings of nature, and let God restore our souls.

Take me, Shepherd God, along peaceful paths. Slow me to a gentle pace where I hear the birds, smell the flowers, feel the brush of spiderweb, and smile. Sit with me in verdant meadows as I dip my toes into cool streams. Teach me to be a grateful steward of your handiwork. Amen.

Many memorial services or services of death and resurrection employ this psalm to bring comfort and hope to the grieving. The psalm acknowledges the presence of grief, of going through dark places, of facing the reality of loss and death. Yet, it offers profound comfort and hope. God is with us through it all.

Many of us have been sustained by the memorizing of the old King James verse, "Yea, though I walk through the valley of the shadow of death, I will fear no evil: for thou *art* with me." Death causes a jumble of feelings and emotions, deep valleys and dark shadows. Yet the psalm carries a promise of moving through the chaos, walking through the valleys. We may journey there for a while; we may return there suddenly when memories evoke a strong pang of loss, but we do not live forever in the valley of death. And we don't walk in the shadows alone.

One friend who was grieving the tragic death of her thirty-year-old daughter from melanoma told me of looking out over the water one night not long after her daughter had been buried and seeing three lighted crosses shining on the water. She received it as a sign of God's presence for her and for her daughter. Yes, they were the masts of three nighttime fishing boats, but it felt like comfort to her. God was with her.

The psalm ends with household comforts, a grace-filled welcome, a place at the table, a cup that overflows. From the fields and streams in the first verses to the tables of plenty in God's presence, the psalm radiates assurance, comfort, and hope in all times and seasons.

Loving God, set a table in my heart for you and for strangers and friends—a big, welcoming table of abundance, kindness, and joy. Give me that openness of spirit and quiet assurance that we will celebrate together for a long time—even forever. Amen.

In the first three chapters of Ephesians, Paul stresses that Christ's death and resurrection have opened the way for Gentiles to draw near to God because the "dividing wall" (see Ephesians 2:14) has been broken down. The last three chapters give instruction on how to live as followers of this inclusive, welcoming Christ. Paul uses contrasting dualisms to point out the different ways to live: light and darkness, good and bad, pleasing and unpleasing to God.

Live as children of light. Be children growing up under the loving care and wise guidance of the faith community. Be like children—curious, joyful, energetic, and rejoicing in what is good and right and true. Discover what pleases God. Let your actions reflect God's grace and love.

Several years ago, a freak Halloween snowstorm knocked out the power in New England homes for many days. My family learned how difficult it was to live in the dark. We were cautious and hesitant in the dark, frustrated and short-tempered. Our productivity declined because of the darkness: All our cell phones, laptops, and everything else that ran on electricity ran out of power. We valued open restaurants only if they had a place to plug in so we could check in. We gained a new appreciation for living in light.

It may not be too far a stretch to think that naming and opposing the darkness of evil, injustice, and oppression will be pleasing to God. Shining a light to expose the darkness of poverty, war, and racism surely pleases God. Children of the light—the opposite of self-pleasing, self-centered people of darkness—seek to bring all individuals and systems into the beloved community of God.

God of truth, awaken me to your love and light, within me and around me. Teach me to walk paths of justice, care for the least and lost, and stand up for what is right. Amen.

This story wrestles with a culture that believed disease and misfortune were God's punishment. Someone did wrong; someone sinned. A person or even parents could cause lasting illness—so the disciples believed, and they want Jesus to settle their bet of who is at fault. The past determines the present, and somehow the past calculation metes out what we deserve.

Jesus changes the equation. God is active in the present, not limited or compelled by the past. The focus shifts to God's grace, which acts to bring healing, light, and insight. "He was born blind so that God's works might be revealed in him," says Jesus.

The complexity of the past brings to mind choices that seemed so good that turned out so bad; ways of coping that helped us survive childhood but that don't work in future relationships or situations. What seemed like a door closing, a disappointing ending, may have turned out to be a surprising opening to something not glimpsed. We can learn from the past and receive wisdom from the past, but Jesus encourages us not to allow our past to control us.

After all, the present can be confusing enough. Consider the many questions this healing raised: Is this really the blind beggar? Is he your son? Who did this? How did this happen? The man's reply: "The man called Jesus made mud, spread it on my eyes." Soon he affirms Jesus as a prophet. He also sees his fearful parents standing before the leaders. He moves from past blindness to the challenges of present-day seeing. Life is not punishment but blessing and challenge. And the One who heals is the same One who accompanies.

Gracious God, lead me from the past into this present moment. Ferret out wisdom from my journey, and place it on my path. Set me free to live with compassion for others, kindness to strangers, and gentleness with myself. Help me see others and myself in the light of your love and grace. Amen.

Seeing, Feeling, Acting   109

FOURTH SUNDAY IN LENT

Sometimes good news is too good to believe. At least it seems that way when Jesus strolls through John's Gospel (John 5, healing one ill for thirty-eight years; John 11, the raising of Lazarus). Here in chapter 9, the healing of the blind man is not met with "hallelujahs" but questions and controversy. The neighbors question if it is the same man. Even the parents are hauled before the authorities to identify the formerly blind son. The Pharisees can't seem to agree on what happened and who is responsible for taking forbidden action on the sabbath.

The authorities may know more theology than the man, but the man speaks from experience—the experience of touch, sight, and a changed life. Even in the face of expulsion from the synagogue for testifying about Jesus, the man clings to his experience, "One thing I know." He believes this good news of Jesus.

This story contains more good news, for Jesus not only heals but seeks. Jesus cares about blindness in his initial touch of the man but Jesus also cares about those separated from the community of faith: the least, the lost, and the outcasts. He searches for the man "driven" out.

It has continued throughout church history. In our time, people who have experienced Jesus' love have been driven from the church for skin color, marital status, or sexual orientation. We celebrate that the church can be a place of healing and forgiveness, but we confess that sometimes it also wounds. Religious authorities, then and now, have been blind to the wideness of God's mercy. The good news is that Christ heals and seeks us all. Thanks be to God.

Holy One, soften our hearts so that your love may flow through us in ever-widening circles. Open our eyes to see you in each person. Amen.

Seeing with the Eyes of God

MARCH 27–APRIL 2, 2017 • DEIRDRE GOOD

SCRIPTURE OVERVIEW: Ezekiel 37 presents a vision of the dry bones that represent the people of Israel after the Babylonian invasion—the people have no life. God calls Ezekiel to see the devastation and to prophesy to the dry bones with the message that they shall live. The psalmist cries out from the very depths expressing both a need and hunger for God and a trust in God's steadfast love and faithfulness. The story of Lazarus's death and Jesus' raising him to life calls forth our own stories and experiences of life and death. It draws us in to a conversation that goes deeper than our intellect. It evokes our questions, our fears, our doubts, and our faith. The Romans text offers the good news that the Spirit that raised Jesus from the dead dwells in us. Each of these texts affirms life after death. Death is not the end; death does not have the final word.

QUESTIONS AND SUGGESTIONS FOR REFLECTION

- Read Ezekiel 37:1-14. How has life come to you through death?
- Read Psalm 130. For what do you cry out to God? Pray the psalm, line by line, knowing that God hears and extends mercy and care.
- Read Romans 8:6-11. How has God changed your mind-set, your attitude, to bring you richer life?
- Read John 11:1-45. What in your world needs to die in order for life to come forth?

Interim Associate Dean of Academic Affairs, Visiting Professor of New Testament, Drew Theological School, Drew University, Madison, New Jersey

Psalm 130:7 speaks of the *hesed* of God when the psalmist employs the term *steadfast love*. Often translated "mercy, faithfulness, loving-kindness, grace, goodness," the wide connotations of the term invite investigation. Scholars propose that *hesed* is relational, describing interaction and mutual relations between two entities. It is active, demonstrated, and even reciprocal: an act of *hesed* encourages and promotes similar actions. *Hesed* in Hebrew scriptures is a noun and in the majority of uses refers to God's activities: God "gives," "sends," "remembers," "shows" *hesed*. Israel depends on God's *hesed*. It is often connected but not limited to God's covenant promises, the covenant community, and the element of fidelity that heals broken relationships. Scholars assert that the greatest *hesed* of God comes when God suspends justice to give grace to forgive Israel.

In the Psalms, *hesed* is the basis for the psalmist's request for deliverance and forgiveness. God remains faithful to Israel and sustains the whole earth. *Hesed* enables humans to relate to God; it is the quality God wants the community to put into practice and the way individuals are to behave toward one another. In 2 Samuel 2:5-6, David promises to do good to the city of Jabesh-gilead because its citizens showed *hesed* in rescuing Saul's corpse and burying it.

In Psalm 130, the cry to God from the depths becomes a cry of hope because the depths of the abyss cannot prevent human anguish or awareness of human iniquity from reaching God. In the closing verses, God's redemption manifests God's *hesed*. God's *hesed* brings a liberating expectation—an expectation that God will act.

O God, give us patience to discern your loving-kindness and mercy. Transform our souls into a reflection of your love and compassion, and grant us strength and peace. Amen.

In Romans, Paul uses the metaphor of "flesh" to contrast the way the world is with the way it should be for those in Christ Jesus. Throughout the letter, Paul tackles a tricky issue: How we are brought into the covenant community of God as those who are heirs of the divine promises.

In the world, this would happen through physical descent or, perhaps, through physical adoption. For Paul, it only happens through the Spirit of God that changes mind-sets, thus moving believers from death to life. However, this is not done through mortal bodies but rather through the divine work of God as God breathes life into those who believe in Christ Jesus. Here Paul sees God's Spirit at work in the lives of the Gentiles.

In Romans 8, flesh connotes physical descent from ancestor to descendant. Flesh here indicates those ancestors with whom God made a covenant and patrilineal forebears of the Messiah. Honor does not accrue through a person's family of descent but rather through the Spirit and promise by means of which God brought heirs of the Abrahamic covenant into being. In dualistic language, Paul contrasts lively spirit with decaying flesh.

The Spirit of Christ dwelling in humans, whether they are Jewish or Gentile, has the power to reorient minds to life and peace—and even to enliven fleshly bodies. Through the Spirit of God, even mortal bodies become life-filled. Paul does not argue that only those descended from a particular parent exhibit a Spirit-inspired mind-set. Quite the opposite: He argues that despite human descent and fleshly failing, God's Spirit dwells in whomever God may choose, slave or free.

O God, give us eyes to see your Spirit at work in the world. Amen.

Psalm 130 was one of Martin Luther's favorite psalms and his paraphrase of it for the Lutheran hymn of 1524: "Aus tiefer Not schrei ich zu dir" is still part of many hymnals. In an English-speaking world the hymn translation is by Catherine Winkworth, "Out of the depths I cry to thee. . . ."

The psalm opens with a cry of suffering, despair, and anguish: "Out of the depths I cry to you, O LORD." A focus on the religious significance of praying can be seen in Christian interpretations of the psalm. In the very act of crying from the deep, this person rises from the deep, says Augustine. "Whoever does not cry out, finds no grace," says Luther. Other interpreters propose that praying the psalm is the means of personal transformation or practice of virtues: devout praying and relying on God's mercy, for examples.

God does not count sins, or else no one would be acceptable. Rather, the psalmist focuses on the character of God who forgives and on trust in the promises that God has made. The psalmist proposes waiting for their fulfillment, stating his or her soul waits for the Lord "more than those who watch for the morning."

To see with the eyes of God is to claim the merciful and loving character of God, which remains steadfast even in the abyss. God is not to be feared because of the wrath of God's judgment, but God is revered because "with the LORD there is steadfast love, and with him is great power to redeem" (verse 7). God's unchanging love is the essence of who God is, and God's power is precisely the power to redeem.

O God, yours is the voice within us when we call to you from the abyss. Show us your loving-kindness and mercy, and grant us peace. In Jesus' name we pray. Amen.

The raising of Lazarus lies at the heart of John's Gospel. Resurrection is the greatest of the seven signs. Jesus speaks enigmatically about Lazarus' illness: "This illness does not lead to death; rather it is for God's glory, so that the Son of God may be glorified through it." Jesus will manifest glory as the communion of present life between believers and God. This sign will glorify Jesus because it will lead to Jesus' death, a stage on the way to glorification. So the Gospel challenges readers to deeper insight. Death is not final.

Jesus intentionally delays his departure for Bethany, heightening the tension of the scene. Lazarus will have been buried for four days when Jesus finally arrives. But hearers need to see in Jesus' absence the symbolic indwelling of Jesus with the disciples. Martha greets Jesus in terrible grief. Yet she speaks of personal transformation: "Lord, if you had been here, my brother would not have died. But even now I know that God will give you whatever you ask."

Their dialogue contains ironic misunderstanding. Noting that Lazarus "will rise," Martha affirms contemporaneous Jewish belief in general resurrection "on the last day." Jesus replaces an established religious belief with self-declaration: "I am the resurrection and the life. Those who believe in me, even though they die, will live." Then Jesus asks Martha (and the reader): "Do you believe this?" She affirms, "Yes, Lord, I believe that you are the Messiah, the Son of God, the one coming into the world." She understands that eternal life conquers death without abolishing it.

In Lazarus's resurrection, readers attempt to see with Martha that death is not final. Jesus has given life as the ultimate sign of the power that gives eternal life on earth, promising that on the last day the dead will be raised.

God, open our eyes to see your glory in the world. Amen.

When we want to identify something, we look at it closely. When we see someone we think we know in a crowded place, we concentrate on seeing a distinctive face or clothing or walk. To identify birds, we look at shape and size. How big is the bird? Is it fat or skinny, long or short? Expert birders identify birds just by listening to their song. Then they look at each part of the bird: is its bill short or long, thick or thin, curved or straight? What shape are the tail and wings?

One spring I went birding with an expert who led a group of us into Central Park. I can now identify a white-throated sparrow and a chipping sparrow. He taught me to pay attention and look. But in my heart of hearts I must confess that I've become skeptical about this common approach to bird-watching for one simple reason: It's fine for identifying species, but it fails to recognize individuality in each bird.

Why might any bird-watcher care about different sparrows of the same species? It's more than simply a matter of paying attention or being more patient; it is a matter of attending to the uniquenesses of the different sparrows. Isn't this the way God sees birds? Isn't it the way God sees us?

Ezekiel the prophet is brought by God to "death valley": a valley of dry bones. Ezekiel spends time walking through these bones to the extent that both he and readers are left despairing and desolate. But God wants Ezekiel to address them. God speaks to the prophet from a perspective he cannot fathom: "Can these bones live?" "O Lord GOD, you know." Where Ezekiel sees dry bones and death, God sees a living, breathing nation.

O God, open our eyes so that we may see as you would have us see. In Jesus' name we pray. Amen.

What do dry bones need to live? In Ezekiel's world, dry bones need God's power to come together by knitting bone to bone with sinews, flesh, and skin. Elsewhere, Ezekiel speaks of the transformation of Israel through the image of new hearts. And dry bones need the breath of life, that is, God's Spirit. It's possible that the prophet Ezekiel here remembers the creation of all humankind in Genesis wherein God forms human creatures from the dust and then breathes the breath of life into human nostrils. Without breath or spirit, there is no life.

So through God's power, the prophet sees reconstituted and revivified bones that "lived, and stood on their feet, a vast multitude." But flesh, sinews, skin, new hearts, and breath of life are not enough, for when the reassembled multitude speak, they do not live because they are without hope. Both they and Ezekiel lament, "Our bones are dried up, and our hope is lost; we are cut off completely." This is the language of exiles describing desolation—not just miles off or in a strange land but in exile in a land where hope does not exist and where Israel is lifeless. This is the vision and the reality that Ezekiel sees.

But God sees differently. Israel's exile and death are not realities in themselves but rather a place where God effects forgiveness and restoration for the people of God. The deep connection God has with the people of Israel exists beyond life, even beyond death itself.

In the height of the fight against apartheid in South Africa, an interviewer asked Archbishop Desmond Tutu if he were "optimistic" about the chances of a nonviolent movement to have Nelson Mandela released from prison and for blacks to receive the right to vote. Tutu replied, "I'm not an optimist, but I am a prisoner of hope."

God of dry bones, may I live as a prisoner of hope. Amen.

FIFTH SUNDAY IN LENT

John 11 juxtaposes Lazarus's death, and by implication, the death of anyone, with belief in Jesus as Word, Light, and Resurrection. Today's scripture enables those who experienced Lazarus's death and we who experience the death of a loved one to see through Jesus' eyes how death is transformed by eternal life in God.

In John's Gospel, Jesus is the Word become flesh dwelling among us, the One who declares, "I am the resurrection and the life." This perspective governs everything spoken and done. Hearing of Lazarus's illness, Jesus declares that it isn't for death but for glorification of God and the Son of God. Jesus' delay in coming to Lazarus confounds and confuses expectations, but it emphasizes that death is not to be feared.

Jesus acts in the knowledge that Lazarus, though dead, is not dead: "Our friend Lazarus has fallen asleep, but I am going there to awaken him" (John 11:11), and that is the will of the Father. So Jesus' absence is not a delay or denial of life but a demonstration of Jesus' sovereign autonomy whether absent or present. Jesus knows what Lazarus undergoes just as Jesus knows what will happen in his arrest and death at the end of his life. Death is part of a larger plan.

All deaths, while real, are not the end. Death's power is limited. John's Gospel presents the transformation of death as the glorification of God opening up the possibility of trust in and unity with God on the part of believers for the world's salvation. It is Lazarus's death that makes real what is possible, even as it confounds human expectations of love and grief.

Go forth created by God's love, redeemed by Jesus' mercy, strengthened by the Holy Spirit. In communion with the faithful, may you dwell in peace. May God's angels lead you, may mercy enfold you, and may you find eternal life. Amen.

God's Unfailing Love

APRIL 3–9, 2017 • BARRY SLOAN

SCRIPTURE OVERVIEW: These texts raise questions about who truly welcomes Jesus and under what circumstances. Isaiah 50 recalls the hostility that inevitably follows servanthood. A moment of acceptance, even welcome, will not hide from the servant the fact of the rejection to come. Psalm 118 claims that the city and the victory and the "one who comes" all belong to God. Any victory declared by human beings is bound to vanish as quickly as the day itself. The Philippians hymn asserts Jesus' own determination to be obedient even to death and God's consequent exaltation of Jesus above all creation. Even in the Gospel accounts, Jesus' entry is one of meekness and humility rather than of power and pride.

QUESTIONS AND SUGGESTIONS FOR REFLECTION

- Read Psalm 118:1-2, 19-29. How do you rejoice in "the day that the Lord has made"?
- Read Isaiah 50:4-9a. The writer notes that for Isaiah, suffering does not signal divine indifference but plays a part in the world's bigger story. When have you interpreted your suffering as part of a bigger story?
- Read Philippians 2:5-11. What earthly traits of Jesus' are evident in your daily living? Do you see yourself living a countercultural lifestyle?
- Read Matthew 21:1-11. Where are you in the Palm Sunday story? How do you respond to Jesus as he enters?

Born in Carrickfergus, Northern Ireland; ordained Methodist minister, currently serving as Director of Evangelism in the Germany Central Conference.

"This is the day that the LORD has made; let us rejoice and be glad in it." Down through the centuries God's children have read, sung, and actively embodied these words from Psalm 118 in faithful acknowledgment of God's unfailing love in and through impossible times. These ancient words have provided comfort and succor in all kinds of contexts both at national and at personal levels.

Their original liturgical context was probably the early Passover festival celebrating Israel's redemption from slavery in Egypt. In fact, present-day Jews still recite Psalm 118 at the Passover meal. It is the last of six psalms in Book Five known as the Egyptian Hallel, which commemorates the Israelite exodus from Egypt. Later in Israel's troubled history the words of Psalm 118 once again took on national significance through the return of the dispirited exiles from Babylon. "This is the day that the LORD has made." This is the day he acted to save us. Approximately three hundred years later, Christians began to read these words through the eyes of Palm Sunday and Easter. They began to cite the words of Psalm 118 as they celebrated the resurrection of Jesus, the Lord's day, the day the Lord has made (acted) . . . to deliver. And still today countless individuals find hope, solace, and encouragement in this ancient text. Why? Because it has to do with love—a love that endures forever. A love that knows no limits, that never gives up. An active love—quite literally one that acts, does, makes, performs, delivers. God's love. God's unfailing love.

Deliverance. Freedom. New life. New hope. These are more than enough reasons to give thanks to the Lord and testify to a love that endures forever!

Lord, help me see, sense, and experience your proactive love for me today. In the impossible situations that I face, remind me of the hope that I have in Christ, my deliverer. Amen.

Today's passage is one of four poems found in the second part of the book of Isaiah (chapters 40–55) that deal with the mysterious figure of the suffering servant. In these poems a faithful and righteous servant addresses Israel. The context is the latter days of Israel's Babylonian exile under a new Persian king named Cyrus who has come to power and established a new empire. God's chosen people live in trying times: their beloved temple in the holy city of Jerusalem desecrated and destroyed, deported as slaves into exile in a foreign land. They now have no king, no Temple, no holy city, and little hope—over a time span of almost seventy years!

Into this context of misery and lamentation come the life-giving words of the suffering servant of the Lord. The very fact that this righteous servant himself suffers helps Israel see God in a new light. God is not distant or disinterested. God is near and has identified with them in the form of this messenger, knowing their suffering and oppression. That makes the words, spoken by the servant all the more comforting. He is qualified to speak of "sustain[ing] the weary with a word" and to be listened to.

The sovereign Lord still surprises us through current revelation in new and unexpected ways. Maybe that's why the first Christians perceived Jesus and his passion (suffering) when they heard these servant poems of Isaiah. One thing is certain though. God's unfailing love often comes to us in unexpected forms. Think about that. And, who knows? Maybe you will be the person who surprises someone today with a word that sustains the weary.

God, thank you for the many persons who support me; I know I am not alone. May I sustain the weary with a word. Amen.

God's Unfailing Love   121

The apostle Paul writes these words to the church in Philippi from a Roman prison. His crime? He follows Jesus of Nazareth. His Christian faith has led to hostility, opposition, and dubious charges being brought against him, leading to Paul's now being, in his own words, "in chains for Christ" (Phil. 1:13, NIV). This is by no means the first time Paul has suffered for being a follower of Christ. He has been flogged and beaten with rods. On other occasions he suffered shipwreck, stoning, and all kinds of troubles because of his faith. And now, he sits "in chains for Christ" to pen a letter to his friends in Philippi. Within a short period of time Paul will suffer a martyr's death. So what does he write?

"Let the same mind be in you that was in Christ Jesus, who . . . emptied himself . . . humbled himself and became obedient to the point of death—even death on a cross." Remarkable words when we consider Paul's setting. No hatred, no bitterness, no hardness of heart. Instead, an exhortation to possess and exhibit the Christlike attitude of service, sacrifice, and self-denial—even unto death. I can think of no other attitude or mind-set that could possibly be more contrary to the ways of the world today. Can anything be more countercultural? more radical?

This is the way of Christ, the way of the cross, the way of godly love—an unfailing love that knows no limits, a nonlimiting love that "unknows" our failures. God calls us to this as followers of Christ. We hear it ourselves but then let it so take hold of us that it becomes *our* countercultural way of life.

Lord, teach me how to be humble, and show me how I can serve others today. To the glory of God the Father. Amen.

Christians find it hard to read today's text without thinking of Jesus' final week on this earth. The disturbing picture of affliction, anguish, and distress painted here so vividly by the psalmist seems to act as a signpost to our Lord's own experiences of abuse and abandonment. The talk here is of eyes weak with sorrow, a body and soul weak with grief, a life consumed by anguish, years consumed by the groans of affliction, hateful enemies, the utter contempt of neighbors. Abandoned by acquaintances, the psalmist faces terror on every side and plots to end his life.

It is, however, the psalmist's exemplary response to his terrible predicament that elicits our attention. "I trust in you, O LORD; I say, 'You are my God.' My times are in your hand." The psalmist places not simply his current reality into God's hands but all times—all situations, all circumstances. These words of the psalmist once again teleport us, so to speak, to the passion of Christ, resonating with Jesus' prayer in Gethsemane, "Not my will but yours" (Luke 22:42). Or from the cross, "Into your hands I commend my spirit" (Luke 23:46).

The psalmist's complete trust in God to act in all times encourages his specific requests of God: "deliver me," "let your face shine," "save me." The psalmist in weakness cries to the God who can save and deliver and whose radiant countenance fosters well-being.

Our troubles may seem tiny in comparison to those we find in this psalm. But they are *our* troubles, which makes them significant to us. May we always have the faith and courage to proclaim, "I trust in you, O LORD. . . . You are my God. . . . Let your face shine upon your servant; save me in your steadfast love."

"I am no longer my own, but thine. . . . I freely and heartily yield all things to thy pleasure and disposal." (A Covenant Prayer in the Wesleyan Tradition; UMH, no. 607)

For the past three years Jesus has shared his life and ministry with his disciples—a small group of simple but committed men who have enjoyed intimate company and fellowship with Jesus and witnessed his miracles firsthand. They have followed him faithfully—if at times questioningly—every step of the way. Yet if we were to read today's passage in isolation, without any previous knowledge of the story, we would not only doubt that these men were his disciples but also that they belonged to his most intimate circle of friends. Judas sells him out for thirty pieces of silver. With a kiss! Peter, who promises he will never fail Jesus, disowns him. Again. And again. In Gethsemane, in what could possibly be described as Jesus' darkest hour, when he needs the love and support of his friends most, they fail him. They fall asleep. Twice! These men, Jesus' closest companions who have been with him all the way, now betray him, disappoint him, disown him, and desert him.

The words of the text speak for themselves. They are heartbreaking. "What will you give me if I betray him?" "Truly I tell you, one of you will betray me." "This very night, before the cock crows, you will deny me three times." "Could you not stay awake with me one hour?" "Put your sword back into its place." "Then all the disciples deserted him and fled."

How well do the words of the text speak for us? We differ little from the Christ-followers of first-century Palestine. Our faith can be just as fickle, our loyalty just as conditional and our following just as hesitant. Lent is a good time to remember that.

Lord, have mercy on me, a sinner. May the power of your unfailing love teach me your ways. Amen.

Why did Jesus have to die? Who was responsible? Was it Judas, who chose to betray him for thirty pieces of silver? Or maybe we could blame Jesus' disciples as a whole. If only they had intervened on his behalf instead of running away like cowards, things might have turned out differently. Surely the rabble also played their part in Jesus' death. When Pilate offered them the chance to let Jesus go free, they scoffed at it, choosing to free Barabbas instead. "Crucify him!" they screamed. It doesn't get much clearer than that. Then we have Pontius Pilate, the Roman governor. He had the power to release Jesus. And he alone had the authority to condemn him to death. "I am innocent of this man's blood," he said as he washed his hands in front of the crowd. But was he? Especially when he felt convinced of Jesus' innocence?

Who was responsible for Jesus' death? We know that Christians have always understood the happenings surrounding Jesus' death as part of God's salvific plan for the redemption of the world. Is God then somehow to blame?

Perhaps we could point the finger at ourselves. Maybe we are to blame. Humankind. Did Jesus not die for *our* sins? Making us in turn responsible for his death?

A complicated matter, a simple answer to all these questions: yes. We all are guilty. God, however, is only guilty of love. Divine unfailing love for us brings death to self before seeing his loved ones suffer. And this love sets us free. Even from death!

Loving God, you would go to hell and back for me. In fact, you already have. In you I am free. Help me to lay claim to this truth in my life today. Amen.

PALM SUNDAY

"Who is this?" This question seems to be on everyone's lips as Jesus processes into Jerusalem on the back of a donkey. Is this the question on the minds of the two disciples whom Jesus sends to the next village for a donkey and a colt? Could they perhaps have been aware that, according to Zechariah 14:4, the Mount of Olives is the place where God will defeat Israel's enemies and inaugurate a new creation? And might they have understood the significance of the donkey ride into Jerusalem? Jesus has walked thus far on foot. Why now, so near to Jerusalem, does he request a donkey? Would the two disciples have understood the messianic prophetic symbolism of this request and quietly asked themselves, "Who is this?"

The crowds that welcome Jesus triumphantly, waving palm branches and laying out their cloaks on the road, would also have engaged the question, "Who is this?" Did they really understand what they shouted as Jesus passed by? Were they aware that the word *hosanna*, although it had become an exclamation of praise, literally meant "save"? And what would or should that salvation look like? Their cries of "Crucify him!" just a few days later suggest that their understanding of Jesus and his salvific work is seemingly incomplete.

When Jesus enters Jerusalem the whole city stirs and asks, "Who is this?" His presence in the world today can effect the same response. Where the body of Christ faithfully exhibits and reflects the unfailing love of God today, people still want to know, "Who is this?" May we be ever willing and able to answer with the words of our text, "This is . . . Jesus."

Stir my heart, O God, and grant me the humility, love, and courage to be your witness today. Amen.

Not What We Expected

APRIL 10–16, 2017 • EMILY ANDERSON

SCRIPTURE OVERVIEW: It is not appropriate to conclude that God disappears at the cross and only emerges again in the event of Easter. Christian proclamation of the cross begins with the understanding that even in Jesus' utter abandonment, God was present. The Holy Week/Easter texts bring together the common themes of death's reality, the powerful intrusion of the delivering God, and the manifold responses to resurrection. Paul argues that the gospel looks to many like nothing more than weakness and folly. The cross symbolizes defeat but is in reality the instrument of power and salvation. Isaiah 50:4-9a recalls the hostility that follows upon servanthood. A moment of acceptance, even welcome, will not hide from the servant the fact of the rejection to come. John 20 honestly faces the reality of death. Paul asserts in First Corinthians that the cross of Jesus Christ reveals the power of God.

QUESTIONS AND SUGGESTIONS FOR REFLECTION

- Read Isaiah 50:4-9a. When have you faced a task with your face set like flint? How did your resolve impact the outcome of your work?
- Read Matthew 27:57-66. When have you attempted to seal Jesus in a tomb? When have you felt anxious or fearful about the change Jesus might bring in your life?
- Read 1 Corinthians 1:18-31. In what ways have you discovered the Cross to be God's wisdom for you?
- Read John 20:1-18. How does Jesus' resurrection signal new life to you? What comes to you "green and fresh" today?

Pastor Head of Staff, New Providence Presbyterian Church, Maryville, Tennessee

"Waste not, want not," Ben Franklin warns. Those of us who are children of the Depression or children of children of the Depression have learned how to squeeze the life out of every single penny. So it strikes us as odd that Jesus not only allows but even applauds what appears to be careless extravagance.

Mary does a reckless thing—embarrassing and perhaps too intimate. No doubt several squirm and look away. "Why was this perfume not sold for three hundred denarii and the money given to the poor?" A laborer's family could live for a year on what that one bottle of perfume cost, and this woman's gone and poured it all on Jesus' feet, for heaven's sake.

Whatever your opinion of Judas, you have to concede his point: The extravagant use of this perfume contradicts all that Jesus taught about simplicity and selflessness. Jesus championed the rights of the poor, called them blessed, and claimed they would inherit the kingdom of heaven.

It seems out of character for Jesus to allow the waste of this expensive perfume, but it shouldn't. The God we see in Jesus Christ is a reckless, passionate, divine spendthrift. The God we see in Jesus Christ is a shepherd who leaves the ninety-nine to go after one lost sheep. The God we see in Jesus Christ is a woman who tears her house apart looking for one lost coin, and when she finds it, invites the neighborhood to celebrate. The God we see in Jesus Christ is a father who throws a party to welcome a prodigal home.

The God we see in Jesus Christ continues to surprise us. If the gospel is anything, it is outrageous; it demands an excessive and extravagant response. There is nothing frugal about the love of Christ or about the lives of those who serve him.

Help us, loving One, to share your outrageous grace with all we meet. Amen.

Imagine the first-century followers of the Way. In the two decades following Jesus' death, the fledgling church has struggled, knowing that a confession of Jesus Christ as Lord was politically subversive in an empire that proclaimed Caesar as Lord. By Paul's day, the Jews had suffered three hundred years of subjugation at the hands of the Romans. A theology developed in some corners that God was coming to clean house: drive out oppressors, destroy enemies, and restore the throne of David. The messiah would literally be the King of the Jews.

Paul writes to encourage the early Christian congregation. He reminds the Corinthians that followers of the Way proclaim Christ crucified, and therein lies the problem. For Greeks who envisioned a god that transcended human life, and Jews who understood God's Messiah in powerful military terms, Christ crucified is indeed a stumbling block.

So who can view the cross as the power of God? "Those who are being saved." The Corinthian community has a reputation for taking pride in its own spiritual wisdom and accomplishments. Paul reminds them that God, working in their midst, chose foolishness, weakness, lowliness—overturning the world's values.

The Christian faith is not about a god of perfection in the way the Greek philosophers wanted or powerful in the way religious extremists preferred. Instead, Christian faith is about a God who laughs and weeps, rejoices and grieves; a God capable of anger and remorse and profound love; a God who, for our sake and the sake of love, suffers. The cross reveals God's wisdom and will for the world.

Amazing love, how can it be that you, my King, should die for me?

This is the third of four "servant songs" in chapters 40–55 of Isaiah. Who is this servant? We can only speculate. Some claim it is Isaiah himself; others say it is a "type" or ideal model of the righteous and faithful servant. But the servant could also be a composite character of the exiles of Israel, still captive in Babylon and longing for home.

Isaiah clearly has no hint of Jesus as the coming Messiah, but early Christians quickly connected these prophetic texts to their Lord. Like the promised servant, Jesus speaks on behalf of Yahweh; he has learned to be attentive to the Lord's direction, and with God's help, he will not be dissuaded in his mission.

We easily see the connection between this prophetic text and the events of Holy Week. The servant's face is set "like flint," and Luke tells us, "When the days drew near for [Jesus] to be taken up, he set his face to go to Jerusalem" (Luke 9:51).

The servant of God faces hostility and suffering: "I gave my back to those who struck me, . . . I did not hide my face from insult and spitting." Despite the troubled nature of his work, the servant asserts confidence in God and contends, "I did not turn backward."

The road of faithfulness, like Jesus' journey through this terrible and holy week, often takes us through dark places and demands sturdy trust. But like Jesus, may we take a stand for hope in God's justice and mercy, a hope that shapes us who claim it into ever more faithful servants of God.

Morning by morning, O God, waken our ears to hear your voice and to share your good news with the world you so love. Give us strength, even in the darkest days, to place our trust in you alone, for you are our help. Amen.

MAUNDY THURSDAY

One evening in December of 2015, Zaevion Dobson was walking home with friends after playing basketball at a neighborhood recreation center. The four stopped on the front porch of an apartment to visit when two men drove by in a car. The passenger fired a gun into the group of teens. Rather than fleeing, Zaevion jumped into the line of fire to shield his three friends from the bullets. He was shot and died instantly.

Jesus rises from the table, ties a towel around his waist, pours water into a basin, and washes his disciples' feet, even Peter's. The Lord and Teacher teaches by example. "By this everyone will know that you are my disciples," Jesus says, "if you have love for one another."

Maundy Thursday teaches us the meaning of costly love. If love were merely a concept or a theory with which we only had to agree in principle, this commandment would be easier to swallow. But the truth is that the kind of love Jesus speaks of involves people—real people with quirks, problems, and flaws that trouble and irritate.

As one writer puts it, "I tend to love with my fingers crossed. I'm ready to love almost everyone, but surely I can't be expected to love the person who has harmed me. Or who does not wish me well. Or who seems hopelessly wrongheaded. Surely I am allowed one holdout. But this commandment has no loopholes."

Jesus calls us to the ultimate tough love. Not just a warm feeling but a willingness to give ourselves away for the sake of another, for the benefit of others. "Just as I have loved you, you also should love one another."

God, help me to love even, and especially, when it demands something of me . . . just as you did. Amen.

GOOD FRIDAY

If you don't know the name of Rollen Stewart, I bet you know who he is. In the 1970s and '80s, Stewart appeared at major sporting events wearing a rainbow wig and holding up a sign reading: "John 3:16." Stewart, an enthusiastic Christian, was determined to get the message out. He showed up at basketball finals, all-star games, between football goalposts, at "Amen Corner" at the Augusta National Golf Club, and behind the pit crew at the Indianapolis 500.

Why John 3:16? Because God so loved that God gave. The idea that the Son of God might be fully human, fully divine, and very much alive seems incongruous to those who prefer that religion be a purely spiritual matter. But Christians refuse to let go of the Incarnation—the idea that a holy God came into this world in the muck of a stable and left it via the painful torture of a cross—that God took on flesh and blood for us.

Now it was the day of Preparation for the Passover; and it was about noon. On the Friday afternoon that Jesus dies, the parade of lambs, goats, and calves into the Temple will have just begun. For the rest of the afternoon, they would be slaughtered while priests caught the blood and poured it on the altar. Outside in the courtyard, the animals were skinned and cleaned according to the law of Moses while Levites sang psalms of praise to God.

So there were two bloody places in Jerusalem that day—one at the Temple and the other at Golgotha. At the close of this day, it was obvious to some who the real scapegoat had been—a flesh-and-blood Savior, the Lamb of God, who sacrificed himself for us.

Lamb of God, who takes away the sins of the world, have mercy upon us. Lamb of God, who takes away the sins of the world, have mercy upon us. Lamb of God, who takes away the sins of the world, grant us peace. Amen.

HOLY SATURDAY

"Make it as secure as you can," Pilate says and assigns a guard of soldiers to work with the chief priests and the Pharisees. Matthew is the only Gospel writer to include these details. It is Saturday, and the religious leaders remain anxious. The public execution of Jesus had taken place the day before, and the matter seems to be settled—finally. The disciples have scattered and are nowhere to be seen.

Saturday is quiet, but here come the Pharisees again: "Remember how he said he was going to rise again? Well, sir, if you don't keep an eye on his disciples, they'll steal his body and then go around talking about a resurrection; and it'll get a whole lot worse around here, if you don't mind us saying so. Why don't you assign a guard to the tomb to be sure nothing happens?"

Frightened people want to make sure nobody shakes things up. The chief priests and Pharisees say they're afraid someone will steal the body. Maybe they fear something else altogether. What if the prediction actually happens? What if Jesus got up and walked out of that tomb? If that happens, nothing will be the same again. If that happens, they have to view the world in a new light, and that prospect is nothing short of terrifying. So let's maintain the status quo.

"Make it as secure as you can," Pilate tells the guard, the chief priests, and the Pharisees. They head off to the tomb with what has to be the easiest assignment in history—make sure a dead man stays dead.

But how do soldiers secure the world against a miracle?

God, you are the one who makes all things new. Save us from our fear of change and uncertainty. Open our eyes, and remind us that with you, nothing is impossible. Amen.

EASTER

Mary supposes Jesus to be the gardener. A few days earlier, in another garden, Jesus' trusted friends could not stay awake and pray, and another betrayed him. Jesus begged, "Let this cup be taken from me."

We hear echoes of the first garden. The writer of Genesis says Adam and Eve hear God in the garden and hide because they are afraid, suddenly aware of how much they stand to lose. And on this Easter Sunday, thousands of years later, we come to this garden where Jesus' body has been laid. Mary Magdalene watched the man she thought was the Messiah die. Everything had come undone.

But this gardener rewrites the script. In the first garden, characters leave in tears. In the garden of Gethsemane, disciples run in panic. In this garden of the new creation, the gardener sends Mary to announce, "I have seen the Lord!" What happens in this garden redeems every garden that's come before it.

Wangari Maathai, an activist with the Green Belt movement, began paying women to plant tree seedlings in Kenya in the 1970s. People laughed. But slowly the trees took root and made the dead places green and full of life again. Now the trees aren't just holding back the desert; they're driving it back.

People thought they were burying Jesus when they put him in the tomb. But they weren't burying; they were planting. And when he sprang up green and fresh, he took that dead, arid place and turned it into a garden, filling it with life.

Christ is risen! Shout hosanna! Celebrate this day of days!

GARDEN

Life in Light of the Resurrection

APRIL 17–23, 2017 • DEBORAH VAN DEUSEN HUNSINGER

SCRIPTURE OVERVIEW: Psalm 16 and Acts 2 fit together, since the latter quotes the former. Both celebrate God's presence in human life and the powerful expression of that presence. In his Pentecost sermon Peter sees a messianic application of the psalm to the resurrection of Jesus. First Peter affirms that resurrection creates community, stressing the faith and love of Christians that arise without the experience of physical contact with Jesus. For later generations, belief and commitment are born out of the witness of others.

QUESTIONS AND SUGGESTIONS FOR REFLECTION

- Read Acts 2:14a, 22-32. When has a life experience made you, like Peter, feel that your faith was a sham? How did you move past that experience into renewed hope?
- Read Psalm 16. When have you perceived God as refuge? How has your faith in God steadied your life? What is your "goodly heritage"?
- Read 1 Peter 1:3-9. What act of power and grace on God's part allows you to reconfigure or reinterpret your life story?
- Read John 20:19-31. When have you employed the power to release others from their sin? to leave them in their sin?

Charlotte W. Newcombe Professor of Pastoral Theology, Princeton Theological Seminary, Princeton, New Jersey

Peter had put all his hope in his beloved friend, Jesus, only to see him cruelly crucified. Jesus had healed the sick, fed the hungry, comforted the desperate, and preached good news to the poor. Through all these signs and wonders, Peter's faith in God must have grown stronger than he could have imagined.

But then his friend was killed—executed for crimes he had not committed. The whole justice system seemed a complete sham. Even worse, Jesus' death implies that Peter's faith in God is a sham. God abandoned Jesus in the time of his greatest need.

Then, far beyond Peter's wildest dreams, Jesus appears to him and the other disciples as one alive. *What can this possibly mean? Could this be the resurrection of the dead that was to come at the end of all things?*

Slowly it dawns on Peter that God had not cruelly abandoned Jesus. Even though Jesus was killed, God had a plan and purpose in mind, a purpose completely unfathomable and deeply mysterious.

Peter comes to realize that Jesus actually fulfills God's promises. Through an astonishing leap of insight, Peter makes sense of Jesus' life and death, and his incomprehensible resurrection.

What had looked like God's cruel abandonment of all their hopes and dreams turns out instead to be part of an inscrutable plan to bring about the fulfillment of God's purposes for redeeming the whole world.

Like Peter, God invites us to reinterpret our lives in light of the reality of Jesus' resurrection. Hope was there all along, even in the darkest hours. Yet Peter could not see it.

Lord, give us eyes to see your hidden purposes among us. Amen.

Knowledge of Christ's identity brings with it an awareness of his living presence. Just as Jesus had not been abandoned to death and Hades but was by God's grace raised from the dead, so we will also be. This is the glad news at the heart of the gospel: the promise of eternal life in Christ.

As we tell others our life narrative, we may, like Peter, recall times of losing all hope in God. We might have believed that God had abandoned us, or that God didn't care about the unjust suffering of our people. Remembering heroes who once gave us hope of a new world tempts us to despair when we recall their being mowed down by lawless gunmen.

Christ's resurrection, now preached by a newly awakened Peter, requires a new kind of seeing. Only with the eyes of faith can we see the hidden Christ at work in the world in spite of human disobedience and sin. As Peter was led to reinterpret his entire life in light of Christ's resurrection, so also are we.

When we see only death, where is the resurrected Jesus alive among us? What signals his hidden presence? Instead of asking, "What would Jesus do," let us ask instead, "What is Jesus doing? Where is our living Lord among us? What glad purposes is God working out in ways that we simply do not see?"

As it dawns on Peter just who Jesus is, he realizes something breathtaking about God and God's purposes. If King David had foreseen and spoken of restoration of life and if Peter is a witness of these glad tidings, then Peter sees into the very heart of God's will for creation. God's life-giving intention for the world is revealed as forgiveness of sin and eternal life in Christ. This good news reconfigures Peter's entire life narrative. And ours as well.

Christ, may we know your presence among us this day, that we may dwell in hope and live with grateful hearts. Amen.

Peter quotes part of this psalm in his sermon in Acts 2:25-28 to support the resurrection of Jesus. So, we as Christians come to the psalm affirming its voice in the life of Israel's faith even as we affirm its apparent witness to Jesus' resurrection.

The psalmist opens with a one-word imperative: *Protect.* That word may also be translated as "guard, keep, preserve." He affirms God's refuge, declares God to be the Lord of his life, and acknowledges God's blessings upon him—no good comes to him apart from God.

The psalmist remembers all the "holy ones," those who have called upon God in times of trouble. They are noble in his sight, and he happily acknowledges his delight in them. They are chief among the blessings of faith, brothers and sisters who through the ages have, in challenging times, taken refuge in God. He contrasts the holy ones, those who place their loyalty and trust in God, with "those who choose another god." He identifies himself as one loyal to God and to God's people.

The psalmist makes a clear choice to serve God. He knows the Lord as the source of his every good. By contrast, those who fail to make a similar choice only multiply their sorrows. So the psalmist wants nothing to do with them. He will not take their names upon his lips. He keeps his focus on the Lord, who is his chosen portion. Such a steadfast gaze on God alone reaps immediate benefit: a "goodly heritage."

Like the psalmist, we too can choose a relationship with God, a God who listens patiently and offers protection and refuge. As we experience the security of that relationship, the expansive nature of that relationship, we will find that our boundary lines fall in "pleasant places."

Gracious God, as we recognize the blessings of our "goodly heritage," help us to acknowledge the saints who inspire us to renewed vision and courage. Amen.

The psalmist maintains a steady communion with God, receiving counsel and allowing his heart to instruct him. How does a heart attuned to God's counsel manifest in our lives and that of the psalmist? It seems to provide stability, a steadiness that promotes an unshakable foundation. The psalmist experiences gladness, rejoicing, and security. When we act on the Lord's counsel and the heart's instruction, what do we experience?

Those who live without attuned hearts remain unaware of God's purposes for their lives. They may doubt the value of their lives, perhaps drifting from place to place looking for love but not knowing where to find it; looking for security, not knowing that they are powerless to bring it about by their own efforts.

Those who keep their hearts secure in God will not be moved. They do not doubt the worth of their lives and are grateful day by day for God's abundant blessings. God daily shows them the path of life.

In verse 10, the psalmist alludes to a time of extreme trouble. Even in that situation, his loyalty and faithfulness to God brings about a happy end: "You do not give me up to Sheol, or let your faithful one see the Pit." We who bless the Lord trust that God will not give us up to the darkness and despair of Sheol. We and the psalmist remain steadfast because we keep God ever in our minds and hearts. Therefore, we experience a fullness of joy that arises out of wholehearted trust. The heart is glad, and the soul rejoices. May we too choose the path of life.

Loving God, we thank you for the blessings of security that come in the wake of knowing that we belong to you. When we understand our lives in the light of your steadfast love and faithfulness we experience the steady joy of knowing that our lives matter. Amen.

Peter and the other disciples do not know what lies ahead. The suffering and death of Jesus has tested them beyond their strength. And yet, they live through it to testify to God's power to bring life out of death, love out of fear, courage and strength out of grief and despair. This new realization of the scope and power of God's grace to save the people reconfigures Peter's entire life story. It gives him a living hope that burns within him his entire life.

Just as Thomas would not believe without seeing, Peter commends those who "have not seen him" yet "love him." The Resurrection brings new birth, inheritance, and salvation to those who love Jesus. The new birth brings relationship within the family of faith. And thus we have a living hope.

We witness God's power at work in the resurrection of Jesus Christ, a power that controls even death. Therein lies our hope for eternal life—both now and beyond this life. Peter tells us that this power is what makes all the difference in human life. Despite the suffering we experience, we can "rejoice with an indescribable and glorious joy."

Genuine faith comes as an imperishable gift that, like gold itself, cannot perish even when tested by fire. God will guard the wavering faith of the disciples, just as God continues to guard our hearts even when we waver in our faith. Our love for Jesus Christ is kept secure, beyond anything that we ourselves can do to secure it. Even though we have not seen the resurrected Jesus, we nevertheless love him. God's action of placing faith in our hearts becomes a source of unutterable joy, for it is beyond all of our own wavering doubts and self-questioning.

Gracious and almighty God, when trials grieve us, may we put our complete trust in you. Strengthen us to act on our love for Jesus even when we cannot see or comprehend your miraculous work among us. Amen.

Christians today depend completely on the testimony of those who have lived by faith for generations before us. Like Thomas, we have not seen the resurrected Jesus with our own eyes. Yet, if believing depends solely on seeing, the living Word of God would never have reached across the more than twenty centuries after his death.

Indeed when it comes to faith, the scriptural witness helps us understand that we all go astray. We need to be taught to see with the eyes of faith and hear with ears attuned to God's Spirit. For this reason, the author of the Gospel of John emphasizes the importance of Thomas's testimony. Universally known as "doubting Thomas," scripture bears witness to his transformation before our very eyes as he becomes "believing Thomas." Once he recognizes Jesus by the wounds in his hands and his side, Thomas exclaims in awe: "My Lord and my God!"

When we cling to God's word, we gain access to a palpable sense of God's peace even amidst trial and tribulation. We lack proof for the incomprehensible event of Jesus' resurrection, and we cannot build a life of faith based on our rational doubts. Instead, we are called to believe in the witness of the early apostles and disciples even though we cannot see or understand how such miracles are possible.

Like the author of the Gospel of John, we reconstruct our life narratives in accordance with a miraculous event that our minds simply cannot comprehend. We are called to believe even when we cannot see. And with the author of First Peter, "Although [we] have not seen him, [we] love him."

Gracious God, reconstruct our life stories in ways that will permit our testimony to be convincing for the generations that come after us. Lead us to live in such accord with your word that our humble witness may be a small but trustworthy parable of love for those who are as yet unborn. Amen.

Life in Light of the Resurrection

The disciples rejoice at having Jesus alive among them. When he appears among them, he shows them his hands and his feet, offers them peace, and sends them to proclaim the good news of his resurrection. Then he breathes on them, giving them the gift of the Holy Spirit.

With this gift comes an admonition that the disciples now have the power to release others from sin. Jesus also makes it clear that his followers can likewise choose to leave others in their sin. These are fearful gifts. Jesus gives to his disciples powers once reserved for God alone. Jesus accepted the power of offering forgiveness that had been given to him. In various controversies, Jesus claims this divine power as belonging to his own vocation. In Luke's Gospel, he prays to the Father to forgive those crucifying him.

Here, Jesus widens the scope of responsibility for freeing others from sin. By breathing his Spirit upon his disciples, he empowers them to release others from bondage. For us, the gift of forgiveness can bring an additional gift—inexpressible peace.

When we receive the Spirit of God, we can cease our endless fretting over who is in the right and who is in the wrong, knowing that we are all under judgment. (See John 3:19.) We can hope in our being made right by Christ's own work among us. We shift our gaze away from blame or self-blame and recognize the miraculous gift of God's forgiveness, which reconfigures the meaning of our entire lives.

Gracious God, we pray for the gift of your inexpressible peace that enables us to forgive even those who have wronged us and to love all those you have given us to love. Amen.

Lord and Messiah

APRIL 24–30, 2017 • MATTHEW CROASMUN

SCRIPTURE OVERVIEW: What is the Easter message, and what are we to do with it? Two dimensions of the responses to God's act of raising Jesus stand out. First, repeatedly the texts speak of public worship. Second, the texts speak of changed lives. In 1 Peter 1 the Resurrection effects a new birth marked by obedience to the truth and mutual love. The two responses—public worship and transformed lives—are not separate from each other in the texts. One leads to the other and back again.

QUESTIONS AND SUGGESTIONS FOR REFLECTION

- Read Acts 2:14a, 36-41. What of Peter's words that follow speak to the heart of the good news: "God has made him both Lord and Messiah, this Jesus whom you crucified"?

- Read Psalm 116:1-4, 12-19. The psalmist declares that he will pay his vows to the Lord "in the presence of all [God's] people." As the author notes, what story will you tell about God's work in your life?

- Read 1 Peter 1:17-23. When have you witnessed God's guiding hand at work in your life, not only in pleasant times but also in disappointment and darkness?

- Read Luke 24:13-35. When have you participated in a Bible study that offered such illuminating results? When have you experienced the inbreaking of God's life at the table of Jesus Christ?

Director of Research and Publications at the Yale Center for Faith and Culture and Lecturer of Theology and Humanities at Yale University; a staff pastor of the Elm City Vineyard Church in New Haven, Connecticut

It's not the sort of message that will win friends and influence people. But it's a refrain of the first several chapters of the book of Acts. (See Acts 3:15; 4:10; 7:52.) You might call it "The Gospel of 'You Killed Jesus.'" "God has made him both Lord and Messiah, this Jesus whom you crucified." We have to wonder whether those who first heard this message might not have heard in this proclamation the very real possibility of a threat. *This Jesus you killed, God has vindicated by raising him from the dead. You killed him. He's back. This can't end well. . . .* We can hear a certain existential anxiety in the response of those gathered in Jerusalem: "What should we do?"

While we often call this story "the good news," we may wonder, *What on earth is good about this news?*

The good news is that though we have made ourselves God's enemies, God nevertheless pursues us in love. We may not literally have crucified Jesus, but we make ourselves God's enemies whenever we oppose God's good work in the world. Yet God still pursues us in love. This One whom we rejected, God has rescued. And now Christ comes to invite us to repent, to receive the gift of the Holy Spirit, and to live into the amazing adventure that awaits.

By the thousands, Peter's hearers do just that. And, as Acts records, the world is changed forever. A people who know that their outright rejection of God cannot dissuade God from pursuing them passionately, a people who know that God manifests that same passion and takes that same posture toward the world around them feel empowered. That's good news that will change your life.

Lord, impress upon me the tenacity of your love. Amen.

So, how did you end up at Yale for graduate school?" Whenever someone asks me this question, I have to decide what sort of story I will tell.

There's the story that says, "Well, I applied broadly and went to the best program that would have me." That's the story I usually prefer in polite company. Then there's the other story. The one that goes like this:

Well, first I applied only to Yale and didn't get in. I was crushed and wasn't sure I could go through the emotional roller coaster of applying again the next year. While I was trying to decide, a young man who knew nothing about me prayed for me and told me that God wanted to grant me favor where I hadn't previously found favor. He went on to tell me things only God knew about my hopes and dreams. I felt completely known and loved by God; it was a pivotal moment in my life.

So I applied again, confident of God's presence with me and received admission to the same program that had rejected me the previous year.

Those are two different stories. Neither is false. They recount the same event, but they tell different stories. I've discovered that it matters very much which story I tell. It matters whether my story is one of natural cause and effect and strategic decisions on the one hand, or one of divine direction and provision on the other. It matters because my past doesn't shape my future nearly as much as does the story I tell myself about my past. The events of the past are over and gone. I carry the story with me.

The psalmist promises to tell a story with God at the center. What story will we tell?

God, give me the courage to testify to your goodness. Amen.

It sticks out like a sore thumb. In the middle of this hymn of gratitude, there it is: "Precious in the sight of the LORD is the death of his faithful ones." A puzzling verse to readers for centuries. The word *precious* may mislead us. The basic meaning of the word is "weighty." For example, in Psalm 139:17, "How weighty to me are your thoughts, O God! How vast is the sum of them!" God's thoughts are weighty; they're difficult for us to understand. We are left to wonder: *Why are we talking about death at all?*

This text can teach us important aspects of gratitude and mourning, of joy and sorrow. God has rescued the psalmist from death. But not all are so fortunate. The psalmist faces the question: How does God *feel* about "the death of his faithful ones"?

When Orthodox Jewish family members paint their house, they leave a patch unpainted as a memorial to the destruction of the Jerusalem temple. The lesson: When we rejoice, we ought to remember those who are in mourning. Otherwise, our rejoicing feels thin, predicated on God favoring us—perhaps even predicated on God favoring us over another. We pair joyful love, the kind that says "we love the Lord because of the good," with awareness of the value of sorrowful love—the kind that says "we love the Lord despite the bad." In this way our thanksgiving remains grounded in reality and hospitable to those who are not rejoicing with us.

Lord, in my joyful gratitude, may I be mindful of those who are mourning. Amen.

Each of us looks for something that will last. In this passage, our instincts about permanence get flipped on their head. The enduring character of what God has done for us in Christ is contrasted to "perishable" silver or gold. If the ads on television serve as an indicator, "perishable" is not the first thing jewelers want coming to mind when we think of silver or gold. These are precious metals, the stuff out of which we make our most enduring artifacts. But perishability is a matter of perspective.

The passage points to two items sturdier than gold or silver. The first is "the precious blood of Christ." The combining of scripture passages suggests we read this in light of Psalm 116:15: "Precious in the sight of the Lord is the death of his faithful ones." Certainly Jesus' death was precious in the sense that it was costly, perhaps too costly to comprehend. His resurrection and continued pursuit of us in love, destined before Creation, draws us into God's eternal intentions for the flourishing of the world. That is secure footing, indeed.

The second source of enduring value is "the living and enduring word of God," described as "imperishable seed," reminiscent of a teaching of Jesus in Luke's Gospel: the word as seed scattered across the world (8:4-15). This word is "the good news that was announced to you" (1 Pet. 1:25). This is the gospel in all its fullness, the message Peter preached at Pentecost: Though we have made ourselves God's enemies, God nevertheless pursues us in love. Jesus' resurrection evidences the unchanging nature of that pursuit. Not even our enmity can turn back the love of God. Not even death can overcome it. If we set our hope on God, we will not be disappointed.

Lord, I set my hope on you. Amen.

Maybe we know this story so well that we find it hard to enter into the disappointment of these disciples, but we can try. These men had big hopes and dreams for Jesus. Now he is dead. "We had hoped that he was the one to redeem Israel." They had hope—not just for themselves but for the people of Israel; now their hope is lost.

Disappointment happens. We share our heart's deepest desires with God not because if we do we're guaranteed to get what we ask for. We express our candid hopes and dreams because God's hands are the ones in which we want to be held if and when disappointment comes. God remains trustworthy.

Luke paints a striking picture: Two men voicing their discouragement to Jesus himself—who listens unrecognized but present. He walks with them and asks what's on their minds. He invites them to narrate their shattered hopes, to tell the story. There's a twist coming, of course—he is risen! But Jesus believes it important that these men express their feelings in this moment of the story. Though God's rescue transforms the desolation of disappointment, it does not erase it. Jesus pauses—asks the question that makes the men stop—and invites them to process what they're feeling.

Disappointment can seem to hide Jesus from our eyes as well. We might wonder, even as Jesus walks beside us, whether he's at all aware of our struggle. But the fact is, recognized or not, Jesus is present in our despair, moved by our sorrow, and ready to hear us out. The key, in any case, is to take our disappointment to God. Sorrowful—even angry—prayers gain us more than merely shaking our fists at the sky.

How has God disappointed you? Dare to be honest and see how Jesus responds.

It must have been the Bible study to end all Bible studies. To be sure, this Bible study has been going for a while now, having begun in earnest when Jesus introduced himself in the language of Isaiah 61 in his first sermon (Luke 4:16-30) and continuing through Jesus' last words in Luke 23:46, "Father, into your hands I commend my spirit," quoting Psalm 31:5. Throughout Luke, clearly the scriptures of Israel are key to making sense of the life and death of Jesus.

Some of this the two men might have put together on their own. The mention in verse 21 that "it is now the third day since these things took place" seems almost too obvious; Jesus has told them what was to happen on the third day (9:22; 13:32; 18:33). But this event is about more than merely connecting a few dots: All scripture testifies to Jesus.

This is the second of three appearances of Jesus in this encounter on the road to Emmaus. First, Jesus is present—though unrecognized—in the disciples' disappointment. Ultimately, as we'll see tomorrow, Jesus is made known to them in the breaking of the bread. Here, Jesus is revealed in the scripture—even as his presence in front of their eyes remains hidden from them.

The challenge for us, then, comes in reading scripture with the expectation that it is a space in which we can encounter the risen Christ. The Bible resembles a building—a cathedral or museum—a space in which the artifacts of God's people, crafted over the course of millennia, testify to Jesus the Messiah. But Christ goes beyond the building's theme; he inhabits this space as a place to encounter us. The questions to us: How regularly will we enter this space, and do we come expecting to encounter the risen Lord?

Pray that the Bible will be a place where you encounter Jesus.

The men's mysterious companion takes bread, blesses and breaks it, and gives it to them. Their eyes are opened; they recognize him—and he vanishes from their sight.

From now on, Jesus is the one made known "in the breaking of the bread." The Gospel of Luke has already made Jesus known in this way. He is the one made known when the hungry are filled, as they were when he blessed and broke bread in feeding the five thousand. (Read Luke 9:10-17.) He is the one made known in the table fellowship of the church, when we remember his giving thanks and breaking bread at the Lord's Supper. (See Luke 22:19.) He is the one made known in the breaking of his body, offered for us—in the very death that had brought about the disciples' disappointment.

When the disciples describe Jesus as the one made known in the breaking of the bread, the disciples aren't merely reporting their experience on the road to Emmaus; they're summarizing their experience of Jesus as a whole. Jesus constantly ate and taught us how we ought to eat—especially in the Gospel of Luke. The key lesson is this: Eat with the poor and the outcast. Use one of the fundamental realities of life—our need for physical sustenance—and watch it be transformed into a site of the in-breaking kingdom of God. Every time we break bread; every time we share fellowship across dividing lines of race, class, and culture; every time we welcome the poor to the table, every time we extend forgiveness, Jesus is made known.

This is especially good news for those of us who need to learn to recognize Jesus without the benefit of seeing him. Jesus is made known to us in the impossible communities made possible at his table. May our eyes be opened to see and our tables be open to receive.

Jesus, help me recognize your presence in my life today. Amen.

Led by the Divine Shepherd

MAY 1–7, 2017 • DIANE LUTON BLUM

SCRIPTURE OVERVIEW: Three of the texts use the image of shepherd and sheep. Psalm 23 and John 10 picture the familiar relationship of trust that sheep exhibit toward the shepherd. The shepherd places himself between the dependent sheep and the aggressive enemy to ward off destruction and exploitation. John 10 and 1 Peter 2 introduce the costly price paid for protection. The sheep's safety comes with immense and undeserved sacrifice. In 1 Peter 2, the shepherd's sacrifice makes possible the return of wayward sheep who have wandered away from the shepherd's protection.

QUESTIONS AND SUGGESTIONS FOR REFLECTION

- Read Acts 2:42-47. How has joining with other believers in prayer, fellowship, and study strengthened your faith?
- Read Psalm 23. What narrow passages of life have you navigated? Upon whom did you depend during that time?
- Read 1 Peter 2:19-25. When have you encountered unjust suffering? What redemptive value did it hold for you?
- Read John 10:1-10. "I am the gate. Whoever enters through me will be saved." How have you allowed Jesus to be the gate to your discipleship?

Retired United Methodist pastor, grandmother, and spiritual director, Nashville, Tennessee

In one of the most memorable of the great "I am" speeches of Jesus in John (I am the vine, and so on), we come to Jesus' description of himself as the good shepherd, known to his flock by way of his voice. This divine voice can be heard, trusted, and followed. Through the guidance of this voice, the disciple finds life in its fullness.

But unlike the contemporaries of Jesus, how many of us in 2017 have even seen a flock of sheep or know anything about the ancient practices of a shepherd? Three decades ago I looked down from what is called the Mount of the Beatitudes across the landscape of Galilee in Israel. Crossing the top of a narrow ridge was an agile man followed by a single file of several dozen sheep. Unlike the herds of cattle I'd seen on the farms of Tennessee, this flock was making a treacherous journey by following their lone shepherd. Led, not prodded from behind or beside, they made their way.

Many children growing up in church, asked to memorize Psalm 23, are introduced to the enduring metaphor of God's care for us as a good shepherd. Over a lifetime we discover Jesus is such a guardian whom we can follow and trust. In these verses of John 10 we learn that before the practices of branding or earmarks, the flock had to recognize and respond to the voice of the one to whom they belonged—or be left behind and lost. In the communal livestock pens of an ancient village, several flocks might be sheltered together. With each new day the shepherd called out his flock, leading them to pasture and water. Safety from predators depended on the willingness of the sheep to respond only to the unique voice of their own keeper if each was to reach full maturity and life.

Loving Shepherd, deepen our capacity to recognize and respond to your guiding voice. Amen.

Thanks to an early familiarity with the idea of Jesus as my good shepherd, the first part of John 10 resonated with my faith and experience. But the idea that Jesus was like a "gate" for the sheep mystified me. Then a teacher made me aware that the technically sophisticated gates of farms and subdivisions in my world would have been centuries beyond Jesus' metaphor in this text. In Jesus' day, shepherds might combine their flocks in one shared village livestock pen. They would have guarded the opening themselves, even as they slept—becoming the gate that guarded against predators and rustlers. A shepherd would literally lay down his life to protect the going out and coming in of the flock.

A gate is a flexible boundary. Jesus, our gate, guides us to safe rest by closing us in against predators and provides for nourishment by opening to green pastures. Like the pilgrims' description of God's protection for their "coming and going" in Psalm 121 (NIV), Jesus keeps us as we go out into the world and leads us safely home for sheltered rest. In the season of life when I pastored congregations, and with my husband, raised our sons (now young adults), we struggled to balance active ministry with sabbath rest. We looked for ways to shelter our sons as well as to bless their growing autonomy. Our journey was fast-paced, and we needed constant guidance. Jesus became for me a gate: opening outward *and* gathering us inward, day by day, season by season.

Do you need to let Jesus be the gate in your discipleship? The gift of this gate promises life in abundance, now and beyond the human journey we know on earth. In life and in death, Jesus the gate promises new life and resurrection power.

Prayerfully imagine a place in your life where you can welcome Jesus as your gate to bless your coming and going.

A professor from a developing nation asked my class what would happen if we lived into a "theology of enough." Since coming to the United States, he had noticed that American Christians were often infected with the economically driven (unconscious) theology of needing, expecting, and striving for more. More of whatever! And to this, young David, son of Jesse and the least likely of his many older brothers to amount to anything (we now celebrate him as composer of this psalm), sings joyfully that his God supplies all he needs. He is not in want, even if he holds a job on the bottom of the career ladder, like tending sheep. This God, like an effective shepherd, provides tender care and enough.

The divine shepherd of this psalm knows the landscape, knows where to find green fields and in which season, knows where to locate mountain brooks and the still pools just below the rocky rapids. In these places, the shepherd nourishes and safely waters the flock. This kind of shepherd is worthy of a deep, abiding trust. This shepherd knows the territory better than my GPS! In places with no maps, we are led to trust this Holy One who sees ahead and provisions our journey.

Our Creator, who leads us beyond fearful striving, invites us into a deepening trust. Can we pause for rest that restores our souls? My Jewish friends have helped me understand that sabbath involves more than simply stopping the work of my week. The joyful sharing of food, drink, and fellowship characterizes sabbath. Abundance is more than counting the places at the table; it is about sharing what we *do* have and discovering a deeper form of abundance and delight. Will you and I discover that sabbath offers a way to the joy of enough?

God, from what would you lead me to pause this week when my loved ones and I practice sabbath rest?

Sheep cannot graze in the same pasture all year, unless it is a small flock in a large, lush pasture. Sheep can overgraze, eating until they consume all the grass, including the root. By then erosion and hunger threaten their survival. A wise shepherd moves his flock to the next safe grazing land by season. In places like Israel and the American Rocky Mountains, the high elevations may green up for summer but quickly dry up or become snowbound before autumn. The careful shepherd leads the flock through narrow, steep passages in order to reach the abundance of the next green pasture. This transit is full of risks: a stumble can turn into a fall; wandering from the path can lead to becoming lost from the rest of the flock, with deadly implications for each sheep.

So it is for all of us; none of us escapes the narrow passages from one chapter of life to the next without the need for the divine shepherd's leading. We often cannot envision the right path until we realize we have been found in God's presence where love casts out our crippling fears. In these valleys of death and shadow we are invited, with saints like John of the Cross, to be held and led by God's hand where and when we cannot see our own way.

Our own wandering endangers us. The fattest, wooliest sheep is at the greatest danger of being upended on uneven terrain. Such a "cast" sheep becomes easy prey in that circumstance—helpless and lost from the flock. The good shepherd has a rod to fight the predator and his crook to right the upended sheep. Our divine shepherd seeks to save us from our enemies and from ourselves.

Lord, come find us with your love when we can't see our way. Amen.

This part of Psalm 23 may mystify the young child who learns this scripture by heart as a prayer. But as that child matures, the invitation to the Lord's banquet of bountiful grace and nourishment will be experienced in real, living human community. Sooner or later, we are positioned to break bread in the presence of someone we believe to be our adversary. And Jesus, our good shepherd, leads the way to transforming love by reminding us that love for our enemies will be one of the ways we are recognized as his beloved flock. (See Matthew 5:43-48.)

The house of the Lord, where we hope to dwell both on earth and in heaven, brings together all of the human family— the ones we like, the ones who are like us, *and* the ones we fear, especially the ones we believe are not like us. We humans draw these lines readily, in our families and in nations, often to our peril. Jesus knows that it may be a saving grace when an "enemy" like the Samaritan crosses the road to rescue a Jewish man left for dead, bringing first aid and underwriting the cost of his ongoing health care. (See Luke 10:25-37.) We glimpse the overflowing love of the table of our Lord when we recall stories like this and when we courageously follow Jesus into relationships like these that reveal communities of God's justice and peace.

How can we grow in this profound practice of love? The psalmist describes feeling at home with God as he dwells in the world. Trusting God's powerful guidance and unconditional love anchors each follower of Jesus as we face every opponent. Find and be found in God's presence by prayer and by praise at the table where enemies can become friends.

Lord, may we feast in your overflowing abundance, especially in living relationship with our adversaries. Forgive us as we forgive others the injuries we cause one another. Amen.

When readers in 2017 read all of First Peter, we encounter the author's apparent acceptance of oppressive institutions of his day: economic, political, and ethnic forms of slavery; inequitable relationships between wives and husbands. But throughout this epistle runs a call to transcend unjust suffering, looking to the powerful experience of Jesus, the shepherd and keeper of our souls. As we listen for the higher and deeper truths that lie at the heart of Peter's letter, we recall the profound suffering of the early generations of Jesus' followers for the sake of their faith. How did they endure? Like Stephen (Acts 6–7), they were known for their love and their forgiveness, in life and in death. This courageous and loving witness gave birth to new generations of Jesus' flock. Death does not have the final word when we trust in this resurrected Lord.

Where have we encountered unjust suffering? As a pastor, I learned that humans, when fearful and anxious, often relieve their anxiety by lashing out at others, usually targeting the most vulnerable or responsible persons and groups. Scapegoating can occur when a child has had a tough day at school and upon coming home melts down. A parent, who doesn't deserve this behavior, may hopefully provide a safe haven for the discharge of this fearful anxiety. But a parent after a rough day can lash out at a spouse or a child and do serious harm. On a grand scale, Jesus became an object of such violence in its deadliest form. Systems of oppression magnify our fearful anxiety. Our suffering can come from systemic or transient forms of oppression. But the transcendent love of God that we see in Jesus can triumph in, through, and beyond unjust—and even deadly—suffering.

Lord, you call us to end the suffering we cause others. Transform us in the midst of our own suffering as we discover that you are our trustworthy shepherd. Amen.

Led by the Divine Shepherd   157

What turns a group of defeated disciples (read: students) into a vibrant host of apostles (read: missionaries)? What sparks dozens, hundreds, and then thousands to adopt a Way of faith and life so contagious that it multiplies to this day in many nations and cultures? Luke writes in Acts that Christians practiced certain essentials: learning the Way and word of Jesus—storyteller and divine Word made flesh; entering into genuine community with others following this Way; sharing meals, resources, and daily prayers.

When any of us embrace the abundant life these practices can bring, joy overflows. Then glad and generous hearts are prepared to face and endure suffering in its many forms. Even in death, love prevails. In broken relationships, forgiveness heals. Every ending can yield a new beginning. Acts 2 gives us a portrait of the body of Christ in its ideal and attractive power.

How can we find an experience of life in Christ like this? Our media in 2017 allows us a multitude of amazing human connections. Media can also fill our lives with superficial relationships that evaporate in the face of broken relationships, poverty, and violence. We long for intimate connections with enough people that we make a difference for good in our world. Such relationships can lead us to share our gifts as well as our vulnerability, deepening our interdependence as a body of faith in Christ. This community of trust in the divine good shepherd leads and equips each of us to shepherd one another. While hundreds come to worship at my church, each Monday I gather with seven others for an hour for prayer and accountability in our discipleship. We try to practice compassion, justice, devotion, and worship. Together we discover the guidance of the divine shepherd.

God, be our shepherd, as in love we shepherd one another. Amen.

Who Are Those Guys?

MAY 8–14, 2017 • BRADFORD BOSWORTH

SCRIPTURE OVERVIEW: Since the beginning, Israel's faith has turned to God in situations of extreme trouble. In such turning, Israel has found God utterly reliable and able to rescue. Today's psalm reading sounds those ancient cadences of reliability. The sermon in Acts 7 takes up those ancient cadences and places them on the lips and in the mouth of Stephen. Stephen's preaching evokes hostility in his listeners. In the end, however, it is Stephen who knows the joy and well- being of life as a gift from God. Both the Gospel and epistle readings turn the faith of the psalm and drama of Stephen's ending toward the concrete reality of the church. They tilt toward the need of a domesticated church to reengage its peculiar identity and its unusual mode of being. The language of "place" serves the practice of risky obedience.

QUESTIONS AND SUGGESTIONS FOR REFLECTION

* Read Acts 7:55-60. When have you experienced the Holy Spirit's nudge telling you, "This is wrong"? What did you do?
* Read 1 Peter 2:2-10. How will we continue to drink of pure spiritual milk so we can repeatedly be called out of darkness into God's light?
* Read Psalm 31:1-5, 15-16. What would it mean for you to say to God, "My times are in your hand"?
* Read John 14:1-14. What tough faith questions have you asked Jesus? What was his response?

Writer who serves and worships at Smyrna (Georgia) First United Methodist Church; a humble member of the priesthood of all believers

This week's scripture references many personalities, some familiar and some not so familiar. I had this image from the classic '60s film *Butch Cassidy and the Sundance Kid*, with Paul Newman and Robert Redford, who play the famous outlaws. The two are perched on a high cliff looking out over a valley thinking they have surely lost the chasing posse by now. Then they notice five horse riders emerging from a dust cloud in hot pursuit of them. And in a line we hear again and again in the movie, a perplexed Butch Cassidy asks, "Who are those guys?" This week we'll discover who a few of them are.

I am writing this meditation in a season of mistrust. Today's passage brings us to what must have been a similar time, although on a smaller scale. In walks Stephen, a well-schooled and credentialed member of the new church in Jerusalem. What does he encounter? He faces division: two separate factions, each with an establishment mentality. Who is this man who has taken such effort to explain God's covenants with the chosen people? Where is Stephen in today's context? Where do we look to find people "filled with the Holy Spirit"? The crowd so blatantly opposes the truth that they cover their ears.

Even when confronted by the onslaught of the screaming crowd, Stephen keeps a laser focus on Jesus. Under attack he willingly gives his spirit over to the Lord. He rejoices in God's glory. Abiding in his Savior, he becomes the Way. And while they stone him, Stephen might well have said, "Father, forgive them; for they do not know what they are doing" (Luke 23:34).

Who is Stephen? Stephen is one who, even in the face of death, stood with forgiving love for those who hated him. May we be so faithful to the way of Christ.

Dear God, fill us with the spirit of Stephen. Amen.

Sometimes scripture throws us a curveball. We read it; read it again and still ask, "What?" Acts 7:58 is such a verse for me. It appears out of place, an anomaly to that which immediately precedes it and that which comes next. Just as God created the moon to guide the tides of the earth's majestic oceans, I discern a purpose in the ebb and flow of my life and that of others. Most assuredly this incident impacts the life of a young man named Saul at its ebb.

Saul believes that he is upholding and adhering to Mosaic Law. As zealous for the risen Lord as is Stephen, so is Saul for the Law. Yet I sense the Holy Spirit at work within Saul. The Spirit, that barely flickering divine pilot light, sends the ever-so-faint message to his soul, "This is wrong." The scripture itself contrasts the hatred of the crowd with the holiness of Stephen.

Saul does not know it yet, but soon he will turn God's witness and join the posse. How rich is this vision of Saul when juxtaposed with the apostle named Paul who pens the wonderful treatise on love in 1 Corinthians 13! Can we believe it is the same person? This blood-stained guy with clothing thrown at his feet in Acts 7 will become one of the most influential people in the history of Christianity.

Do we dare ask, "If Saul, why not me?" This verse in Acts reminds us that God made us for holiness not hatred. We are worthy! Both the ebb and the flow of our lives turn toward the author of our salvation.

Who is this guy? Saul/Paul is one whose life was changed from hatred to holiness. May it be so for us!

Father, open our eyes to see your purpose at work in our lives. Amen.

In this letter, Peter begins to develop thoughts about the household of God and the unity of that household—the deep connections within the household. In October 2010 I attended the North Georgia Men's Walk to Emmaus #144. I have never been the same. I took time away to be with God and others. I listened to the presentation over the three days' time of the "short course" in Christianity. I was seated with seven other men at the Table of Peter. We shared our insights and reflected together. As a result of that placing, I decided to read the Gospels from the perspective of Peter. A year later I presented a devotion for a group of men serving on another Walk. First Peter 2:2-3 served as the starting point for my devotion.

My biannual involvement in Emmaus Walks as part of the servant team provides spiritual renewal for me. None of my other routine prayer and meditation practices comes close to the impact of this three-day experience. During my pilgrim journey in 2010 I tasted and saw that the Lord is good. I was like a newborn baby then and feel like a newborn baby each time I return as I gain new insights into the Christian life from others seated around the table. Each time I return in a slightly differing role with a new group of men, I glimpse our Lord's abundant and unmerited love. It is life in grace, the presence of Jesus.

The holy ground for these walks with the risen Christ is called The King's Retreat. When all the servants and pilgrims show up on the Thursday of a three-day Emmaus Walk, we are all running—some of us away from God again. Before Sunday's conclusion, we have stopped running.

Who are these guys? They are faithful pilgrims seeking an ever-deepening walk with Jesus Christ by slowing down to hear his voice and to share in fellowship around a table. May we seek such times with Christ.

Abba, thank you for your pure, spiritual milk so we may grow toward our salvation. Amen.

Even the least Bible-literate people among us have some clue about David, to whom this psalm is attributed. We may recognize him through popular culture's portrayal of the man in the David and Goliath story or perhaps the legendary lore versions of his lustful failing toward Bathsheba. These two views of the man stand at opposite ends of the reputation spectrum. When we dig deeper in scripture to gain a more complete picture of David, we read of a life that evokes both our sympathy and our anger. He attempts to live as a child of God even with the demands of being king. The pressure is on!

Through the words of these verses we get a view of the man after God's own heart. So much is expected of him, and he knows where to turn when the demands come. I can empathize with David whenever I take on a leadership role. When folks question my decisions, I question their motives. My enemies are the voices of my self-will woven into the fabric of my ego. My refuge is the place, a safe space, of quiet surrender where I can listen, those enemies quieted now.

David turns to the Lord as well. He turns to the God he has come to know as refuge, rock, and fortress. He asks that God lead, guide, take out, and redeem. He turns his life over to God in confidence: "My times are in your hand." When we, like David, place our lives and times in God's hands, we discover a God who comes to deliver, to shine the light of well-being, and to save.

Who is this guy? David is one who, even in the ups and downs of his faith, remained a "man after God's own heart." May it be so with us!

Lord, today take us to that quiet place of refuge where we will know your will for us. Amen.

Who Are Those Guys?

Peter is the disciple who seems to be in the right place at the right time. On the seashore of Galilee, fisherman Simon, always ready for an adventure, hears the call of invitation and says in so many ways, "Yep, I'm in!" Dropping his nets, he kisses that life good-bye. And so it goes: the camping trip up a mountain and the witness of the Transfiguration; Peter, who impulsively and without hesitation jumps out of the boat, then instinctively moves *toward* his Messiah. Yet stories of Peter moving *away* from the Lord offset some of these events. He finally denies knowing Jesus.

Who better to help us find our identity in Christ than Peter? He knows from personal experience about long-term commitment to Jesus: "a stone that makes [us] stumble, and a rock that makes [us] fall." But Peter has learned that God builds the house, and Jesus Christ is the cornerstone. The pupil becomes the teacher. And commitment to this understanding makes believers "living stone[s]" who are precious in God's sight.

We are constantly called back into the covenantal relationship as God's chosen people, called to move toward God. It is a daily endeavor that occurs moment by moment. When I move toward the Wonderful Counselor, words flow more freely onto the page. But when uncertainty and fear of failure creep through the cracks in my confidence, I move away from living confidently as a child of God. Fortunately, this scripture speaks to us when we want to turn away and deny the claim that we "are a chosen people, a royal priesthood, a holy nation."

Who is this guy? Peter was the impulsive rock on whom Jesus would build his church—a man who at one time moved away but with the taste of God's goodness on his tongue was "called . . . out of darkness into his marvelous light"!

Lord, may we ever move toward you. We are your chosen ones. Amen.

Two days ago I turned sixty-four. When I was twelve, my father died suddenly just weeks short of his sixty-fourth birthday. I am a break-the-cycle sort of guy. I have now outlived my father. As part of my birthday celebration, a friend and I planned a hiking trip to Cloudland Canyon State Park in Georgia, to majestic Cherokee Falls. This trail happened to be a challenging trip! We are not avid hikers, and we did not know the way as first timers on the trail.

The hike to the falls was long and arduous and even more so on the return, with the day growing longer. We began to question our physical abilities and our mental faculties. *Were we still on the same trail?* We were second-guessing everything. But the yellow markers along the trail reminded us we were indeed on the right path.

Jesus is preparing his closest friends for his departure. We can only imagine how emotional the time is for all gathered. He tells them, "You know the way to the place where I am going."

Jesus assures them and us that we already know the way, and it is he. We can break the cycle of our desert wandering and become those who live in the world but not of it. He marks the path for us by calling us God's people. Before we know it, along the way we begin to see glimpses of heaven, our Father's house. We have stopped running away. Jesus assures the disciples of an ongoing existence in fellowship with him.

God offers many "dwelling places." God's grace abounds in falling water. Shimmering, sparkling crystalline facets of abundant love make up the many rooms of God's house.

Who are these guys? They are Jesus' closest followers, to whom he promised eternal communion with him. May we hear and believe that promise.

Yahweh, when we wander away from your will, help us find our way back to your precious Son again and again. Amen.

Who Are Those Guys?

My mother repeatedly drove home to me as a child the importance of telling the truth. I have learned if I am not honest with myself or true to myself, then it is hard for me to be honest with others. The fourth step in Alcoholics Anonymous is "Made a searching and fearless moral inventory" of ourselves. At this step a high percentage of those in recovery drop out of the program. They can't get honest with themselves.

We "overhear" Jesus' final discourse with his closest friends. Jesus continues teaching to the very end. We are there to learn about ourselves, to draw closer to the truth. Thomas and Philip figure prominently in this scripture. At first pass we may want to fall back on traditional characterizations of Thomas as the doubting one and to interpret Jesus' response to Philip as a rebuke. By now we know that his response is a teaching tool.

Being honest with ourselves or humble as Jesus would have us, we remain teachable. We have so much to understand about ourselves and the ways of God in the world—so much truth still to find. If Thomas and Philip, still hungering for the word in Jesus' final hours, do not ask these questions, what would all of us have missed in Jesus' answers?

How many instances in our school days did we hesitate to raise our hand to ask a question and have another classmate ask that very question? We looked around the room, and everyone was taking notes. The notes I scribbled down as a result of Philip's and Thomas's questions are these: "[You] will do greater works than these," and "I am the the way, and the truth, and the life."

Who are these guys? Philip and Thomas are two disciples honest enough to express doubts and to ask questions of Jesus. May we be free to do likewise and be open to hear the answers Jesus gave to them!

Father, may we always be of humble heart and know there is
so much more to learn about the truth of your word. Amen.

Following Christ in All Circumstances

MAY 15–21, 2017 • JUDY WOOLDRIDGE

SCRIPTURE OVERVIEW: The psalm and the Acts reading address the ways in which the concrete faith claims of the community have credence outside that community. They undertake to make the faith credible to outsiders. On the basis of personal testimony, the psalm invites the nations to share in the new life given by God who has saved. Paul makes concrete confessional claims about Jesus in response to the religious inclinations of his Hellenistic listeners. The Gospel and epistle readings focus on the needs of the church community and seek to offer pastoral consolation. The psalm and Acts readings are a "journey out" to the nations and to attentive nonbelievers. The Gospel and epistle readings are a "journey in" to the life and needs of the church.

QUESTIONS AND SUGGESTIONS FOR REFLECTION

- Read Psalm 66:8-20. Recall a time when God did not let your feet slip.
- Read Acts 17:22-31. What are your unknown gods? What are your known gods that become idols in your life? How do they affect your relationship with the God who made the world and everything in it?
- Read 1 Peter 3:13-22. When have you suffered while doing good? What did you learn about God? about yourself?
- Read John 14:15-21. How have you experienced the Advocate's companionship and guidance?

Adult Sunday school teacher and member of the Adult Spiritual Formation team, Belle Meade United Methodist Church, Nashville, Tennessee; retired Product Development Specialist, LifeWay Christian Resources

As I stood at the Acropolis and viewed the Parthenon and various crumbling edifices, I felt overwhelmed by the ruins and broken statues of gods and people. More than an ancient history fact, for the people in that day the gods resided in shrines made by humans. As I took the short walk down to the Areopagus, a word referring to the civil council that met on Ares (Greek god of war) or Mars (Roman god of war) Hill, I felt overwhelmed again as I stood where ancient Athenians stood as Paul delivered his sermon on Mars Hill.

In previous verses, we find a perplexed Paul viewing a city full of idols, a brazen Paul arguing in the synagogue and the agora, and a confronted Paul at the Areopagus answering to Athenian philosophers. In verses 22-31, Paul with temerity gives his sermon at Mars Hill, addressing the plurality of Greek religion and citing an altar to an unknown god observed in Athens. Piety probably caused Greeks to create this altar out of fear they might offend a god unknown to them. Paul proclaims the God they don't know as the one true divinity.

Echoing Isaiah and Old Testament prophets, Paul offers those gathered the God who made heaven and earth as the one true God who doesn't live in shrines made by people and as the one who needs no support from humans. Paul stresses that God provides life and breath as well as the unity of all humanity through God's creation of all nations "from one ancestor." Pointing to how we all search for God, he meets the Athenians on their own ground by quoting two Greek philosophers—"In him we live and move and have our being" (sixth-century BCE poet Epimenides) and "We too are his offspring" (third-century BCE Stoic, Aratus). Paul, in his wisdom, tempers his proclamation with some accommodation of Greek interest.

God, may I look beyond the brokenness and ruins of daily life to the joy of living and moving with you. Amen.

Paul in verse 29 offers a classic Jewish and Christian argument against the polytheism of that day. If we as humans are truly "God's offspring," then we shouldn't think that gold, silver, stone, or even an image created by our own endeavor can adequately represent God. As God's offspring, divine nature is of our kind and not that of gold, silver, or stone. As a creation of God's, we engage in worship of the Creator, not in worship of something created by our own design and skill. Paul's preaching against the idolatry of that time sounds very much like Old Testament discourses on idolatry.

Paul returns to address the ignorance of the Athenians. Their acts of piety avail them nothing because they don't know or worship the one true God. Previously, God has overlooked humanity's ignorance, but now the time of the Athenians' ignorance has ended because they know of the one true God through Paul's proclamation. Now is the time for repentance. Paul challenges them to turn from the worship of gods created by their own design and turn to God. Without calling him by name, Paul mentions Jesus in verse 31 and refers to his resurrection. Paul meets the Athenian intellectuals on their own turf and connects them to the potent message of the gospel.

When I consider the polytheism of that time, I am amazed that people could worship so many different gods. Yet, when I step back from my amazement, I am troubled by what I see today. Like the Athenians, we have erected multiple gods that we worship daily. Consider money, job, status, and possessions, to name a few. Paul offers us a powerful message for those times when we create personal idols. God doesn't punish us for our ignorance but does call us to repentance and change.

Help me, God, to turn from my personal idols to worship only you. Amen.

The psalmist affirms, through national and individual thanksgiving, God's providential deliverance. Verses 1-7 call Israel to acknowledge God's power in bringing the people out of Egypt; verses 8-12 call the "peoples" to offer praise to God for seeing them through trials; verses 13-20 offer an individual's thanksgiving upon entering the Temple to fulfill his vows to God for God's intervention and saving grace.

Often we experience difficulties; we feel backed against the wall by circumstances; burdens overwhelm us. Yet, just as God kept Israel "among the living" and brought them to a "spacious place," God provides the same support to us today. God's care takes us to new places and experiences.

In some ways, verses 13-15 sound like bargaining with God for favors. Yet, the psalmist's promises are heartfelt—verses 16-20 describe the psalmist's deliverance. Three key concepts stand out in these words: (1) God hears our prayers; (2) God does not reject our prayers; and (3) God's love remains steadfast and constant.

"Has not let our feet slip" in verse 9 is my favorite phrase in today's passage. In January following bilateral knee replacement in August, several inches of ice coated my pathway to the carport. The inconvenience of being trapped in the house was secondary to my fear of falling and damaging the surgeon's masterpiece. Friends reminded me to stay in the house; a neighbor risked his own bones to fetch my mail. After two weeks, the neighbor and I agreed to try and loosen the ice. As we worked with a hoe and a snow shovel, the neighbor reminded me not to slip on the ice. Sure footing was important on the ice but sure footing is important in all of life. God alone provides that kind of assurance and protection.

Thank you, Father, for your ongoing providential deliverance! Amen.

THURSDAY, MAY 18 ~ *Read 1 Peter 3:13-17*

In today's verses the writer moves from husband and wife references in verses 1-7 and entire household references in verses 8-12 to the entire community. Verses 13-17 challenge readers to strive for good in the midst of trouble, disaster, and distress.

According to verse 14, you are "blessed" even if you "suffer for doing what is right." The writer seems to reiterate Jesus' teachings in Matthew 5:10-12. And these words seem like a paradox to us—how can we be happy or delighted to be suffering? We naturally respond to difficulties by feeling unhappy and unfairly treated. But in verse 15 the writer challenges us to move beyond our "poor me" attitude to worship and communion with Christ. That worship occurs in the heart, independent of any building or visible objects.

Just as Christians in that day and time felt persecuted by a culture that viewed Christianity with a suspicious eye, we face similar attitudes today. But the consistency of a relationship with Christ can put to shame any detractors who attempt to undermine us.

In the early 1990s I made three trips to Romania where I trained a group of individuals who were developing and publishing Christian curriculum materials for use in churches. Still fresh in the hearts and minds of these individuals were examples of what it took to develop and maintain a personal faith through the years of Soviet rule. I may have had "the answers" about writing, editing, and publishing curriculum materials, but these persons had "the answers" about keeping the faith in the midst of adversity. One phrase in verse 15 stands out as part of what enabled these Christians to survive their culture and environment—"in your hearts sanctify Christ as Lord."

How can I daily "sanctify Christ as Lord" as I face life's difficulties?

The writer offers in verse 18 the basis for all that follows in today's passage—Christ's suffering that led to resurrection and new life for us. Verses 19-20 lend themselves to varying interpretations. Martin Luther indicated that he couldn't say with certainty what the writer meant! (Luther, *Commentary on Peter and Jude*, p. 166) Verse 19 brings to mind the creedal tradition of the church in Christ's preaching to those in prison and attending to the souls who died in the flood. No one lies beyond God's redemption! Perhaps the best application is this: Christians follow Christ's example by living upright lives in the face of difficulty or opposition. We can do this with confidence because of Christ's actions.

The righteous (Christ) died for the unrighteous (believers). Just as the original recipients of these verses are to maintain a life of holiness in the midst of opposition, so are we. What does that mean in a world divided over cultural and societal issues, crippled by fear of threats and terrorism, plagued by fractured communication, and filled with hate and distrust? We recall verse 14: "Do not fear what [the world] fear[s] and do not be intimidated." And we go back to our sure redemption through Christ's self-sacrifice—suffering, death, and resurrection.

Verses 21-22 move from the image of rescue from the Flood in verse 20 to the image of baptism. As we recall our baptism we are challenged to remember our salvation and the impact of that salvation on our lives. Again we are led back to the charge that new life in Christ calls us to lead lives of holiness in the midst of opposition!

God, use the remembrance of my baptism to empower me for endurance in the face of life's anxiety and distress, and help me discover the meaning of a life of holiness. Amen.

Clearly the Gospel writer intends these words for the church and the broader Christian community. The first message to the church is that obedience indicates or reflects our love for Christ. That obedience manifests from our following Jesus' example. Up until this point, Jesus had comforted, helped, defended, and taught the crowds and his disciples to whom he speaks in today's passage.

The second message in the form of a promise is that Jesus will ask the Father to provide "another Advocate" who will be with the community forever. We find this reference to the Advocate only in the Gospel of John. Other words used for this promised One in various translations of the Bible include these: *Advocate, Comforter, Counselor, Helper*—all roles Jesus had played in their lives. A good and reassuring meaning for this term is "the one called alongside." This Advocate will be the "Spirit of truth" who will abide in the Christian community. Jesus provided Christians with a divine agent of truth for living in this world. What the disciples most cherish is what will hold them together in a world that will not always value what they value.

Not only will the Advocate be "with" the early Christians; the Advocate will be "in" them. And the call for obedience to Christ and the promise of an Advocate offer hope to those in faith communities today. But we have to remember that the promised Advocate, the gift of the Holy Spirit, comes with this condition: "If you love me," Jesus said, "[and] keep my commandments." And that's seldom easy.

Gracious God, may we abide in the Advocate today as we face the world. Strengthen us to be the body of Christ. Amen.

Today's verses highlight the promise of the continuing presence of God and Christ within the Christian community. Verse 18 reflects Jesus' speaking to the feelings of loneliness in the disciples. First, he reassures them that they will not be left alone or *orphaned*, a term that conjures up various meanings. I envision an overwhelming aloneness or desolation, the feeling that probably resides in the heart of the disciples at this time. Second, Jesus tells them, "I am coming to you"—meaning that the Advocate will provide the same support and sustenance they have known during his life among them.

Jesus goes on in verses 19-21 to make a strong statement about his future and an even stronger statement about the challenge ahead for all disciples. "In a little while" he will leave them through death, but "on that day" following his resurrection, they will know that he lives again in the Father.

The challenge for Christians is that believing requires more than mental action. Belief encompasses more than knowing rules or commandments—it integrates knowledge and obedience into a way of life. An effective made-up word for this kind of obedience is *followship*. Disciples live in service and obedience to the Son whose commands come from God. The verse goes on to indicate that not only will Jesus love such disciples, but he will also reveal himself to them.

I often fail to integrate knowledge and obedience. Sometimes I take the quickest or the least painful way rather than the way of challenge. I will busy myself in the kitchen rather than sit and visit with the homeless persons I've volunteered to feed. Or I might pretend not to see a friend who is visibly upset. From this time forward, I shall accept this challenge gladly.

> *O God, may we accept the challenge to integrate our knowledge with our obedience into a life of* **followship**. *Amen.*

In the Power of the Spirit

MAY 22–28, 2017 • JOYCE HOLLYDAY

SCRIPTURE OVERVIEW: The entire Easter season focuses on the new governance that breaks the grip of all that is old, tired, deathly, and enslaving. The psalm shows the church using the ancient language of enthronement. Now it is Jesus through whom the drama of God's power is brought to fruition. In Acts, the community accepts the new governance as a bold witness in the world, sustained by a disciplined life of prayer. The epistle reading addresses people who are in the midst of suffering, hurt, and need. They are enjoined to powerful hope for the time of God's eventual and full triumph. The Gospel portrays the church under the power of God's resolve, being given a wholly new identity and vocation in the world.

QUESTIONS AND SUGGESTIONS FOR REFLECTION

- Read Acts 1:6-14. Having received the power of the Holy Spirit, how is your life unfolding?
- Read Psalm 68:1-10, 32-35. When have you sensed God's absence? How did you attempt to fill that void?
- Read 1 Peter 4:12-14; 5:6-11.When has God restored you?
- Read John 17:1-11. Where do you see Jesus as you go about your daily life?

Founding pastor of Circle of Mercy congregation in Asheville, North Carolina; author of several books, including *Then Shall Your Light Rise: Spiritual Formation and Social Witness* and *Clothed with the Sun: Biblical Women, Social Justice, and Us*

The warmth of the bread and the sweetness of the wine still linger as Jesus' friends receive his tender gazes while he kneels and wipes their feet. But already the seed of betrayal has been planted in Judas's heart; the authorities conspire, and the executioners sharpen nails. Jesus describes the suffering to come, and suddenly a chill fills the room.

As the darkness encroaches, Jesus delivers a detailed, loving farewell that spans three chapters (14–16) in John's Gospel. He tells them not to fear and offers them peace, promises them the Holy Spirit as an Advocate in his absence, and commands them to "do the works that I do" (John 14:12).

Then Jesus turns his eyes to heaven and offers a final, fervent prayer, including these words: "I glorified you on earth by finishing the work that you gave me to do." He has welcomed, listened to, taught, healed, fed, and forgiven people. Jesus has brought those on the margins to the center. His work is done.

Now Jesus takes leave of those he loves. But he lets them— and us—know where to find him: "Truly I tell you, just as you did it to one of the least of these who are members of my family, you did it to me" (Matt. 25:40). Whenever a hungry person is fed, a stranger welcomed, or a prisoner visited, Jesus himself has been so served. He's still with us in the soup kitchens, at the borders, in the jail cells, inviting us to finish the work he began.

For many years, every Saturday morning at the Sojourners Neighborhood Center in inner-city Washington, DC, volunteers gave out food. Always before opening the line, we joined hands, as a beloved, longtime neighbor offered a prayer. May her prayer be ours today, wherever we encounter Jesus.

We know, Lord, that you're coming through this line today, so help us to treat you right. Amen.

In the spring of 1988, a young man active in the anti-apartheid movement named Sfiso was showing me around his black township. Eight rifle-wielding members of the South African army leapt from an armored personnel carrier and ordered us to the military tower. In the interrogation room, an officer threatened to put Sfiso back into prison, where for ten months he had been held in a cold cell and tortured. Sfiso reached calmly into his back pocket and took out his small New Testament. Holding it up to the officer's face, he declared, "Sir, I am a Christian." Silence descended as the arrogance of evil met the quiet power of the gospel.

Sfiso's action was the most courageous I had ever witnessed. He told me afterward that he was not against white people but against injustice. Sfiso and his colleagues in the freedom struggle were working for a unity based on their belief that every human being is a beloved child of God—from the most exploited laborer to the cruelest perpetrator of racist violence.

Jesus makes visible God. The disciples' relationship with him allow them to know God. Now, as Jesus faces death, he prays that his disciples "may be one, as we [Jesus and God] are one." A few verses later, he prays, "I ask not only on behalf of these, but also on behalf of those who will believe in me through their word, that they may all be one" (17:20-21). Unity is on Jesus' mind in his final hours on earth—for his friends and for those of us who follow in the path of discipleship after them.

As Sfiso taught me almost three decades ago, such unity requires extravagant mercy and costly forgiveness. This is part of the price for those who "have kept [God's] word" (17:6)—and for those of us still striving to do so.

Merciful God, give me the strength to forgive, and help me never to underestimate the power of your word. Amen.

The children's story from church remained vivid in the minds of her three-year-old triplet sons as a mother from my congregation wrestled them into their pajamas one Sunday night. "I'm Jonah!" crowed Will proudly. "I'm the big fish!" piped up Connor in response, puffing out his cheeks and spreading his arms wide. Jack's shoulders slumped, and a crestfallen look overtook his face as he sighed sadly, "I guess I have to be God."

In the story as Jack heard it, Jonah was a superhero. The big fish was . . . well, a big fish. And God operated as a disembodied voice behind the scenes with a bit part.

Our psalm today tells us that Jack got it wrong. Its verses celebrate the constant provision and presence, protection and promise of God. God watches over vulnerable widows and orphans, gives homes to the desolate, leads prisoners to prosperity, and provides for the needy.

When our ancestors in the faith spent forty years in the Sinai wilderness on their journey out of slavery toward the Promised Land, God showered them with quail and manna, reminding them of the steadfastness of divine love and care. They were being handed a lesson in how to live justly and generously with one another, trusting God's provision.

When God seems absent, we're tempted to fill emptiness with the accumulation of possessions; when we fear the uncertainty that lies ahead, we need the assurance of the psalmist's words. The God who guided our ancestors to freedom as a pillar of cloud by day and a pillar of fire at night—who made the astounding choice to take on flesh and enter into the world with all its pain and joy in the person of Jesus Christ—is active among us still. The Holy Spirit is ever present, hovering close— beckoning us to live justly and generously as well, trusting in God's promises.

Loving God, help me trust in your care and provision. Always. Amen.

ASCENSION DAY

At first, Jesus' friends are "startled and terrified, and thought that they were seeing a ghost" (24:37). They simply cannot believe it is Jesus. He offers his wounds as proof. They have to see before they will accept the truth. I urge us to remember this scene when we feel tempted to try to hide our wounds or weaknesses: These prove our humanity.

Just to make sure that his followers knew that it's really Jesus in the flesh, he asks for something to eat. He takes a piece of broiled fish, and they watch him eat it. I picture him smiling as he swallows it. And I'm guessing those gathered shed more than a few joyful tears. His friends are beginning to believe. By the time he recounts the events of the previous days and anoints them as witnesses, they are sure.

So the group follows him to Bethany. He lifts his hands and blesses them. And then he disappears again—carried up to heaven and out of their sight.

We would think that Jesus' ascension would send his friends into a major depression after their hopes have been raised and then so quickly dashed again. But they return to Jerusalem "with great joy." Something they can't yet see or understand lies in store for them. Without knowing fully what it meant, they cling to the promise that they will be "clothed with power from on high."

These disciples trust in the God that the author of Ephesians describes as the One "who by the power at work within us is able to accomplish abundantly far more than all we can ask or imagine" (3:20). We may not always know or understand what is in store for us, but we can trust that God sees what we cannot.

Gracious God, help me to trust in your promises and to live in joyful hope. Amen.

I met six-year-old Kyle just before Christmas several years ago. He excitedly offered to recite the story of Jesus' birth from Luke's Gospel. He got to his favorite part—where the angels appeared to the shepherds and proclaimed, "Glory to God in the highest, and on earth, peace!" But his mind went blank. He thought hard. Then he started again confidently, attributing these words to the heavenly host: "Glory to God in the highest . . . and I'll huff and I'll puff, and I'll blow your house down!"

God's vision is peace, but our world is plagued with huffing and puffing: gale-force winds of war that sweep the globe; tornadoes of terrorism that strike and spin off in perpetual cycles of vengeance; hurricanes of hatred that divide person from person and nation from nation; untamed tempests unleashed by our grasping abuse of the planet.

Today's words from First Peter about suffering and persecution may seem foreign to our ears, but such is the lot of many of the world's people. The cries from homeless shelters and refugee camps, from safe houses and rickety boats on the run, remind us that the world's huffing and puffing creates many victims.

Those who "keep alert," who pursue the truth and resist the evil that lurks like a devouring lion, cannot help but be buffeted by the persecuting blasts. Our calling is clear: to stand in the gaps with the world's victims, working to make God's promise the world's reality.

We are not alone. Whatever comes, God will "restore, support, strengthen, and establish" us. What power those words hold! To be established implies a groundedness that enables our survival of any wind that comes along. May we hold our ground, working for the day when we can join the angels in proclaiming with joy, "On earth, peace!"

Steadfast God, anchor me in your word and your love, so that I may work for your peace. Amen.

The writer of Ephesians paints a royal portrait of Jesus seated next to God in the heavenly places, "far above all rule and authority and power and dominion" with "all things under his feet." It depicts Christ enthroned and almighty—a far cry from the humble Jesus who was born in a stable, lived among the outcasts, and breathed his last on a criminal's cross.

Several years ago, on Christmas Eve in a shelter for home-less women, Sheila accused Mary of stealing her coat. Mary called Sheila a string of very creative synonyms for "prostitute." Sheila shot back that Mary was a "no-good good-for-nothing." Mary replied proudly, "I'm an aristocrat of the highest order, with the Rothschilds on my mother's side and the three wise men on my father's." End of argument. Sheila couldn't top that.

That night, as I pondered the claim of wealth and royalty that erupted out of Mary's poverty and vulnerability, I thought of the words of another Mary. Awaiting her miraculous son's birth, she proclaimed that God had "brought down the powerful from their thrones and lifted up the lowly; . . . filled the hungry with good things and sent the rich away empty" (Luke 1:52-53).

I imagine Mary and her friends at the shelter saying to the kings on their thrones, "Move over, it's our turn now." Jesus brings a whole throng to the heavenly places. Those of us who claim to follow him, who are willing to have "the eyes of [our] hearts enlightened," can also lay claim to these "riches of his glorious inheritance." But we must be humble to be exalted and learn to see the world and all God's children through the eyes of Christ—which are the eyes of the heart.

Compassionate God, give me discerning eyes to see your truth and a loving heart to act on it. Amen.

Although two Gospel writers don't even mention it, Luke clearly values the Ascension. He ends his Gospel with the event and opens his second volume, the Acts of the Apostles, with a recounting of it. In verse 5 of Acts 1, Luke reminds Jesus' followers of the promise Jesus made before his death: They "will be baptized with the Holy Spirit not many days from now." Then in verse 8, he recalls Jesus' words, "You will receive power when the Holy Spirit has come upon you." How significant were these words that they were the last message Jesus gave to his followers!

We find in the very next chapter the fulfillment of the promise on the day of Pentecost, which we celebrate next Sunday. The Holy Spirit anoints the gathered crowd in a rush of wind and tongues of flame. That morning all languages are understood. And by the end of Acts 2, believers hold all possessions in common, caring for the needy, breaking bread together, and praising God.

Jesus did not leave a blueprint to follow, a plan to execute. Events unfolded when open hearts received the power of the Holy Spirit. Here, for a moment, among the believers in the Jerusalem church, Jesus' prayer "that they may all be one" finds fulfillment.

In a world buffeted by winds of war and division, those of us who follow the Prince of Peace feel compelled to ask what force is stronger than these powerful gales and gusts? Only a bold and grace-filled wind like the one that filled the room at Pentecost—the kind that stirs people of good will to lavish compassion, extravagant mercy, and just sharing of the common wealth—can tame the hateful blasts. If we are open to receiving the power of the Holy Spirit, we too become part of the fulfillment of Jesus' final, fervent prayer for the world.

Anointing God, open my heart to the fullness of your power and strengthen me to receive it with courage. Amen.

The Coming of the Holy Spirit

MAY 29–JUNE 4, 2017 • BRONSON C. DAVIS

SCRIPTURE OVERVIEW: The foundation of the Pentecost festival is that series of events recorded in Acts 2, a decisive proclamation that links new life in Christ to the activity of the Spirit of God. At the heart of the church's new life is its experience of the crucified, risen Lord, a reality also recalled in the John 7 reading. Psalm 104 celebrates the power of God in endowing the heavens and the earth with life, an endowment that is linked to the work of God's Spirit. First Corinthians points the reader to the reality that the gift of life, having once been made, remains with the Spirit-led person in the form of a heart reoriented to new and marvelous deeds of witness.

QUESTIONS AND SUGGESTIONS FOR REFLECTION

- Read Psalm 104:24-34, 35b. God's gift of Spirit animates the life and well-being of creation. Today, breathe in God's Spirit; breathe out God's praise.
- Read Acts 2:1-21. The church is the Holy Spirit's creation to continue Jesus' mission. What part are you playing in the ongoing drama of ministry and mission to the world?
- Read 1 Corinthians 12:3b-13. The writer asserts that "every day, people of diverse gifts . . . model by their example how the Christian life is to be lived." How do you express your valuing of those who differ in worship style, theology, or doctrine?
- Read John 20:19-23. The writer says that Jesus' call to his followers "is no easy assignment; it is not without peril." How has being a Jesus-follower been difficult for you?

Member, First United Methodist Church of Fort Worth; serves on the Board of Trustees of Brite Divinity School; also served seven years on the Board of Directors of the Westar Institute, the group that began with the Jesus Seminar

No doubt many people look askance at the many denominations that make up Christianity today. Wouldn't our witness to the world be more effective if we were unified and spoke with one voice?

There is, however, a certain beauty in diversity. Different faith traditions appeal to different folks. Some love the rituals and symbols of the high church, the celebration of the Eucharist with all the glorious imagery; others emphasize a more emotional approach to worship, sway with the music and work to let the Spirit move them. Some prefer an intellectual approach to God, a call to rationally understanding the scriptures and how they relate to the worshiper in the modern world. And for still others, the Christian experience is all about service. Paul writes,

> For just as the body is one and has many members, and all the members of the body, though many, are one body, so it is with Christ. For in the one Spirit we were all baptized into one body, . . . and we were all made to drink of one Spirit.

We all share in that Spirit and the oneness of Christian community no matter what our denomination, no matter how we approach the altar, no matter which aspect of the Christian experience we emphasize. Our variety exists to build up Christian community.

Our church homes should embody the fellowship and understanding God desires. With the abiding of the Spirit, we can be part of a loving community that exemplifies Jesus' teachings. Our unity amid our diversity brings the kingdom alive as we prepare to be God's people in the world with all the responsibilities that entails.

Gracious God, we give thanks for our churches and we ask your guidance in helping us to be responsible, committed bearers of your Spirit. Amen.

This psalm splendidly captures the sense of gratitude and wonder we feel as we move through this joyous season. It also underscores the providential care in the form of sunshine and rain that makes possible the bounty of spring.

I take issue with the notion that God would "hide his face" and "take away his breath" thereby causing hardship and difficulties. That makes God seem too capricious, arbitrary, and even whimsical. However, the psalmist stresses our dependency and all creation's dependency upon the self-giving care of the Creator. Life certainly presents challenges: We get sick, relationships end, financial problems present themselves, and family members and close friends die. During those times, being part of a church community of love and friendship creates a balm of comfort and healing.

The church came into being seven weeks after Jesus' cru-
cifixion. The Holy Spirit inspired Jesus' followers at this point and provided the spiritual strength for them to go forward following the devastating loss of their leader on the cross. The disciples and their successors surmounted many obstacles in the first three hundred years after Jesus' death: the destruction of Jerusalem, persecution by the Roman Empire, and struggles among themselves.

Nearly two thousand years later we can join in the psalmist's celebration of the divine glory, "O Lord, how manifold are your works! In wisdom you have made them all." The Spirit breathed new life into the disciples just as God breathed life into creation. The church helps us appreciate those works and the wisdom of the Creator. Today we celebrate the manifold works of God and all those who make church possible for us.

Gracious God, we give thanks for the many ways creation bears witness to your Spirit. Amen.

Beginning with 1 Corinthians 11 through chapter 14, Paul addresses many issues related to corporate worship—the life of the body, the group that works as a team. Modern life provides many opportunities to serve on teams, including sports teams, school project teams, work teams and church teams. Our experience on teams helps us realize that people come to the effort with a wide variety of God-given talents. The key to team success comes in weaving these talents into a coherent whole.

Paul writes, "To each is given the manifestation of the Spirit for the common good." Once again the Spirit is at work—in creation, in us, in the distribution of God's gifts. We do not develop these gifts; they are not accomplishments. They are gifts of the Spirit. And no one gets all the gifts. So as we come together in the body, we hope the "team" can use the varied talents of its members to achieve its objectives.

The church and our faith communities are our focus this week. Since the initial work of the twelve apostles chosen by Jesus and then the efforts of millions working on behalf of the church through the two thousand years of Christian history we see examples of people inspired by God to carry out the church's mission. At many points charismatic leaders stepped forward: Augustine, Martin Luther, John Wesley, John Paul XXIII, Mother Teresa, and many others. All these leaders differ in outlook but share the skill of inspiring people to work together to accomplish important objectives.

Every day, people of diverse gifts quietly work to make the church a responsive community of believers who model by their example how the Christian life is to be lived. May our manifestation of the Spirit work for the good of all.

God, we thank you for the rich life we value as members of the church. May we witness the influence of the Holy Spirit in all our undertakings. Amen.

Can you imagine the devastation the disciples feel after their leader's crucifixion? We cannot fathom what they anticipate as they enter Jerusalem in what would become the final week of Jesus' ministry. They have been promised that they will "sit on twelve thrones, judging the twelve tribes of Israel" (Matt. 19:28) with the restoration and renewal of the true nation of Israel. They had no doubt forgotten Jesus' warning: "If any want to become my followers, let them deny themselves and take up their cross and follow me" (Mark 8:34). Most no doubt forgot the warning and embraced the promise of Palm Sunday.

All those dreams were crushed on the following desperate Friday. What does the future hold for these unsophisticated men? There are no MBAs among the group, no skill in planning and sales. Probably none can read. So their first reaction to seeing their slain leader once again has to be both astonishment and elation—hope embodied.

A first appearance and Jesus' first words, "Peace be with you." The disciples rejoice, but Jesus gives them little opportunity to glory in the moment. Instead he issues the fateful directive, "As the Father has sent me, so I send you." Most critical is that he then "breathed on them and said to them, 'Receive the Holy Spirit.'" Jesus speaks their call and commission. And yet again, the Spirit as new life and empowerment comes to the fore.

The origin of the church has divine roots, Spirit roots. The Holy Spirit would serve as the disciples' guiding light. Surely they experienced some concern and unsettling as they wondered how the Holy Spirit would support them as they went out into the world to fulfill Jesus' commission.

Creator God, we give thanks for the courageous disciples who, with Spirit-infused lives, picked up and carried on Jesus' ministry to the world. Amen.

The Coming of the Holy Spirit   187

This first-day-of-the-week meeting is how the Gospel of John describes the Great Commission. He wraps it in the risen Jesus' first appearance to the disciples and makes it into a simple, direct charge to go into the world without him but with the guidance of the Holy Spirit that he breathes on them.

Jesus sends them out to share the news of his resurrected life with all the world. The significance of the meeting in the upper room is not about his coming back from the dead; it is about the disciples' coming to understand that he now expects them to fulfill his ministry. This is no easy assignment; it is not without peril. Yet, somehow they must overcome their fears and rest their confidence in his gift of the Holy Spirit.

Would it not take a profound faith to go out from this room with the comforting presence of Jesus into a world they knew firsthand could be hostile? Jesus didn't issue road maps or how-to handbooks. They had not always been successful in their endeavors or in their faith judging from the various Gospels that describe their lives as disciples prior to Jesus' crucifixion. And yet, here Jesus places all his faith in them.

Jesus has stated several times in John's Gospel that when he leaves them, he will provide the gift of the Spirit, which will remind them of all that he has taught them. The Spirit will also bear witness to the meaning of who he was and will provide a source of deep, consoling peace.

The Spirit did indeed support and console the Jesus-followers as they began their ministry of witness without his physical presence. We don't know the stories of these twelve men as they go from this place, but we know the results and can admire their courageous lives. This Spirit-breathed commission resulted in the eventual spread and influence of Christianity.

Gracious God, may we sense the support of the Spirit as we do your work in the world. Amen.

What a week this has been—the highs of Pentecost with the appearance of Jesus to the disciples after the devastation of his loss, the coming of the Holy Spirit into their lives, and the incredible challenge of the Great Commission! Their lives have been in turmoil since Jesus' final week of life, and now an unknown future down an uncertain path beckons with only the guidance of the Holy Spirit. Can you imagine putting your head down to sleep that night after receiving your mission from the Holy One?

Jesus chose these simple, country men to enter an unrelenting three years of life experience. They have seen unbelievable events and viewed life from perspectives they could never have imagined. Their lives have been transformed; there is no going back. They now will carry their own crosses to spread the teachings and actions of Jesus.

Peter's quoting the prophet Joel helps them set their marching orders as it lays forth the prophecies of salvation. With the coming of the Spirit, the time for waiting has past. The disciple community is to set out in mission. They will tell those they meet of the signs of God's kingdom, and "everyone who calls on the name of the Lord shall be saved."

Peter uses Joel's prophetic insights to mobilize the disciple community, along with the others gathered to hear him speak. For the writer of Luke's Gospel, the divine inspiration of all scripture makes these words from Joel particularly significant to the fledgling Christian community. With this impetus, the Spirit-breathed disciples move into the world to bear witness to Jesus Christ. And that has made all the difference.

God of all, we give thanks for the efforts and sacrifices made by the early followers of Jesus. It has made all the difference in our faith and in the world. Amen.

PENTECOST SUNDAY

Pentecost celebrates the coming of the Holy Spirit to the followers of Jesus some fifty days after his death on the cross. (The word *Pentecost* means "fifty" in Greek and is borrowed from a Jewish holiday that occurs seven weeks after Passover.) The disciples have gathered in "one place"; at Peter's direction they await the baptism by the Spirit.

The author of Acts portrays this event in dramatic fashion, beginning with a sudden gust of wind accompanied by fiery tongues that settle on each participant. The great noise attracts people in the nearby community who are astonished to hear the acts of God recited in their own native languages.

Peter then delivers his first sermon to his fellow disciples. He has overcome his painful denial of Jesus and emerges in Acts as the clear leader of the disciples. He speaks of the fulfillment of what Jesus has commanded them to do. First, they are to remain in Jerusalem until they have received the Spirit. Then they will be his witnesses, carrying out Jesus' mission and ministry.

It is not hard to imagine how difficult the past seven weeks had been for the disciples and other followers of Jesus. Their world had come to an end. What were they to do? What were they to say? Where were they to go? They need direction. They need affirmation. With the coming of the Holy Spirit, their ending becomes a new beginning as the Spirit brings life and power. The words of Joel that Peter quotes in verses 17-21 move from being words of destruction and death to words of new life on the lips of Peter. The magic of Pentecost: the coming of the Holy Spirit, which brings life. These followers now become empowered believers who will become the church.

God of us all, we greet this day with joy and thanksgiving as your empowered people. Amen.

Grace for God's Community

JUNE 5–11, 2017 • ELAINE EBERHART

SCRIPTURE OVERVIEW: Trinity Sunday is an appropriate time for the church to reflect on the dynamic tension between what we know of God and our attempts to formulate and articulate what we know. The Genesis text demonstrates that the God of Israel, the creator of heaven and earth, is unlike other gods and must be served and worshiped exclusively. The psalm asserts the same power of God but is more explicit about the implications for human life of God's governance. The Gospel reading reflects on the gift of God's presence in the church, a presence marked by moral expectation and demand, as well as assurance. The epistle reading voices the strange convergence of God's authority and God's remarkable grace known through the presence of Christ.

QUESTIONS AND SUGGESTIONS FOR REFLECTION

- Read Genesis 1:1–2:4a. God takes a break. When do you allow yourself to step away from the busyness of the world for some much-needed sabbath time?

- Read Psalm 8. This song of praise exalts the order and majesty of creation. We, like the psalmist, ask, "God, why do you care for humankind?" How do you respond?

- Read 2 Corinthians 13:11-13. What ways can you envision yourself acting to calm disagreements and tension within your church community?

- Read Matthew 28:16-20. Jesus gives his disciples clear instructions: Go, make disciples, baptize, teach. How is your discipleship evident in your "going"?

Works in the Department of Development for Mayo Clinic, Jacksonville, Florida; an associate at Green Bough House of Prayer in Scott, Georgia

According to this Creation account, the created order, including human existence, begins in darkness when "a wind from God" sweeps over the face of the waters. Though God separates light from darkness and day from night on the first day, God does not eliminate the darkness. It remains part of the created order. God's creation of the sun, moon, and stars on the fourth day illuminates the day and the night and marks the seasons. Though light shines in the darkness, darkness remains.

As Christians, we often speak of shining God's light into the dark places of our world, and many places could use God's light to expose injustice and human need. But we may miss valuable aspects of God's grace if we are scared of the dark. Seeds germinate in the loamy damp soil before a sprout emerges in the sun; sometimes new life in us begins in darkness too. Though we grow in our knowledge of God's way of love when exposed to the light of our community and the beauty of creation, we also come to know God and ourselves in new ways when nothing seems clear to us. We find new depths of understanding about our relationship with God when clouds obscure the moon and stars, and we must make our way step by step, trying not to fall over the roots and rocks in the path.

We do one another a disservice if we insistently connect darkness to a lack of faith. Acknowledging darkness as part of our Christian life and caring for those who are in the midst of uncertain places is part of what we are called to do and be for one another. Indeed, we might ask God to make our experiences of darkness rich with possibilities for knowing God's presence.

How have you connected to God in a new way through an experience of darkness?

Genesis tells us that creating the world took work. Separating light from darkness and water from dry land required divine effort. Through labor born of God's creative imagination and love, animals and humans come into being. So when God hallows and blesses the last day of Creation, God puts a holy imprimatur on time set aside for rest.

Though it seems paradoxical, today we must *work* to find sabbath time. Distractions surround us, and turning off the channels in our minds, all playing at once and competing for attention, takes an act of will that many of us struggle to find. We receive opportunities to purchase calm moments through phone apps on meditation or tropical vacations promising us the chance to correct our sleep deprivation. Trying to buy rest sometimes affords us only new worries, however, with none of the needed respite from our full lives.

We do not leave busyness at the doors of our churches, and our communities of faith may add new responsibilities that require our effort and focus. Cooking for the soup kitchen, serving as a teacher for the youth Sunday school, organizing the church's recycling center are all vital tasks to which God may call us. But God also calls us to rest; sabbath is as important to our lives as service is.

As a Christian community, we are called to rest at least once each week when we gather for worship. God's Spirit recreates our hearts and minds in the time when we sing, pray together, hear good news spoken to weary hearts, and gather around God's welcoming table. Even if we cannot escape our worries for that time, we are invited to share ourselves and our concerns with our brothers and sisters who will bear our burdens with us and remind us of the promise of rest.

Where is God offering rest to me and to my community of faith?

Cotton fields and woods surround the retreat house I visit in Scott, Georgia. Few houses line the road that leads to the Green Bough House of Prayer. I see a horse or two and a rooster that announces dawn at all hours of the night and day. Unlike my home in the city, there are no high-rise condominiums, no office buildings sprawling block after block, and no strip malls. Compared to the places I live and work, the quiet and simplicity of the setting attract me and others to find our way there when we can.

A year or two ago, another retreatant shared a time-lapse video of the night sky at Green Bough. It still may be out in cyberspace somewhere. As wonderful as the video is, it only hints at the awe-inspiring skies I see when I walk out of the chapel onto the porch after night prayer. Undimmed by the artificial light of the city, the stars and moon and planets are so vivid that I am overwhelmed when I experience them after I have been away long enough to forget their power.

On a clear night, the majesty of the sky is almost too much to take in. I walk in the yard outside the guesthouse and turn until I think I have taken in every view of the dome above my head. Only when my neck begins to cramp do I reluctantly climb the steps and sit in a porch rocker for a more comfortable view, one that I can sustain until I go back inside to sleep.

I like to think that the psalmist had a similar view that prompted the words of praise to God for all that God has created. Like the psalmist, I find it difficult to comprehend that I am as important to God as those beautiful stars.

Thank God for experiences that confirm God's presence as Creator.

The psalmist and the writer of the Creation account in Genesis put humankind at the pinnacle of Creation, and biblical translations use words like *dominion, rule, and subdue* to describe the role of humankind in caring for the earth. Is there any way to understand those words apart from a hierarchical relationship between humans and the rest of the created order?

If you drive almost anywhere in the southern United States, you soon will see how our efforts to subdue creation often backfire. Kudzu covers thousands of acres of southern fields and forests, and its rapid growth and deep roots make it difficult to eradicate. Even with the time and expense of efforts to remove it, the spread of kudzu is a relatively benign misstep when compared to the extinction of animals and plants and the pollution of our air and water. How can the damage we have done in exercising dominion over the earth be part of the plan of the One who loved the world into being?

Notice that the affirmation of God's sovereignty frames human dominion. Perhaps that is where dominion resides: within the sovereignty of God. The psalmist tells us that it is impossible to look at the work of God's fingers and not be moved by the majesty of what God has made and entrusted to us. Perhaps our communities of faith lack the awe and delight necessary for us to long to protect our earth as if it were our child. If we honor the earth as God cherishes it, our decisions about how we live and what we value will change. Our communities of faith will weigh in on the difficult questions about how to balance the needs of humans while caring for the earth because these are not simply political issues; they are spiritual questions that lie at the heart of what it means to be the people of God.

How can my faith community experience the awe of creation and hear anew God's call to care for the earth?

Paul offers advice to the Christians at Corinth and hints of a troubled past relationship between him and the church. Though he urges the community to love the member of the Corinthian church who spoke against him, Paul also defends and justifies himself as an apostle and bearer of truth. He asks the hearers to open their hearts to him and their pocketbooks in support of the church of Jerusalem. He ends the letter by encouraging the church to heed his words and live in peace with one another before closing with a benediction for the church.

How well most of us know that living and worshiping in a Christian community is difficult and often contentious, a petri dish in which conflicts grow wildly from the smallest particles of misunderstandings. In the Corinthian community, we can imagine that hearing Paul's letter might have been met with some eye rolls. Put things in order? Agree with one another? Live in peace? These directives are easier said than done, Brother Paul. Without the grace of the trinitarian God whom Paul names in his benediction, there can be no concord or unity of effort in the church. Even periods of harmony among leaders or consensus following a particularly hard church decision are often followed by an unraveling of peace within the body of Christ.

Our Creator God, author of the order of creation, creates us and our communities for love. Jesus redeems us for love and provides an example of love that seeks unity and peace. The Spirit moves among us and sustains our community when we lean into possibilities for love and work to dismantle dividing walls. Even when agreement is impossible, the Spirit enables members of the community to love through conflict and to will the good of sisters and brothers though disagreement persists.

Imagine God as Creator, Redeemer, and Sustainer moving through your community of faith to bring unity and peace.

The risen Jesus promised the members of his community that he would be with them always. He would be with them when their mission met resistance. They would know his presence when they were afraid. He would embolden them with his authority as they pronounced good news and the coming of God's reign.

To see their beloved teacher alive again after the crucifixion must have been exhilarating and comforting. Maybe it even seemed too good to be true. Is the too-good-to-be-true part in the minds of those who doubted? And do they have a change of heart after Jesus challenges them to continue his mission and promises his presence with them always?

I will admit that I might have been among the doubters on that day, and I do not think that I would have been alone. Many of us waver between doubt and belief, between assurance and a deep longing for assurance. Someone we love may be sick or dying, or we may be grieving a relationship that has ended. At other times doubt arises from the routine, when worship services begin to run together, and we have lost sight of the new thing that God is doing in our midst.

When we find ourselves in a season of doubt, someone assures us of God's nearness. Someone bears witness to the Spirit. Someone exchanges the peace of Christ with us in a way that reminds of us the love from which nothing can separate us. Someone hands us the bread and cup with the promise that through a holy mystery, God is present and available.

Jesus gives "authority" to all who gather that day: the steadfast and those who doubt. That authority comes from the One who possesses all authority.

Thank God for the witness of others when it is difficult for you to believe.

TRINITY SUNDAY

Jesus commands the remnant of his community to make disciples everywhere, baptizing in the name of the triune God those whom they invite to join God's mission of love and justice. It is hard to imagine a more ambitious command or a grander scope for the community's work after Jesus completed his ministry on earth. And Jesus gives this commandment both to those who worship him when he appears to them on the mountain and to those who doubt. The Great Commission is not just for the high performers, those whose faithfulness he counts on, those who have demonstrated that they fully understand the mission to which he calls them and the One who calls them to that mission; Jesus gives the Great Commission to all members of the community.

Though the travels of the disciples are documented in the Acts of the Apostles and by early Christian writers, there is no definitive proof of the distances their ministries took them after Jesus' death. Regardless of the number of miles they journeyed, we know that they offered healing and preached the good news of the coming of God's reign of justice and mercy.

We may be called to travel no farther than the town in which we grew up, but even there people with hurting hearts long for the affirmation that they are beloved sons and daughters of God. They need the good news that we celebrate: We are loved into life to follow and serve the risen Christ. They need the rite of baptism that initiates us into Jesus' community on earth and seals us as Christ's own forever. They need the invitation to join God's community of doubters and believers who are sustained by the Spirit and who are supported by brothers and sisters who walk the road of discipleship together.

Who are the people around you who need the good news of God's love, acceptance, and abundant grace?

Self-Emptying Power

JUNE 12–18, 2017 • NIALL MCKAY

SCRIPTURE OVERVIEW: Two threads run through all the readings. One is the claim that God is powerful over all things. Psalm 116 makes this claim most eloquently with its assertion that God "has heard my voice and my supplications." The story of the promise of Isaac's birth demonstrates that it is God and God alone who gives life. Matthew situates the call of the disciples within the larger context of Jesus' mission and understands their work to be the consequence of God's decision to send workers. Paul emphasizes God's power by recalling that God's act of reconciliation comes within the setting of human alienation and hostility. The second thread is that of the unworthiness of those whom God chooses.

QUESTIONS AND SUGGESTIONS FOR REFLECTION

- Read Genesis 18:1-15; 21:1-7. When has God presented you with a laughable opportunity? What incredible offer would you like God to propose to you today?
- Read Psalm 100. How do you create a future of hope by recalling God's faithful action on your behalf in the past?
- Read Romans 5:1-8. When have you looked for a superhero in a crisis situation? Who came to your aid?
- Read Matthew 9:35–10:23. What field of harvest is God calling you to? Do you yearn for wheat rather than potatoes? How do you go about an attitude adjustment?

Minister, Uniting Church in Australia; research associate with Stellenbosch University in South Africa; committed to reading the Bible for the sake of enabling justice, forgiveness, and hope

Over the past few years the challenge of hospitality and welcome for refugees fleeing war and persecution has once again confronted wealthy Western countries. Countries in Western Europe, North America, and even Australia have been divided in their response to those who have arrived on our shores fleeing persecution. Sadly, many of us, even many Christians, have failed in our calling to provide welcome to those who have sought sanctuary. Under the cloak of national and economic security, we have let fear and self-interest dominate our actions and our words.

The Genesis account of promised blessing to Sarah and Abraham provides a helpful reminder to all people of faith about the blessing that arises from generous hospitality. As the strangers arrive at the camp, Abraham and Sarah engage busily in all the normal matters of welcome—food, water to wash up, and a place to rest. They engage in hospitality not begrudgingly but, instead, with a spirit of abundance that can only arise from a deep sense that meeting a stranger is, in itself, a blessing. Meeting a stranger is not a time for fear but a time for gratitude.

The promise of new life that comes later is not a matter of *quid pro quo*—it is neither a payment nor a reward for hospitality. Rather, it is blessing that comes unsought and unearned—as faithfulness and welcome create a space where generosity and blessing overflow. In this encounter, like so many others in the stories of Abraham and Sarah, risk leads to blessing. The strangers, the ones our natural instincts tell us to fear, actually bear God's promise. Across the ages the Israelites returned to this story to affirm and confirm an identity rooted in radical and generous hospitality. As Christians we do well to remember this heritage—especially when people need shelter and welcome.

Loving God, may your love and faithfulness inspire us to generosity and graceful welcome. Amen.

A kind of stunned bemusement sometimes emerges unbidden at times of surprise, especially when our clearest thinking and best analysis make us expect failure. When success emerges through a confluence of unlikely circumstances or an improbable intervention, we cannot help laughing, especially when the prediction and analysis of the experts is confounded.

Sarah meets the announcement of her pregnancy with a disbelieving laugh, an unbidden snort at the absurdity of a promise that seems impossible to fulfill. Sarah's initial laugh is wry and skeptical, born of a deep sadness and hope unrealized. But it is also truthful, for it sees the world as it really is. For most of us life is terribly predictable. The future flows on linearly from the past. New and amazing things do not happen. The elderly do not give birth.

Consider the stunned bemusement, then, that Sarah and Abraham must have felt when Sarah becomes pregnant. Against all odds, something different is happening in her life, something unexpected and joyful. And, when the child is finally born, the laughter of skepticism and bemusement is transformed into the laughter of joy. Sarah's life is not predictable or driven by fate. Indeed God is faithful, and God's promises are honored.

From start to finish, the lives of Abraham and Sarah involve risk, promise, and trust in the face of their own best judgment. They travel to far-flung lands, deal with powerful rulers, and attempt to establish a new communal life—even when they have no children of their own. Despite their human fallibility, their lives become a testament to the way that trust in God is met by God's faithfulness. The story of Abraham and Sarah certainly inspire much of the New Testament—including Romans 4; Galatians 3; Hebrews 11; and James 2. May it continue to inspire us today.

Surprising God, transform our laughter from wry skepticism to overwhelming joy. Amen.

Sometimes we find it hard to be joyful and offer praise to God—especially when our present circumstances overwhelm us. The pressures of life—expectations, busyness, illness, worry, addiction—fill our lives and our minds. Perhaps we need to step back from the details of our lives and look at the bigger picture. Perhaps even try and glimpse life from God's perspective.

The Psalms are a collection of writings that move among the pressures of life—of enmity, oppression, and despair—to the bigger view that acknowledges God's authority, love, and presence in all things. Because the psalmists are well aware of their own frailty and destitution, we can identify with their experience. And yet, at the same time, almost every psalm concludes with a renewed trust in God that helps us escape the mire of everyday worry.

Of all the psalms, Psalm 100 is one of the most hopeful. It reminds the people to rejoice and sing praises because of God's faithfulness. Moreover, the psalmist here clearly takes the long view: God's faithfulness is not a singular event but spans the generations. It reaches back into the far-distant past to our foundational stories. This allows us, in turn, to imagine and create a future that relies on this same faithfulness.

At a basic level, taking the long view is liberating, for it frees us from being consumed by the day-to-day pressures of life. But at a deeper level, the witness of Psalm 100 means that we do not simply react to what happens to us. We can step back and acknowledge the blessing of life. We are able to envision a future in which this blessing is shared further and wider. Let us hope in a future where the whole creation makes a joyful noise.

Eternal God, may your faithfulness over the ages give us hope for the future. Amen.

Humans expend a lot of effort in trying to make peace with their gods. We tend to attribute value and worth to many different (false) gods: success, wealth, tribal or national loyalty, self-determination. Yet the gospel of Jesus Christ tells us that these ideas are mere distortions of the reality they purport to represent. These ideas do not deserve our allegiance because they are false. Take wealth, for example. Elevating wealth as an ideal, as our society so often does, simply illuminates wealth's failure to meet emotional needs. Chasing wealth does not lead to abundance but instead to lives of poverty, fear, and despair.

In Romans 4–5 Paul draws upon the faithfulness of Abraham and Sarah to show that trust in the living God affords us a kind of real peace. This authentic peace grows from true relationships built on endurance, character, hope, grace, and suffering. Just as Abraham and Sarah often faced alienation, persecution, and despair in their lives of faith, their faith in a God of loving providence prevailed.

In Romans, Paul engages in lengthy theological explorations about how the early church may best live out lives of faith in the God of Jesus Christ. But at the core of it all is his clear belief that Jesus enables humanity to be reconciled with a loving God, to be at peace with God through faith.

Paul's belief in making peace with God through Jesus Christ is audacious but totally grounded. When we trust that God loves us faithfully through the ages, we will never be disappointed. Our future is one of hope. For the early church and for us, making peace with God means that we will be able to make peace with ourselves and with others—even with our enemies.

Reconciling God, may we make peace with you and all human-kind. Amen.

The number of movies about superheroes seems to have exploded in past decade. Some scholars have suggested that the popularity of superhero stories develops because they take the place of local folk stories, myths, and fairy tales that have shaped moral and communal identity over centuries. Superhero movies tend to raise questions about the corruption of power, about vigilantism and justice, and about whether even someone with superhuman powers can be regarded as completely righteous. The best superhero narratives consider the internal struggles of the protagonists who realize that even when their intentions are good and they try their best, they often don't measure up because of their own fallibility or because of impossible social expectations.

In the middle of his extended theological explorations, in Romans 5 Paul touches on the question of righteousness in the saving plan of God. He begins by asserting that it is up to God to recognize and define righteousness in people's actions—as he does with Abraham. Yet, perhaps even more importantly, in Romans 5:6-8 Paul reminds us that the saving life and death of Jesus does not depend on our righteousness. Salvation is for all—the righteous and the unrighteous alike. This does not deny the importance of righteousness. Living lives that God might declare righteous is central to the calling of the faithful. Yet Paul clearly notes that human failure to become righteous—or worse, becoming self-righteous against others—does not deny the power of Jesus to save, redeem, and make whole. Superhero films show most clearly that superhuman power will not save us. Christians, however, hold to a different story. We believe that only the sacrifice of the cross and the self-emptying of power by God can save.

> *God of all hope, help us recognize the true righteousness of our servant king Jesus. Amen.*

A few months ago I attended a funeral for my friend John. John had been a minister for over fifty years, mostly serving as a rural parson in agricultural communities in Australia. During the eulogy, his sons recounted tales of how John helped the farmers of his community in practical ways, and they remembered fondly harvesting the golden wheat in the warm summer sun. Less romantic was the time later in John's ministry when he ministered in a community of potato farmers. This time, helping with harvest was far less glamorous and mostly consisted of thick mud, sore backs, and the irremovable stench of rotten tubers. But John did not help with potato picking and wheat harvesting for their aesthetic or romantic value but rather as ways of helping out his flock and living out his ministry.

The Gospels contain many stories with explicitly agricultural metaphors. The sending of the disciples in Matthew 9–10 seems no exception. The account begins romantically enough: "The harvest is plentiful, but the laborers are few; therefore ask the Lord of the harvest to send out laborers into his harvest." Yet even before their commissioning, the disciples' task is clear based on Jesus' actions: He has been teaching, healing, and proclaiming. The disciples will have to key off Jesus' own attitude toward the crowds: "He had compassion for them." And the disciples will go in Jesus' authority. Matthew makes it abundantly clear that being on a mission from God is not a romantic endeavor but rather a difficult and perilous undertaking. As disciples of Jesus today, the mission (and the risks) are the same. We are to bring in the harvest—even if it more often resembles picking potatoes in the mud than harvesting wheat in the sun.

God of sun and rain, help us to be faithful disciples in all times and places. Amen.

Many churches in the small country towns where I grew up have large wooden boards affixed to the back wall. On these boards are recorded, usually in faded yellow-gold text, the names of soldiers who died in the World Wars. Often the names are listed directly under the words *For God, King and Empire.*

This kind of memorializing seems incongruous to me. Australia was a very new country with a small population when these wars occurred. We also have a long cultural suspicion of authority that goes back to the convict era. Remembering those who died in conflict is common and occurs in many countries —but to encompass that tragedy and violence under the British king and empire grates against the slightly rebellious Australian spirit. Certainly many of the soldiers criticized the British hierarchy. More terrifying to me, however, is the blasphemous co-option of the God of Jesus Christ into this kind of memorializing. Using God to justify war is a distortion of our faith.

In Matthew 10 we read not of the establishment of grand kingdoms and empires but of a movement that will face persecution, usually enforced by the governors and kings. The confronting reality of Christian discipleship is that it puts us at odds with many human institutions—including our good citizenship to the state. Following Jesus demands an ultimate loyalty that makes everything else secondary. In the ancient world, Christian faithfulness was met with persecution. Perhaps, however, in the so-called "Christian West" we have faced a more insidious problem. The state has generally not persecuted the church but rather co-opted God for its purposes. War and sacrifice in the name of God, king, and empire? Or forgiveness, peace, and salvation through God alone? We cannot choose both.

God of peace, may our highest loyalty be to your kingdom. Amen.

Intimacy, Promise, and Threat

JUNE 19–25, 2017 • SHARONNE PRICE

SCRIPTURE OVERVIEW: Implicit in the story of Hagar and Ishmael is the threat to Isaac and to God's promises to Abraham and Sarah. The psalmist captures the terror by unnamed forms of destruction that may threaten an individual or people. Paul raises the specter of that most universal threat—death—but does so within the context of the new life won by Christ's resurrection. Matthew describes various ways in which the enemies of Jesus threaten his disciples because of their association with him.

QUESTIONS AND SUGGESTIONS FOR REFLECTION

- Read Genesis 21:8-21. When have you felt burdened and outcast? What was your experience of God's hearing you where you were?
- Read Psalm 86:1-10, 16-17. Do you pray in the confidence that God hears and will answer your pleas? If not, how could you learn to pray in that manner?
- Read Romans 6:1b-11. Paul speaks of dying to self and rising with Christ. How has your Christian faith given you a sense of freedom from sin?
- Read Matthew 10:24-39. What makes God's presence real to you? How does God's intimate knowledge of you—the number of hairs on your head—make you feel?

Executive Office, Pastoral Relations and Mission Planning, Uniting Church, South Australia

The pain of abandonment fills this part of the great saga of Abraham. The story thus far has been laden with difficult choices: the decision to leave Ur and all its familiarity and then to leave Sodom and Gomorrah to God's judgment after striving to find clemency; leaving Lot's wife because of her fated disobedience. And now after all that faithfulness, we have a story of ruthlessness.

We recognize the themes of invitation and hospitality throughout this story: Sarai's invitation for Abram to lie with Hagar, the Egyptian slave; the kindness shown by Abram to the strangers who visit; promises and covenants, including the circumcision of Ishmael, the slave woman's son, along with all the males of the household; and God's promises, not only to Abram but also to both Sarai (Sarah) and Hagar about their sons, now flourishing and growing in strength.

But a dark thread runs through this narrative. In Genesis 16 we read how Hagar, having conceived, has mocked the barrenness of her mistress. Sarai responds by treating her badly so Hagar runs away into the wilderness where God encounters her as she rests by a spring of water. And now, some years later, we find Sarah's jealousy and Abraham's response resulting in Hagar being driven into the wilderness to the point of death. Experiences of being "in" and "out" weave through the story.

Through all of this drama of inclusion and exclusion, jealousy and suspicion, brinkmanship and desperation, human kindness and yet disturbing injustice, one thing remains constant: God, who hears "the voice of the boy where he is," keeps God's promises, providing sustenance to the outcast in need and treasuring the life of Ishmael. "God was with the boy."

God who hears the voice of the abandoned and the homeless, help us to keep our own promises to protect and nurture those who bear the brunt of an unjust world. Amen.

Abraham faces a difficult situation. The mothers of his precious children are jealous of each other, and he knows he cannot maintain the situation—a distressing time. The teller of the story does not belabor the point, but Abraham's choices will influence the path of this story of God's intervention in his life and the formation of a great nation.

Abraham, risking everything, has been faithful to God. In the most surprising, even laughable ways, God has kept the divine promises. Abraham has wealth and fruitfulness, and here are two boys who perhaps will father the great promised nation. But Sarah states that Abraham must cast Hagar and Ishmael out. Abraham, who has demonstrated his love for Ishmael and has included the child in his family, turns to God and receives comfort. God makes another promise: "I will make a nation of him also."

This story pulls at our heartstrings. How can Hagar's life be so devalued, and how can a child of promise be sent away with meager provisions to die in the desert? I find myself outraged that because Isaac is the more "legitimate" heir and that this story is written from the perspective of the "chosen ones" —descendants of God's direct intervention—it seems OK for Abraham to make this horrendous choice. However, I am pulled back to reason when I realize that God's grace pervades every episode in this great saga. God's reassurance is there for Hagar and Abraham, and the nurtured Ishmael grows to adulthood with both strength and skill. I need to read this story with an eye not on human injustice but on God's intimate interest not only in the grand plan but in every precious life.

God of the big picture and the grand plan, help us to see your grace at work in the challenges of our small stories and in every detail of our lives. Amen.

Intimacy, Promise, and Threat 209

This psalm is the only one ascribed to David in Book III of the Psalms. Familiar Davidic themes run through it. We may wonder, *How many times does David need to cry out to God? How often is his life threatened? And how does he manage to get himself in such messes?* Some scholars believe that the Hebrew people found this psalm particularly significant when they were in exile; for centuries it has found its way onto the lips of the faithful.

Whether in times of war or difficult circumstance, personal trouble or ill health, this psalm captures the depth of feeling that accompanies the person whose back is against the wall, that moment when only God can make a difference. I find it interesting to explore the form of the psalm. The petitioner begins by crying out to God, begging God to come near and hear, reminding God of her/his devotion and absolute faith and trust in God's goodness. In this sense, it has the feel of coming into a royal court, showing absolute respect to the Lord who alone can help. Only God's power can save.

The psalm serves as a timely reminder of the respect God deserves. Though we often speak of our relationship with God like we are intimate friends, in times of trouble we become painfully aware of our smallness and the need for God to be God—great, majestic, omnipotent. God is creator and we are creature; though we sometimes like to think otherwise, it is good to remember that reality. I don't mean to imply that God is aloof and disinterested and needs our groveling adoration. God remains as near as the breath we breathe and more willing to be with us than we can imagine. "For you, O LORD, are good and forgiving, abounding in steadfast love to all who call on you." No matter the circumstance, we can turn to and trust in God.

Teach me your ways and hear me when I call, God of grace and mercy. Amen.

My brother Lance was born with a hearing disability, and I learned early in my life how to communicate well with him. We needed to be attentive to each other, and he needed to ensure his ear was "inclined" to his small sister if he was to understand and participate in a conversation. I always found it frustrating when other people or sounds distracted him, or he simply didn't want to hear.

"Incline your ear, O Lord" is the first plea of this psalm. The psalmist shouts words to this effect: "Take particular notice of me, Lord God! This is about me this time! I need your favor right now!" In Australian lingo, this is the equivalent of "Look at me, look at me, look at me!" Prayer and a sense of being heard always involve relationship and attention.

The personal prayer acknowledges and recognizes God, but only one verse (outside of today's reading) articulates the psalmist's trouble: "O God, the insolent rise up against me; a band of ruffians seeks my life, and they do not set you before them" (v. 14). This is no casual prayer. It details a direct intimate relationship centered in promise and faithfulness—a covenant. The psalmist is confident of the right to seek God's help and in the belief that God will respond.

This is no "flick a quick prayer out when I'm in trouble just in case God really exists and will help me." Unlike my brother who could choose not to hear me, God "will answer" the psalmist. The God to whom the psalmist prays does not get distracted; the Lord is "good and forgiving, abounding in steadfast love." The psalmist and his God: a fostered, attentive relationship of intimacy and grace that encourages me to examine my own attentiveness to God so that I too may cry out with confidence, "Incline your ear, O Lord, and answer me."

Teach me your ways, O God; may I grow in my understanding of your power and grace. Amen.

Surely Jesus' teachings and actions bring extreme responses. The words of this particular passage come on the heels of the Sermon on the Mount, some healings, and the call of the twelve. This is Jesus' first set of teachings, and they scarcely offer an encouraging pep talk. "If they have called the master of the house Beelzebul, how much more will they malign those of his household!" "Do not fear those who kill the body but cannot kill the soul." "I have not come to bring peace, but a sword." I could go on, but the picture is quite clear. Jesus demands everything of the disciples and, by inference, of us.

Living as we do in a culture that prizes individual worth, where we choose our words carefully when speaking to one another, these words shock us. Does Jesus really mean all that he declares? His words utterly confront. The gentle Jesus meek and mild, full of grace and mercy, surely holds much more appeal. Yet the truth is, we cannot and dare not domesticate him, reducing him to some form of niceness.

Jesus confronts. He confronted then, and he confronts us still. He confronted the complicity of religious leaders collaborating with power. He confronts our easy conformity to the particularities of culture. He confronted all the ways in which people were excluded by gender, purity sanctions, or race. He confronts us today as we struggle with the issues of asylum seekers and religious intolerance. He confronted those who no longer put God first in their lives—even over family. And he confronts us with that same question he put to Peter, "Do you love me more than these?" (John 21:15). Discipleship is costly. It demands our all!

> *Jesus, revelation of God, teach us your ways and sustain us as we try to follow you. Forgive our inadequacies, and guide us this day. Amen.*

A balding friend remarked, "I try to make life easy for God. No one will have trouble counting the hairs on my head. Oops, there goes another!" It never fails to get a laugh. In the midst of what could sound like a tirade, Jesus pulls the disciples into a circle of compassion and love. He offers them the secrets of the kingdom. It used to be a mystery, but all is in plain sight, he says, so proclaim it from the rooftops. We can imagine a stuttering disciple countering with these words: "But, Jesus. We'll get slaughtered." To which Jesus answers, "Oh, don't worry about that . . . you are more precious than sparrows." *Worth more than sparrows? God counts the hairs on my head?*

As harsh and demanding as Jesus' words with his disciples seem, grace is never far away. The disciples have received their commission. Here Jesus makes the connection between master and slave, teacher and disciple. And then he speaks the words "do not fear" or "do not be afraid" three times. The disciples will become as the teacher, but they have nothing to fear—they are of more value than sparrows.

In a time when people are more likely to be ridiculed than praised for being Christian, we remind ourselves of Jesus' promises to his followers: "I also will acknowledge [the one who acknowledges me] before my Father." Jesus promises eternal life, the gift of the Spirit that leads into all truth, and his everlasting presence.

Without the gift of grace and the empowerment of the Spirit, none of us can live up to Jesus' invitation to discipleship. None of us has that innate capacity. But in the divine presence, absolutely affirmed as beloved and cherished, right down to the hairs on our head, anything and everything is possible—even the possibility of transforming the world for good.

Loving God, may we hear your word of grace and serve you without condition or restraint all the days of our lives. Amen.

Intimacy, Promise, and Threat 213

The fight for freedom from apartheid lies deep and strong in the memory of many people who lived through it. Steve Biko, murdered in September 1977, had been a trailblazer who believed that his people would be freed from oppression only when they were freed in their minds and they started to believe in freedom. He said, "It is better to die for an idea that will live, than to live for an idea that will die." Biko knew he was fighting for a new South Africa, a South Africa where there would be opportunity for his children and his children's children. He would not give up. It is the way of the martyr. It is the way of Christ. "No one has greater love than this, to lay down one's life for one's friends" (John 15:13).

Paul takes up this notion of dying to self and being raised with Christ in his letter to the Romans. It goes beyond theological nicety. He lives almost every day of his Christian life as a man under threat. He has been threatened with death and escapes with his life. He is a man who travels the world proclaiming the good news of Christ to people who at best have little understanding, and at worst hate him. So the idea of dying to self holds a certain poignancy, and later he too will be martyred.

In this passage, though, Paul reflects on the nature of salvation, on the way in which Christ deals with sin. For Paul, identifying with Christ and dying to self is the key. We come to know the absolute freedom that is born of faith as we die to all that has a hold over us and, in the process, come to know the joy that is born of new life, resurrected life, life in the Spirit of Christ. This is true freedom—to live for a good cause and to die to all else. What greater cause exists than to follow Christ?

Almighty God, who through the mystery of the cross and resurrection brings the gift of eternal life, grant us the courage to die to self so we may rise with Christ to the joy of your eternal kingdom. Amen.

Hard Conversations

JUNE 26–JULY 2, 2017 • BRIAN MCCAFFREY

SCRIPTURE OVERVIEW: Not only is God's call on Abraham unthinkable; it jeopardizes the long-delayed but now realized promise. Yet in the end, Abraham's faith and God's grace prevail. Psalm 13 is the classic example of a psalm of complaint. It shows that a prayer of complaint is a vigorous, active form of hope in God. Thus the psalm moves from a situation of need to a resolution in joy and confidence. In the passage from Romans 6, Paul juxtaposes three pairs of opposites: sin versus righteousness, freedom versus slavery, and wages versus gifts. For Paul, sin is a power that exceeds the abilities of human beings to contest. Only God is a match for the power of sin. We cannot earn or achieve eternal life; it is a gift from God. Matthew 10 makes a strong claim about the identification of believers with Jesus and, in turn, with God.

QUESTIONS AND SUGGESTIONS FOR REFLECTION

- Read Genesis 22:1-14. We do not often face such demands from God as the one Abraham faced. What hard situations has God called you to? What hard conversations followed?
- Read Psalm 13. The psalmist asks God to pay attention and take his situation seriously. When has that been your request of God?
- Read Romans 6:12-23. When have you felt like a scout earning merit badges for God? How has obedience from the heart helped you reorient your life?
- Read Matthew 10:40-42. What "cup of cold water" might you offer to someone in need?

Retired Evangelical Lutheran Church of America pastor and long-term care chaplain, living in St. Paul, Minnesota

Throughout our life we try to avoid hard conversations—the ones that may embarrass, leave you feeling a fool. Hard conversations have an impact on our relationships; they don't remain the way they were. We sense a wedge driven between ourselves and another or we glimpse a greater possibility that vastly changes our sense of self, our relationships, and our perspective on life and death—and life again.

A Jewish scholar, Martin Buber said there are only two kinds of encounters/conversations: the first being I-it, a monologue where you purposefully manipulate the other in order to get what you want. There is no need to listen. However, the other conversation, I-Thou, is based on respect where a true dialogue can occur, where listening to the other holds the potential of our being changed by the encounter.

Our passage today begins with a hard word from God to Abraham though it doesn't quite meet the requirement for conversation. God calls, Abraham responds. God's request imperils the promise, the greater possibility that an heir offered Abraham and Sarah. Couched in the language of testing, God demands Isaac as a sacrifice. Does Abraham trust God and obey out of faith, or does Abraham desire relationship only for reward?

Call, response, request, silence. The conversation ends in Abraham's obedience. He readies the wood and donkey and sets out with his servants and Isaac. Only as they reach the place of sacrifice do words come as Abraham addresses his servants: "Stay here . . . the boy and I will go over there; we will worship, and then we will come back to you." Father and son set out with wood, fire, and a knife. Isaac himself inquires, "Where is the lamb for a burnt offering?" Another hard conversation, but perhaps they walk toward a miracle.

When did your prayer time last involve a hard conversation between God and you?

Today's reading offers several hard conversations that remove the smile from Abraham's face. God's demand for a sacrifice will remove the laughter that Isaac has brought to Sarah and Abraham's life. Isaac carries the wood for the sacrifice while Abraham carries the fire and knife. That knife can cut the tension in this story. Isaac calls to his father who replies in the same manner to which he replied to God: "Here I am," adding the words "my son." And with Isaac's question, "Where is the lamb?" another hard conversation begins. Listen to the ready deceit in Abraham's voice as he responds to his son's inquiry: "God himself will provide the lamb." As they continue walking, surely Abraham wonders if this child of the promise will really become the sacrifice.

With altar built and wood laid on, Isaac no longer has a reason to ask about a lamb. As the glint of Abraham's knife flashes above, another conversation begins. It too opens with a call to Abraham. And yet again we hear Abraham's standard reply: "Here I am."

Does Abraham's obedience win the day? Does it bring to the fore a different conversation than the hard ones up to this time? Yes! God tells Abraham not to lay his hand on Isaac. So Abraham names the place: "the LORD will provide." Disaster averted; promise intact. Obedience or faith rewarded? The text says God tested Abraham. So how did Abraham do? Verses 16-17 give us the answer: "The angel of the LORD called to Abraham . . . and said, 'Because you have not withheld your son, your only son, I will indeed bless you, and I will make your offspring as numerous as the stars.'"

Today I shall have a hard conversation with God about the demands of faithful obedience.

Rich Melheim says that by the end of the day we should be able to name a high and a low—and we should pray about both. That really is a countercultural discipline. We know that in regard to the news, "if it bleeds it leads." We all long to stay far from the world's ugliness. Some will build a protective wall against the big hurts of life. Others will deny the world's reality by choosing to see only the good.

Our psalm of complaint opens with the psalmist posing some pretty hard questions to God: "How long, O LORD? Will you forget me forever? How long must I bear pain in my soul?" The psalmist's questions imply that not only is he suffering, but God is responsible! The petitioner speaks in desperation. God has left him to his own devices and neglected his needs.

After the five questions, the psalmist lays out his demands: "Consider, answer, give light." He pleads for God's attention. Only God can "give light to [his] eyes," restoring his vitality and well-being. Only God can bring vindication against his enemies.

Sometime in our life, chaos inevitably breaks through our defenses, turning our world upside down and calling our most treasured beliefs into question. Saint John of the Cross called it "the dark night of the soul." We, like the psalmist, may find ourselves in circumstances of total despair and cry out to God, "How long, O LORD?" This hard conversation may initiate a fresh perspective. Both we and the psalmist may look at our troubles and believe God is not only absent but the cause of our difficulties. So we call to God to attend to us and answer us. Then in God's steadfast love, God will consider and answer. God will bring us light.

Today I shall have a hard conversation about my sense of God's absence in my life.

"God, if you don't come to my rescue, l am going to die" is a lament frequently heard in the Psalms. Freud said that the fear of death is the great motivator in life and is one commonality among us all. We seldom speak with our loved ones about death. We're a little superstitious—afraid that if we mention death, death will hear us. We think that if we don't talk about dying, death won't notice us or our loved ones. However, some people long to have just such a conversation with their loved ones. They and we want to feel sure that when death comes, someone knows our heart and will be our voice when we can no longer speak for ourselves. A movement called Dinner with Death opens with the topic of our first experience of death. We have to start our hard conversation about death by pulling back the curtain.

The only one who can save the psalmist is God. He asks for God's consideration and attention largely so God won't be embarrassed by the enemy's humiliation of the psalmist. God's sovereign power is at stake. If God does not revitalize, the psalmist will "sleep the sleep of death."

Death is certain, but is it the final word? And is it a conversation the psalmist wants to entertain? When Christians talk about death, I hope we hear the whispers of the One who has much to say: the Word of God that took on flesh, the light that the darkness will never overcome, the shepherd who promises provision, the resurrected one who tells us not to fear. Death has been swallowed up in victory, and we will hear the trumpet sound. And clearly by verse 5, God *has come* to save and the psalmist's heart rejoices in God's salvation. No doubt the psalmist heard God's whisper: "I'm right here." Have we?

Today I shall have a hard conversation about my expectations of the Holy One and God's action in my life. I will listen to God's promises.

Hard Conversations

FRIDAY, JUNE 30 ~ *Read Romans 6:12-14*

I recall a cartoon in which the lead character, Andy, walks by a fence with a NO TRESPASSING sign nailed to it; on the other side of the fence is an apple tree with the most tempting of apples. Suddenly on Andy's shoulder, the devil appears and begins whispering all the reasons Andy should have one of those apples. Then on Andy's other shoulder appears an angel whispering all the reasons that it would be wrong for him to have an apple—a fairly familiar plot. God doesn't always expect us to make the right choices, but we have the power to choose. God never tires of giving us the opportunity to choose life.

All the dos and don'ts in scripture used to annoy me because I heard in them the rigidity of the law rather than the gospel of grace. I heard *do* these things in order to gain God's love; but God's love is already certain.

Paul juxtaposes three elements in Romans 6:
- sin opposed to righteousness
- freedom opposed to slavery
- wages opposed to gifts

In today's verses we consider sin and righteousness. Unlike the cartoon character mentioned above, sin for Paul is not doing something bad or failing to do something good. It is not temptation; it is a way of life. Sin, like going over to the dark side, is a force, a power that entraps us. We are either enslaved to sin or engaged with God in righteousness. We choose sin without God or righteousness with God. Paul leaves no wiggle room. We hope and pray that what God has begun will be brought to completion.

Today I'll have a hard conversation with God about how I live.

My dad died when I was young. My family rarely attended church, so the most positive influence in my life was Boy Scouts. I learned to love the outdoors, and I developed skills in many areas: camping, cooking, first aid, canoeing, and orienteering. I became a leader, a camp counselor, and camp director before I became a chaplain. Scouting's ideals shaped me; the Scout Oath and Scout Law remain with me. While rules may confine, ideals can open us to something greater.

Most of us consider ourselves to be free individuals, making choices, selecting values. Paul tells us that we are "slaves of sin." But we have a choice. The second set of opposites calls us to choose freedom or slavery. We may be living as slaves to sin or as free persons living in the righteousness of God—either choice requires obedience. As Christians we find ourselves "obedient from the heart to the form of teaching to which [we] were entrusted." We have sat under the "teaching," which has shaped us—much like my experience with scouting. Paul raises the question as to what we gained from our slavery to sin. What did we find so compelling?

How has the gospel of Jesus Christ allowed you to overcome the pervasive power of sin? And so Paul moves to examine the third set of opposites: wages versus gifts. We may ask what is the payoff for obedience to God, for commitment to the gospel of Jesus Christ. And Paul tells us: "The wages of sin is death, but the free gift of God is eternal life in Christ Jesus our Lord." Notice the distinction between "wages" and "gift." God grants us the gift of eternal life—a gift so precious we could never earn it. We do not get merit badges for choosing obedience to God. We are invited to follow so that we may know freedom and realize the promise Paul speaks of: "The end is eternal life."

Today I will have a hard conversation with God about obedience and freedom.

In the verses prior to the ones in today's reading, Jesus reminds us that the gospel can break families apart; it can set men against their fathers, daughters against their mothers. But going into a mission field and taking the good news of God's love often creates a more enduring community than some people experience in their biological families—especially when the good news is welcomed. The relationship between the messenger and those who receive the message is key to all of us receiving the rewards of relationship with God. In Matthew 25 Jesus reminds us that when we welcome even the least of his brothers and sisters, we welcome him.

While serving my first pastorate, my wife and I divorced. She expected her family and home church to disown her; they did not. I expected the members of the small rural church I served to say they could not have a divorced pastor; they did not. Most of the church members supported and encouraged me. Many of them had weathered their own storms in life. They had experienced what it meant to be offered a cup of cold water. God's grace was truly active in both these instances.

I trained as a chaplain in a major Minnesota hospital, serving on the Women's Oncology unit. Daily I would visit women who were struggling to survive. A group of older women became my teachers. Many of them had life stories filled with suffering and loss. Inevitably at the close of the visit they would say, "Through it all pastor, God has been good." Circumstances do not determine God's goodness. In these moments of ministry, where I not only gave God's good news but received it as well, all of us received the reward of God's grace—the sure knowledge that sometimes even a cup of cold water can bring us into the presence of the Almighty.

Today I will have a hard conversation with God as to whom I welcome.

Trust in God's Leading

JULY 3–9, 2017 • MARYSOL DIAZ

SCRIPTURE OVERVIEW: The Genesis text tells of Abraham's quest to find a bride for Isaac from among his own people. In opting for Isaac, Rebekah makes herself the instrument for the preservation of the promise; God's intentions are sure. A hymn honoring the marriage commitment is a good pairing with Genesis, since the Song of Solomon addresses the sweetness of love. Romans 7 depicts a battle of human life. Here the strong desire to do good and serve God rightly is threatened by the enemy of sin. Jesus' prayer in Matthew recalls that knowledge of sin's defeat often comes to those "infants" to whom God has granted revelation.

QUESTIONS AND SUGGESTIONS FOR REFLECTION

- Read Genesis 24:34-38, 42-49, 58-67. How difficult is it for you to trust that God will act for your good, even if you find yourself waiting?
- Read Song of Solomon 2:8-13. Whose voice have you known as beloved? How did it waken you to creation's beauty?
- Read Romans 7:15-25a. How might you let God's understanding love make a change in your actions?
- Read Matthew 11:16-19, 25-30. Jesus offers rest for our souls. How do you tap into that wonderful offer?

Pastor, Evangelical Lutheran Church in America, Puerto Rico

I believe that we are born with a natural tendency to doubt. When I was five, my parents arranged a family day at the beach. My cousins and sisters found their way into the water quite comfortably. I didn't know how to swim, so I played with sand on the shore. I felt safe sitting in the sand, bathed in sunscreen, building my sand castle.

As I put the finishing touches on my masterpiece, an uncle interrupted my play with a question: "Do you know how to swim?" I looked up, trying to avoid the rays of the sun, and replied, "No." He picked me up in his strong arms and, in spite of my resistance, assured me that he would not let me drown. I didn't have much of a choice. He held my right hand with his left and wrapped his right arm around my body securely. My fear of the deep and my fear of drowning soon dissipated as he held me close and allowed me to hang on.

Abraham is up in years; he wants to secure a wife and family for his son Isaac. He sends his trusted servant to seek a wife for Isaac. In the verses that immediately precede today's passage, Abraham's servant has met a lovely young woman at the well, a woman who offers him the hospitality of a drink of water and a place to stay for him and his animals. He "gazed at her in silence to learn whether or not the Lord had made his journey successful." Perceiving the enormity of the task before him, the servant will not eat until he tells of his errand. Trusting that God will guide him in order to accomplish what his master has asked of him, he commits his way to the Lord, trusts him, and knows he will act. (See Psalm 37:5.) May we be so obedient and discerning.

Dear Lord, give us the determination and the disposition we need to commit our ways to you, trusting and knowing that you will act. In Jesus' name we pray. Amen.

Not being in control of events and not being able to predict the future, I have learned to live in trust, which offers the gift of waiting. While many consider not knowing a weakness, those who live in trust discover a richness in not knowing. Our not knowing can lead to an openness, a time of waiting to embrace what God holds in store for God's beloved.

Abraham's servant has been praying. He has opened his heart, and God has directed his steps. Now in Rebekah's home, he rehearses his experience by the well. With God's leading he has decided that Rebekah is the wife he has come seeking for Isaac. After engaging Rebekah, he bows his head in joyful thanksgiving and praise and worships the Lord. God has listened and answered his plea. He has walked the road trusting, praying, and praising God.

Then in verse 49, he repeats words often spoken in transactions: "Now then, if you will deal loyally and truly with my master, tell me; and if not, tell me, so that I may turn either to the right hand or to the left." The servant is left to wait for the reply. Will this relationship come to fruition?

We cannot escape waiting. Such is life. We are always waiting. What can we learn from this truth that all would prefer not to have to endure? On the one hand, it encourages us to pay attention. It reminds us that we need to "Be still, and know that I am God" (Ps. 46:10). In so doing, we learn to see through the eyes of discernment. Above all, waiting can teach us that God's love will lead us. A mutual relationship with God will lead us to green pastures and wells of abundant grace that anoint us with God's unending provision and love.

Heavenly Father, thank you for the gift of trust. Guide us through the unknown as we stand before you, knowing that you are our refuge and our strength. In Jesus' name we pray. Amen.

Where do you go when you find yourself in the midst of a painful event in your life? Who will embrace you with compassion? Naturally we desire to be with loving friends and family when we experience troubling times.

Abraham acknowledges his son Isaac's mourning the death of his mother. Recognizing that he already suffers from old age, Abraham feels driven to make every effort to provide his son with someone who will bring love and understanding into his life. Compassion moves the heart of a loving father. Sharing troubling times exemplifies compassion at work.

Rebekah chooses to return with the servant to Isaac. Those of her household bless her before she sets out: "May you, our sister, become thousands of myriads; may your offspring gain possession of the gates of their foes." And so we hear an echo of God's promise to Abraham of descendants as many as the grains of sand. The promise endangered by Isaac's being a bachelor moves toward a bright future. Isaac takes Rebekah; she becomes his wife, and he loves her.

That is how it is with God. God's love comes to us bearing an invitation, offering a future of promise. We, like Rebekah, step into relationship. We cannot escape God's love. Psalm 139 describes eloquently how even if we "settle at the farthest limits of the sea . . . your hand shall lead me, and your right hand shall hold me fast." Hope and compassion flow from the heart of our God and remind us that we are not alone.

Gracious God, I accept your invitation to relationship that steadies me in troubling times. Amen.

My colleagues and I get together once a week for coffee at a local bistro. We share stories and pastoral concerns. After many years of ministry together, we were surprised to hear that the oldest member of our group had been adopted when she was only six months old. I asked her if she had ever thought about who her real parents were. Her answer has resounded many times in my mind: "That day my parents had the opportunity to pick out any one of the babies that they had before them. They chose me. They are my real parents."

Song of Solomon is a collection of love poems. Today's reading describes a mysterious passion that draws two people together. It reminds me of my baptism and suggests the mystery of God's great love for creation and our response. God's love and Christ's passion bind us together in one spirit. At baptism, God chose to seal me with the cross of salvation. God adopted me as a beloved child for everlasting life and gave me the faith that declares that Christ is my bridegroom and the Eucharist is our marriage feast. God speaks to me from the cross, from the garden—an insistent lover. I serve God with joy and thanksgiving.

I came across a faded black-and-white picture recently of my cheerleading days in high school. Those days came back in a flash. Everything seemed so simple then. We easily forget the obstacles, concerns, needs, and spur-of-the-moment situations that blur our ability to remember. One fact to remember: God chose you. Jesus sealed you with the cross on Calvary. When all has faded, and life has lost its color, our loving and faithful God will continue to lead the way with passion and love beyond our understanding.

Loving Lord, united in one spirit we ask you to shed your everlasting love upon your people as we strive to serve you with joy and thanksgiving. Amen.

Scarcely a day goes by without a struggle between what I want to do and what I finally end up doing. I face an ongoing battle with my sinful nature. God's awareness of my struggle makes it all the worse. *God knows.*

God knows who we are, and we allow people to know who we are as well. Yet, don't we fear showing our dark side? We tend to hide our weaknesses and sinful selves from others. And while the voice of our sin is strong, the voice of God's forgiveness is stronger.

Paul does not address evildoers; he speaks to good, conscientious Christians who, despite their best intentions, fall prey to sin. As we often say, "The spirit is willing, but the flesh is weak." We face the divide between willing and doing, and that is part of our human condition. God does not encourage dwelling on sin; God invites us to experience a new heart and a new spirit. "Cast away from you all the transgressions that you have committed against me, and get yourselves a new heart and a new spirit! . . . I have no pleasure in the death of anyone. . . . Turn, then, and live" (Ezek. 18:31-32).

Nothing we do can overcome sin's power; that task falls to God who has accomplished it through Jesus Christ. We cannot escape our sinful nature, but God can take all our mixed motives, good or evil intentions and turn them to divine service.

Henry Nouwen taught that "we can carry in our heart all human pain and sorrow, all conflicts and agonies . . . because God's heart has become one with ours." And as Paul reminds us so eloquently in Romans 8:39, nothing in creation "will be able to separate us from the love of God in Christ Jesus our Lord."

Heavenly Father, lead us to seek you in our daily lives that we may come face-to-face with your love and understanding. We long for our hearts to become one with yours. In Jesus' name. Amen.

A highlight of my recent pilgrimage to Israel came in observing an aged rabbi walking toward the Western Wall. He did not walk alone. Five young men followed close behind. They followed in his footsteps, bodies inclined and taking each step with some difficulty, the same way as their teacher. They imitated him because they were his followers.

In the Jewish tradition, being a follower of the local Jewish rabbi brought honor and distinction. The followers sit at the rabbi's feet to learn. They study his vocabulary and his response to the facts of life. Their principal virtue comes in serving him, even in the most insignificant of tasks. They remain determined to be like him.

In the Christian tradition, Jesus comes to us speaking two simple words: "Follow me!" Jesus invites us to follow: to share his passion serving those seeking the way to salvation. In these verses, Jesus expresses his thoughts about "this generation." "This generation" has been exposed to the ministries of John the Baptizer and Jesus: John, the sober, austere man who calls for repentance, and Jesus who comes proclaiming the nearness of the kingdom and who sits at table with many different kinds of people. "This generation" labels one as crazy and the other as a drunkard and glutton. People had heard the good news proclaimed by both men and have chosen to follow neither. They do not dance or mourn.

Jesus knows the father. He has intimate knowledge of our Creator. True wisdom has been hidden from the wise and intelligent. We are those who follow. We sit at the feet of the cross and listen. We follow in the steps of Jesus' public ministry and go in peace to serve our Lord. It is the Jesus way.

Most gracious Lord, may we share your promises with those in need and follow you with joy and thanksgiving. Amen.

Trusting in God's Leading   229

Throughout his public ministry, Jesus addresses people who are overworked or carrying heavy loads due to political and religious oppression. He offers them an alternate way: "Come to me, all you that are weary and are carrying heavy burdens, and I will give you rest." His ministry stands in stark contrast to earthly rulers whose yokes weigh down and oppress. Jesus offers a yoke that in the Greek suggests suitability. The yoke of Jesus is to learn from him. To learn his way. To follow it. This schooling comes from the hand of a "gentle" teacher.

And Jesus makes it clear that a high IQ or lofty position does not give us an inroad to God's wisdom. Instead, God has "revealed [divine wisdom] to infants." To infants? Why to infants? They receive what is given, and they come with no preconceived ideas about God. How can we open ourselves to receive what God offers in this way? What do we need to release about our understandings of God's work in the world—and how God works in the world?

Jesus and God "know" each other in an intimate way. We come to knowledge of each only through divine revelation. Jesus' calling anoints us with hope and joy. When we follow, we find rest for our souls. His way puts us on the road to recovery. He will set us on the path of true life where active benevolence becomes our desire as we freely serve. Living in the light of freedom and dignity for every person, especially the deprived, will not be a burden. It will in fact point the way to true refreshment.

We commit our way to the Lord, trust him, and know that he will act. We go forth sent by our gracious Father.

Jesus, I yearn for your "easy" yoke. I want to learn your way and find rest. Amen.

The Promise and Work of God's Word

JULY 10–16, 2017 • JOHN ADCOX

SCRIPTURE OVERVIEW: Genesis 25 marks the beginning of the narrative of Jacob's life. The theme that stands out in starkest relief is the election of Jacob to be the heir to the promise—Jacob, who has no claim to be the heir except that which the grace of God bestows. Psalm 25 reflects a general sense of alienation. Yet the psalmist expresses confidence in following God's paths and truths. Paul sets out two polarities in Romans 8: those who "live according to the flesh and those who "live according to the Spirit," a cosmic duality related to the rule of sin and the rule of God. The parable of the sower and the seeds in Matthew 13 is an object lesson in the mysterious grace of God.

QUESTIONS AND SUGGESTIONS FOR REFLECTION

- Read Genesis 25:19-34. When in your life have you experienced favoritism from a parent, friend, coworker, or boss that created division?
- Read Psalm 119:105-112. The psalmist promises to follow God's law every day in every aspect of his life—despite his circumstances. When did you last renew and affirm your commitment to God through daily obedience?
- Read Romans 8:1-11. How have you attempted to fill the "God-shaped" hole in your life?
- Read Matthew 13:1-9, 18-23. What kind of soil are you? How bountiful a harvest do you produce for God?

Chief Executive Officer, Gramarye Media

The story of Jacob and Esau is a story of violence that begins before birth. It's a story of trickery, of deceit. There's even an element of parental strife, as father, Isaac, and mother, Rebekah, play favorites. On the surface, this isn't the cheeriest of stories.

But then, I don't believe we're meant to read scripture on the surface. There's something more here. This is a story about answered prayers—of direct and personal relationships with God. Isaac prays for a son; Rebekah prays for understanding. Both receive an answer. But there's still more.

It's a story of supplanting—Jacob is born holding his brother's heel, and his name means "holder of the heel" or "supplanter." Of course, Jacob later takes a different name: Israel. Names are important in the Bible. Jacob has a destiny.

On the surface, it's hard to sympathize with Jacob, the trickster who steals his brother's inheritance and, later, the blessing. I imagine, though, that the Israelites held a different view. Israel, after all, was a tiny nation surrounded by empires—Egypt, Assyria, Babylon, and then the Persians, Greeks, and Romans.

An all but inevitable awareness of their situation must have made the Israelites appreciate stories about underdogs, about reversal of the so-called natural order between strong and weak. We see that reversal again and again in Genesis. Don't we like to cheer for the underdogs too? For the weak who, with God's help, somehow triumph? Especially when *we're* the underdog?

In this story, God reminds us that we too can overcome the so-called natural order and triumph. We're not predestined to suffer oppression or defeat. God roots for us; we are born for something greater—something of spirit, not just of the world.

O God, may we remember that you know all outcomes and that you will guide us when we pray . . . and listen—especially when we read and reread the scripture that troubles us. Amen.

Today's verses talk about commitment—fierce, unshakable, and, yes, even loving commitment in the face of the harshest adversity. The psalmist fiercely declares his strong commitment. More, the psalmist speaks out of pure and utter joy in his promise. Near the end of today's passage, he sings,

> Your decrees are my heritage forever;
> they are the joy of my heart.
> I incline my heart to perform your statutes forever.

The psalmist makes a profound commitment: to obey God's commandments forever. He promises to follow God's law *every* day in *every* aspect of his life. How many of us have the courage to make a commitment like that? Can we promise to obey God every single day?

The psalmist's life isn't all that easy. He states, "I am severely afflicted," and "the wicked have laid a snare for me." But the psalmist sticks with his commitment. That's pretty amazing, especially when we have trouble making that kind of commitment in the face of minor annoyance—when work's been especially stressful, when bills are due, and when someone has the gall to cut us off in traffic.

But here's the significant part. The psalmist tells us why he makes that kind of commitment, even in the face of danger and suffering. The surprise? It has nothing to do with reward, fear, duty, or obligation. The psalmist promises to obey God completely and in every way—because he finds joy in it. God is the source of all joy, all comfort—even in the face of suffering and despair. Read these words again: "Your decrees are my heritage forever; they are the joy of my heart."

Dear Lord God, help us to remember that you make your laws because you love us. When we follow them, we find joy, comfort, and peace. Amen.

The Promise and Work of God's Word   233

The majesty of creation is central. The heart of the image in this section is life, specifically, life springing joyfully from water—rain and snow from above. This very rain and snow cause the earth to bloom with life, "giving seed to the sower and bread to the eater." If you've ever taken a biology class in school, you know the importance of rain and snow to life.

Here, though, the water means more: "So shall my word be that goes out from my mouth," God says. This is not a simple metaphoric glimpse into the water cycle. This is about God's word that gives life, creates and succeeds in God's purpose. It is water for the soul, water of life—a thing of the world becoming something of spirit. That theme runs throughout this week's scripture readings. God's word does not return empty.

The word of God accomplishes God's purpose—repentance, renewal, and salvation, just as waters wash clean and bring forth life. This is God's work done by way of God's word proclaimed, "You shall go out in joy, and be led back in peace; the mountains and the hills before you shall burst into song, and all the trees of the field shall clap their hands." All creation celebrates the promise and work of God's word. The God of renewal and pardon invites repentance. We are called to turn toward the living God, for the water of God's holy word nourishes our joy.

God of creation, send your water to wake new life in us. May we follow your word and be ever mindful of your path. Bring us back to your living water. Amen.

This passage begins with some pretty good news, doesn't it? Verses 1 and 2 promise that there is no condemnation for those who are in Christ Jesus. The law of the Spirit of life in Christ Jesus has freed us from the law of sin and death. God calls us to the law of the Spirit out of love and forgiveness and offers us rebirth and renewal.

After the introductory verses, the text gets a little harder. It mentions *flesh* or *the body* several times. "God condemned sin in the body by sending his own Son to deal with sin in the same body as humans, who are controlled by sin" (CEB), even going so far as to equate the body with selfishness. "[God] did this so that the righteous requirement of the Law might be fulfilled in us. Now the way we live is based on the Spirit, not based on selfishness" (CEB).

That seems rather harsh, doesn't it? Some context will help. For Paul the realm of the flesh refers to the arena of sin; the realm of the Spirit reflects that which is ruled by God. The body itself is neither good nor bad. It all depends on the body's function. When we use the body as God intends, the body is good. When the body opposes God's intention selfishly, it becomes sinful. "People who are self-centered aren't able to please God" (CEB)

I think the key point comes in verse 9: "But you aren't self-centered. Instead you are in the Spirit, if in fact God's Spirit lives in you" (CEB) and in verse 11, "If the Spirit of the one who raised Jesus from the dead lives in you, the one who raised Christ from the dead will give life to your human bodies also, through his Spirit that lives in you" (CEB).

When Paul talks about flesh and spirit, he is talking about two ways of living: the life before Jesus enters and after.

Lord, remind us that when you are with us, our flesh and our spirit is strong. Amen.

The author Rob Bell reminds us that Bible stories aren't just about characters from history. Bible stories are *our* stories. In some way, God is talking to you, to me, to all of us through the accounts in the Bible.

Jesus now seems to rely on parables as his chief means of getting his point across. A definition from Sunday school says that a parable is an earthly story with a heavenly meaning. When Jesus talks about the kingdom of heaven, he's talking about a change in the world that lies before us, a radical change—at least to those people sitting by the lake. Something physical, made of dust, will become something . . . more.

How do you explain the ineffable to the people gathered by the lake and to all of us through the many generations that follow? You use story. That's why stories are sacred. Reducing them to mere history trivializes them. These stories live, even today, right here and now, and they help us recognize glimpses of the kingdom when they come shining through.

Until now, the people haven't understood Jesus' mission as the Messiah, and so he brings them along carefully, slowly. It's a profound message. I've heard commentators suggest that Jesus used parables not to illuminate but to conceal the truth from unbelievers. After all, they argue, why would people suddenly understand Jesus when he spoke in parables if they didn't understand when he spoke plainly?

I think Jesus meant to be heard, then and now. We're to keep reading them, exploring them, and praying about them. Again, there's more here than we see on the surface. The surface is dust. Beyond is spirit. The stories he told are about us. Even more, they're love stories: the stories of the powerful and eternal love between Creator and created.

 God of love, may we hear your story of everlasting love today and always. Lead us to deeper understanding. Amen.

Jesus explains the parable's meaning. Notice that in these verses Jesus talks to the disciples privately. Jesus is God incarnate, omnipotent, and eternal. It must surely have occurred to him that these twelve men would tell others, who in turn would tell others again, and so on until someone thought to write his words down. Jesus talks to the twelve, and he addresses us too.

So if these are our stories, who are we in this particular story? Are we the soil that sits there, waiting to see what happens? Are we the seeds that simply fall to the ground? Are we the sower?

Notice that the farmer isn't talking to the ground; he's scattering seeds. And he scatters indiscriminately. He's defined by his own action not by the action of the soil (that which experiences his witness). His witness comes in the form of action, of service. Are we the farmer? Yes, indeed. We scatter gospel seeds wherever we go.

Are we the soil? You bet. The seed falls on us, all of us, all the time. It's falling on us right now. Our receptivity is key. And we make choices. If we don't understand, we're the path. If we don't have roots, we don't last. Thorny? As verse 22 reminds us, "The cares of the world and the lure of wealth choke the word, and it yields nothing." You get the idea.

We are soil with hearts and brains. Thinking, feeling human beings raised from that same soil, from dust, to become filled with spirit. We can think, we can consider, we can question, we can pray. And through his parables, Jesus calls us to be good soil, to bear fruit and produce. For those of us who hear and understand, the harvest will be bounteous—"in one case a hundredfold, in another sixty, and in another thirty."

God of love and wisdom, may we provide fertile soil for the seeds of the gospel. Amen.

Over the past week, we have talked about how God calls us to obey, to trust, to pray . . . and yes, even to struggle to understand, even in times of trial. Remember the words from Romans 8:10-11 (CEB):

> If Christ is in you, the Spirit is your life because of God's righteousness, but the body is dead because of sin. If the Spirit of the one who raised Jesus from the dead lives in you, the one who raised Christ from the dead will give life to your human bodies also, through his Spirit that lives in you.

So I'd like to pose a final question. Why Christian? Blaise Pascal, a seventeenth-century Christian philosopher, contemplated the happiness of humanity. He contended that we contain an "infinite abyss [that] can be filled only with an infinite and immutable object; in other words by God." Pascal speaks of the God-shaped hole in our lives.

What is the driving force behind what you do? Is it the Christian call to service and Christ's reign, here and now? The call to service isn't about rejecting the world; it's about transforming it, sanctifying it. It's a call to bring forth glimpses of the kingdom here on earth.

Ultimately, the choice that Christ calls us to is a joy subtler but more profound. The kingdom of God is far greater than what the world gives. It is of the spirit. We are Christians called to serve, not because we fear hellfire and brimstone but because we feel a joy that is greater than any we have ever known.

Why Christian? Not because it's easy or comfortable. Certainly not that. But because it fills the God-shaped hole— because it speaks words of life.

God of all, give us strength to follow you. We ask you to fill the holes in our lives and speak to us your words of life. Amen and amen.

Unexpected Grace

JULY 17–23, 2017 • ELMER LAVASTIDA ALFONSO

SCRIPTURE OVERVIEW: This week's texts depict a broad span of settings of God's activity, from Jacob's encounter in solitude to the broader context of creation itself in Romans. The texts also tell of God's commission of human agents, weak and inadequate, to carry out divine tasks. Jacob may not be totally aware of God's plans for him, but the reader knows. Paul declares that the people in whom the Spirit of God dwells are very much in tune with the pain of creation. They also long for God's final deliverance. Just at the point of the reluctance of God's agents to carry out the tasks, the parable from Matthew about the wheat and weeds gives hope. God will take care of the weeds in God's own time. Psalm 139 is a moving statement on the ubiquitous nature of God's presence.

QUESTIONS AND SUGGESTIONS FOR REFLECTION

- Read Genesis 28:10-19a. When have you "wakened" to acknowledge that you were in a holy place? What did you do to memorialize the place?
- Read Psalm 139:1-12, 23-24. Do you regularly take time in a set-aside place for an intimate relationship with God? If not, what steps could you take to ensure that relationship? *GOOD QUESTION*
- Read Romans 8:12-25. Do you feel close enough to God to call God "Abba"? Why or why not?
- Read Matthew 13:24-30, 36-43. What are you doing to discourage the growth of evil in your life? How does your garden grow? *GOOD QUESTION*

Retired Baptist pastor, founder of an interdenominational center, teacher of New Testament at Eastern Cuba Baptist Theological Seminary

According to modern-day atlas measurements, Jacob has traveled fifty miles from Beersheba to Bethel the first day. His fear of his brother's revenge probably spurs him on as he makes that lengthy trek. He wants to put as much distance as possible between him and Esau's brutal wrath. We can also make the best of poetic language when it says "because the sun had set." The growing darkness of twilight can invoke romance, or in Jacob's case, apprehension. But the tired young man grabs the minimum element for a night's rest—a rock as a pillow.

Jacob could not possibly surmise the outcome of that night. He only knows that he is heading toward Haran to find a wife among his mother's relatives and be secure there for a while. But grace surprises him. More than a dream—it is a vision, a confirmation of his personal participation in the patriarchal project. His father's blessing before parting has now received approval from Yahweh with the added promise of divine protection at all times until the full plan becomes reality.

We are not always running away from infuriated brothers or traveling far from home to find a spouse, but we have experienced foreboding sunsets of life. We have lain down to sleep out of sheer exhaustion still carrying heavy loads of anguish and uncertainty, even of fear. But our God surprises us with divine grace when we least expect it and takes our situation far beyond immediate solutions. God doesn't just mend things; God makes things new!

Before the close of this day, take some time to review your pilgrimage of life and note how many times the God of Abraham, Isaac, and Jacob has actually brought you a Bethel experience just when you thought there was only a night to endure.

God Eternal, help us to trust your guidance even when we cannot see beyond the next hour of existence. Thank you for your unexpected grace that grasps us along the way. Amen.

This division of the Genesis text allows us to distinguish two moments of the event—one where God takes the initiative and a second one where Jacob is the protagonist. It seems that verses 16 and 17 occur just as Jacob wakes from sleep, but dawn has not arrived. He gains another view of the place where he has settled for the night: God is here!

Then three expressions follow: "I did not know it," "he was afraid," and "how awesome is this place." They offer an interesting sequence from ignorance through fear to admiration—or perhaps we would say *adoration*.

Many years ago while in a forced labor camp, I sat in the dark on Christmas Eve and felt haunted by loneliness and fear. Many sad and bitter thoughts rushed through my mind because "I did not know" that God was with me there. I felt so scared that when I heard the guard screaming my name to present myself at the entrance gate, I decided not to answer. But the second call and third shout shook me to my feet, and I ran to the gate. There stood an unknown cousin of my mother and her husband, two elderly persons with a hug and a kiss and a small gift in their hand—soda crackers and guava jam! At that hour of the night I gathered with several brothers in the faith, and we feasted in great thanksgiving. How awesome!

Jacob then converts the very stone that served as his pillow into an altar and acknowledges that lonely place as "the house of God." Did you recall your own Bethel experiences yesterday? Turn each one into a service of thanksgiving and praise! Build your own altar!

O God, thank you for accompanying me each hour of the day and night. May I be sensitive to your presence so that I can truly discover you and worship you in my own Bethel experiences. I shall pour oil on those altars. Amen.

Unexpected Grace   241

This meditation fits Jacob's experience surprisingly well. He could have written and sung this poem as he poured oil over the improvised altar at Bethel. And yet it belongs to another millennium! Which implies that as centuries pass, God remains the same as does the manner in which humans relate to God.

In his youthful years David, the attributed psalmist, also knew the experience of displacement and uncertainty. Before he wore the crown, he was an outlaw in his own nation. Surely as he matured he became aware of God's intimate knowledge of his life: "You search out my path and my lying down, and are acquainted with all my ways."

This prayer asks for nothing; the psalmist simply considers the intimacy of relationship with God—an intimacy that leads to amazing knowledge of the psalmist. The psalm manifests astounding theological discernment beginning with verse 7. We find it difficult to understand such an unqualified presence. The psalmist acknowledges that God hems him in "behind and before." He can go nowhere that God is not—God surrounds him. Even the darkness is not dark to God. He with Jacob can affirm, "Surely the Lord is in this place!"

Even though we will never fully understand God, we are invited to acquaint ourselves with the divine. Friendship requires intentional cultivation. In our desire to hide on the periphery, wander in the fringes, escape to the sea, we miss the depth of the experience with the Eternal, a God who never gives up the pursuit of relationship. Such intimate relationship takes time and space.

"Nearer, my God, to thee, nearer to thee!" I want to enjoy your great and tender love; may I feel your presence. Amen.

Eighty-six years ago today my parents married in the city of Havana. Every time I look at their wedding picture, I think of the psalmist's words in verse 16: "Your eyes beheld my unformed substance." One day while in my teens, my mother confessed that I had not been a planned child. Really? Then she went on to say that I was actually unexpected grace.

The technological revolution of our times gives us the idea that we have absolute control of life. And yet as we face the contingency of each day we must frequently recall our creatureliness in the face of a Presence that transcends time and space.

The last two verses offer a timely climax with the two petitions: "search me" and "lead me." It is a dialectic process in which we know and, at the same time, we are known. Paul writes to the Galatian Christians, "Now . . . you have come to know God, or rather to be known by God" (4:9).

Instead of fearing transparency, total openness guarantees meaningful guidance. This transparency encourages the psalmist to submit gladly to God's examination: "Search me, O God, and know my heart; test me and know my thoughts."

Each of us comes into the world as an "unexpected" grace from God. This psalm focuses on strong relation. This God pursues, offering health and well-being, having knit us together in the womb. Indeed we are fearfully wonderful! Such knowing is beyond us. Yet, as we "come to the end—[we are] still with [God]." Thanks be to God.

Dear Father, may I find the way everlasting through total openness to you. Amen.

This week we have been blessed by the depth of ancient Hebrew poetry in Psalm 139, and today we stand amazed at the apostle Paul's declaration that we become adopted sons and daughters of God. Paul, a Pharisee and former student of Gamaliel, no longer claims exclusive filial relation to God as a Jew; instead he feels admitted to the universal family in Christ through the work of the Holy Spirit. No legacy, no talent, no personal effort, simply the witness of the Spirit to our spirit while we are "led by the Spirit of God." We gain an intimacy that Jesus himself expressed when he called God "Abba"—an unexpected grace! We, as children of God, are joint heirs with Christ—heirs both of his suffering and his glory.

In verses 18 to 25 Paul reflects on the mystery of suffering viewed from one perspective: that of creation. Excessive individualism in theology has separated salvation from creation. And yet they belong together: "Creation itself will be set free from its bondage to decay and will obtain the freedom of the glory of the children of God." We suffer and groan together with creation, but as children of God we enjoy in advance the hope of transformation because of "the first fruits of the Spirit."

Romans presents a treatise on the meaning of salvation: why we need it, how to experiment with it, and the expected results. We try to imagine the impact of this letter on the first-century congregation in Rome. Many of them, like Paul, were converted Jews who needed this explanation of unexpected grace in Christ. Today, for other cultural reasons, we also need to renew the experience of being "led by the Spirit of God."

Abba Father, revive in me the precious hope of my salvation. Amen.

SATURDAY, JULY 22 ～ *Read Matthew 13:24-30*

Chapter 13 begins a sequence of three sets of parables. Eugene Boring says that "in the preaching of Jesus, parables were not vivid decorations of a moralistic point but were disturbing stories that threatened the hearer's secure . . . world of assumptions by which we habitually live" (Matthew, *New Interpreter's Bible*, 299). Even this simple agricultural scene lends itself to varied interpretations.

Is Jesus reflecting on the presence of evil in the universe? Or is Jesus speaking against building boundaries of exclusion? This scripture challenges us to discover its meaning for our times. The way good mixes with evil in our communities and worldwide continues to baffle us. Surely our Lord would not ask his followers to remain passive in the face of evil! In a subtle way he advises that an opportune time for action, for decision, exists. The weeds will eventually be eliminated but not in the fashion that the servants propose. Their approach could have caused damage instead of healing.

As we consider evil in our midst, we may find ourselves questioning God's nature and approach: "Master, did you not sow good seed in your field?" The servants move from observation to a plan for action: "Do you want us to go and gather them?" And the reply comes, "No."

God sheds eternal wisdom on human pathways. With no fixed recipe, God invites us into a risky adventure where we discover what is valuable and what is not. We trust the guidance of the Spirit of God as we mark each day's pilgrimage.

Lord of the harvest, I constantly need your direction and inspiration to take my daily steps. I ask for your guidance today. Amen.

Unexpected Grace   245

In the opening verses of chapter 13, the disciples question Jesus' use of parables in preaching, to which he answers that they are stories in code. He does not preach to entertain or amuse; he preaches to reveal truth to those who have an interest.

Clearly these verses that interpret the parable bring to mind the final judgment: "the furnace of fire" or shining "like the sun." They may promote anxiety as we consider whether we're weeds or good seed. The harvest does come.

When I read the original parable in verses 24-30, I do not perceive the punitive tone as I read in today's interpretive reading of the parable. Instead the weeds are simply gathered and burned, and the wheat taken to the barn. Jesus did not conceal the destiny of evil, but he did not capitalize on fear as a path toward God. I remember my mother confessing that her conversion resulted from her fear of death and hell. Only later did she come to appreciate salvation as an experience of love. We try to avoid turning the good news of the gospel into foreboding alarm. Jesus' conversations with the hurting people of his time avoided condemnation and emphasized unexpected grace.

The parables of the mustard seed and the yeast separate the initial parable and its explanation. On the other side of the explanation we read of treasure hidden in a field and the pearl of great price. The emphasis lies with discovering what is of value and then giving all in order to make it our own.

I have had experiences in my ministry as a prison chaplain with men considered dangerous by the officers and yet sensitive to the announcement of God's grace for them. Even more, they bear the fruit of that grace in the midst of so much hurt and limitation. "Let anyone with ears listen!"

Divine Shepherd, come and prepare a table of your grace even though I am surrounded by evil. Amen.

Treasures from God

JULY 24–30, 2017 • CHRIS FOLMSBEE

SCRIPTURE OVERVIEW: In the Genesis text, Jacob the trickster is tricked. Yet through a combination of patience and perseverance he ultimately wins Rachel, which sets the stage for all that follows in the story of Abraham's family. Psalm 105 addresses a forgetful community that has lost touch with the God of the Exodus. Remembering becomes a powerful experience when it focuses on both God's actions and God's judgments. Romans 8 also serves as a reminder of God's way, of God's movements from knowledge to action, from saving grace to promised glory. The scribe of Matthew's short parable brings out of the storehouse both what is new and what is old. There is no true future without a remembrance of the past.

QUESTIONS AND SUGGESTIONS FOR REFLECTION

- Read Genesis 29:15-28. When have you experienced a setback due to poor treatment at the hands of someone you trusted? What did you learn?
- Read Psalm 105:1-11, 45b. How do you "seek God's face"? How do you offer thanks to God?
- Read Romans 8:26-39. Consider Paul's three questions and formulate a one- or two-sentence answer of your own.
- Read Matthew 13:31-33, 44-52. How do the parables about what the kingdom of God is like surprise you? How do they shock you?

Adult Discipleship Director, Church of the Resurrection, Leawood, Kansas

Jacob, a master deceiver, meets his match in Uncle Laban who one-ups Jacob and turns the tables. He leaves Jacob no choice but to concede to his demands and work another seven years for the woman he loves. Jacob, filled with an irritation that probably turns to rage, finally must feel what his father, Isaac, and brother Esau unquestionably felt when he deceived them both. Jacob's own deceit of stealing the birthright and the inheritance forced him to flee. His deceit has served as the impetus for this frustrating journey.

We use phrases like "what comes around goes around," "reap what you sow," and "come full circle" to describe what happens when a person's actions result in consequences for the person. Unmistakably this is one of those moments for Jacob. Some would say Jacob gets what he deserves. One thing is certain. Jacob's past decisions have finally caught up to him.

It is hard to imagine or feel the suffering dispensed by another until the giver of the suffering experiences it personally. Jacob, probably for the first time in his life, experiences a deep sense of wrongdoing and possibly even remorse for his collective transgressions.

Like Jacob, we have deceived others in one way or another. We've also probably experienced the consequences of our trickery. Perhaps the memories and the feelings unsettle us as we reflect on our actions. For this very reason we should not be too quick to judge Jacob and Laban for their individual trickery. And for this reason as well, we should quickly forgive when the tables turn and we find that we are the ones offended.

God, may I strive to be a righteous person. May I also be gentle and gracious to all those who are reaping what they have sown. Amen.

Paul eagerly desires that Christians in the church in Rome understand the role of the Spirit in overcoming weakness. Paul, no stranger to weakness himself, declares that the Spirit works as an advocate for us, praying what we do not know to pray ourselves. Paul helps us realize that often we cannot see within our own hearts to discover what limits us or keeps us from being the follower Jesus calls us to be. Therefore, the Spirit prays for us as God searches our heart, and we discover the shortcomings in our lives that keep us from being the person God created us to be.

We are called to live fully human. It has been said that when we get to heaven and meet God, God isn't going to ask us, "How come you weren't more like so and so." Instead, God will ask, "How come you weren't the person I created you to be?" When our weaknesses are uncovered and we experience transformation or conformity toward the likeness of Jesus, we live into our true image—people created to bear the image of God, which is a holy love.

People who have accepted the invitation to proclaim the gospel by living into the image in which God created us through holy love are justified. The saving work of Jesus covers us. As a result of this gospel living, we exemplify human weakness made spiritually strong.

Our own right doing does not make us strong. We become strong through the grace of God who creates good from our bad (weaknesses), the saving work of Jesus who covers us, and the ongoing advocacy of the Spirit who guides us toward a life of transformation and conformity.

God, through the power and presence of the Holy Spirit help us see our weaknesses. Strengthen us and use us as examples of what it means to live the way you intended. Amen.

WEDNESDAY, JULY 26 ～ *Read Psalm 105:1-11, 45b*

The word *thanks* may be one of the most widely used words in the English language—or any language for that matter. To say thanks is to acknowledge gratitude for the generosity of another. In this psalm, however, we may better translate the word *thanks* as "praise." When we offer praise we go beyond merely saying thanks. We express more than gratitude; we express worship. Worship involves bowing down before God, demonstrating that we acknowledge God as ruler of the universe. God is God and we are not.

The psalmist wants us to sing songs of praise and worship that honor the Lord, that communicate extreme appreciation for God's active involvement in redeeming humans, that reveal to the outside world God's love for all humanity. God is an everlasting presence whose love compels human beings to love God in return and love others as a result of God's love for us.

God's great activity of redemption displayed through God's mighty works of miracles, wonders, judgments draw God's worshipers to "seek his face," to live in continuous pursuit of God's presence, to remember all that God has done for humankind—and for us personally. We worship God most fully when we obey God's laws. God has faithfully kept the everlasting covenant with us. What results from that covenant? Land, portion, inheritance. The psalmist recalls Israel's salvation history of miraculous action, faith in God's promises, a future of hope, and lives of well-being. "Praise the LORD."

Help me, God, to move past a flippant "thanks" to you and replace it with songs of praise that emerge from my faithful obedience. Amen.

Small beginnings mark the growth of God's reign. A tiny, seemingly insignificant mustard seed can yield a flourishing tree—a tree large enough for birds to live in, produce buds from which to multiply other trees, and provide an awning for rest. This parable reveals the workings of the kingdom of God. Thousands of tiny acts of love lead to a new kind of people who multiply into an even greater number of acts of love—all the while pointing to God.

Just like a mustard seed, the yeast seems insignificant. However, just as the mustard tree begins with a tiny seed to produce a great harvest, the yeast is "worked all through the dough" (NIV). The kingdom of God brings a "leavening" to every aspect of life.

Imagine what the Jews in Jesus' day, who were expecting a king who would lead a political and military revolt, must have thought when Jesus presented the image of the kingdom of God as a tiny mustard seed and yeast. They must have found it difficult to comprehend how Jesus could be a king at all, let alone the Messiah.

Jesus' teaching in these two parables, however, articulates that the reign of God works peacefully and from small and humble beginnings. Jesus will not lead a violent revolt to conquer the Romans. Instead, Jesus leads a quiet and humble movement characterized by peace, hope, and love.

Each of our specific acts of love, regardless of their seeming smallness, reveals that the kingdom of God exists and flourishes. In God's economy, there is no rich or poor, large or small—just multisized acts of love and compassion, all of which point to God's rule and reign.

God, help me to see that all the good I do, no matter how insignificant I may think it is, points to your reign over both the physical and spiritual world. Amen.

Treasures from God   251

Paul writes to the church in Rome and raises three momentous questions to help the members understand more clearly their relationship to God through the person and work of Jesus Christ. First, "If God is for us, who is against us?" The short answer to this question is "no one." God is the only one who can judge us. Since all sin, regardless of what or to whom it is directed, is against God, God is the only one who can bring charges against us. Because of the death of God's son, Jesus Christ, and our freedom from the captivity of sin, God will not bring charges against us—God is for us, not against us.

Paul asks a second question, "Who is to condemn?" The short answer is Jesus Christ who not only died but also was raised to life! Jesus will not undo his salvific work on the cross —it is once and for all. Jesus' sacrificial act clears our guilt and liberates us. Jesus has provided that freedom. In addition to liberation, those who trust in Christ have new life—a gift that only God can give—and this gift of life comes with Jesus' continuous intercession on behalf of all believers.

Finally, Paul raises a third question: "Who will separate us from the love of Christ?" Christians affirm that Jesus makes us more than conquerors. Regardless of our adversary, worry, fear, or suffering, God's love provides a way out. We are indeed victors not victims.

As believers we live into the future knowing that God's timeless, ceaseless, and limitless love envelops us. Clearly Paul desired the church in Rome to understand its relationship with God through Jesus as one beyond the temporal. New life in Jesus Christ brings a personal and permanent love.

Help me, God, to remember your great love for all people, even me. May I live into your unfailing, permanent love. Amen.

The kingdom of heaven is worth all that we have or ever will have. Today's parables indicate the kingdom's unparalleled worth. What is God's kingdom? The kingdom of God is both a future event and a present reality. The kingdom of God is inaugurated in the life of Jesus. However, God's reign also remains a future event as we await the final consummation in which all things will be made new. Therefore, due to its present reality in the person of Jesus and its coming in the final days, we celebrate its worth, and we exhibit earnest hope.

Jesus' teaching in the parable of the hidden treasure and the hidden pearl points out that the kingdom of God is worth every sacrifice whether we stumble upon it or set out to find the treasure intentionally. One man discovers the treasure, pulls together all he has, sells it, and buys the field from the owner. The merchant intentionally looking for pearls comes upon the greatest pearl ever. He immediately sells all of his other great finds to ensure his rightful ownership of the greatest find. Upon their discoveries, both men, with no hesitation, sell all for the treasure. Their discovery of the kingdom reshapes their priorities and focuses their thought. Treasure seeking is costly.

Like the one who randomly discovers the treasure hidden in the field and the merchant who deliberately searches, we are called to give all we have to participate in a costly discipleship. This devotion and commitment on our part carries eternal significance as the parable of the net reminds us: "So it will be at the end of the age. The angels will come out and separate the evil from the righteous and throw them into the furnace of fire, where there will be weeping and gnashing of teeth." Discovery and discipleship are matters of life and death.

God, may I willingly give up all that I own for the treasure of your kingdom. Amen.

Treasures from God　　　　253

Laban tricks Jacob into working another seven years for the woman he loves, Laban's daughter Rachel. We don't know from the passage what kind of worker Jacob is. We know that the first seven years seemed like a "few days" to Jacob because of his great love for Rachel.

Most of us work hard when the work results in some direct and tangible benefit to us. We work for recognition, more money, the ability to give others a life we didn't have, to climb up another rung of the proverbial ladder. I hope that every Christian works hard to honor God with his or her ethic and theology of work.

Jacob works for fourteen years in order to marry his love. We learn in Genesis 30 that under Jacob's care the family wealth has grown exponentially. (Read verses 25-30.) Jacob the deceiver met his match. However, he worked hard and persisted, giving all he had for the love of his life.

What if we worked hard for many years without seeing the results we hoped for? Would we still honor God with the way we put our hand to the plow, so to speak, in our efforts to work diligently? God calls us to care for creation, which goes well beyond our personal interests and rests on God's interests. After Jacob marries Rachel, he works for Laban another seven years—twenty-one years in total. Would that our commitment to kingdom work were so focused.

God, may I be the kind of worker who pleases you in all that I do—even with no tangible benefit to me. May I serve in a way that brings glory to you. Amen.

Seeking God's Presence

JULY 31–AUGUST 6, 2017 • EMILY M. AKIN

SCRIPTURE OVERVIEW: The heavyhearted psalmist gives voice to the feelings of many when he states, "Hear a just cause, O LORD; attend to my cry." In the Genesis text Jacob wrestles with a "man." At one level, this story is about human struggle with God, but at another level the story tells of a human being's struggle with himself or herself. Yet even in the midst of our struggles, the enduring word is one of God's grace. Romans 9 also deals with suffering: Paul's personal anguish over Israel's failure to receive God's messiah, the Christ. Matthew 14 reminds us that God's mercy is real. Obedient disciples become agents through whom God's provisions are served to hungry people.

QUESTIONS AND SUGGESTIONS FOR REFLECTION

- Read Genesis 32:22-31. When have you felt like you were wrestling with God? What impact did it have on your relationship with God?

- Read Psalm 17:1-7, 15. In what ways does your faith give you strength in the face of adversity? Reflect on a difficult time when you felt God's presence.

- Read Romans 9:1-5. How do the words of Peter in Acts and Paul's words in Romans shape your understanding of the Jewish faith?

- Read Matthew 14:13-21. How hungry are you for Jesus? Are you willing to nibble and snack, or are you starving for substance and sustenance?

Freelance writer and church musician, Union City, Tennessee

Jacob, while God's man, is a fighter. He struggled with Esau, his twin, while still in the womb. During birth, he grabbed firstborn Esau's heel. Later, he cheated Esau out of his birthright. He tricked his father, with his mother's help, into blessing him instead of Esau. This incident forced him to leave home. He went to live with Laban, his uncle—the man who deceives the deceiver. After years with Laban, God tells Jacob (Genesis 31) to take his family and return home.

Needless to say, the trip home has to raise Jacob's anxiety level. *How will his brother receive him?* Jacob has fared well in his years with Uncle Laban. Jacob sends the caravan of wives, children, and livestock ahead. He remains alone for the night. Why? Doesn't he feel an obligation to watch over his family? Does he want some alone time to pray and seek God's guidance?

Whatever the reason, Jacob gets more than he bargains for. As he wrestles with the man, he cannot prevail. The man could probably have beaten Jacob easily, but he does not. Perhaps God tests Jacob to see if he has the fortitude to be the heir to the covenant and leader of the chosen people. Jacob realizes he is striving with someone powerful, and he demands a blessing.

Jacob gets his blessing and remains forever changed. He has been tested and proven worthy. All of us wrestle with God at times. We lift fervent prayers seeking answers from God. We may have hard decisions to make. Perhaps a serious illness looms for us or for a loved one. In the face of tragedy, we ask God, "Why?" We demand answers, wrestling with God to understand why these situations happen. May we be as persistent as Jacob so that we may receive God's blessing, whatever our circumstances.

Bless all who struggle to understand God's will for their lives.

We recall the Jacob who fled his home. We remember the Jacob so weary that with a rock for a pillow he lay down to sleep. That was the Jacob who needed divine attention; Jacob wakened from his dream affirming that God "is in this place." On the eve of his return home, Jacob once again finds himself alone and in need of attention. Once again God comes—in a more physical fashion this time. Jacob hangs on and prevails to gain a blessing.

Jacob walks away from the wrestling match a changed man. From this time on, he will limp because the stranger struck his hip. And he has a new name. Jacob is now Israel, meaning "he wrestled with God." If a name creates expectations, Jacob has improved his lot. The most common meaning of the name of Jacob is "supplanter," one who tries to take the place of another. The old name implied an untrustworthiness. Yet God entrusts the covenant to him, selecting Jacob to join the company of the patriarchs. In the Old Testament, God speaks to the people in this way: "I am the God of Abraham, the God of Isaac, and the God of Jacob." (See Exodus 3:15; Matthew 22:32.)

A limp and a new name, a new identity, mark the man Jacob-Israel. He names the place Peniel because he recognizes the face of God. He has wrested a blessing and a new understanding of God's activity in his life.

A pastor once stated that God wants to wrestle with us. If this is true, God does not want to hear puny prayers. God wants us to pray passionately, demanding answers. We can grab on to the promises of God, saying, "I will not let you go until you give me an answer." Perhaps, if we pray bold, fervent prayers, we too will know that we have been with God, forever changed by the experience.

God of Abraham, Isaac, and Jacob, show me how I can serve you today, in the name of the Father and of the Son and of the Holy Spirit. Amen.

Seeking God's Presence   257

"You said if I cleaned my room, did all my homework, and fed the dog, we could do something special." Youngsters asking favors of parents often start their pleading with such logic. They go on and on, telling the parent how well they've fulfilled the requirements for the granting of the favor. Most of us have been on both sides of this negotiation, either as the one pleading the case or as the judge who must be convinced.

The psalmist's approach to God reminds me of such conversations. Wanting God to save him from his enemies, he tells God how righteous he's been, how he's resisted temptations like associating with evildoers. Next, he progresses to "God, are you listening? I have something to ask you." The psalmist believes that God in God's steadfast love will save him. He has remained true to the covenant; he has kept the faith and lived righteously. God will answer prayer. But it seems to me that while he's confident of God's support, he seems unsure that God's answer will be to his liking.

How often have we pleaded our case before God, noting our long list of good behaviors that would surely warrant God's intervention on our behalf? Our prayers often contain too much talking and not enough listening. We overstate our case. We know God is aware of our behavior—the good and the bad. We know God judges, but we forget that God also forgives.

Like the psalmist, we affirm that God answers prayer. "I call upon you, for you will answer me, O God; incline your ear to me, hear my words." We, like the psalmist, have experienced the steadfast love of God in other times and other places. God will incline God's ear and hear.

Lord, help me listen for your voice and seek your will daily. May I welcome your answers. Amen.

The psalmist says in verse 15, "I shall behold your face in righteousness; when I awake I shall be satisfied, beholding your likeness." He thinks that his righteousness will allow him to see God's face. For him, as for us, seeing is believing. If we cannot experience something with our senses, we have difficulty believing it is real. The Common English Bible adds a sense of longing, a need to be filled with God's presence: "I will be filled full by seeing your image."

Seeing God suffices for the psalmist. But some of us want more—an experience of God that draws in all our senses. We want to feel the breath of the Spirit, the wind and fire in our souls. We long to smell the fragrance of the Son. (See 2 Corinthians 2:14.) We desire to hear God's voice clearly, for we know that God does speak. (See Acts 22:14.) Psalm 34:8 suggests we can taste God's goodness, the sweetness of God's presence.

The world saw God in the person of Jesus Christ in the flesh. Jesus' contemporaries did not understand all he tried to teach them. But he told them he would be with them always. Once he left this world, God sent the Holy Spirit as their (and our) guide and comforter. The Latin root words mean "with strength." The Spirit exists to make us strong in mind and spirit so we can cope with whatever comes our way.

The Spirit emboldens us to ask for God's help, to take refuge in God's steadfast love. Then in our righteousness, we shall see God face-to-face. The open, loving relationship will allow for full communion. God hears and answers.

Today, let us praise God, the Three-in-One:
Praise God, from whom all blessings flow;
Praise God, all creatures here below;
Praise God above, ye heavenly host;
Praise Father, Son, and Holy Ghost. Amen.

Seeking God's Presence

As a first-year public school music teacher and church musician, I looked forward to observing Good Friday and Easter. I wanted the children in my classes to understand why Good Friday was a holiday. When I described the significance of the day, one child raised his hand. He said, "I live across the street from the people who killed Jesus." I moved on with my lesson, not knowing how to respond. I shared this experience with other teachers. One of them offered an explanation. "His neighbors are Jewish." I was speechless. It never occurred to me to blame the Jews for Jesus' execution.

In today's reading, Paul grieves for the Jews who have not accepted Jesus as Messiah. Paul was a Pharisee, so strong in his faith that he relished persecuting Christians. But Paul came to believe when he came face-to-face with the Lord. Here, he states that he would relinquish his relationship with Christ in order to bring the Jews to belief in Jesus' messiahship. He goes on to list the many gifts God has given Israel. And yet the question remains: *Has God rejected God's chosen people?* Paul attempts to hold Israel as chosen by God through the unfolding of the plan of salvation that will save *all* people.

Many Christians have friends or family members needing repentance and the peace that forgiveness brings. We may grieve or become frustrated that they do not share our beliefs. We may fear that they will fall outside the fold. But we, like Paul, affirm God's loving plan of salvation that includes the entire world.

Lord Jesus Christ, we pray today for all who do not know the joy of repentance, forgiveness, and communion with you. May we trust in your plan of salvation. Amen.

Can you imagine having crowds follow you everywhere, wanting you to solve their problems? Pastors and teachers can probably identify with the exhaustion Jesus and his disciples must have felt in this situation. Jesus has heard of the death of John the Baptist. Perhaps he has many reasons to keep a low profile—but the crowds follow.

The people want to see him, to hear him, and to experience his healing touch. Disregarding his own need for time alone, Jesus feels compassion toward the people, so the healing and teaching begin. Perhaps they lost all track of time. I wonder, though, *why would people in that day and age leave home without provisions?* Did their eagerness to see Jesus make them absent of common sense? Perhaps the urgency of being with Jesus precluded their planning for their physical needs.

Jesus charges the disciples with the task of feeding the crowd. In the middle of nowhere, what can they do but ask the crowd to share? They find little—just five loaves and two fish. But when Jesus blesses and breaks the loaves, it feeds more than five thousand people. Jesus met all the people's needs that day—men, women, and children.

We often ask God for help with our physical, emotional, or spiritual problems. We may feel inadequate for the task ahead. There never seems to be enough time or enough resources to do what we need to do. We lose hope when obstacles seem insurmountable. But we can feel confident that God will come to our aid, displaying the same compassion as did Jesus that day.

Compassionate God, we lift in prayer our pastors, teachers, government leaders, and others who serve God's people. Give them strength to cope with the demands placed on them. Amen.

Jesus hosts the multitudes, feeding people's spiritual and physical hungers. While Jesus' blessing and breaking works an amazing miracle in a tight spot, the disciples play an important part. Jesus does not lay out a grand plan before them. They simply follow Jesus' direction without question. They gather food and collect the leftovers and thereby participate in a miracle of compassion that goes far beyond their understanding. William Barclay, in his Bible study series, states that Jesus teaches a lesson with the blessing and distribution of the food: All gifts come from God. Barclay also notes that Jesus wants the disciples to learn their role, to receive gifts from Jesus and to distribute them. Today, many of us live in such abundance that we have trouble imagining that people do not have food to eat. But many do not. Some cannot care for themselves; some fall on hard times. As modern-day disciples, what role do we play in sharing God's gifts with others?

In my city, a local church sponsors an event each Thanksgiving called "The Feeding of the 5000." Organizers solicit donations of money and food items from the community. They recruit people from other churches to cook, serve at the church, and deliver to homes a traditional Thanksgiving meal to those who sign up. When the call goes out for volunteers, local disciples of Jesus come together from all over the county to make it happen.

Emulating the original disciples, these Christians meet a felt need of those who hunger. Grateful for the bounty they receive from God, they give what they have. It's a joyful day for all involved. Jesus still takes, blesses, and breaks what we bring—all our gifts from God. And we participate once again in the miracle of compassion.

"Mine are the eyes through which the compassion of Christ must look out on the world." (Paraphrase of a prayer of Teresa of Avila)

Faith through Discomfort

AUGUST 7–13, 2017 • DAN WUNDERLICH

SCRIPTURE OVERVIEW: The Genesis text begins the story of Joseph. Things would have turned out very different for Joseph (and for Israel) had it not been for the watchful care of the One who called Israel into being. Psalm 105 briefly recites the saving events in Israel's life, and this week's portion remembers the story of Joseph, stressing both the hiddenness and the crucial significance of God's mercy. In Romans 10 note the manner in which Paul brings the past to bear on the present in terms of God's saving activity. Notice also Paul's insistence on the universal availability of salvation. The Gospel lesson of Jesus stilling the storm points to the inexplicable wonder of God's redeeming love, which can be appropriated and answered only in doxology.

QUESTIONS AND SUGGESTIONS FOR REFLECTION

- Read Genesis 37:1-4, 12-28. The writer says, "Not all the challenges we face are a divine plan." Do you agree or disagree? Why?

- Read Psalm 105:1-6, 16-22, 45b. How well does your memory serve you in times of distress to recall God's presence and past action?

- Read Romans 10:5-15. In what situations have you chosen to rely on God?

- Read Matthew 14:22-33. The writer says that comfort and safety should not be our "primary criteria when discerning and acting on God's will." Do you agree? Why or why not?

Serves in extension ministry through the Florida Conference of The United Methodist Church, hosts the "Art of the Sermon" podcast; writes regularly on worship, creativity, and communication at DefiningGrace.com

When we look at the family tree of the patriarchs, we find a series of "gold stars." Abraham literally had many sons, but Genesis 25 tells us that he gave all he had to Isaac and sent the others away. Isaac and Rebekah each had a favorite son, and as a result their fraternal twins would live in conflict for decades. In the preface of our passage today, the scripture tells us that Jacob "loved Joseph more than any other of his children," leading Joseph to arrogance and his brothers to hatred.

The gold-star label can be uncomfortable. For all the perks of being favored, the favored one may pay a price in the response it can evoke from others. But whom do we blame? The father who played favorites? The son who let it go to his head? The brothers who felt slighted?

Favoritism runs up and down this family tree, poisoning relationships. The effect finally compounds itself to the point where the divinely promised offspring sell their brother into slavery and lie to their father, saying that his beloved son is dead. This problem goes beyond relational to systemic.

Broken relationships and broken systems continue to compound themselves in our world today. Poisons like prejudice, greed, and violence lead to injustices like poverty, hunger, and human trafficking. It would be charitable to call these injustices uncomfortable. These injustices are, more accurately, sinful and destructive.

Sadly, we experience these injustices in the church as well. But the Joseph narrative offers good news: When faithful people awaken to what God is doing in and through them, they can become a force for good—repairing broken systems, restoring relationships, and blessing the world around them.

God, we pray that you open our eyes to the injustices in the world around us. Make us instruments of your love. Amen.

W hy do bad things happen to good people—specifically me?" Distant tragedies from around the world can lead some to question God, but how many more crises of faith result from personal challenges?

Lots of bumper sticker slogans attempt to address issues of personal theodicy. Perhaps the most popular is this: "God won't give you more than you can handle." While meant to encourage, the unintended message is that God causes our pain. As we will see later this week, God does not have a problem handing out uncomfortable assignments on occasion, but sometimes God gets too much credit. Not all the challenges we face are a divine plan; many are the consequences that result from human free will or the laws of nature.

Today's text does not mention God—which is significant since Genesis seldom fears crediting God's words or actions. Instead, we read about a series of poor decisions. Israel sends Joseph out alone to check up on brothers who hate him. The brothers plan murder out of jealousy. Nervous Reuben convinces them to throw Joseph in a pit instead, intending to come back and rescue him later. Yet, for some mysterious reason, he leaves Joseph alone with them (see verse 29). The now unsupervised brothers add greed to the mix, capitalizing on the opportunity to sell their brother into slavery.

God may not have caused these actions, but scripture tells us that God was with Joseph through it all. It is not some intentional level of suffering that God calibrates on our behalf that helps us get through it all. Rather, it is God's presence that helps us face whatever challenges come our way.

God, we give thanks that you are with us during difficult times.
Help us to recognize where you are present and active, working
all things together for the good of those who love you. Amen.

Everyone loves a good story, and central to a good story is conflict. Few best-sellers focus on the perfect day where everything works out. Romantic comedies end when the couple gets together because happy, stable relationships are fun to be in but boring to watch.

Yet, we can hesitate to share our own stories because they contain conflict or challenges. Our culture demands perfection, and we worry about what people will think. It is even worse at times in the church where it can seem like everyone else is always smiling and their lives are always "blessed." We hear sermons about struggles, brokenness, and pain, but we are supposed to nod sympathetically in support of whomever the pastor is talking about—because it is surely *not* us.

Psalm 105 summarizes the story of God's chosen people from the humble beginnings of a wandering family through the dramatic exodus from Egypt. Interestingly, the psalmist does not pull any punches. The history is a difficult one: homelessness, slavery, and abuse. When the people are not paying the price for their own poor choices—like selling a brother into slavery—the challenges often result from not being big and strong enough to stand up for themselves.

Many would deem this story embarrassing, but those who comprised the canon essentially put it in their greatest hits! They not only retell but celebrate the story. Why? Because in spite of their failures, the God who promised to look out for them kept that promise. Because even when a great and overwhelming challenge faced them, it was never too great for God.

The stories from our past that make us the most uncomfortable may actually be our best source of hope for the future.

God, give us the courage to share our stories so that your faithfulness in the past will give strength and hope for today and beyond. Amen.

I am guilty of overlooking small details in familiar stories like Jesus walking on water, but recently a single word jumped out: Jesus *made* the disciples get in the boat and head out onto the Sea of Galilee. He *made* them.

If this seems out of character for Jesus, there is a good reason. This story presents the only time Jesus is the subject of this particular verb. He does a lot of inviting but not much compelling. Yet, this soon-to-be stormy boat ride is one that Jesus essentially forces the disciples to take.

Perhaps Jesus had to *make* them because the disciples protested. They likely remembered a previous trip during which a storm arose quickly over this same body of water causing them to fear for their lives. (See Matthew 8.) We do not know if Jesus anticipates the coming storm, but such a storm is always possible. In fact, if we follow the sequence of events that Matthew gives us, Jesus sees the storm envelop the boat before he even begins his trek down the mountain and out onto the water.

This boat ride goes beyond discomfort for the disciples—it carries the possibility of danger. Yet neither potential nor real storms bother Jesus. Comfort and safety are not his top priorities, nor should they be our primary criteria when discerning and acting on God's will.

But Jesus does not leave them alone. He walks into the center of the storm to be with them—the very heart of Incarnation. God is not some distant being, calling the shots while avoiding the dirt and danger. Instead, Jesus becomes human, and we know him as Emmanuel—God with us.

> *God, forgive us for the times we protest or even deny your call because it is a challenge. Instead, may we look for your presence and the ways in which you walk alongside us. Amen.*

Discomfort in life can come from many sources—natural consequences, other people, broken systems, and even God. However, sometimes we bring the discomfort on ourselves.

"Lord, if it is you, command me to come to you on the water." Peter shouts this request to what appears to be Jesus walking upon the stormy Sea of Galilee. We have to wonder—*what is Peter thinking?*

Though he is a fisherman by trade, Peter likely still had a healthy fear of deep water. The Old Testament—the scriptures he knew—painted deep water as home to sea monsters. And when Jesus encountered a man possessed by many demons, Jesus returned the demons to the abyss via pigs drowning in this very body of water. (Read Luke 8:26-39.)

Yet, far from land during a predawn storm, Peter asks Jesus to command him to get out of the boat and walk over the top of deep water. Peter does not simply ask for a miracle—he puts his life at stake in an act of faith.

Peter does not have to do this. Jesus does not ask him to. And he certainly doesn't make this request because it looks like fun. This mysterious figure is almost to the boat, and Peter's companions are terrified. So he shouts this request to verify Jesus' identity. Peter essentially asks Jesus to use him to prove that Jesus is who he claims to be. Is there a better request from a disciple?

Peter would willingly risk everything to protect his friends and help them all know Jesus better. By the end of this passage, they declare Jesus as Son of God for the first time. What are we willing to risk for the world to know Jesus?

God, fill us with a desire to see others come to know you. May that desire lead us to take risks in trusting you. Amen.

When it comes to the inconsequential, we can easily admit that we're wrong. For example, I am comfortable saying I was wrong to think guacamole tasted bad just because it looked funny. The more important the issue, however, the harder it is to confess failure. To do so requires a fight against strong internal forces like fear and pride.

When we look at scripture's offer of salvation, it begins and ends with God, but it must include our admitting to the greatest failure of them all: We are sinners who have broken the relationship that matters the most!

It is easier for me, as someone who was raised in the church and who is now a pastor, to accept the label of "sinner." I have been familiar with it my whole life; I have personally experienced God's grace and mercy; I now teach and preach about forgiveness regularly. But what does today's passage sound like to someone who has yet to come to faith?

Even understanding God as loving and merciful, the idea of turning our lives over to an all-powerful being and admitting that we have been wrong about something this important is intimidating. Fear and pride thrive in situations like this. Accepting that we need saving requires a belief in God's judgment, which is certainly an uncomfortable concept.

We tend to forget what it is like *not* to be Christian. We say that becoming a Christian is the most significant decision we have ever made, but we forget how scary that can sound. As we read this passage tomorrow, with its beautiful call to evangelism, let us remember that Jesus had great understanding for those who found faith difficult and experienced frustration with those who thought they had it all figured out.

God, give us compassion for those who have reservations about faith. Help us not judge but rather embody your patience and love. Amen.

Faith through Discomfort   269

We close this week by reading one of the most beautiful yet practical calls to evangelism in the Bible. Paul has just explained his concept of salvation, but he understands that not everyone will "get it" on his or her own. For this reason, God has called, equipped, and empowered us to help carry the message of God's grace and mercy. By working back through the process logically, Paul lays out the progression.

Reliance on God comes as a result of belief. Belief comes as a result of hearing the gospel. Hearing comes as a result of someone proclaiming the gospel. Proclaiming comes as a result of being sent. And—hint, hint—it is going to take everyone playing his or her part to fulfill the mission of God, who is Lord of all and generous to all.

Which of these steps do we find easy and comfortable? Belief? Hearing the gospel? Proclaiming the gospel? Being sent? If we are honest, for the majority of us none of them is easy or comfortable—at least not in the beginning. Ask a pastor how attendance at evangelism events compares to fellowship events, and you will get the picture.

Yet, we have seen this week that comfort is not God's primary concern. It is not God's desire for us to suffer, but the unwavering source of contentment and joy is not our physical and emotional condition moment to moment. Rather, it is God.

Nor is discomfort a stumbling block to God's will being worked in the world. The One who most clearly embodied God's will in the world faced death on a cross. It is often through, not in spite of, discomfort that God achieves incredible things in and through people who place their trust in God.

God, remind us of your eternal love for us, especially when we face the discomfort and challenges that come our way. May we be an active part of your will being done on earth as it is in heaven. Amen.

Reconciling Love

AUGUST 14–20, 2017 • KARLA KINCANNON

SCRIPTURE OVERVIEW: Genesis 45 portrays Joseph in a moment of triumph. The trials of the past are over, and his trembling brothers are now in his power. Joseph acknowledges God's hand in the events of his life and is reconciled to those who attempted to do him harm. Psalm 133 is a brief but exuberant song to the spirit of unity and fellowship that can exist among the members of the family of God. Paul delivers a resounding "no" to the idea that God has rejected Israel. God's election is irrevocable. The story of Jesus and the Canaanite woman in Matthew 15 illustrates the wide umbrella of God's mercy. The woman's faith and persistence serve in a curious way to minister to Jesus. As she becomes a means of God's grace to Jesus, he extends God's mercy to her.

QUESTIONS AND SUGGESTIONS FOR REFLECTION

- Read Genesis 45:1-15. What relationship in your life needs reconciliation? How will you help bring it about?
- Read Psalm 133. How healthy is your church family? Is there need for greater unity among the members?
- Read Romans 11:1-2a, 29-32. What wounds in your life have brought you a greater understanding of God's mercy?
- Read Matthew 15:10-28. The writer says, "The work of Christians is to love others, not to change them." Is this difficult for you?

Director for Spiritual Formation at Aldersgate United Methodist Church, Alexandria, Virginia; affiliate faculty member at Garrett-Evangelical Theological Seminary

The day of reckoning has arrived. Joseph comes face-to-face with the brothers who had betrayed him. When they met for the first time in years, his brothers did not recognize Joseph; but he knew who they were. His brothers do not know that Joseph not only survived the ordeal but has risen to a place of power and privilege in Egyptian society. Now that Joseph is a powerful governor, his brothers fear the power of his office. Their survival lies in Joseph's hands.

In today's text, the brothers meet Joseph, and he identifies himself as the vulnerable innocent they had sold into slavery. Now the tables are turned, and the brothers find themselves in a place of precarious vulnerability. They fear Joseph will act in a manner similar to the way they had treated him.

Joseph has a choice to make. He can act out of his hurt to even the score or reach out in a gesture of reconciliation. We sometimes try to assuage our wounds through acts of revenge, but it seldom brings lasting relief. Though revenge may bring short-lived satisfaction, it's often followed by regret, pain, and loss of dignity.

Joseph chooses a way forward other than revenge. He is God's man; God has worked throughout his life to bring good out of evil: "God sent me before you to preserve life." His tears signal a cathartic healing. He lets go of past hurts. Without this healing, he may have exacted revenge. His familial bonds of love are stronger than his desire to get even. Joseph takes the higher road and assures his brothers of a life of abundance despite five more years of famine. The brothers' inability to speak turns to weeping among the brothers with many hugs exchanged. This is the path to abundant life: forgiving those who have harmed us, loving those who have done us wrong.

Remember a time when you were tempted to exact revenge. Offer the situation to God for healing. Ask God for courage to be a bearer of Christ's forgiving and reconciling love.

Fortunately for Joseph's brothers, Joseph has experienced a change of heart as the familial bonds of love rekindle within him. He begins to heal from the trauma of having been separated from his family in his youth. His heart becomes tender as he weeps, releasing years of pain. Not desiring to punish his brothers, he does not even ask for an apology. He wants to be reconciled with his family.

Though Joseph yearns to resume his rightful place within his family, he cannot achieve it from his position of power. His brothers are too afraid. If Joseph wants to reconcile with his brothers, he must find a way to relate to them not as the powerful governor but as one of them. In a subtle move, Joseph addresses the fears of his brothers by relinquishing his power. In a moment of vulnerability, he asks his brothers to come closer, and thereby removes the "official" barrier—no longer their governor but their brother.

Reconciliation does not happen automatically and often occurs in increments, as it does for Joseph. Christianity has at its heart a downward movement of surrendering power in favor of relationship. God, in Christ, became vulnerable so that we could be reconciled to God. What a remarkable God we have, who surrenders power so that we are able to come closer to the source of reconciling love.

Reconciling God, as we move closer to you, we are drawn into deeper relationships with one another. Heal the brokenness of our lives and create in us a forgiving heart. Grant us the courage to be willing to move toward forgiveness and reconciliation in the example of your son, Christ Jesus. Amen.

Our psalmist begins by celebrating family unity, declaring unity as good and pleasant. The image of oil signals God's favor, for oil was used to consecrate and bless. God intends that families be healthy and whole, living in peaceful unity.

Healthy families are a gift. In our earliest years we form attachments in our families that enable us to love and be loved, developing the ability to form lasting relationships. We learn our identities from our families and how to trust. Healthy families usually form healthy individuals who can live in unity.

However, the psalmist does not intend God's blessing to be for the individual family alone. Some biblical scholars believe that the focus of this psalm is on the unification of the two kingdoms of ancient Israel. The psalmist's message reaches to address all the people of God, all God's children.

The church often functions as a family, and its unity is fragile. Conflict commonly occurs in the local American church. Studies suggest that at any given time about one-fifth of congregations have active conflict within their ranks.

Avoidance is an automatic response to conflict; however, Jesus calls us to be peacemakers. We do not gain peace by avoiding conflict; rather, we move into the center of conflict in order to create peace, even if that conflict is within the family of God. Reconciliation is part of the mission of the church to the world and must be practiced within the walls of the church if the mission is to have authenticity.

The oil and dew of the psalm signify bountiful well-being. The peace and harmony within the shared community in this psalm depict life as God intends.

Pray for your family and your church today. God desires us to dwell together in unity.

Family unity is fragile. Harsh words spoken in the heat of anger too easily wound and estrange individuals from their families. Unity breaks down temporarily, if not permanently. The Bible records many stories of family members in dispute, from the very serious, as in the stories of Cain and Abel or Jacob and Esau, to the minor skirmishes like those between Mary and Martha. Human differences make unity a challenge to maintain, whether unity of the family, the church, or between nations.

In our current time we have difficulty creating unity. We eagerly judge others rather than attempt to understand behavior. We objectify those who are different from us, easily dismissing them and making them the enemy. Yet, the psalmist makes it clear that God desires unity for the whole human family.

Christians who take the call to unity seriously participate in the ministry of reconciliation of which Paul speaks in Second Corinthians. Working toward unity is no easy task; it requires a learned skill set. Merely desiring reconciliation is not enough. Those who work toward unity must learn how to "listen for understanding, speak the truth in love, use their imagination to picture a better way forward, and be forgiving."*

How would your life differ if you worked for unity by practicing these four skills? Instead of judging others, what happens inside of you when you listen for understanding? How does this way of listening change your perspective on those whom you encounter? What does speaking the truth in love mean to you? How might you practice it?

---

*Stephanie Hixon and Thomas Porter, *Engage Conflict Well, Version 1.4* (Washington, DC: JUSTPEACE Center for Mediation and Conflict Transformation, 2011), 3.

What steps toward forgiveness can you take this day? How might you imagine a future of unity in the broken places?

I entered ministry at a time when my denomination was just beginning to recognize the presence of women as ordained clergy. My early years in ministry were full of struggle. Changing cultural norms seldom comes without conflict; the apostle Paul knew that well! As a young woman I felt bruised by the conflict. I wondered if God had rejected or forgotten me. Those early experiences taught me much about God's mercy.

When we are wounded, part of our identity may go into hiding. In order to protect ourselves against future pain, we develop defenses. Our defenses help us survive, but they can also imprison us. Reinforced defenses can become masks. We begin to think we are the person we pretend to be.

Our gifts are closely linked to our identity and to the call that God has placed on our lives. But gifts go into hiding too. We fear letting our light shine, worried that we might experience the perceived future pain we are trying to avoid.

The good news in today's passage is that God's mercy sets us free to use the "gifts and the calling" God has given us. They are "irrevocable." God's foreknowledge, a means of grace that goes before us, woos us into our calling and the use of our gifts. Though we have each been wounded by life in different ways, God works to heal us, yearning for us to come out of hiding to use our gifts for the healing of the world.

The wounds that life inflicts do not signal God's rejection but rather opportunities for God's mercy to heal us, integrating and reconciling painful experiences within our being. In the process, we discover in God's mercy new energy for living.

Reconciling God, send your mercy into our wounded lives and make us whole. Help us respond to your love by loving others. Amen.

Many of us feel passionate about church or family traditions. Years ago my family changed one of its Christmas traditions. Family members were very vocal about what we left out of our traditional celebration! Change is difficult.

The Pharisees believed that practicing their traditions kept them connected to God and the community. They believed in the correctness of their approach. Previous generations had passed down their beliefs to them. Sadly, many Pharisees were blind to the harm done to persons when the law excluded individuals from community. They did not understand the ethic of love that motivated Jesus to place people's needs before religious practice.

Jesus bases his message of reconciling love on relationship, not rules. Jesus builds bridges between people, inviting everyone to the table—washed and unwashed. It is not religious practice that separates people; it's what we carry in our hearts. When we harbor judgment, hatred, or deceit; when we objectify others, failing to respect the human dignity of each person, we defile ourselves. We cut ourselves off from others.

For centuries the church has focused its energies on defining who is included and who is not. It has sometimes acted more like the Pharisees; other times it has more closely resembled Jesus. When the church boldly welcomes others—as segments of it did during the civil rights era—it behaves like Jesus. Though racism still exists, we are learning what it means to set more places at the table.

What would it look like if the church were to embody Jesus' reconciling love fully? Who would be welcome at the table?

God, grant us purity of heart to love as Christ does. Amen.

Reconciling Love

SUNDAY, AUGUST 20 ～ *Read Matthew 15:10-28*

This scripture tells the story of Jesus' conversion to his own ethic of love. Through his encounter with this Gentile woman, Jesus grows in awareness of the far-reaching nature of God's love.

Initially, we witness Jesus discriminating against this woman on the basis of gender and race. He intends to dismiss her, proclaiming that his message is limited to the "lost sheep of the house of Israel." She is an outsider, undeserving of God's love and grace. How puzzling to see Jesus' actions resembling those of the Pharisees!

But Matthew invites us to use this encounter to examine the hidden chambers of our own hearts. Do we treat others who are different from us as inferior, believing them to be less worthy of God's love? Do we feel superior to others because we have more money and status, a different ethnicity or race, a certain gender or sexual orientation, a specific denomination or religion? If so, we have cut ourselves off from the Jesus community, just as Jesus initially cut himself off from relationship with the Canaanite woman.

Jesus believes he came to convert the misdirected house of Israel and, yet, this encounter reflects his own misperception and misdirection. Through the Canaanite woman's wit and persistence, Jesus comes to understand that his message of God's saving love is meant for everyone! God intends to leave no one out—no one. Furthermore, Jesus does not try to change the woman before he responds to her. He requires no conversion. He accepts her as she is and acknowledges her great faith. The work of Christians is to love others, not to change them.

Lord Jesus, you love us abundantly, without limit or condition. Help us to love as you love. Convert us to your ethic of reconciling love that the world may live in unity and peace. Amen.

Reconciling Love

Courageous Faith through Obedience

AUGUST 21–27, 2017 • BO PROSSER

SCRIPTURE OVERVIEW: All the texts bear witness to the rich and powerful sovereignty of God, who generously gives life. In the Exodus text, both the future of Israel and the future of God's plans for all humanity are imperiled. At one level, the infant is saved only by the cunning of his mother and sister and by the compassion of the Egyptian princess; but, truthfully, Moses is saved only by the grace of God. Psalm 124 looks beyond the birth of Moses to the moment of the Exodus and celebrates with great joy God's redemption of the people. Only by God's help can humans find life and freedom. In Romans 12 Paul calls for the transformation of the person through the power of God. We are to "be transformed," thus placing primary emphasis on the activity of God in the life of the Christian. The Gospel reading is a confession of Jesus' identity as the Messiah. Matthew emphasizes the rootedness of the church in the disciples' recognition of Jesus' messianic nature.

QUESTIONS AND SUGGESTIONS FOR REFLECTION
- Read Exodus 1:8–2:10. When have you had a scary experience that God's "grand plan" made successful?
- Read Psalm 124. Looking back on your life, where can you see God's hand guiding you through rough times?
- Read Romans 12:1-8. Take time to answer the writer's question: "How are you using your gifts in your church and in your community?"
- Read Matthew 16:13-20. Who do you say Jesus is?

Coordinator of Strategic Partnerships with the Cooperative Baptist Fellowship, Atlanta, Georgia; author, teacher, sought-after speaker and storyteller

Just when everything is going great; the journey seems smooth, and we think we have finally arrived, the scenario shifts again. We cry to God, "I've been faithful! Why is this happening to me?" The children of Israel find themselves in a similar position.

"A new king arose over Egypt, who did not know Joseph." (Uh oh!) All that Joseph has stood for, the good works he has done, is erased in a moment. The children of Israel flourished under the cooperative spirit that Joseph had instilled in them. Joseph had forged strong relationships with the Egyptians, and Israel had continued to grow.

"A new king arose over Egypt, who did not know Joseph." This king chooses to remain ignorant of the good work that Joseph and past leaders have done. This new king is afraid. He fears the growing Israelite population in his country, fears that the Israelites might turn on him, fears that he can't "rule" over them. So he returns to the bitter oppression of the past.

"A new king arose over Egypt, who did not know Joseph." The days of cooperation and mutual respect have ended. This king brings harsh work and selfish demands. The taskmasters brutally afflict the Israelites! The focus is to break the spirit of the Israelites and stop their continued population growth.

Yet, as often happens with God's people, God's blessings continue to abound. And the more abuse the Israelites face, the more they flourish.

Where do you struggle in your own work, life, faith? What history are you ignoring? What do you need to resist in your life? How is God blessing you in the midst of your struggle?

O God, give me courage today—courage to press on, to seek abundant life. O God, give me wisdom today that I will choose the right things to do. O God, give me faith today to trust you regardless of what may come my way. Amen.

The king is still on a rampage! Since backbreaking slave labor and brutal treatment has not stopped the growth of the Israelites, the king goes directly to the "labor and delivery room"! He gives an order to the Hebrew midwives, Shiphrah and Puah, "Kill all the male babies born!" The king's fear leads him to cruel and immoral leadership.

The midwives fear and respect God more than they fear or respect Pharaoh; they refuse to kill the male babies. Israel continues to flourish even in the face of tremendous persecution. Because of their courage and obedience, the midwives are rewarded with God's blessings, protection, and families. These women looked right into the face of evil and refused to be intimidated. What courage! What role models!

A king planning to kill all Jewish male babies could also have killed disobedient midwives. Yet God's blessing and protection meets the midwives' resistance. God stays faithful to God's people. Always has, always will!

There have been many such brave women in our Christian heritage. Women who, in spite of trial and death, have followed God with courage and with faith. I am a product of strong women of faith. These strong faithful women taught me how to be a godly man. They modeled for me the disciplines of Bible study, prayer, worship, and leadership. How different my life would have been—how different the church would be if not for strong women of courage and faith!

Who are the women who have influenced your faith journey? Who are the women who have nurtured you in your Christian growth? How does your fear affect your decision making? How does your courage keep you close to God?

Thank you, God, for women of courage and faith who model for us a way of life. May we follow their example, and be bold for the sake of your world. Amen.

Courageous Faith through Obedience

The call to act on God's behalf is a scary one. When God called me to follow and become a disciple of Christ, I had to walk down front and tell the preacher. Scary! When God called me to ministry, I had to sit before an ordaining council and share my call experience. Scary! In seminary, I had to articulate my call before learned scholars. Scary! Since seminary, I've had to share my thoughts as to why I believed God was calling me to work in particular congregations. Scary!

God's call never comes without risk or an element of fear. Yet, I serve a God filled with love and grace who casts out fear. The God I serve controls the process; God knows the "grand plan"! I didn't always get my dream job. At times fear has threatened my faith. Sometimes God doesn't work the way I expect. Yet, most times God has used my shortcomings to lead me to successes beyond my imaginings. God remains faithful like that!

Imagine a mother having to hide her precious son to save his life. Imagine a sister having to babysit down by the river knowing that her brother could be killed. Imagine a daughter rebelling against her father, the king, and raising an Israelite child as her own. Imagine a powerful, fearful king, willing to kill innocent babies. Each player in this passage serves as an instrument within God's grand plan. None of them knows the outcome of his or her actions. All have to sacrifice, some at great cost. God's guidance in this passage reminds us of the courage and obedience God desires. Are you willing?

When has God surprised you by turning "failures" into blessings? How are you like the women in this passage? How do you move beyond your fear to follow God's guidance?

God, help me to set aside my plans and follow yours. May I act with courage and in faithful obedience to you. Amen.

If is a powerful little word! The English language defines it as a conjunction that introduces a conditional thought. "If it had not been the LORD who was on our side" can bring to mind thoughts of death and destruction. Ultimately, though, this little *if* leads to wonderful verses of praise.

If allows us to examine what might have been without actually experiencing the pain. *If* allows us to think the worst without experiencing the worst. *If* might best be used at the front end of a decision. However, in this psalm, the writer uses *if* in hindsight. In looking back, the psalmist recognizes that the hand of God has been upon Israel for a long, long time.

This recollection carries power. The psalmist now can see clearly how God has guided Israel through everything from natural disasters to the threat of powerful armies. God has been and is now with us, guiding us, protecting us. And, the psalmist raises the question of what would have happened *if* not for God. The psalmist looks back into ancient history and perhaps also deals a bit with recent memories. And the "song" includes the joyful refrain, "Blessed be the LORD."

The word *if* helps us connect our history with our reality. God is always active, always guiding. I shudder to think what would have happened to me *if* God had not been my protector, my shield, my shepherd, my guide. Thanks be to God; blessed be the Lord!

From what *ifs* has God protected you? As you look back, where do you see the hand of God in your life? As you look forward, what hope do you glimpse in God's continued guidance in your life?

Thank you, God, for your ever-present protection and guidance. Thank you that the ifs *in my life have not overtaken me. Blessed are you, O God! Amen.*

Many point to the megachurches of our era as the superstars of our faith movement. The average megachurch will usually run more than one thousand in attendance each week. These churches fall in the categories of multimillion dollar budgets, multistaff ministries, expansive programming, and an international reach. These churches are important to God's reign and provide great ministry throughout the world.

However, the average US church has about seventy-five to one hundred people in attendance each week. These smaller congregations meet weekly, dutifully living out the Great Commission in their own right. All vital congregations minister faithfully, serve responsibly, worship creatively, and share obediently.

Paul suggests that the members of the church at Rome "be transformed" by the renewing of their minds. Christians, when shaped by the gospel of Jesus Christ, change the way they think. Behavior follows thinking. Paul also reminds the members of the richness of their congregation. He does this in the context of serving obediently, living humbly, and sharing freely. Paul notes the spiritual gifts at work in their church. He does not rank these or emphasize one gift more than the others. Paul encourages the Roman Christians to use their giftedness to become *more* of what they already are. Paul speaks in generalities concerning the gifts. While understanding the gifts is important, putting these gifts to use is much more important!

How has God gifted you? How are you using your gifts in your church and community? Are you more about "knowing" God's gifts or "using" God's gifts? What shifts might you need to make? How have you conformed to this world? What transformation are you seeking today by your renewal in Christ?

God, help me not to discount my gifts! May I seek ways to serve your church and your people faithfully. Amen.

We can access entertainment news twenty-four hours a day! Many television channels dedicate themselves solely to celebrity news. We can read about the lives of celebrities on the Internet, in the checkout line, even in daily papers. And you know the old saying, "There's no such thing as *bad* publicity!"

In Jesus' day, publicists, tabloids, and agents did not exist. So Jesus asks his disciples, "Who do people say that the Son of Man is?" I don't think Jesus has a concern about ratings or celebrity rankings. He merely sets the stage for the next question! But the disciples quickly rattle off all the local "gossip" about their rabbi: "Some say John the Baptist, but others Elijah, and still others Jeremiah or one of the prophets." I imagine there is some fun in the conversation and that they all have a good laugh about some of the responses.

But then, Jesus shifts the conversation by saying something to this effect, "Well, that was fun; but who do *you* say that I am?" And, suddenly, the disciples confront a new reality. It's not enough to know *about* Jesus; we are called to *know* Jesus. And Jesus desires that we know him deeply, intimately, and consistently. How will you answer Jesus' question?

Whatever your response, Jesus is the Messiah, the Son of the living God. Today perhaps you need to have the courage to claim Jesus as Lord for the first time. Perhaps you need to reclaim Jesus as a priority relationship in your life. Whatever the answer, know that Jesus loves you unconditionally. Who do you say that Jesus is? What do you need from Jesus today?

Jesus, forgive me when I have not known how to answer your question. Give me the courage and faith to claim you today and always as Savior and Lord. Amen.

Some defend the freedom of every believer. Others claim that a believer is free until conflict arises with an authority figure; then we must submit to that authority. Whatever you think, the freedom of every believer is a gift of grace given from the ultimate authority: God through Jesus the Christ. We always affirm an individual's right to think and believe as he or she sees fit. But we also understand that the ultimate authority resides in the grace of God through Christ.

We use all the senses God gives us to live into God's revelation. Jesus pronounces Peter as "blessed." Peter surprisingly pays attention to God's revelation and dares to answer beyond the tangible evidence. He freely expresses his faith. He knows *about* Jesus, and he *knows* Jesus. And he dares to risk what he knows with a public affirmation: "You are the Messiah!" And Jesus confirms his belief.

The Apostles' Creed affirms, "I believe in Jesus Christ, [God's] only Son, our Lord." Many of us repeat this every Sunday. We believe like Peter believed. We risk like Peter risked. We proclaim like Peter proclaimed. We are free to do so and find blessing in our belief.

Within the freedom of every believer, we are free to read and interpret the Bible as we interact with God's Spirit. We are free to pray thoughtfully as we work out our own salvation with fear and trembling. We live freely within the essence of our personal and corporate confessions of faith. And upon courageous believers, like Simon Peter and you and me, Jesus will build his church.

What are you willing to risk to proclaim Jesus as Lord? How are you like Simon Peter? What needs to happen for you to become bolder in your faith?

God, help us to pay attention. May we boldly proclaim our faith to all who seek your grace. Amen.

The Challenge in the Call

AUGUST 28–SEPTEMBER 3, 2017 • GENNIFER BENJAMIN BROOKS

SCRIPTURE OVERVIEW: In Exodus 3, Moses is moved to inspect the bush because it is an oddity, and in so doing he encounters the presence of the living God. Not even Moses could be prepared for the challenge that ensues. Psalm 105 recites God's great acts of mercy in Israel's life; in this instance, focusing on Moses and Aaron. The key verb here is "sent," and its subject is God. In Romans 12, Paul takes the notion of covenant demand and expounds on it. Christians are called not simply to keep rules; they are transformed and readied for new life in the world. Paul provides an inventory of new life for those who are changed and renewed by the gospel. The Gospel reading is one of Jesus' most acute reflections on the obedience expected of the faithful. He announces his own destiny of suffering obedience and invites his disciples to share in that radical destiny. For the faithful, there is no "business as usual"; it's a divine call that brings challenge.

QUESTIONS AND SUGGESTIONS FOR REFLECTION

- Read Exodus 3:1-15. Have you experienced God's call to something you felt ill-equipped for? What did you say to God? to yourself?
- Read Psalm 105:1-6, 23-26, 45c. How difficult is it for you to praise God in the midst of turmoil? Why?
- Read Romans 12:9-21. Where in your life do you have opportunities to bless those who curse you?
- Read Matthew 16:21-28. What does your call to discipleship in Christ cost you?

Ernest and Bernice Styberg Professor of Preaching and Styberg Preaching Institute Director at Garrett-Evangelical Theological Seminary; dean of the ACTS DMin in Preaching Program; elder in the New York Annual Conference

Moses feels overwhelmed. His life has evolved in ways that he never imagined when he was a favored son in Pharaoh's house as the child of royalty. Learning his true identity sends him on a journey full of peril, but he has found a place of security in the household of the priest of Midian. But God has a plan for his life that also lies beyond his imagining, and God shows up with a call that challenges who and what he understands himself to be.

The wilderness to which he has journeyed is probably the last place he expects to see the light of God, to experience the fire of God's presence, to stand in the radiance of God's glory. Nor does he expect to hear his name called and to be brought face-to-face with the God of his ancestors. No wonder he is afraid. Perhaps he senses that this call from God will catapult him into places unknown and force him to face unimaginable challenges.

But isn't that the common story of those whom God calls to speak a word of freedom, of justice, and of the amazing love of God to the people of God? When we find ourselves in wilderness places, we often come face-to-face with the glory of God that shines into our lives from unexpected places. But like Moses, we can become fearful.

Fear of what awaits us causes us to hide ourselves, to refuse the challenge of our call to service in God's name. But we cannot escape the light of God's glory. The darkness of the wilderness cannot overcome God's amazing light that shines all around us as we accept the challenge of offering the word of God to the people of God.

Eternal God, shine your light on us that we may move beyond fear to reflect the light of your glory. Amen.

Overcome by fear, unconvinced and unwilling to take on the challenge of facing both a beleaguered people and the might of Pharaoh, Moses protests repeatedly. In return he receives the assurance of divine presence that will direct and empower his mission to the glory of God. All Christians who, like Moses, face the challenge of accepting God's call need to hear this witness.

Oppression and injustice seem to be the order of the day for many individuals and groups in our society. Violence to body and spirit plagues our communities in cities and suburbs and rural villages. We may well wonder whether God still hears the cry of the people. Certainly we need prophets to speak a word of liberation. The task is overwhelming, and the people of God are overwhelmingly reluctant to accept the challenge.

But God still calls prophets in this day to speak truth to power and to seek liberation for all people. The demand for justice resounds in the voices of the #BlackLivesMatter movement. People of color everywhere cry out in protest against the marginality of an existence that is forced upon them by hegemonic systems that control their lives. Will we answer God's call and face the challenge that it represents? Or will we Christians, individually and corporately, remain silent, ruled by fear?

God's promise of presence to a reluctant Moses is the same promise on which all who answer the call to seek freedom and justice for the oppressed can depend. God assures Moses and every reluctant prophet and Christian across the ages and today: "I will be with you." Our acceptance of that call and our worship of God are ever and always by faith, and our response to that divine directive reflects God's glory.

Glorious God, empower us by your presence to seek justice and freedom for all. Amen.

The Challenge in the Call

This psalm that ends with a brief reminder of Moses' mission that brought freedom to Israel begins as a song of praise. It calls the people of God to remember the works of God among their ancestors and offer their own praise as they testify to the greatness of God as a source of their own empowerment. How do we sing the Lord's song and offer praise and thanks to God in the midst of trouble and oppression?

In African American churches even in the time of slavery and Jim Crow domination and despite the challenges of life African Americans face as persons whose full humanity is often ignored, the people have faithfully sung their praises and offered their thanks for the goodness of God. They worship and give glory to God for life even when that life is toil and trouble. Like the Israelites of old, they speak faithfully of a God who has brought them a mighty long way as they sing heartily: "If it had not been for the Lord on my side, where would I be?"

We continue to see evidence of the victimization of African Americans in substandard education, inadequate housing, a flourishing school-to-prison pipeline, an overwhelmingly African American prison population, food deserts in their communities, and double-digit unemployment. And yet the worship in African American churches is exuberantly joyful and celebrative, praising God's glorious presence that empowers them to answer the call and face the challenge of serving God faithfully, despite the heinous reality of systemic oppression at every level of society and even in the Christian church.

God calls the people of God to experience the glory of God's presence. We can do so as we remember the promise of God in the best of times and the worst of times, to bring freedom and justice through God's unfailing presence.

Holy One, give us eyes to see your glory and hearts and voices to praise you always. Amen.

Paul's directives for Christian living seem challenging at best and perhaps even impossible to fulfill. For Paul, love is the foundation of the Christian life, and all his admonitions emanate from a call for genuine love. But here he is not simply talking about the emotion expressed between individuals. He directs his instructions to the community with the hope that his entire list of strictures will build up the community by making clear the meaning of genuine love, the one essential of Christianity.

Paul's words speak directly to John Wesley's requirement of holy living for the people called Methodists. Wesley called on Methodists to demonstrate the love of God and neighbor by living a holy life both individually and in community as a testimony to their Christian identity. For the individual Christian, Wesley's "The Scripture Way of Salvation" begins with repentance and new birth and leads from justification through sanctification to Christian perfection. From the community, Wesley required social holiness that actively responded to the needs of the saints with peace and harmony within and beyond the community.

In this post-Christian era, the church, known more for its divisiveness than its love and so often remaining silent in the face of injustice, encounters a challenge. Paul's words remind us that we are called as Christians to be the people of God who show genuine love through holy living and who live in peace and harmony as the beloved community. Only God's presence and grace make living the Christian life possible. God's grace alone enables us to live holy lives, individually and corporately. May we live in the light of God's empowering presence.

Gracious God, empower us by your Spirit to be guided by love in all things. Grant us your presence and your grace so that we can become the beloved community. Amen.

The Challenge in the Call

Living peaceably with everyone is difficult in a violent world. Daily we hear news reports of death and destruction that result from human greed and oppressive structures. Even Christians find it hard to overcome the desire to repay evil for evil. And yet that is what God calls us to do. We are called to bless and not curse those who do us harm; to strive for peace, leaving retributive justice to God; to show love at all times and in all places. But ensuring that we allow love to rule in all situations presents a serious challenge.

Paul here connects a believer's love of God with service to neighbor. Living holy lives as Christians in the world demands that we hold fast to God if we intend to follow the path of love set by Christ. Living in harmony, even in the church, presents a challenge, as does showing hospitality to strangers, especially those who do not look like we do and whom we consider "other" because of difference in gender, race, class, sexuality, age, ability, or any other social definer. And yet that is God's call on our lives: to "live peaceably with all."

Living holy lives that demonstrate love requires that we acknowledge the *imago dei* (image of God) in each person and live actively in God's presence. By so doing we will be able to see and respond to their needs and seek justice for all. Paul's words offer a guide and, by the ever-present grace of God, we can follow it and live lives of genuine Christian love.

Christ our Savior, help us walk closely with you as we seek to follow your example and be people of love. Amen.

Jesus has been preparing his disciples for what is to come. He has met the challenges brought by the established leaders of the community, and he has continued to respond with love and compassion to the needs of the people. But his eyes are set on Jerusalem, the location of the ultimate challenge embedded in his call. He understands the absolute nature of his messianic identity, and he is ready to make the supreme sacrifice.

Knowing what is to come, Jesus wants to prepare his disciples. He tries to ensure that those he has called, those who have walked with him during the years of his earthly ministry, are also ready for the final act. But they fear facing the stark reality of his call and mission as Messiah. Peter, the self-selected spokesperson, rails against a message that he considers inappropriate for the Messiah.

Fear greatly deters the work of ministry. The call of Christ, to love as Christ loves, offers a great challenge, and we are sometimes afraid to step out into the unknown. Like Moses, we offer many excuses, or like Peter, we refuse to listen to the word that Christ speaks into our hearts. We often make excuses or protest our ability to do the work of God, to live fully a life of Christian love. Most often it is because of fear. We forget that those whom Christ calls he empowers.

God prepares us for a holy life, and God's presence supports us as we step out and live fully as Christians. We can face the challenge of Christian discipleship through the presence and grace of God.

Christ, you are our Savior and guide. Help us to follow your lead in the assurance that we have been empowered by your grace. Amen.

The Challenge in the Call   293

If we want to follow Christ, we must follow, obey, and approach life with a new way of thinking. When we answer the call to follow Christ, we start anew. Our new birth enables us to lay claim to a new will directed by Christ and a new purpose that leads to eternity with Christ. Jesus' call to radical discipleship individually, coupled with Paul's radical message of holy living for the beloved community, defines our call to the Christian life. It's the challenge Jesus extends to all who would follow him. Jesus' teaching has an eschatological focus, but we live in the present. Peter shifts his focus from the realm of heavenly thoughts to those of the world; he begins to think in an inappropriate way. As Jesus tells Peter: "You are setting your mind not on divine things but on human things." Peter, in his understanding of Messiah, cannot fathom anything other than stunning success.

Each of us faces the challenge of being Christian. Christ directs us to love God with our whole selves and to love our neighbors as completely as we love ourselves. Living a life that evidences such love is the epitome of a holy life: one that seeks justice for all, shows kindness and compassion to all, and walks in humility with God.

The Christian life depends on faith in Christ and a denial of self for the good of the community. It is a life in which thought and action based on love align and reflect the kingdom of God. We meet the challenge only by living in Christ's presence and reflecting Christ's light to the glory of God.

Glorious God, we stand in your presence. May we truly reflect your light in the world, through Jesus Christ our Savior. Amen.

The Challenge in the Call

Searching the Scriptures

SEPTEMBER 4–10, 2017 • MARK H. STEPHENSON

SCRIPTURE OVERVIEW: Exodus 12 provides instructions for keeping the Passover. Yahweh defends those who seek Yahweh's shelter. In the end, the people stand liberated from all false loyalties and allegiances, and vow allegiance to Yahweh alone. Psalm 149 sounds a strong note of realism. The rule of Yahweh binds Israel to an understanding that the social order must reflect the moral integrity of the world's ultimate King. The reading from Romans 13 marks a point of transition within Paul's letter. Paul here urges his readers to trust that faith in Christ makes a difference. Matthew 18 speaks to the importance of trustworthiness in the life of the believing community and provides measures for the restoration of confidence and for reconciliation.

QUESTIONS AND SUGGESTIONS FOR REFLECTION

- Read Exodus 12:1-14. In the Passover meal, no one is excluded from the table. Where in your life can you be more inclusive?

- Read Psalm 149. If you wrote a new song to celebrate and recall a "mighty act of God" in your life, what would the song be about?

- Read Romans 13:8-14. Reading these verses of Paul's letter to the Roman church, how would you define your neighbors? Are there neighbors, whether close by or far away, with whom you need a closer connection?

- Read Matthew 18:15-20. When have you spoken privately to a member of your faith community about an offense against you? What was the result?

Fourth-generation Methodist minister, Cape Town, South Africa

Passover brings ancient Jewish tradition to life. It reminds us of God's faithfulness and the endurance of a people. The Passover celebration serves as a reminder of the endurance of the Jewish people, who have survived and thrived several thousand years as an identifiable congregation of believers with the same core values and vision. Jewish festivals proclaim that God's faithfulness in the past carries into the present, giving us hope for the future.

Central to the Passover ritual is the sharing of a meal. The original meal included unleavened bread and a young lamb seasoned with desert plants ("bitter herbs") and roasted over an open fire. The Passover meal commemorates their ancestors' final meal as captives in Egypt.

Moses' deliverance began in a personal encounter with God. At the burning bush, Moses heard God declare, "I am the God who is and who will be active in whatever you are called to face" (AP). This encounter reveals God's pattern of working. God meets us where we are and pledges to accompany us wherever we go. As we worship, praise, and honor the Lord our God, believe in a God who is active in and through history, and remember God's deliverance, God frees us to flourish as God's people. All this comes at God's initiative.

The Hebrew people do not choose to be the people of God; God chooses them. (See Exodus 6:7.) Their ritual acts proclaim their faith that God will act soon to deliver them once more. This is the hope of a suffering people. God can still bring about a radical change in the world order.

The great reality undergirding all Hebrew faith is not the Jews' grasp of God but God's grasp of them.

This passage recounts God's passing over the blood-marked door frames of the Hebrew homes in a death-dealing mission. Every home that did not have the blood on its doorposts and lintel would lose its firstborn—people and animals.

Passover reminds the Jews of who they are as a people and where they have come from. They are a delivered people. One generation hands the message to the next. In this story, they prepare themselves for leave-taking. The ritual meal conveys the Hebrew people's preparation for travel and their faith in God's promises. Each aspect of the meal holds meaning, even the bitter herbs that remind diners of the Hebrews' suffering under the Egyptians. The fastened belt, the sandaled feet, and the staff in hand signify the haste with which the Hebrews celebrated the first Passover, ready to make their march to freedom. They eat unleavened bread, which reminds them of the quick escape from Egypt.

Through no merit of their own, the Hebrew people stand in a unique relationship with the living God. Their enduring presence reminds the world of who God is and what God has done. And so it is for us.

Christians recognize that the sacrament of Holy Communion echoes much of the sentiment reflected in the Passover. In 1 Corinthians 5:7, Paul calls Christ "our Passover lamb" (NIV). We feast in God's presence as we reflect on lives filled with grateful memories of past mercies. Like the Hebrews of old, we should be dressed and ready for the journey of spreading God's love throughout the land.

Holidays (Holy Days) are annual reminders of what God has done for us. How often do you reflect on this fact?

When we glimpse God's greatness and goodness as never before, we sing a new song. The psalmist calls us to catch sight of the awesome nature and sovereignty of God and sing a new song in word, faith, and deed. We can walk confidently into darkness because no matter what else we find there, we will find God.

The words of the new song still live. They challenge and stimulate us by calling into question many of our accepted values. Singing a new song is an act of faith that stands on the mighty acts and gracious promises of God. And God's people wield a two-edged sword. We are no longer powerless. The sword brings order and garners "glory."

Many of us coast through life, failing to sing a new song and reach our God-given potential. As disciples, we need the two-edged sword of spiritual discernment and instinctive recognition of divine authority. We Christians see these qualities in Jesus. My country, South Africa, the Rainbow nation, desperately needs that spirit today. We're squandering the peace that Nelson Mandela and so many others fought to establish. Now is our time to pursue the values we want for the world.

When we read the Psalms, we hear clear and strong voices of politics, economics, citizenship, prayer, and penitence. God has entered our world and whatever we face, we know that God is with us. We are "glad in [our] Maker." Isn't it time for us to sing a new song?

Praise the Lord! This is the victory of God's people.

Paul writes his letter to the Romans form Corinth. He clearly states the gospel that he preaches. To ease the Jewish-Gentile tensions, Paul desires that fellowship cooperation develop in the early church. How does this occur within a community of diverse believers? What has to happen that we view one another in a different light?

Believing, trusting, obeying, hoping, loving—these verbs direct a disciple's life. God is love. God longs to bless, not punish; to give, rather than take away. The divine nature is always to have mercy—to show hospitality not hostility and to fill our lives with good things.

God's love cleanses, renews, restores, and forgives. Even though we try our best to follow Jesus' commandments to love others—even our enemies—we are not always very good at it.

In the law of love, all means *all*. We have a responsibility to love our neighbors. This means seeing that others are fed, clothed, and housed. Paul reminds us that love is the only law we need. When we open our lives to God's grace, we catch a glimpse of what love is all about. If God sees something special in us, surely we can see it in others.

The Holy Spirit does not sing a song of revenge. The love that breaks into history in the person of Jesus Christ is full of mercy, forgiveness, and reconciliation. Jesus' death and resurrection reveal an ultimate love that bonds faith and life. Nothing now, in life or death, can ever separate us from the love of Christ. God is love.

God, help us share your unending love with others by tending to their spiritual and physical needs. Amen.

Jesus' call to love our neighbors sounds easy until we realize he is referring not only to those who live next door or nearby but also people everywhere. Suddenly the scale of the challenge and the enormity of our responsibility overwhelm us. The list is endless, for there is virtually no limit to human need within our world. We have grabbed greedily at the earth's resources with no thought for the future.

Paul insists that the secret to life is knowing how to respond with God's love, grace, and spirit. Paul appeals to Christ's love for us as the incentive for us to love others. This is the source of our inspiration in our duties toward one another.

Light shines in the darkness. Daylight comes, and Paul urges his listeners to stop doing things that belong to the dark. Living out the Christian life makes a difference, and the time to do it is the present: "It is now the moment for you to wake from sleep." Jesus becomes the essence of life. He teaches us to look properly at the ordinary things of life—something as natural as a flower in the field—and we will see God's hand behind it.

Life takes on a new direction when we choose to walk in the light. If we really believe that God holds the world in trust for us, we need to live in such a way that we lead through our actions: We "put on the Lord Jesus Christ."

O God, in love we take up our responsibility for our neighbors.
May we value all parts of your handiwork. Amen.

We can easily turn a blind eye to injustice; we believe an action is wrong but leave the problem to others to sort out. Much in life seems to suggest that evil has defeated good. Confronting others may well prove costly, but at times it is a necessary discipline.

Jesus urges us to take time to look at ourselves. He offers practical advice for us to address conflict in our Christian life: "If another member of the church sins against you, go and point out the fault when the two of you are alone." He outlines three more stages to deal with the problem if meeting one-on-one doesn't work: (2) Meet with one or two witnesses. (3) Meet with church leaders. (4) Walk away. Conflict resolution sometimes requires outside help. Grace permits us to ask God to speak according to our need, that God may direct our actions and words.

Open-mindedness doesn't mean that we must accept everything. When we have to deal with the realities of life, we may find ourselves amenable to reconsidering our opinions. Whatever the conflict, however dark life may seem, God has promised that light will ultimately break through. Faith reminds us that from the darkness of Calvary dawned the day of Resurrection—light that can never be extinguished.

We all discover this message for ourselves. Putting our faith into practice wherever we find ourselves is the test of commitment. The light of Christ shines through us. As the prophet Micah puts it, we are called to "do justice, . . . love kindness, . . . walk humbly with your God" (Mic. 6:8).

What might open up to you if you choose to go one way rather than another?

If we as Christians are to make any impact on society, any significant difference to the world we live in, then we need to work with those in our own fellowship and with those within and beyond the wider church to get there. All too often our relationships turn persons *away from* the church instead of drawing them *toward* it. Where do we go wrong?

Jesus teaches us to search for meaning, for truth, and for God. He urges us to seek openly and honestly and insists that we will find. We will discover life in abundance.

In knowing Christ we receive a heavenly foretaste of all that is to come. In this scripture passage, Jesus invites us to make that connection between heaven and earth. But it comes with a warning: Whatever we bind on earth will be bound in heaven and vice versa. What qualities do we want to bind to ourselves for all eternity? Love, joy, peace, kindness?

 Everything that Jesus introduces and represents he calls the kingdom of God. It's the place where God smiles on what happens. Here God does what is needed. If we cannot see signs of God's coming kingdom, perhaps we are looking in the wrong place or for the wrong things.

Kingdom signs mark Jesus' practice. He reminds his followers of his presence when they join together in his name. In God's kingdom people connect with one another and feel that they belong. God will not rest until God's will is done and God's kingdom is established, on earth as it is in heaven.

May we never lose the vision of what life can become or stop working for it.

The Ever-Present God

SEPTEMBER 11–17, 2017 • REGINA FRANKLIN-BASYE

SCRIPTURE OVERVIEW: Exodus 14 narrates the Exodus event in stylized liturgical statements. It tells of God's utter commitment to Israel and of Israel's fearful doubt. This is a narrative "toward faith." Psalm 114 is a buoyant, almost defiant celebration of the Exodus, in which all the enemies of Yahweh are put to embarrassing flight. It is recalled that Yahweh's sovereign power to liberate is decisive for the world, as it is for Israel. In Romans 14 Paul struggles with the issue of freedom within obedience and moves us beyond the letter of the law to its spirit. For Paul, the attitude of faith shapes human conduct. The parable of the unforgiving servant in Matthew reminds all would-be disciples that law must be tempered with mercy in their dealings with one another if they expect to receive mercy from God.

QUESTIONS AND SUGGESTIONS FOR REFLECTION

- Read Exodus 14:19-31. How can you tell when God is guiding you? When in your life have you wondered if God was still there? Reflect on those times.
- Read Psalm 114. "Judah became God's sanctuary, Israel his dominion." Substitute your name for Judah and Israel in this verse and pray the words several times. How does it feel to be called God's sanctuary and dominion?
- Read Romans 14:1-12. How do you observe a weekly sabbath? Are there businesses in your community that close for a sabbath? How does that practice affect you?
- Read Matthew 18:21-35. Whom do you want or need to forgive? Why and how might you avoid this issue? How will you pray about this?

Fellow in thanatology—the study of death, dying, and bereavement; a ministry focus on grief and loss

303

God's omnipotent presence is made known to the Israelites as "angel of God," and by a "pillar of cloud." God serves as a protector, going before the Israelites and later behind them. This divine presence "steps" between the army of Egypt and the Israelites.

God serves our lives in similar fashion. Because of God's omnipresence, we can depend on God to serve in multiple capacities throughout our lives. Sometimes God steps out in front, guiding and directing our paths. Other times God goes behind us, protecting us from seen and unseen dangers. God also walks beside us as our loving and faithful companion.

Like the Israelites we frequently witness God at work in our lives. When God goes before us, we feel confident and become more aware of divine presence. We become trustworthy and more dependent on God. When God moves behind us, we may feel abandoned, lonely, and afraid. Sadly, we lack confidence in the presence of the Almighty in our lives.

As the Israelites witnessed God's miraculous work, they feared God while believing in the Lord and also the Lord's servant Moses. They sang a song afterward praising God for God's mighty acts and for their newfound freedom.

I encourage you to sit quietly and reflect on a time when you sensed God's active engagement in your life. Then reflect on another time when you felt abandoned by God. Link these thoughts together as you develop a keen awareness of God carrying and sustaining you, even when you felt all alone.

Gracious God, I am aware of your presence, and I thank you for carrying me through difficult times, never leaving my side. Heighten my awareness of your presence as I realize you will stand with me and see me through. In the holy name of Jesus I pray. Amen.

My family and I were returning home from our daughter's volleyball game one evening. During our commute home, we found ourselves in the midst of a major traffic jam as an eighteen-wheeler had overturned on the freeway. The rescue of passengers, cleanup, and restoration of the highway became an incredible challenge for city employees. We were stuck in the midst of this metal congestion with nowhere to turn. Our experience was daunting, as we were getting hungry, irritable and tired as night fell upon us. After a long, three-hour experience, we finally inched up to our freedom and the ability to drive the normal speed limit.

We all began rejoicing in our freedom, thanking God we had made it though such a dreadful experience, which permitted us to appreciate what lay ahead. Because we had been trapped for such a long time, our future looked bright. We realized the value of the little things we usually take for granted.

God revels in God's people. With God as redeemer, the Israelites leave Egypt. They consciously decide not to turn back. They depart from a difficult land and experience. With God's help, they face their future with certainty. Israel is their new home and new land, and they become more appreciative of their future based on the challenges they have faced in the past.

When have you felt trapped during a difficult situation? How did you cope during your challenging experience? What emotions did you feel before, during, and after this trying time?

Thank you, Lord, for our freedom. Thank you for delivering us out of darkness into light. Thank you for delivering us from bondage into safety. Thank you for never leaving our side. Amen.

The Ever-Present God

God saved the Israelites from the advancing Egyptian army, and during their time in the wilderness they witness God's power at work in astonishing ways. As the Israelites begin to cross the Red Sea, the psalmist says that "the sea looked and fled." Then they are able to cross on dry land. The psalmist recounts that later God brings water from a rock that quenches their thirst. Those present watch in amazement as they witness these extraordinary acts of God.

This is a song of praise that recalls the miraculous ways that God delivered the Israelites from Egypt. Sea, mountains, hills—all give way to the Creator. The earth itself trembles. The created order changes before their eyes. This song of praise reflects God's power. Yahweh has acted on their behalf; nothing can intimidate them!

Today we witness God's miracles all around us: Babies are born; flowers bloom seasonally; days turn to night. God exhibits divine power and sovereignty daily. Even as we witness tragedies, we watch the omnipresent and miraculous works of God play out.

Meditate on the mighty works of God—within your family, your community, your workplace, or around the world. Be present and mindful of God's great miracles that still occur today.

Creator God, you have sustained us during challenging times, and yet, during your miraculous and saving works you continue blessing and protecting each of us. Help us always to be mindful and grateful for your sovereign power and saving grace. Amen.

The Jewish community had particular observances: the observance of sabbath and distinctive dietary restrictions. As these Jews become followers of the Way, they feel that Gentiles who came into the fold should follow these practices as well. The Jewish community insists that Gentiles observe and practice the same rituals and days of observances as they do. Criticism and judgment surface as worship patterns are not followed according to their beliefs. The differences in worship and food regulations apparently cause enough friction among believers for Paul to address these issues.

In the Christian community, we acknowledge sabbath by setting aside a special day to rest and abstain from work while worshiping God. Because we live in a melting pot of cultures and a wide variety of faith traditions, it behooves us to be open to the ideas and ways others express and observe their faith traditions. Paul notes that the well-being of the faith community itself is more important than these petty quarrels over special days and diet. He raises this question: "Why do you pass judgment on your brother or sister?"

Let us be open to the faith traditions, practices, and customs that others bring to the faith community. We need to be willing to invite someone into our worship settings and practices while remaining open if they are unwilling to engage as we do. As we open ourselves to differing understandings, we can unite on many levels.

Lord, help us to be open and accepting of the many ways and rituals others use to observe and worship you. Help us to grow more loving and more accepting of one another. Amen.

My reflections on parenting remind me of those times when my children failed to meet my expectations. Children's disobedience can wound the hearts of their parents. During their formative years and while they live with us, we continue our role of teaching and training in the art of forgiveness.

As a mother, I am naturally inclined to forgive my children. Being forgiving and offering a means of grace is to be expected. So what does this mean for Jesus and Peter? Peter has been traveling with Jesus for three years. He has witnessed healing, proclamation, forgiveness of sin. He has, in many respects, spent formative years being trained and taught by Jesus. And it appears that Peter's question: "Lord, if another member of the church sins against me, how often should I forgive?" is more preemptive than having a basis in reality. Peter seems to believe that at some point we stop forgiving.

Some of us believe that as well. Some of us know we need to forgive but find ourselves unable to let go of past hurts. They are too deep. So when Jesus responds, "Seventy-seven times"—a limitless number, we must reconsider our relationships with those who have hurt us.

As a parent, I recall times when my children, both of whom had been forgiven for earlier offenses, withheld forgiveness from one another. And Jesus' parable provides a key here. A debt is forgiven for an enormous amount, but that person is unwilling to forgive another of a small debt. For many people forgiveness is a hard practice. But should we not have mercy on others, just as we have received mercy ourselves? How often should we forgive? "As many as seven times?" No, Jesus replies; "not seven times, but . . . seventy-seven times." May God have mercy on us all.

Loving and faithful God, help us to forgive others as we grow in your love and grace. Amen.

With God as protector, the Israelites set out. Ahead of them as a "bodyguard" goes the angel of God, while the pillar of cloud moves with them, both in front and behind, giving light for continued travel. I cannot imagine experiencing nightfall while light emerges from the sky. This "pillar of cloud" appeared in such an organized fashion: "The cloud was there with the darkness, and it lit up the night; one did not come near the other all night." This divine manifestation is the work of God's miraculous power. The cloud brings light for the Israelites; they need clear vision while remaining separate from the Egyptians.

God intervenes in a direct way through Moses, who stretches out his hand over the sea. The water parts, and the Israelites walk across on dry land. The Egyptians pursue; and as their chariots get mired, even they come to the realization, "The Lord is fighting for [the Israelites} against Egypt." Their thoughts of turning back come to naught as the waters close and drown them. Not one of Pharaoh's army remains. The Israelites see the sobering reality of the Egyptians dead on the shore, which brings fear and belief.

I have experienced God's mighty acts in my life, acts that only later I acknowledge as God's hand at work. When we finally do realize that God has acted mightily in our lives, as we recognize God's miracles of "the right time" or "the right place," should we not stand back in awe and wonder at the way these God-circumstances have unfolded?

Reflect on areas of your life where events went dramatically in your favor and remember: this God acts to save—with an angel ahead and a pillar of cloud behind.

Almighty God, thank you for guiding our footsteps while providing for our needs. Thank you for watching over us and for the many ways in which you protect us daily. Amen.

The Ever-Present God

This passage reminds us that we should accept one another's differences and cultural practices relating to the ways we serve and honor God. Maintaining the integrity of the body of Christ carries more weight than "right" ways of doing or believing. It is God who issues the welcome to all. Paul encourages those within his community to speak ways of peace, along with words of affirmation and acceptance. Routinely taking this approach will help us experience a more loving and peaceful community and world.

Considering others beliefs and practices, particularly those that move us out of our sphere of comfort, may create feelings of anxiety in us. We usually want to hold to our familiar ways. However, our willingness to permit and engage in other ways of worshiping and honoring God allows us to affirm other approaches as valid.

As a hospital chaplain I witness a great variety of cultural beliefs while serving patients and family members. Respecting spiritual boundaries is an essential practice of my vocation. As I remain open to others, I discover endless possibilities that await a given visit. Creating opportunities to learn and understand the ways of another is critical in our melting-pot society.

Reflect on a time when you observed Christian religious practices that differed from your own. If you participated in the practice, what emotions surfaced? How did you resolve those emotions?

Creator God, I offer thanks and praise for those who are different from me. May I acknowledge the validity of their ways of honoring you. Amen.

Presence and Provision

SEPTEMBER 18–24, 2017 • HAKYOUNG CHO KIM

SCRIPTURE OVERVIEW: The reading from Exodus 16 concerns Israel's primary memory of food given in the wilderness, given where there are no visible sources of life, given in the face of restless protest, given wondrously and saving Israel from both hunger and despair. The verses from Psalm 105 recall the marvel of God's grace during the wilderness years and the people's joyful response. In the Philippians text Paul wrestles with the question of God's will with respect to his own leadership. Paul not only explains the meaning of his incarceration but goes beyond that to explain the meaning of his life: "Living is Christ and dying is gain." Matthew 20 reminds the reader that in the kingdom of heaven God's mercy is often surprising, even offensive. People are valued not because of their economic productivity but because God loves and engages them.

QUESTIONS AND SUGGESTIONS FOR REFLECTION
- Read Exodus 16:2-15. What experiences have strengthened your trust in God?
- Read Psalm 105:1-6, 37-45. Spend a moment recounting God's faithfulness to you in the past. Does recalling those times encourage your obedience to God today?
- Read Philippians 1:21-30. Paul acknowledges the importance of his physical presence to the Philippians. Whose physical presence makes a difference in your life?
- Read Matthew 20:1-16. What situations in your life make you question God's fairness? When have you been envious because of God's blessing of another?

Retired United Methodist elder, New England Conference; spiritual director, author, living near Boston, Massachusetts

This psalm-hymn praises God for steadfast faithfulness to God's people. Because it recounts some of the Exodus event and wilderness sojourn, we could also describe it as a history-psalm. The psalmist calls on God's chosen people to remember the mighty deeds of Yahweh in their salvation history.

The first six verses of introduction include the call to praise: "O give thanks to the Lord, call on his name, make known his deeds among the peoples. Sing to him, sing praises to him; tell of all his wonderful works."

The psalmist, in speaking to the "offspring of [God's] servant Abraham," calls on them to remember God's mighty acts of providential grace. The main purpose of the divine acts of salvation are these:

1) To make known God's wonderful deeds so that the circle of God's family will expand to all people.

2) To inspire the people's obedience: "That they might keep his statutes and observe his laws. (v. 45)

3) To glorify the name of God by singing hymns in praise of God's attributes of goodness, mercy, compassion, justice, and steadfast love.

4) To praise the God of salvation who acts for good in our lives and in the world.

Lifting voices in song remains a chief way that we praise God. Singing praises together unites minds and hearts, breath and voices—indeed the whole being—in praise.

Faithful God, we thank you for the story of your providential work. We praise you for the truth that you keep your promises to those who trust and obey. Amen.

Today's passage continues the recounting of God's faithfulness by reminding "future" generations of Israelites of the Exodus, the time of wilderness wandering, and the entry into the land of promise.

Moses and Aaron, God's servants, confronted the pharaoh of Egypt, asking that he free the Israelite people. Pharaoh agreed as the last of the ten plagues against the Egyptians came to fruition. Pharaoh and his people feared that even worse disasters would befall them so they were glad to see the backs of their former slaves. And the Israelites do not leave empty-handed.

These verses reveal a tender, compassionate God who protects and leads the Israelites in the wilderness, providing quail and manna from heaven in abundance and water from a rock.

On their wilderness journey the Israelites experience God's presence through cloud and fire. They find themselves sustained in the desert wandering through God's provision. Despite the difficult circumstances of wilderness life, God's presence and sustenance make even the desert a place where life springs forth: "He remembered his holy promise, and Abraham, his servant. So he brought his people out with joy, his chosen ones with singing." God remembers and leads the people through the wilderness, upholding them with steadfast love. The people are to obey the law not from a fear of punishment but out of gratitude and fidelity for what God has already done.

We too find ourselves sustained by God's presence and provision in times of wilderness wandering. We can easily stumble in our spiritual journey toward the land of promise unless we strive for radical trust and joyful obedience. Thanks be to God!

Covenant-keeping God, we thank you for remembering your servant Abraham and for leading us all to a land of promise. Thank you for your presence and provision. Amen.

The passage opens with the whole congregation's complaining against Moses and Aaron for the lack of food in the wilderness after deliverance from Egypt. But God knows that they actually voice complaints against God. Yahweh sends quail in the evening and "bread" in the morning. The people gather enough for each day's portion. It reminds us of the words "Give us this day our daily bread" in the Lord's Prayer.

To this day the manna remains a mystery. "What is it?" the people ask. Moses answers, "It is the bread that the LORD has given you to eat." By this the people are to acknowledge the Lord as God.

In this passage some form of the word *complain* appears seven times. It is one of a series where the whole "congregation" of Israel complained against human and divine leadership in the wilderness. (See Exodus 15:24; 17:1-7; Numbers 11:1; 14:1-4, 26-27; 16:11; 17:1-5.)

Why do the people complain after experiencing God's wonderful works in the Exodus event? Why do they doubt God's care and provision? We can list some root causes of this spiritual symptom we call complaining (grumbling, murmuring):

They forget God's wonderful works on their behalf.
They are not content with what is given them.
They do not trust God, the true Shepherd.

God desired the well-being of the Israelites, and God desires our well-being. The next time we find ourselves complaining habitually, let us search for the root causes of the problem. Then, we can take action(s) toward spiritual renewal and wholeness.

God, thank you for caring and providing for us just as you did for your complaining people in the desert. Amen.

From prison Paul expresses his Christian hope using these words: "For to me, living is Christ and dying is gain." These words come from a man who faces death by Roman executioners at any moment. Though he tends to lean toward living, dying is a very real possibility: "I am hard pressed between the two: my desire is to depart [from the flesh] and be with Christ, for that is far better; but to remain in the flesh [body] is more necessary for you." Paul views neither life nor death as failure. Both have their advantages. In death he will be with Christ and find fulfillment, but he acknowledges that for the Philippians, his remaining with them as a teacher is more beneficial. He gives expression to his confidence in Christ in order to encourage and foster confidence in the Philippians.

Paul no longer views the world through the earthly eyes of someone who aspires to worldly success and acclaim. Rather, his view is that of Christian hope, a "forever" home with the exalted Christ. This Christian hope changes three things for Paul because he no longer lives with the fear of death:

1. Paul's focus shifts from his wants to others' needs. Christ's love for Paul makes him love others more than self.

2. Paul's view of what matters in life changes. He wants his life to reflect well on the cause of Christ.

3. Paul's understanding of suffering as a privilege increases. In seeing life with a vision suffused with the Holy Spirit, he counts his suffering as blessing. He invites the Philippian Christians not only to believe in Christ but to suffer for him as well.

Paul comes to the end of his physical life having found something to live for and to die for—Jesus Christ.

> *Eternal God, thank you for Paul's confident faith in the Resurrection that inspires us to fruitful living by turning suffering into service. Amen.*

Paul writes to the Christians at Philippi to reassure them of his own well-being and to thank them for the gift they have sent to him. It appears that the congregation at Philippi experiences a minor bit of disunity—a matter Paul never names. To inspire their confidence, he exhorts them to "live your life in a manner worthy of the gospel of Christ." He puts forward a vigorous spiritual training program for discipleship:

- standing firm in one spirit;
- striving side by side with one mind for the faith of the gospel;
- not being intimidated by opponents;
- believing in Christ and suffering with Christ.

This constitutes Paul's call to faithful discipleship. Before our calling as disciples of Christ, we understood ourselves as forgiven sinners who have "escaped like a bird from the snare of the fowlers" (Ps. 124:7). Out of our thankful hearts for the justifying grace of the Spirit, we dedicate ourselves to live the new life in Christ. Dedicated Christians grow spiritually through the teaching and example of Jesus. And the Spirit of Christ in us continually sanctifies us through the spiritual disciplines. This process may sometimes involve harsh and painful trials in life; Paul has no greater desire than to suffer for Christ, and he sets them an example.

As disciples growing in the Spirit, we readily open our hands and hearts to the Lord in discipleship. We stand firm against domination and enslavement. We no longer love things and use people. We reach out to people in need with compassionate love. May we strive to "live [our lives] in a manner worthy of the gospel of Christ."

Righteous God, thank you for the story of Paul's example of faithful discipleship. We praise you for being the transforming God who woos us to radical trust and joyful obedience. Amen.

Jesus faces an audience generally trained in the Jewish doctrine of merit. The immediate context of the parable concerns Peter's question about what he and his fellow disciples will receive for following Jesus.

So Jesus tells a story. An owner of a vineyard needs extra workers for the full harvest before some of the grapes rot. He goes to the marketplace at different times of the day and asks, "Why are you standing here idle all day?" The owner picks up a crew at six in the morning at a fixed daily wage. And he adds workers at 9 AM, at noon, 3 PM, and again at 5 PM, an hour before quitting time.

At the end of the day, the manager hands out the wages. Those who started last receive the usual day's wage. Surprisingly, all the workers receive the same amount; but those who worked more hours are furious and complain about unfairness. Certainly those who worked fewer hours were grateful for a full day's wage for their families' sustenance.

In a sense we note two opposing groups: the owner and the laborers; those who labored all day and those who labored a short while. *Not fair!* These words come to our minds as we consider the owner who pays everyone the same, including the laborers who work all day.

The owner keeps his promise to pay in full, and he shows grace to those in need with his generosity. God is generous to all and divine grace is sufficient to meet everyone's needs.

The parable does not look at unfair labor relations with a worldview of scarcity and a value system of self-interest. Rather, it centers on God's economy of provision—an economy not based on merit but on grace.

Merciful God, we praise you that you are a gracious God who gives enough provision to meet everyone's needs. Amen.

Throughout the parable, the owner of the vineyard is the dominant figure. He instructs his manager to pay the workers, and he addresses the laborers who think they have been wronged. The owner replies to one of the complainers by saying, "Friend, I am doing you no wrong; did you not agree with me for the usual daily wage? Take what belongs to you and go; I choose to give to this last the same as I give to you. Am I not allowed to do what I choose with what belongs to me? Or are you envious because I am generous. So the last will be first, and the first will be last."

The owner does not take offense at the complainer. His words imply reproach, but the tone remains friendly. The owner does not argue; he does not justify himself. He merely ask questions that force the hearer to answer in the affirmative. Most of the workers experience the owner's generosity. The disgruntled employees remain totally blind to the owner's benevolence until the mask that veils their discontent is removed by the question, "Are you envious because I am generous?" In the kingdom of heaven equality is the rule. The work performed by the disciples, and for that matter by any one of Jesus' followers, is transcended by a reward equal for all, even though the work itself may vary.

God's gift is sheer grace. In the kingdom of God the principles of merit and ability may be set aside, so that the principle of grace triumphs. We are workers for the kingdom of God and being chosen to be kingdom workers entails joyous privilege.

Ever-present God, thank you for your gracious nature that ensures all a place in the kingdom. Amen.

It's time to order!

Upper Room Disciplines 2018

Regular edition: 978-0-8358-1624-3

Enlarged-print: 978-0-8358-1625-0

Mobi: 978-0-8358-1626-7

Epub: 978-0-8358-1627-4

bookstore.UpperRoom.org

or

800-972-0433

Did you know that you can enjoy

The Upper Room Disciplines

in multiple ways? Digital or print?

The Upper Room Disciplines is available in both regular and enlarged print, but are you aware that it is also available in digital format? Download a copy to your Kindle or choose an EPUB version for your e-reader. Whatever your preference, we have it for you today.

What is a standing order option?

This option allows you to automatically receive your copy of *The Upper Room Disciplines* each year as soon as it is available. Take the worry out of remembering to place your order.

Need to make changes to your account?

Call Customer Service at 800.972.0433 or e-mail us at

CustomerAssistance@upperroom.org.

Our staff is available to help you with any updates.

Fearlessly Faithful

SEPTEMBER 25–OCTOBER 1, 2017 • TERRY SHILLINGTON

SCRIPTURE OVERVIEW: The mercy of God is a theme that surfaces this week. In Exodus 17 Israel is not sure that God is faithful or reliable. By requesting water and voicing an urgent need, Israel appears to be testing God to discover God's power and inclination. Psalm 78 praises Yahweh for grace in liberating the people from Egyptian bondage. Yahweh's mercy sustained and supported them. Philippians 2 begins with a statement about the need for human kindness and compassion and then moves to the work of mercy that motivates human love—the incarnation of God in Jesus Christ. In the reading from Matthew, the mercy of God, which is extended to those who normally receive no mercy, illustrates not only the inclusive nature of God's grace but also how different the kingdom of heaven is from the kingdoms of this world.

QUESTIONS AND SUGGESTIONS FOR REFLECTION

- Read Exodus 17:1-7. When has your "speaking out" been met with negative response? Have you ever felt you were standing too "close to the cross"?
- Read Psalm 78:1-4, 12-16. Today, *listen for* God rather than *speak of* God.
- Read Philippians 2:1-13. When have you emptied yourself and become a servant?
- Read Matthew 21:23-32. How well do your actions match your words in terms of obedience to the commands of Christ?

A mostly retired minister within the United Church of Canada; social activist; husband, father, and grandfather

The year was 1988. My denomination (The United Church of Canada) had taken a difficult social justice position. Some had left the church in protest. Others had loudly complained—still others had celebrated the church's courage. As the church leadership met that fall in a regional meeting, rather somberly (perhaps feeling some self pity), the president of our conference offered a comment I have never forgotten. He said, "We are not used to standing this close to the cross."

Being a leader can be exciting. We may enjoy taking bold stands and being part of a progressive moment. Civil rights protesters must have found those heady days of the 1960s exciting too. We all lead in some way or other. We all find ourselves invited to take bold positions—on climate, race, peace, and a host of other issues.

But sometimes these stands and this "speaking out" can be hurtful. Moses, in our Exodus reading, discovers that his people do not appreciate his bold leadership. He has led them as God has instructed, but they snap at his heels in protest. What a painfully wrenching time for Moses!

We too need to be ready for those times when being a Christian is not easy. We may slide into thinking, *People will always appreciate my leadership. I should be thanked and respected.* If we have made significant sacrifices or gifts, we desire honor.

In those painful times, we remember that we too are called to stand "close to the cross." We are challenged to speak boldly, even if unappreciated. We are to stand for right and truth, even if untruth seems more fashionable. For such days we will need to remember the saints and prophets of the past. Their stories of courage and stubborn faithfulness can help us continue fearlessly in our own journey of faithful living.

Holy Spirit, give us courage to endure the hard times and love for those whose ways seem to be at odds with God's truth. Amen.

No one can fight like Christians." I heard this angry, frustrated lament from my mother when I was a teen. My parents' tiny rural church was closing (in the face of rural depopulation), and the members were disposing of the church furnishings. Neighbors were scrapping about who should receive what and what should happen to some of the items.

We have all known congregational disputes and conflicted situations. Often these situations do not involve grand theological issues. Frequently they revolve around smaller issues: music, the welcoming of newcomers, or idiosyncrasies of the pastor. Moses finds that he too has some cranky, short-tempered followers among the Israelites wandering in the Sinai desert.

In today's passage Moses finds his power amid these travails. While the story describes locating water for the people in the wilderness, we also hear Moses moving from lament to courage, from a "pity party" to bold action.

When we face grumpy, ungrateful followers and crabby Christians, we can easily grow cynical and cranky ourselves. But this passage offers a more healing approach. Just as Moses unpacks his laments before God, we too probably need to identify in prayer our own hurt, disappointment, and wounds. It can be healing simply to sit down with our pastor, with a safe friend or colleague, and name our own sorrows and wounds as we face difficult times. This enables us to set anger aside and seek a more healing, compassionate response.

God assures Moses, "I will be standing there in front of you." In the tough times, we too can trust in God's presence. Then, as Moses does, we can move ahead boldly to offer our gifts anew, trusting the Holy One will go with us, finishing what we start.

O God, help us to face our challenges, name them, rest awhile
in your presence, then return to serve you afresh. Amen.

For years, I used these words as part of baptism preparation with young couples. On one of the three evenings, I would invite them to name some of the special Christians in their lives, ones who had influenced them, and to tell what made them significant. At first they would sit and stare blankly, unable or too shy to name anyone. After I prompted them with a few stories, their own stories would emerge. They would thoroughly enjoy telling these stories of the special people of faith in their lives.

The psalmist takes an exuberant delight in the stories of the past—the marvelous activity of God, the special people in that past, the wonders and truths tucked away in history. The Israelites persistently and consistently retell the stories of God's wonders. This psalm invites us to do the same, to savor the faith stories of the past. We tell these tales because they nourish us. We take courage in these saints of the past when we have lost our own.

In many religious traditions, the parents commit at their child's baptism to telling him or her these faith stories. But we all need this refreshing of memory. We need to rediscover that we are all rich in such tales. Here are some questions that may call your stories to mind:

- Which biblical stories move you the most?
- Who of your previous ministers or church leaders helped to shape you?
- Which family members have taught you about faith?
- Which contemporary Christians inspire you?

We not only recall these stories; we look for opportunities to celebrate them with other Christians.

Thank you, God, for sending us many heroes of our faith who can challenge us to greater obedience to you. Amen.

Our age often seems bedeviled by huge global issues that defy simple answers. We have ongoing controversy over climate change and what we ought to do. We are faced with refugees from war-torn countries and our obligations to them. We debate war and military actions in distant lands—should we be there? My own land, Canada, suffers ongoing anguish over how to do right by our aboriginal peoples. These are all huge issues, marked by complexity and few simple answers.

Some, perhaps many, feel inclined to opt out of the confusion and anguish. It seems so much easier simply to do our work and play, raise our families, and ignore these political-social dilemmas.

A careful reading of today's passage from Matthew suggests that is exactly what the chief priests and elders do with Jesus. They ask under what authority he acts. Jesus turns the question back to them—what do they think? Because any answer they give would commit them to some action or stance, they opt for silence. "We do not know," they mumble finally.

If we retreat from the issues of our day, wring our hands, and declare we can do little, we have responded as the chief priests and religious leaders did so long ago. They opted to duck the question and stay on safe ground. But from the Gospels, we sense a call to respond. We can follow the news and become better informed. We can read up on issues or affiliate with organizations around particular concerns. Then we can respond in Christian action and witness out of an informed stance.

Christians are to respond faithfully, living out what they believe. We may experience stress and make mistakes, but silence ("we do not know") is not a faithful choice.

Holy God, give us wisdom and patience to be faithful amid our own confusion. Amen.

Fearlessly Faithful

A woman in my congregation named Carolyn keeps a low profile. She has never held high office in the congregation, never been a volunteer lay preacher, never chaired a committee, and does not make impressive speeches at congregational meetings. Lots of regular church attenders would not know her.

But any parent of children in the church knows who Carolyn is. She has served as superintendent of the church school for decades. She has loved each generation of children, known them by name, and in turn been loved by them. Now a gray-haired grandma, she has been a key person in the faith of so many children.

I am reminded of Carolyn's quiet but rich contribution to my congregation as I listen to Jesus' sharply worded parable of the two sons, one who says he will go and serve but does not. The other, with much less fanfare and promise, actually shows up and does the job. Jesus is maybe giving a dig at the Pharisees who cut a wide swath in the community as religious people but have not welcomed Jesus. Jesus looks for consistency between word and deed.

We all may feel some discomfort with this parable's challenges. How easy to sing the hymns with their glowing promises and commitments! As one who has preached countless sermons over the years, how easy to enjoy the praise of congregants! How easy to speak as if we were environmentalists or justice seekers or open and welcoming! How challenging to live the values of forgiveness and compassion! How difficult to be truly welcoming of the stranger, the refugee, and the person with special needs!

What areas of faithfulness are hard for us to live daily? Where do our words not quite match our actions? This parable calls us to confession and offers us new beginnings.

O challenging God, help us to meet you with honesty and humility. Amen.

I am honored to have a six-year-old grandson who imitates me in many things. No father participates in his life. I tend to be the family member who transports him to his activities, and I am frequently the one who cycles with him on weekends. He often wants to do the things I do—right down to personal quirks, whether layering cereal preferences or eating fresh raspberries with a toothpick.

I find this imitation both touching and sobering. I try to be mindful of the example I set. Clearly, we all need some role models, some healthy individuals who mark out for us what being a whole, healthy person truly is.

Paul writes that Christians are to place Jesus Christ in this place of honor. "Let the same mind be in you that was in Christ Jesus." Some commentators have said this is the earliest attempt to define who a Christian is. We are to have the mind and spirit of Jesus, the Christ. We are to grow into humility so that we care about the welfare of others more than our own.

Paul lays out a challenging path for our faithfulness. I do not believe that he wants us to become doormats, submissive and unassertive. But clearly he urges us to set aside personal ambitions, the need for prestige, and personal accolades. As the mind of Christ grows in us, we require less for ourselves; we will care more about the needs of others.

Wow! This may seem a steep hill to climb! I prefer to view it as the journey of faithfulness that may take a lifetime. Our world needs more humble Christian witness. As we seek such maturing in faith, we may learn from the Christians around us who carry this mark of faith.

Holy Spirit, may humility and genuine caring grow in me day by day so that I may care for all your children. Amen.

How easily we can forget our purpose once we get underway. How readily a meeting can be subverted and diverted by a side issue or question! How quickly in our relationships we forget our vows and commitments when faced with temptations!

Paul describes in glorious imagery Jesus' offering of himself in humble service. The reading closes with these words: "Every tongue should confess that Jesus Christ is Lord, to the glory of God the Father." I belong to a denomination (The United Church of Canada) that has a strong history in social action. Often we view any scripture passage as a call to justice.

However, this passage does not take us there. After describing Jesus' self-emptying, becoming a servant and entering into human form, and being raised into glory by God, a different ending surprises me. We do not rush out to save the world. Our first task comes in getting down on bended knee, offering praise and bearing witness. These verses remind us that our first Christian task is not to do justice or to be humble and gentle. Those aspects, while critical, are not our primary task. First we are called to join the choir. We are to stand, open mouthed in wonder and amazement. We sing in praise and live lives of praise and thanksgiving for the saving acts of God for us and for our neighbor.

Then acknowledging God's work in our lives, we work out our "own salvation with fear and trembling." We live out our response in the action of daily life. But first Paul challenges us to take our worship seriously. This is our first calling—to sing out in praise, to offer thanksgiving and prayer, to stand humbly as ones who need saving and transforming. Is this a piece of our faith life we need to deepen?

Calm us, amid the world's rush and hurry, O God, that we may be amazed at how you have reached out in love to each one of us. Amen.

Fearlessly Faithful

God's Grace in Life's Disorder

OCTOBER 2–8, 2017 • THOMAS EDWARD FRANK

SCRIPTURE OVERVIEW: The Decalogue in Exodus 20 need not be considered a litmus test of righteousness or religious purity but rather a declaration that lies near the heart of the covenant relationship between Yahweh and Israel. The Torah is the way the people say yes to God's saving initiatives. Psalm 19:1-6 links the gift of the Torah to other acts of divine creation. The balance of the psalm celebrates the strength and beauty of the Torah and moves the reader behind the Torah to its Giver, thereby proclaiming the gospel of the well-ordered life. In Philippians 3 Paul speaks of himself as leaning into the future in response to the manner in which Jesus Christ has invaded his own life. The parable in Matthew 21 presents a direct and bold affinity for living in accordance with the gospel, producing "fruits of the kingdom."

QUESTIONS AND SUGGESTIONS FOR REFLECTION

- Read Exodus 20:1-4, 7-9, 12-20. If you are unable to live out the Commandments, which ones would you remove from the list?
- Read Psalm 19. If you monitored your speech for a day, how would you describe the tone and content? What one gift would you petition God for?
- Read Philippians 3:4b-14. How is your church and its people a sign for those who need hope and new life?
- Read Matthew 21:33-46. Where in your church, among the members and in the various meetings and activities, have you seen evidence that folks "have forgotten who owns the vineyard"?

University professor and chair of the Department of History at Wake Forest University, Winston-Salem, North Carolina

Imagine the Israelites at Sinai. They have fled from Pharaoh, rushed headlong through a miraculously parted sea, and then traveled on into a barren desert wilderness. Suddenly, it dawns on them that they are in the middle of nowhere, following an eighty-year-old man who has promised them a land of milk and honey. But first they must stop at this mountain, Moses tells them, and hear what the Lord has to say.

When Moses had received his charge from the Lord to go to Pharaoh and say, "Let my people go," he had been at the foot of this same mountain—also called Horeb. (See Exodus 3.) Horeb means "wasteland" and that was an understatement! "We would rather go back to Egypt," cried the people, hungry, thirsty, and exhausted. (See Exodus 16:3.)

The Lord sent manna with the dew, but the people whined, "What is it?" (16:15). The Lord made water flow from a rock, but the people soon thirsted again (17:1-7). Now the Lord calls the people to the mountain—shrouded in darkness, thunder, and smoke—to hear a word.

The people tremble, for they cannot see the wasteland for what it is: a place of grace, where in their neediness they can learn to rely on God. In the fear and despair of their lives, can the Lord have a word for them?

Read Psalm 114. How has God spoken in your wilderness?

The people Israel stood skeptically before a rock at Meribah, waiting for Moses to produce some water in the wilderness. "What did you bring us out here for, to kill us with thirst?" they cried. But Moses struck the rock with his staff, and water flowed to quench the people's thirst. (See Exodus 17:1-7.)

Similarly, I stand before the rock of the Ten Commandments. Where is the water here? Is there life for me in these formidable "thou shalt nots?"

These are only ten of the hundreds of commandments and laws in the Torah (the first five books of the Bible). Christians do not pay attention to the others, though, such as what to do with an ox that gores someone. What is it about these ten that is so compelling?

Jesus repeated them to the rich young ruler as the basis on which the man could be saved. (See Matthew 19:16-22.) But Jesus went on to say that they were not enough, that the young man should sell all his possessions and give the money to the poor—then he would be perfected in God.

And perhaps that is the water from the rock. The Decalogue comprises ten words (*deca-logos*) of life, intended to keep my life centered, focused, and balanced in God. They remind me of what God has done for me. ("I brought you out of Egypt.") They relieve me of the young man's burden of constant work, achievement, and accumulation of possessions by letting me rest in the wondrous grace of God, the Creator of heaven and earth. ("Remember the sabbath.")

Jesus said, "Follow me," and the poor fishermen dropped their nets to come along. But hearing the same call, the rich young ruler turned away. Which one am I?

Read Psalm 1. Where do you find the waters of life?

God's Grace in Life's Disorder   331

Nowhere in scripture is the unity and order of God's creation more eloquently displayed than in Psalm 19. Nature and humanity exist in perfect harmony. For humanity's part, the law of the Lord provides a trustworthy order of life that is righteous, sure, clear, pure, true. Such a life tastes good, sweeter than honey.

As if to mirror that perfection of human order, nature itself proclaims the glory of God in the wonders of the heavens. The daily course of the sun across the sky signals God's faithfulness. Indeed, these are joyous rounds, the sun acting like a newlywed emerging from the wedding tent, an athlete exhilarated with the race.

Then the jarring language of warning, error, fault, and insolence strikes a sour note. Where does that come from? What is evil doing in this perfect universe?

I am thrown again into the continual human struggle for a life of integrity and justice. LORD, . . . *Why do you hide yourself in times of trouble?* wonders the psalmist (10:1) "The voice of the LORD shakes the wilderness . . . and strips the forest bare" (29:8-9). So I call out for God's help in a world quaking with chaos.

I cannot always expect to look at the heavens with Psalm 19 eyes. Shaken by the death of a parent, upset by the divorce of good friends, distressed by the faces of hunger and poverty, I cannot glibly mouth such words of orderliness and glory. My tongue is tied, and the Spirit must give me the words to speak. And what does the Spirit whisper to me to say? "O LORD, my rock and my redeemer."

In "the meditation of my heart," how am I learning to trust God, Creator of beauty, Redeemer of a troubled world?

Paul, an extremely righteous man under the law, observed all the commandments. His outrage with the people claiming that Messiah had come led him to persecute them.

But then something happened that turned all these achievements to rubbish. The sabbath "attendance pins" and the prescribed daily prayer routine came to seem outdated, useless.

It's risky, this throwing out everything from a past life. Every time I clean out my closet, I stall over the sweater Grandma gave me or my favorite old jeans.

What's wrong with keeping these things another year? I wonder. There is really nothing wrong with Paul's life; the world could benefit from more righteous people. Why does he turn away from his old life? Does he find it empty, unfulfilling?

No. This is simply my attempt to explain Paul's actions out of my own needs. Paul saw nothing wrong with his life. He just met Jesus, that's all. And after he meets Jesus, nothing is ever the same again. "The value of knowing Christ Jesus"—his voice soaring now—"surpasses everything."

Paul was not among the Twelve. He witnessed none of Jesus' miracles, heard none of his parables. He did not parade with him into Jerusalem, and he was not at the cross. He never sought Jesus at all. But Jesus found him.

I go to church, sing the hymns, give my offering, volunteer to teach. I know how to be a pretty good church member, but what I really want is for Jesus to find me too.

God of Messiah, hear my longing for Jesus to find me. Amen.

God's Grace in Life's Disorder

I often wonder if Paul's contemporaries doubted his sanity; or, at the least, wondered that he made up what he said had happened to him.

"You say you met this Jesus on the road that runs up to Damascus?" some may have inquired.

Others may have mocked him, "What did he look like? He was executed years ago."

But Paul is nothing if not tenacious. He will not let his experience or his vocation slip away. The resurrected Lord has spoken his name, that he knows for sure. And even if his skeptics doubt the experience, they cannot long question the fruit of Paul's calling.

Because of his call, Paul willingly suffers just as Jesus had. His fearlessness comes not out of naïveté but out of courage. He plans to witness to Christ's power to change lives even if it costs him his safety, his home, or his life.

Once he has heard the call, Paul can even forget the past, his guilt, his obsession with saving himself by practicing the law. Now he sees the prize, an all-surpassing life in Christ. And through his witness, people down through the centuries have been drawn to listen.

So Paul's life itself became a sign of what people who did not know Christ for themselves could hope for. Is my life, and my congregation's life, such a sign?

How is my life a witness to my calling in Jesus Christ?

Jesus' journey has at last brought him to Jerusalem. Daily he teaches in the Temple courtyard where disciples would gather around their various rabbis to hear the word of God interpreted, listen to stories, and debate. It soon becomes apparent that Jesus' stories have an edge to them. People gather around him, some hoping for a heated debate, some to hang him up in something heretical.

"Once upon a time, . . . " Jesus begins, and a story unfolds that, like a bad TV show, is laced with murder and mayhem, the tenants so obviously crooks, the landlord so obviously innocent that when Jesus asks his listeners what the owner should do, they are unanimous: Throw the bums out.

"Once upon a time," the prophet Nathan had said, "a rich man stole, slaughtered, and ate a poor man's favorite pet lamb." "Oh," cried King David, "that's awful! He should pay dearly for that." Nathan looked at the king—who had just taken Uriah's wife as his own and arranged for Uriah to die in battle and said, "You are the man." (See 2 Samuel 12.)

But Jesus tells his story in a more direct fashion. "You," he says to the scribes and Pharisees, "have forgotten who owns the vineyard."

I sometimes wonder if I am not a Pharisee. I find it hard not to think of my faith as a possession. I catch myself thinking of *my* church, *my* sanctuary, *my* pew, *my* beliefs.

What a relief to know that nobody owns God's creation or our faith in God's purposes. It all belongs to God alone and comes to us by God's grace. And that means I am free to follow Jesus, even to Jerusalem, even to a cross.

If I am only a tenant, a sojourner in God's creation, then how should I treat the earth and those who sojourn with me?

God's Grace in Life's Disorder   335

I suppose everybody has a favorite house. My childhood memories still gather in the spacious, rambling rooms of my aunt's home. My eye roams from the vastness of the wraparound porch, to the living room's high ceiling with its wooden beams, up a stately staircase to the chain of bedrooms linked around a huge central bath, to the mysterious stairs leading to a toy-filled attic, back down the stairs to the sunlit kitchen.

It is not only the spaces, of course. It is that I have always felt at home in this house, where there is always room for me. Jesus is the cornerstone, he tells his listeners, upon which a great house will be built. According to Peter, as we are filled with gifts and graces by the Spirit, we become living stones. Aligned with the cornerstone, Christ, we are built up into a spiritual house where God lives. (See 1 Peter 2:4-5.) We receive our calling to be stewards of the household.

Stewardship is not ownership; rather, it is finding the particular grace or gift God has given me and using it for the good of the household. (See 1 Peter 4:10.) When I discover how my gift fits in, I am truly at home in the house. (See Ephesians 4:11-16.)

At table with his disciples for a last supper, Jesus washed their feet, blessed and broke bread, and served them a cup of wine. Then he spoke to them of God's house and its many rooms. You will have a place there, he says. (See John 14:2.)

As I grow in Christian discipleship, I am gradually finding my place in the household. I am learning how God wants me to use my gift. But the best part is that there is room for me here because Jesus is the host.

"How lovely is your dwelling place, O God." Amen.

Supplicate, Sing, and See

OCTOBER 9–15, 2017 • WEN-LING LAI

SCRIPTURE OVERVIEW: The narrative in Exodus 32:1-14 reflects on the blindness of the people, but the focus is also placed on Yahweh's intense anger and on Moses' intervention. Yahweh's mercy prevails, and Moses is revealed as the quintessential mediator. Psalm 106 recalls the folly of the people in making the golden calf. The sinfulness of the Israelites is laid to their forgetfulness. The inability and unwillingness of the people of God to remember is a damning sin that calls for a tough response. The Philippians text stresses the need for faithfulness to the gospel. Matthew's version of the parable of the wedding banquet offers a negative example of faithfulness in the form of a guest who comes to the wedding without the proper attire.

QUESTIONS AND SUGGESTIONS FOR REFLECTION

- Read Exodus 32:1-14. How do you demonstrate allegiance to or dependence on God's faithfulness in your life? What "golden calf" diverts your attention?
- Read Psalm 106:1-6, 19-23. Reflect on those times when you recalled the past, lamented, and cried for mercy.
- Read Philippians 4:1-9. Conflict creates discord. How do you handle conflict in your spiritual journey? in your church?
- Read Matthew 22:1-14. God continually invites us to divine encounters—with God directly and with others. How seriously do you take God's invitations?

A certified candidate for elder in the United Methodist Church; local pastor witnessing God's love in action via Walnut Valley United Methodist Church in New Jersey. Made in Taiwan; she loves God, her husband, Dave, and her kids Anna and Geoffrey

The Israelites who follow Moses out of Egypt have experienced some significant traumas! During the liberation process from the oppressive Pharaoh, they have crossed the parted Red Sea and witnessed the massive drowning of their pursuers. They also have learned to trust the Lord for their survival in the wilderness. They have learned to rely on God both for food and for water. And Moses, as their leader, helps bring them to this trust through his own obedience to God's commands. No wonder the group's anxiety escalates when Moses takes a long time before coming down from Mount Sinai.

We can also understand why the traumatized Israelites would go to the next in command with their request. They ask Aaron to make gods for them as a coping mechanism to soothe their anxiety when they become apprehensive and impatient while wandering in a strange place. The fretful people willingly give up their precious gold earrings toward the making of an idol. They willingly sacrifice relationship with the one true God for a golden idol. Moses has left them too long.

Tough times and tribulations that we have experienced in the past or face now can make it more difficult or quite impossible to stay close to our Maker. God may seem absent from our midst. As disciples of Jesus, we must willingly acknowledge how our untended wounds may impact our relationships with the Divine and with each other. Using temporary or unhealthy practices to substitute the authentic relationship with God will only delay our reconciliation with Yahweh.

Ultimate Healer, help us face and repair our individual and collective wounds from life's traumas so we may live joyfully as your faithful creation. Amen.

What does God's monologue to Moses in today's scripture remind you of? Does it sound like the prologue of a judge who is about to sentence a group of lawbreakers? Or does it sound more like a rant of a parent who needs to discipline unruly children?

The Lord expresses anger at the Israelites' disobedience and disrespect. As would many parents, the violated One wants to teach and hold the newly freed and undisciplined people accountable for their behavior of creating and settling for substitute gods to ease their anxiety. In fact, the sanctions that God is ready to distribute include renunciation ("*Your* people, whom you brought up out of the land of Egypt") and rejection ("Let me alone, so that my wrath may burn hot against them and I may consume them") as serious consequences of their actions. We can only wonder how God responds to our undisciplined behavior as we purport to be followers of the Christ. How close does God come to rejecting us altogether, saying, "I've had it with you!"

Ironically, God not only discusses the divine plans with Moses but also wants to reward him with a favor ("of you I will make a great nation"). I remain unconvinced that God behaves like earthly parents and wonder if such anthropomorphic presentation of the Divine helps drive home the point of what can happen when people turn away from God.

What has made you turn aside from God's ways? What false gods have you created to meet your own needs while ignoring God's provision?

Loving God, who always provides, thank you for loving us even when we disobey or distance ourselves from you. Help us follow the way that you have sanctified in blessing and caring for us. Amen.

In the four verses from Exodus 32, Moses builds a convincing case that averts God's wrath against the Israelites. By mentioning God's powerful involvement and mighty intervention in bringing the people out of Egypt, Moses—the great advocate of the disobedient people—skillfully reframes the situation and the judgment of the Divine. In addition, Moses intentionally redirects the focus and energy of the Powerful One to God's original promises to multiply descendants of Abraham, Isaac, and Israel.

I never question the fulfillment of God's promises because the experience of divine presence, provision, and protection demonstrates unmerited amazing grace. When and how often have other people's supplications on our behalf changed our situation or direction? As Moses enthusiastically petitions for "his" people, how have you heard his rejoicing in what God's powerful and mighty hand delivers? When Moses calmly and gently reminds the Lord of past divine promises, Moses also provides a model for our supplication with thanksgiving while making our requests known to God. Given God's response to the people's disobedience helps us bear in mind that God's mercy and wrath are great. Moses' intervention helps temper God's judgment on the people and turn it toward mercy.

Who has intervened for you? What worries do you have today that you can turn over in prayer and supplication with thanksgiving to the Lord who will provide? When and where have you witnessed God's awesome intervention in your life, which has readied you to claim the grace God offers?

 Lord, who is present, thank you for your continuous presence and participation in my life! Today, I lift up _____ for your intervention as you know that person's needs. Thank you for providing and protecting this person in ways that only you can perceive. In Jesus' name I pray. Amen.

How does your body respond when you recite today's psalm aloud with sincerity and gusto? You've not read it yet? Try it now before you continue reading the rest of this meditation.

My heart beats differently when I verbally thank others, especially God! When I loudly proclaim, "Praise the LORD!" from my heart and the top of my lungs, I cannot help but smile and draw in extra oxygen as I remember the Maker's love and grace. Sometimes as I thank God, tears well up as I recall the times when I have really messed up and do not deserve anyone's forgiveness and care—especially God's. Yet I still receive grace.

Often, I experience peace beyond all understanding and sleep more deeply when I take time to confess or tell Yahweh about how I have messed up or distanced myself from God and others. Somehow, my heart and mind gain strength to face and resist the world's temptations when I praise God and confess my sins. The psalmist confesses both the sin of his current community and that of the ancestors. He alludes to the events in this week's Exodus text, and he states the reason for the Israelites' disobedience in verse 7: "Our ancestors, . . . did not remember the abundance of [God's] steadfast love."

In order to praise God, we must remember God's loving provision. And as Paul notes, we continue to practice whatever is true, honorable, just, pure, pleasing, and commendable. "Happy are those who observe justice, who do righteousness at all times." At *all* times—that's a big request.

For what would you like to thank God today? What will you confess as an act of emptying yourself to make room for God's presence and participation in your life?

Lord, who is peace, help us stay close to you and follow your will and way by confession, prayer, and supplication with thanksgiving. Amen.

The psalmist mentions several major offenses that the Israel-ites at the base of Mount Sinai commit. Then he dramatically sings about how Moses stands in the breach to change God's mind about destroying the Israelites. Today's psalm verses capture the essence of the ancestors' sins at Horeb while the Exodus passage fills in the details of how they wronged God in an effort to ease their own anxiety. The people make a calf of gold to worship, thereby breaking the first two commandments related to loving God wholly and making no graven images.

How do you perceive the "lessons" sung or told in today's scriptures? I do not believe that the songs and stories of the Bible exist to scare people into avoiding sin. I believe that the retelling of people's experiences with God reminds us of God's response to human iniquity: God's love and grace.

Intrinsic value resides in the telling, hearing, and processing of others' and our own experiences. Storytelling about interactions with God can provide comfort and counsel in the midst of tribulation. When stories are told, songs then follow to help us further remember God's provision through the rhythms and intonations that synchronize with our mind, body, and spirit.

How does your life keep rhythm with the beat of God's commands? What stories about God's presence and participation have you been telling? How can you synchronize your heart, actions, and soul with the beat and words of the Divine?

Lord, who listens and sings to us always, we thank you for never giving up on us! Help us learn the songs and stories that you compose with our lives. Amen.

How would you respond if I publicly announce that you need to be of the same mind in the Lord with someone with whom you are in conflict? I always wonder about the fine points the Bible leaves out. I imagine the details of the conflict between Euodia and Syntyche to be too famous, too juicy, or too unworthy to bring before the live studio audience in Philippi. Perhaps the disagreement between the two is so well known that it bears no repeating!

Lack of authentic mindfulness can foster lack of unity, which can lead to unfaithfulness in community. Paul first admonishes the Philippians to "stand firm in the Lord." He then stresses the need for unity. Regardless of the reason for the conflict, Paul encourages the two women to "be of the same mind in the Lord." He urges others in the community to come alongside the women and support them in this matter.

Paul goes on to urge the readers to rejoice in the Lord always, to let gentleness be known to everyone and not to worry but in everything let their requests be made known to God. Is he also addressing the two women while reminding himself about how to live and function in a community or as a disciple of Jesus? Paul lists the qualities of true community and suggests that the Philippians make those their focus as they come together mindfully. Then he closes with this admonition: "Keep on doing the things that you have learned and received and heard and seen in me." He sets himself forth as an example.

What conflicts in your community need people, including you, to come together to resolve or reconcile in order for the ministry or mission to produce fruit? Whose example do you choose to follow?

Patient God, who loves and teaches us always, thank you for promoting much-needed reconciliation and healing. May we seek you always and everywhere. Amen.

What exactly does Jesus mean when the king hosting his son's wedding banquet says, "Many are called, but few are chosen"?

I have struggled with this parable because the king's violent tendency and angry actions significantly conflict with my understanding of God's nature. The God I know reflects both patience and gentleness and does not choose to give love and grace to certain people over others. Therefore, I believe this parable conveys a picture of a merciful God who relentlessly pursues our presence and participation in the grand plan to love.

Whether we refuse or promptly respond to God's invitation to discipleship, God does not love us any less or more. But God may call upon others who are willing and able to show love and care, while waiting for us to answer perhaps another call or a new opportunity for participation in kingdom life.

 We do not passively wait for Yahweh to choose or invite us; instead, God patiently awaits our response to the invitation. Some commentators deem "the wedding robe" to represent a new way of life we accept or begin when we accept the invitation to discipleship. The difficulty comes in accepting but doing nothing. There is no authentic Christian faith without living a new life. Failure to do so will lead us ultimately to the pain of weeping and gnashing of teeth.

What new life are you ready to live in order to further God's kingdom on earth? What will you need to choose or avoid in order to fulfill this invitation to the wedding feast?

God, who knows and still loves, help us tenaciously seek, courageously sing, and clearly see your invitation to new life. Amen.

Show Me Your Ways

OCTOBER 16–22, 2017 • ARTHUR MCCLANAHAN

SCRIPTURE OVERVIEW: In Exodus 33 Moses successfully argues that without Yahweh's merciful presence Israel is no nation and that Yahweh's and Moses' efforts have come to naught. Psalm 99 mentions Yahweh's royal rule, which brings to mind the human agents of that rule: Moses, Aaron, and Samuel. Each of these leaders facilitated Yahweh's conversation with the people and Yahweh's rule over them. The opening lines from First Thessalonians raise a question about the church's understanding of evangelism. Paul and his coworkers experience a change in themselves because of the Thessalonians, who become a living proclamation of the gospel by virtue of their ready acceptance of it. In the Gospel reading, Jesus answers a question with a question and confuses his "audience" both then and today.

QUESTIONS AND SUGGESTIONS FOR REFLECTION

- Read Exodus 33:12-23. When have you most longed for a glimpse of God's glory? How did God give you the assurance you needed?

- Read Psalm 99. Where in your life is forgiveness needed to restore a loving relationship? How have you experienced "a forgiving God"?

- Read 1 Thessalonians 1:1-10. As your Christian faith has developed, how have you seen it move "from head to heart to hands"?

- Read Matthew 22:15-22. How do you give to God "the things that are God's"? What are some of those things Jesus wants you to give?

Ordained United Methodist elder; Director of Communications, Iowa Annual Conference. Author of *Be Filled: Sermons on the Beatitudes*

It's frustrating when you recognize someone but can't call the name. It's on the tip of your tongue, but it's not coming. Even finger snapping doesn't bring the name to consciousness, as if hand movement magically generates recall.

My friend Bill has the uncanny ability to recall instantly the name of everyone he's ever met! Ten years or ten seconds ago, he can name the person in his sight line, when they last met, what they were last doing, a bit about their personal story, and something about their family.

Moses and the Israelites have known God. God never abandoned them in the wilderness. God provided for them—they had "no shortage" (Exod. 16:18). God guided their journey and kept them safe. They need no jogging of the memory to remember who God is.

But then at the foot of Mount Sinai, the Israelites, in their anxiety about Moses' absence on the mountain, choose to create a different god—a god of gold. Moses averts God's anger toward the people, and in the verses prior to these, God tells them to journey on to the Land of Promise, "but I will not go up among you" (Exod. 33:3).

We pick up that conversation in today's verses. Moses feels compelled to request more from God. In a simple, direct exchange, Moses asks, "Show me your ways, so that I may know you." I'm pretty certain that God's reaction must have been, "Really? What more do I need to do?" Yet, without God's presence, the Israelites are no people. Their distinctiveness as a people is known by God's presence. Moses once again advocates for the people, and God concedes, "My presence will go with you."

What about your knowing God and God's presence makes your living distinctive?

Loving God, may we come to know you more and more each day. Amen.

I like my hammock. With it hanging between two pine trees, I can climb on, wait for the gentle swaying to stop, and gaze out on the lake that reflects the blue of the sky and the green of the pine trees that ring the shoreline.

There's not much better than to settle in and rest. Peaceful, quiet rest. Rejuvenating, still rest. What a gift those moments are! The buzz and breakneck pace of most days fades away. The task lists are forgotten. The numerous obligations vanish. Rest. Renewing rest. Ahhh—the way life should be!

The conversation between God and Moses continues. God assures his called one yet again that he and the people of God need not be anxious because God will continue to accompany them—guiding, protecting, providing. "My presence will go with you."

And likewise important is God's second promise: "I will give you rest." God knows that the generations-long trek in the wilderness will be arduous. Daily living will be far from easy, and the wilderness living will stretch on for years and decades. Even so, God's faithful assurance is strongly gentle, "I will give you rest."

Many of us hear this blessing of God echoed in Jesus' extraordinary invitation, "Come to me, all you that are weary and are carrying heavy burdens, and I will give you rest" (Matt. 11:28). Or, to put it another way, when daily life turns into a struggle, and we feel like some ancient beast of burden, Jesus will be an oasis of restful peace.

When living seems too much to manage, circumstances too difficult to cope with, the future too gloomy to consider—call time out. Stop and discover the nurturing, renewing gift of the Holy One . . . rest.

God, in the midst of life's busyness, grant us the sacred space of *blessed rest. Renew us. Nurture us. Calm us. Amen.*

To have an identity is to be unique, to be distinguished, to have connection with others, to have history, to belong. In late 2014 a worldwide gathering focused on the plight of global migration. The circumstances of consensual journey and forced displacement detailed the ever-shifting movement of humankind. Perhaps the most disturbing revelation focused on war refugees. They flee their homes and homelands in search of safety, which is often short-lived. As they make their way to new places, many become victims of the excruciating dangers of their perilous journeys or of disingenuous promises of freedom and security extended by the unscrupulous.

Many who do escape armed conflict find themselves in a doubly disturbing predicament. They are no longer in their place of origin, with known ways and language. And then, to compound that misery, they frequently discover that their home areas no longer exist and, in some cases, even their country vanishes.

Simply put, they have no identity. No place to call home. They hardly know themselves any more.

The Exodus journey was like that, in a way . . . and yet very different. The people of that pilgrimage have a tangible sense of God's presence with them. They are not abandoned. Moses exclaims to his Creator, "We shall be distinct, I and your people, from every people on the face of the earth." Moses lays claim to a unique identity that finds expression in the mutual relationship of God to God's people and they to their God.

Quite a number of years ago a claim was boldly, publicly declared, "I am somebody!" That's true—uniquely and individually. We are all somebody, and our lives matter, most especially in relationship to the Creator God.

Who are we, O Lord? We are your people. We are somebody! Our lives matter. For this we most humbly thank you. Amen.

"Love means never having to say you're sorry" according to Erich Segal's novel (*Love Story*), written nearly fifty years ago. That philosophy deems responsibility for hurt feelings unnecessary. Regret becomes irrelevant. Remorse simply doesn't exist.

If Segal's philosophy had been prevalent in the early 1990s, then Nelson Mandela's release from Robben Island prison on February 11, 1990, would have been just another day's news item. South Africa's president F. W. deKlerk's promise would have merited little notice. But it was something much more than that! It was the beginning of righting a twenty-seven-year-long wrong, the first small step toward the Truth and Reconciliation Commission with its restorative justice and redress of abuse by way of rehabilitation.

Thankfully, our God is one who hears the cries of the needy. Psalm 99 names three of Israel's intercessors: Moses, Aaron, Samuel. "They cried to the LORD, and he answered them." The psalmist, in recounting the history with a covenant God, touches on the Exodus experience in his reference to "the pillar of cloud" and "the statutes." This sovereign God is "a forgiving God."

We pray, "Forgive us our debts, as we also have forgiven our debtors" (Matt. 6:12) in the prayer of our Lord. The woman who anoints Jesus' feet with the ointment from the alabaster jar was forgiven many times and because of that forgiveness she can show "great love" (Luke 7:47). Perhaps that's the core truth of relationship: When we can say that we're sorry then we can be forgiven. When we can be forgiven, we can forgive. When we can forgive, we can experience restored relationships. Restored relationships foster love, which brings life to God's community!

Forgiving God, may we willingly say we're sorry for the hurts and wrongs we've done. Help us to forgive others who've done so to us. In that way we can truly love one another. Amen.

A small brown rock sits on my desk amid other sentimental stuff—wind-up clacking teeth, a challenge coin from a police department I served as chaplain, a tiny carved wooden elephant from Nigeria. The unassuming rock has a word etched on one side—*gozo,* a Spanish word translated as "joy." The rock reminds me of a lesson learned in a caring, multiethnic community. *Joy.*

"You received the word with joy." Paul, Silvanus, and Timothy commend that first-century community for the way they've received the message of the gospel. They've imitated the ways of Paul and his companions—and, even more importantly, they've become imitators of Jesus Christ.

Thessalonica, the capital city of the Macedonian region, boasted a city of more than two hundred thousand people—Greeks, Romans, and Jews. It was a regional hub because of its hot springs. As a naval station, prominently situated along a military highway, it was a wealthy city, a center of commerce, but one known for cult worship and licentious behavior.

The Thessalonians receive the word with joy and not only imitate Paul and his companions but turn "to serve a living and true God." They move their faith from head to heart to hands and become missionaries themselves. Paul states, "You became an example to all the believers in Macedonia and in Achaia." The rapid growth of the Thessalonian church and its commitment leads to the persecution of the emerging religious community.

Even so, the Thessalonians "received the word with joy." Perhaps it's precisely when times are most difficult that we can discover or rediscover our solid foundation in joy. That little brown rock on my desk reminds me of this every day!

> *Holy One, bless our lives with joy. Lead us once again to an awareness that you are always with us—and in your presence we discover everlasting joy. Amen.*

Playing favorites isn't fair! While nepotism isn't illegal, the practice of giving family and friends special opportunity and privilege can have demoralizing effects on others. Morale crashes. Mistrust builds. And those who don't get a chance walk away frustrated.

Title IX of the Education Amendments Act of 1972 ensured that boys and girls would have equal opportunity in sports. One aspect of the 1964 Civil Rights Act was the creation of the US Equal Employment Opportunity Commission. The notion of the "glass ceiling" and equal pay for equal work remains a topic of debate in political campaigns. This matter of impartiality comes up in conversation in today's scripture.

The Pharisees set out to trap Jesus with his own words as he challenges the order they so zealously uphold and the tradition for which they demand respect. Not being courageous enough to engage him directly, they send some of their followers to challenge the one recognized by the people as the One. Instead of asking a religious question, they disguise their antagonism in the veil of secular political cover—taxes.

As so often happens in public forums, they preface their question with disingenuous speech. If Jesus says people aren't obligated to pay taxes then Herod will engage Jesus, and the Pharisees will be off the hook. Yet, ironically, in their question's preamble the Pharisees' disciples speak an essential truth about Jesus: "You do not regard people with partiality."

Jesus' invitation is universal: "Come to me, all you" (Matt. 11:28). When Jesus plays favorites, his favorite is *everyone*! ❧

Thank you, O Lord, for including me in your eternal community. Thank you for inviting all, for welcoming all to you. Amen.

Sometimes the unbelievable complexity of life brings amazement. Shorthand and lingo get batted around, effectively excluding anyone who hasn't been part of the conversation from the beginning. Sometimes people use big words for the sake of using big words.

On the other hand, at times "conversation" is so starkly simple that it confuses the folks who prefer a more complicated vocabulary. That's precisely what happens in the encounter between Jesus and the disciples of the Pharisees who at long last believe they will trap Jesus in a chargeable offense.

The Pharisees' disciples pose an "earnest" question, having opened with flattery: "We know that you are sincere, and teach the way of God in accordance with truth." Then comes their zinger: "Is it lawful to pay taxes to the emperor, or not?" No way Jesus can answer this and remain in favor with the crowd *and* with the emperor. So Jesus does not answer. Jesus turns the tables on them and asks for a coin. He then becomes the questioner: "Whose head is this, and whose title?" A coin with the image of Caesar on it belongs to Caesar. A human being stamped with the image of God belongs to God. People can choose. Rather than falling into their trap, Jesus simply tells them to give "to God the things that are God's." When his questioners hear this, they are "amazed" and leave.

That's it. It's basic. Give God what rightly belongs to God. A few moments of your day. A few of your thoughts. Some observation of what's around you. Some listening for sacred sounds, perhaps even filtered through the noise of the world—your entire being.

Simplify it. Silence it. That's it! You'll be amazed.

What's amazing, O God, is that you show us who you are. We experience you in our very being! Amen.

Redeem the Time

OCTOBER 23–29, 2017 • PAT HANDLSON

SCRIPTURE OVERVIEW: Deuteronomy 34 narrates Moses' death and Joshua's succession, both the end of Moses' life and the continuation of his influence. Psalm 90 is ascribed to Moses, and the tone suits the setting portrayed in Deuteronomy 34. In First Thessalonians Paul continues his recollection of the relationship between himself and the Thessalonians. Paul and his coworkers acted out their love of neighbor, a love that is possible only because of their prior love of God. The Gospel places Jesus in a setting of controversy with the religious leaders of the day. The exchange about the greatest commandment demonstrates that the religious authorities in fact observe none of the commandments because of their inability to understand properly what Jesus calls the "first" and "second" commandments.

QUESTIONS AND SUGGESTIONS FOR REFLECTION

* Read Deuteronomy 34:1-12. How is God speaking to you about your life? What endings seem imminent? What new beginning is God forming you for?
* Read Psalm 90:1-6, 13-17. Notice all the references to time. How do you experience time when you perceive God's work in your life? How do you measure time when God seems absent?
* Read 1 Thessalonians 2:1-8. What relationship is God using to form you spiritually? Who are you tenderly sharing the gospel and yourself with so that God is using you in someone else's life?
* Read Matthew 22:34-46. The writer states, "It is impossible to love God without also loving those created in God's image." What are the implications of this statement on your life? the life of your church?

Pastor, Cookeville First Presbyterian Church, Cookeville, Tennessee

My Bible ascribes Psalm 90 to Moses. Perhaps the servant of the Lord wrote these words in anticipation of his death in order to ease the suffering of those he would leave without his leadership and guidance. Today the words of this psalm continue to comfort those who have lost a loved one.

Some people live in one house all their lives; others may move many times. Our common reality is that none of us really lives anywhere but in the Lord. For a people wandering in the wilderness for forty years, this is good news indeed. God provides a home and *is* their home. Before the mountains were formed, before the earth took shape, God already was and will ever be.

When we consider the scope of the universe and the idea of eternity, we face another reality. We are small and our time is short. Like grass that comes and goes, our lives are over quickly. The psalmist challenges us to make the most of whatever time we have. He petitions God for some kind of balance between joys and sorrows. That challenge lies before us in the present as well. All our technology has made little difference in the overall life span of a healthy human being. We still have a limited amount of time to make an impact on our world. Finally, the psalmist asks that God guide our hands, so that the impact we do make will be pleasing and beneficial to God and the world.

We find ourselves caught between the two "turns," one in verse 3 and one in verse 13. In verse 3, God speaks, bidding humans to turn back to dust. In verse 13, mortals implore God to turn and have compassion. The brevity of our life as humans on this earth and our yearning for God's help while we are here frame our being.

Loving God, grant us wisdom and courage to make the most of every day of life we're given. Amen.

Surely Moses knows in his heart that this will be his last trip up a mountain. Alongside the God he has followed faithfully for over forty years, Moses goes to his death willingly, his service now ended. Certainly, if anyone deserved to enter the Promised Land, it was Moses. But, like the patriarchs, Abraham, Isaac, and Jacob, he labored trusting that God's promise would be realized by a future generation. Moses accepts God's divine judgment.

We may recall a harsh penalty issued by God to both Moses and Aaron: "Because you did not trust in me, . . . you shall not bring this assembly into the land that I have given them" (Num. 20:12). By the time of the scriptural account for today, the penalty remains, but God's mercy has come to the fore. Moses will glimpse the long-awaited Promised Land. Moses cannot see the length and breadth of the Promised Land, but God blesses him with a divine vision that allows him to take it all in and be satisfied that his work in preparation for entrance into the new land ensures that the wandering Hebrews have a permanent home.

The people mourn Moses' passing for thirty days and then community life resumes as usual, which reminds us all to remain humble. We are all sinners, falling short of the goals of the kingdom and dependent upon God's grace. Moses is buried in an unmarked grave, in an undisclosed location. This may have further demonstrated his humility, but it also prevented any idol worship or veneration of Moses' body.

Moses was chosen by God to lead the Hebrew people from slavery in Egypt to the Promised Land. He was blessed with the physical prowess to perform those grueling duties over forty years, starting when he was already eighty years old. His powerful presence, late in life, inspired all people.

Almighty God, "servant of the Lord" is the best epitaph a person could hope to have. May we so live that we will be remembered in just such a way. Amen.

How do you follow Moses, a prophet unlike any other? Moses knew God so well that they spoke "face to face, as one speaks to a friend" (Exod. 33:11), and Moses had performed signs and miracles in front of all the people. Joshua may have felt woefully unequal to the gargantuan task ahead after Moses had led the Hebrew people to the border of the Promised Land.

It now becomes Joshua's job to lead the Hebrews across the border to occupy the land promised them from the time of Abraham. One big obstacle remains. Other tribes and nations occupy the land God promised.

The forty years of wandering may have fostered an unrealistic expectation that taking possession of the land would be quick and easy. So Joshua will simply approach those already living there and explain God's plan, and they will all agree to leave or live under Jewish authority! Joshua knows it won't be that simple, however. He has already surveyed the land as one of twelve spies for Moses. Ten of those spies report that the occupants of the land are too strong for the Hebrew people to defeat. Only Joshua and one other tell Moses that with God's help, the Hebrews can prove victorious over the people living in the Promised Land. He voiced his optimism even while remaining realistic.

Another factor works in Joshua's favor as he takes the reins of leadership. He knows that he, like Moses, has been chosen by God to lead. Moses, in laying hands on Joshua, completes the transfer of authority. The Hebrew people recognize Joshua's authority and agree to follow him as they had Moses. Filled with the spirit of wisdom, Joshua will know the right time for a military effort and when the time would require patience.

Mighty God, help us to recognize our calling and take our place among the people committed to following your path. Amen.

This may be the oldest letter in the New Testament, written before the Gospels and yet long enough after the death and resurrection of Jesus that people are starting to doubt their faith. Another issue that troubled people whose faith may have been weakened by the delay in Jesus' return was the many traveling preachers who were out for personal gain.

Paul feels the need to distinguish between self-serving ministers and a true apostle. The word *apostle* helps us understand the distinction. It means "one who is sent out with a mission and a message." Through many examples, Paul reassures the Thessalonians that he is a genuine apostle. He has not personally profited by his preaching. In fact, it has caused him considerable harm. Leading a committed Christian life is not necessarily easy. Often it involves sacrifice and suffering. Paul's lifestyle and experience certainly bear witness to that fact. He mentions three characteristics of the true apostle: (1) courage to proclaim the gospel of God; (2) integrity, acting without "deceit or impure motives or trickery" (including greed); (3) the distinctive relationship of apostle to convert: "like a nurse caring for her own children." This deep care leads to a vulnerability between Paul and those to whom he has proclaimed the gospel of God.

For Paul, the costs are well worth the effort. He and his companions have shared "our own selves." He does not chronicle the results of their efforts, but he notes that "our coming to you was not in vain." Paul cares deeply for this young congregation, even though they are a far distance apart and can only hope to see one another rarely: "You have become very dear to us."

Loving God, help us to recognize the true path to discipleship and to maintain the relationships that strengthen our faith. Amen.

Paul approaches every group with a variety of arguments, believing that if one doesn't work he will try another. Paul reminds the Thessalonians of his experience and of their own. He asks that they recall his gentle approach and willingness to overlook his status as an apostle, though he notes that he could have taken advantage of status had he so desired.

Paul encourages the Thessalonians to remain strong in the faith by his own example. He endures despite the persecution he suffered while in Philippi. By his example, Paul teaches us all to persevere. Faith does not guarantee anyone an easy ride. It does promise us strength and guidance for living through the difficulties that inevitably arise along life's journey.

Paul commends his ministry team to the Thessalonians as honest and hardworking. True faith doesn't try to trick people into becoming followers of Jesus. Nor should it be used to build up the reputation or influence of any individual. Pleasing God is far more important than pleasing mere mortals. We can easily get distracted by desiring the approval of friends and neighbors and forget that God may have different priorities for our lives.

Paul in his apostleship does not emphasize quantity of converts but integrity of relationship with God through Jesus Christ. He asserts the authority of his position; he has "been approved by God to be entrusted with the message of the gospel." Paul is not being arrogant in this claim. Paul lets his readers know that in order to claim any authority, he views his work through the lens of the gospel, the good news of Jesus Christ, his death and resurrection.

Loving God, may we always be aware of the path that leads to you, and may the Holy Spirit ever be our guide. Amen.

It's not a good idea to argue with Jesus. Throughout the Gospels, many people question and challenge Jesus. Leaders of his day felt threatened by what they perceived as unorthodox teachings and his apparent disregard for the law when strictly interpreted. At the same time, they can't understand or explain the power Jesus has to heal, so they look for ways to destroy him. At first, their goal is defeat by humiliation. Many times his opponents thought they had trapped him. Each time, Jesus turned the tables, leaving them defeated and even embarrassed by his powerful responses.

Today's text teaches us a lesson about Jesus' divinity. By bringing up the lineage of David and David's role as the greatest of Israel's kings, Jesus makes it clear that the true Messiah has to be more than merely mortal. Though the Messiah is generations removed from the original King David, that person will be more powerful than David and will rule with more authority. David will be invited to sit next to the Messiah in a distinctly subordinate role. Such a ruler can only come from heaven. All earthly rulers will fall short of this standard.

The Pharisees strongly advocate for traditional order. All power flows from David. They can't conceive of an earthly ruler with more power than their greatest king, nor can they accept the idea of a heavenly ruler coming to earth. The last point seems crucial since the Pharisees know Jesus is speaking about himself and they do not want to admit they stand on the wrong side of the argument, in opposition to God's chosen Messiah. Jesus has silenced them. After this devastating defeat, the Pharisees decide that Jesus has to die.

Holy God, guide us by your Spirit that we may never find ourselves in a position opposite your beloved Son. Amen.

In one of their last attempts to defeat Jesus in the marketplace, the Pharisees get together to challenge him with a controversial question that will divide his followers and weaken his popularity among the crowds. Everyone has familiarity with the Ten Commandments. Dedicated students of the commandments attempt to rank them in order of importance. Such an exercise is doomed to failure as people can never come to a consensus on this topic. The Pharisees imagine that by asking Jesus this question he will become part of the controversy. No matter which commandment he may choose, scholars will criticize the choice.

Rather than falling into the Pharisees' trap, Jesus responds in a way that confounds them and creates a new way of understanding what it means to be children of God. Instead of choosing one of the ten, Jesus turns to the crucial prayer of the Jewish faith. The Shema (Deuteronomy 6:4-5) is part of every Jewish family's daily routine. From scholars to uneducated peasants, everyone listening to Jesus will know that reference and understand the rationale behind Jesus' response. Then Jesus does something even more remarkable. He expands the commandment to love God by extending that love to include neighbors as well.

Jesus has plenty of scriptural support for his addition of neighbors and the implication is clear: It is impossible to love God without also loving those created in God's image. Bible scholars today still talk about the two tablets of the law, those commandment having to do with our love for God and those understood as directed toward our love for neighbors. As followers of Jesus, we face a constant challenge to give our time in service to both God and neighbor.

God of all, clear our minds and strengthen our hearts, that everything we say and do may serve and glorify you. Amen.

The Word at Work in You

OCTOBER 30–NOVEMBER 5, 2017 • WILL WILLIMON

SCRIPTURE OVERVIEW: The texts remind us that human decisions, relationships, communities must be rooted in the reality of God. In his vision recorded in Revelation, John sees all communities, all nations, shouting before God's throne that salvation comes only from God. The story of the crossing of the Jordan in Joshua 3 illustrates this principle: apart from Yahweh's grace, Israel's life could not be sustained. Paul does not deny an authority due him because of his previous relations with the Thessalonians. At the same time, he can reverse the image and speak of himself as an orphan when separated from these people (2:17). The possibility of mutuality emerges out of a clear acceptance of the authority of the gospel. The scribes and Pharisees are singled out in Matthew 23 for flaunting their positions and for engaging in pious activity so as to be praised and courted by others. Their craving of honorific titles illustrates their failure to acknowledge the empowerment of Jesus as teacher and God as Father.

QUESTIONS AND SUGGESTIONS FOR REFLECTION

- Read Joshua 3:7-17. What miracles have you seen God perform lately in your life? in the life of a friend?
- Read Revelation 7:9-17. How do you reconcile a God of judgment with the writer's statement that "God will settle for nothing less than a standing-room-only heaven"?
- Read 1 Thessalonians 2:9-13. How is the word of God at work in you?
- Read Matthew 23:1-12. When have you been humbled in being faithful to Jesus' call on your life? Is being humbled a sign of true servanthood?

Professor of the Practice of Christian Ministry, Duke Divinity School, Durham, North Carolina

"I will be with you as I was with Moses," God says to Moses' successor, Joshua. The Exodus from Egypt is ending. But now Israel faces the challenge of living in a strange new land. God promises to go with them into this new place to keep making a way when people think no way exists.

In other words, God tells Joshua, "If you thought miracles (dramatic interventions by God) are over, think again." The God who made a way by pushing back the sea in Israel's exodus now pushes aside the Jordan, making a way into the Promised Land. The miraculous, interventionist, active love of God goes with them. What God intends for God's people, Israel cannot accomplish alone. The miracles continue.

I hope you went to church yesterday and experienced God's presence. I pray that God did things *to* you and *for* you that you could not do for yourself. But as you go through your workaday Monday remember: God actively loves 24/7.

During a dormitory Bible study a student asked, "How come Jesus almost never says or does anything important to people in church?" As a clergyperson who spends lots of time at church, I found the student's statements annoying!

As you go about doing all sorts of nonsacred, nonreligious things on this mundane Monday, keep looking over your shoulder. The life you live is not your own. Your actions may not be the only action in your world. God not only speaks to you but works in you. When confronted by some seemingly insurmountable obstacle, "There is no way for me to cross that deep, dangerous river," be prepared to be proven wrong. You do not journey alone. Even though you are a modern, thinking person who remains unsure about the possibility of the miraculous, the miracles continue.

Think of a time when God made a way for you when you thought there was no way.

Halloween," the psychologist explained, "is a creative way of dealing with our deepest fears by putting on a scary mask, a costume, and making fun of our fear that something horrible lurks in the dark." If that's true, Halloween is a sad trivialization of the church's All Saints Eve, a pitiful attempt to lay aside our deepest fears merely by mocking them.

"My mother attempted to reassure me, when I would wake terrified of the night, 'Honey, there's nothing to fear in the dark,'" recalled a friend. "After I lost my job, endured my daughter's terrible illness and my husband's infidelity, I now know—Mom was wrong."

Christians do not deny the darkness. We admit the reality of evil and pain even in this often beautiful world. We are able to be truthful about the forces that lurk because we have been let in on the last act of the play, the final chapter of the story, the outcome of the battle.

When Revelation 7 lifts the curtain on our ending, we catch a vision of the world when God at last gets what God has always wanted. In the end, when all is said and done, when the forces that cause us sometimes to suffer and weep are defeated, the once-crucified Lamb shall reign "at the center of the throne." Every fear defeated, every tear wiped away, not because of our creative denial of the darkness but rather because of the victory of the Lamb.

We don't have to don a happy-face mask and make fun of our fears. We have a story about where this wonderful, sometimes terrifying life is headed. At the end we do not find fearful oblivion, evil's triumph, eternal tears. In the end, God.

Let the good news of tomorrow's All Saints Day be your comfort today and into eternity.

Lord Jesus, we know that you love us, and that keeps us going. Amen.

ALL SAINTS DAY

John gives us a vision of the triumph of God's will for human-kind. What is our end, the destination toward which we are headed? Revelation sings of a well-populated, joyfully crowded eternity where "a great multitude that no one could count, from every nation . . . all tribes and peoples and languages," sings, "Salvation belongs to our God!"

My church is shrinking. Our losses indicate our unfaithful limitation of the scope of God's expansive salvation. Revelation is clear: God's realm is not restricted to one age group (my church's median age: sixty), a single social or economic class (we are comfortably middle-class), one race or language (we speak English in our worship). God wants it all—a great, innumerable crowd.

My wife, Patsy, serves on the Invite and Welcome Committee of our church and therefore worries about a task that ought to consume the whole congregation. In what ways do our practices limit the boundaries of God's people? How do we unintentionally exclude some "tribes and peoples and languages" by the way we worship? The grand, inclusive, expansive vision of Revelation 7 tells us what God wants, and it's our job as the church to want what God wants.

"Sadly," a congregant told me, "my son who was brought up in the church, as an adult is not a Christian."

Thanks to Revelation 7, I, knowing of God's determination finally to have "a great multitude," replied, "You should say, 'Not yet a Christian.' You tell your son to keep looking over his shoulder as he goes into his fifties. God's got ways. Revelation 7 says that God will settle for nothing less than a standing-room-only heaven."

What can I do to spread the good news that God's family is "a great multitude"?

I teach a seminary course on "Ordained Leadership." Among my maxims for aspiring church leaders: "Leadership is necessary for any organization that needs to move from maintenance to vitality." "Leaders ask the right questions believing that followers will come up with the answers."

Leadership, so rare among us, is even more challenging when leadership is attempted in the name of Jesus. Good leaders are usually known for their gifts, self-confidence, ability to use power effectively, and skill in motivating others. In Matthew 23, Jesus contrasts worldly wise leaders with the qualities of leadership in his name as if to say, "The world's great leaders . . . . But you . . . "

Leaders in the body of Christ are not all-knowing teachers but perpetual students; not the powerful, dominating parents but the vulnerable children; not the great masters but the humble servants.

In the light of this week's Gospel lesson, the greatest challenge for the Christian leader comes in not getting in the way of our true leader, Jesus. It's tempting to think that the good things that occur in my congregation are due to my astute leadership rather than to undeserved gifts of the Holy Spirit. I too easily delude myself into thinking that my sermons are heard because of my stellar speaking rather than to God's relentless determination to be revealed to God's people.

Thus the theologian Karl Barth said that Christian leaders ought to point beyond themselves to Christ. Christian leaders help people be more faithful to Christ rather than more attached to them. We lead in the name of the One who taught and led by using a basin and towel and washing his followers' feet.

Jesus, keep teaching me that I may teach as I have been taught by you. Amen.

The Word at Work in You   365

Have you ever tried to be humble? A person who brags about having achieved humility probably hasn't. Maybe that's why Jesus doesn't say to his disciples in his criticism of religious leaders, "Don't be like them. Humble yourselves." He speaks of humility as something *done to* you rather than *by* you.

Have a problem with pride? Have an exalted opinion of your abilities? Try being a leader in Jesus' name, and God will fix that. You will be humbled.

The day I was exalted as a bishop, a wise bishop told me, "This job will force you to your knees." Earlier, I had interviewed retired bishops, asking them to characterize the episcopacy. Their main response: Powerlessness.

"As a bishop, you have a front-row seat to see the problems and failures of the church, but the rules and procedures mandated by *The Book of Discipline*, competing caucuses, uncooperative clergy, and reactionary laity tie your hands," one explained.

How ironic that those to whom the church has given the most power are humbled by their impotence.

Maybe my question ought not be, "What can I do to be more successful, effective, and powerful?" Rather, "Have I been so infrequently humbled because I've attempted too little in the name of Jesus?" Or, "How have my leadership failures shown that I may be faithful to Jesus?"

Jesus promises, "Follow me; attempt to teach, to lead, or to love in my name and I promise: You will be humbled."

This is good news for those who hope to align our lives with the One who taught his followers, "The greatest among you will be your servant."

Lord, humble me by giving me tasks that remind me of my limits and my need for your grace. Amen.

Alabama's legislature passed the meanest anti-immigration law in the nation. I wrote a letter protesting the spiteful law. An immigration activist asked, "But what are you going to *do*? Your letter is just words. What about action?"

Paul says that in this faith, it's never "just words." Paul led fledgling churches through letters, praising the church at Thessalonica for receiving his words "not as a human word" but as "God's word" so that these words were "at work in you believers."

All God had to do to create the world was to say the word. The gospel spread like wildfire throughout the world through witness, letters, and sermons. A couple of centuries after Paul wrote these words, the church defeated the Roman Empire without firing a shot or raising a platoon, all on the basis of a bunch of words called scripture.

Why are you a Christian? Why you are reading these words? I bet that God used words to "work in you"—nonviolent, noncoercive but powerful-in-the-hands-of-God words.

Tomorrow in church, through hymns, scripture reading, prayers, and a sermon, you will hear and speak only words. Be warned: Scripture tells a story of how an active, revealing God seizes these human words to do God's work in the hearts and minds of people like you. By God's grace little words like *grace, love, go,* and *invite* burrow into your soul; they ignite, push, and prod you to do something beautiful for God. It's then that you acknowledge Paul's truth-telling: Just through words, God is "at work in you."

And by the way, that sorry law was erased without violence or mayhem, with nothing but words.

Lord Jesus, who not only loves us but also speaks to us, who speaks to us in order to change us, go ahead, speak to me. Amen.

The Word at Work in You　367

In the Sundays after the 9/11 tragedy, my church experienced a 20 percent jump in attendance. Three months later, our new attendees were gone; attendance slipped back to pre-9/11 levels.

Why? Some speculated that the new folks came to church and the boring worship, hackneyed sermons, and cold congregations reminded them why they had stopped attending in the first place! I theorized that people came to church in their distress seeking comfort, consolation, and care only to be encountered by Jesus. Sure, sometimes Jesus comes to us with healing and compassion. But often he comes with judgment, summons, critique, and command.

Take today's Gospel lesson. There had to be lots of hurting people around Jesus that day. The burdens of leadership and teaching can be heavy. But Jesus offered them stinging criticism, making sharp separation between his ways and theirs.

Sometimes we come to church and receive comfort and affirmation. But what we mainly receive is the living Christ in all of his sometimes prickly, demanding, sovereign glory.

A member of my congregation emerged one Sunday saying, "I have had a terrible week with my diagnosis and my son's continued problems. I was at the end of my rope, looking for help with my burdens."

"I hope that you received compassionate help in today's service," I said.

"No, I didn't," she replied. "I came here seeking Jesus' aid and instead Jesus had the nerve to give me an assignment!"

As you attend worship today, take care! Jesus may offer you more of himself than you asked for. He may speak a word to you that you have been avoiding all week. He may have more faith in your ability to be a faithful disciple than you have in yourself.

Lord, give me the grace to hear when you speak to me and then the courage to do your will. Amen.

Listen to the Teachings

NOVEMBER 6–12, 2017 • GEORGE HOVANESS DONIGIAN

SCRIPTURE OVERVIEW: This week's passages speak of ultimate commitment or of the return of Jesus or they speak in parables that reflect a protagonist who has been delayed in an anticipated appearance. Living so far from the time of the texts makes it difficult to appreciate the urgency with which the issues arose in various communities and the crises they precipitated. Eschatology, however, is not to be thought of merely as a speculative venture in which curious religious people gamble on a time when the world will end. In the Bible, the coming advent of God demands from and warrants for the people of God a distinctive style of life. In Joshua 24, Israel receives an opportunity to define itself by identifying its God. First Thessalonians 4 comforts anxious believers who are worried about the fate of their deceased parents. Jesus' resurrection is not an isolated event, Paul argues, but the beginning of the resurrection of all people. The prospect of Jesus' return forms the basis for hope.

QUESTIONS AND SUGGESTIONS FOR REFLECTION

- Read Joshua 24:1-3a, 14-25. When have your ministry activities become so time-consuming that you lost your connection to God? How can you regain that connection?
- Read Psalm 78:1-7. Which of the teachers in your life are you most grateful for? Why?
- Read 1 Thessalonians 4:13-18. How concerned are you with the end of time? What would you say to someone who claimed to know when the "end of the age" would be?
- Read Matthew 25:1-13. What part has fear played in your journey of faith? What does fear have to do with receiving God's love?

Pastor in South Carolina; author of several books, including *Three Prayers You'll Want to Pray* and *A World Worth Saving*

"Give ear . . . to my teaching," says the psalmist. Today we choose to listen. Tomorrow we may choose another voice, but today we listen. The psalmist invites us to listen and to be attentive to the teachings. Those teachings are the focus of the four scripture passages this week. We will listen, in the words of the psalmist, to things that our ancestors have told us. These topics for remembrance explore the history of salvation, the glorious deeds of the Lord. The entire psalm details the history of God's mercy for Israel. The psalm also encourages its hearers to tell the next generations about these deeds of God. This portion of Psalm 78 tells us of the establishment of the covenant with the nation. Israel will remember God's gracious action on behalf of the people. They may also remember their subsequent acts of rebellion against God and the invitation to renew the covenant. Give ear to my teaching and remember.

Why should we give ear to this teaching? Why remember? We remember not simply to allow ego to reign in us as we admire the good old days. Our remembrance points us to new actions of God on behalf of the people, and such remembrance directs us to receive God's continuing new deeds. Our remembering God's grace in the past prepares us to live with those promises into the future of God's reign.

Like you, I have experienced gifted teachers and less accomplished ones. I have learned from all of them. The lessons range from basic life skills to the intricacies of music, algebra, and theology. I invite you to reflect on those who taught you ways of faith and discipleship; offer a prayer of gratitude for teachers.

Give ear to my teaching, and remember. What actions will you remember today that will open you to God's grace and new creation?

O Holy Spirit, give us courage to endure the difficult times and love for those who do not perceive truth as we do. Amen.

G ive ear . . . to my teaching." Chapter 24 begins with a speech from Joshua and closes with his death. A portion of our text forms the beginning of Joshua's valedictory speech, an address that offers remembrance and hope. Joshua recalls the history of Israel. Today's text offers Abraham as the first with whom God made covenant. To remember Abraham means that we remember both Sarah and Abraham and the grand promise made by God to the old couple that they would have offspring.

Before we jump to the history, allow the opening of this narrative to seep into your awareness. Joshua gathers the twelve tribes and brings together the community leaders, those whose vocations reflect knowledge of God. They are the judges, tribal heads, and elders. We assume that they know the fullness of the story, and yet Joshua feels compelled to remind them of their history. Is the reminder necessary because the tyranny of everyday life has so trapped these leaders that they have lost sight of God? Do busy church leaders today also need that reminder? Sometimes we get so caught up in activities that we forget the larger purpose of the bustle. The busyness of church interferes with our connection with God. Listen again to the teachings. Take time to hear through contemplative prayer and meditation, and remember the grace of God's compassionate love.

The opening of Joshua's speech reminds us of Abraham and Sarah and the seemingly impossible birth of their son Isaac. To remember Abraham and Sarah calls for our recollection of a time when each of them heard God's voice through divine messengers (Genesis 18). While Abraham may have responded to God in faith, Sarah laughed at this promise. No matter their response, they paid attention. How today shall we pay attention?

Open us to hear the wonder of your loving voice, gracious God,
so that we may grow as followers of Jesus Christ. Amen.

Listen to the teachings! Sometimes in our zeal to follow the ways of God, we discern odd paths. This week's texts remind me of William Miller, an American Baptist who studied the Bible and eventually came to believe that the Second Coming of Christ would happen in his lifetime. Pressed by contemporaries, Miller declared that the Second Coming would happen sometime between 1843 and 1844. Miller is one of many disappointed prophets who predicted the Parousia. If Miller and others, including many contemporary people, would pay attention to Jesus, they might be more cautious in their declarations. The parable of the ten bridesmaids is one of four parables that concern judgment and the return of Jesus. This text and the passage in First Thessalonians sometimes cause discomfort. Here the discomfort may stem from the descriptions of the wise and foolish.

Listen to what Jesus actually says in this parable and not to the many other voices that try to identify when the bridegroom will show up. Jesus introduces the parable of the ten bridesmaids in a simple way: "The kingdom of heaven will be like this." We remember that Jesus began his public ministry by declaring that the kingdom had drawn near—and that John the Baptist said the same. Here the declaration of the kingdom includes advice to be alert. If we listen to Jesus, we become more alert to the ways of God's kingdom and reign. What do we notice as the kingdom draws near? What signs of the kingdom become revealed as we pay attention? One sign that leaps at me from this text is the small group of bridesmaids. They point me in turn to the banding together of small groups that work together as a community of faith, love, and justice. A more important question: How can we remain open to the ongoing revelation of God's spectacular future? Listen to the teachings.

Open us to see signs of your kingdom in our midst, compassionate God. Amen.

Listen to the teachings! What emotional response arises in you as you read today's text? Many people read Paul's text as though it foretells the exact way in which the "end" will arrive. This Thessalonians text raises concerns for a large number of people because they pay attention to rumors.

Read the text and listen to what it holds. The passage begins with a reminder of the hope that we have in the resurrection of Christ. In a very straightforward way, Paul speaks to those who grieve the death of loved ones. Here is a reminder to continue in the hope of Christ, even in grief—for resurrection does not happen without death. The passage ends with a plea to the community to offer encouragement to one another. In between these verses Paul attempts to describe the presence of Christ with believers at the end of the age. We grapple with this text. Some people read this and other end-time passages in fright. They live with a theology of fear, forgetting the basic biblical message to "fear not." Some liken this passage to the ways in which people throng roadways to greet a king and then return with the king to the city. N. T. Wright connects this passage with the new heaven and the new earth of which Jesus spoke. Hope stands as the ultimate message in this text.

The passage closes with the words "encourage one another." I hope that you hear much encouragement within the body of Christ. No matter our understanding of the end times, we need to hear hope and encouragement, the two primary themes in this text. This passage reminds me of the closing lines of "A Statement of Faith of the United Church of Canada": "In life, in death, in life beyond death, God is with us. We are not alone. Thanks be to God" (UMH, 883).

Season our lives with encouragement, gracious God, so that we may live as people of hope. Amen.

Listen to the teachings! The kingdom of heaven will be like ten bridesmaids who await the groom. With the delay of the groom, five bridesmaids do not have enough oil to complete their task. At the end of the parable, the five bridesmaids cannot enter the wedding banquet and the groom says, "I do not know you." Jesus concludes by saying, "Keep awake therefore, for you know neither the day nor the hour."

How do you hear those words? Are they somber? Do they produce fear of judgment? Listen to Jesus with a sense of hope. The words conclude a parable about a wedding festival—a joyful event. The ten bridesmaids need to have prepared for a tremendously joyful celebration, an event that marks goodness, love, and blessing. Why would they come unprepared?

First Thessalonians 4:13-18 and today's passage help us realize that we have fallen prey to the twenty-first-century invasion of fear. Fear—whether of terrorism, infectious diseases, street violence, or immigrants—becomes a lens through which we see the world. That fear transfers itself to the way we read the Bible. Instead of reading the Bible as God's gift of love, we read it with fear in the background. When fear becomes a perspective, we miss joy and hope; we focus instead on condemnation.

Rather than looking with fear, live like the bridesmaids who look forward to the arrival of the groom. They prepare with joy for something better and for a greater joy. That seems the place of prayer in our daily discipleship: We listen to God as we read scripture. We pray and open ourselves to God's grace for the day so that we may be open and receptive to the greater joy that will be ours.

God, in your compassion, help us to stay alert to the joy that arrives each day as a foretaste of what will yet be. Amen.

Listen to the teachings! Joshua reminds the people of God's faithful history with them. He invites them to revere and serve God. The people respond positively, but then comes a hard portion of this text: Joshua does not affirm this facile response from the people; instead he tells them that they cannot serve the Lord because God is holy and jealous. He points out some potential problems in the relationship. Despite that challenge, the people affirm faith in God. Joshua challenges them yet again, saying that they will serve alien gods. Again the people respond that they will serve and obey God.

How do we listen for the voice of God in this text? Our times offer many temptations to serve many deities who are foreign to the God Joshua speaks of. We face countless temptations each day, ones that range from our reactions to one another or to problems and on to our choice of activities and the ways we use time. Each morning when we wake, we reaffirm our awareness that the love of God is fresh and new. How does our morning prayer keep us fresh to God's grace throughout the day, especially as we deal with the tyrants and demands that are part of each day's schedule? These demands can become the alien gods. Like Joshua and the twelve tribes, we too need an alertness to see those things that tempt us to turn from God.

Notice also in the verses that follow today's reading that Joshua sets a stone under an oak tree and states that the stone will serve as a witness to the people's choice. What physical item reminds you of your choice to serve God? Some people wear a cross—whether as necklace or tattoo. Others keep another religious object to serve as a reminder. I think each of us carries a living reminder of grace and obedience: the voice of conscience and the voice of the Holy Spirit.

O God, help us face our challenges, name them, rest awhile in your presence, and then return to serve you afresh. Amen.

Listen to the teachings! We close this week with our starting point of Psalm 78 and its recounting of God's compassionate love for Israel. Throughout the psalm we read of God's interaction with Israel. Reading this history displays the constancy of God's love through human faithfulness and human rebellion. In this history we also see confession, absolution, and renewal.

The psalmist invites us to remember God's actions on behalf of Israel and, by extension, God's actions for us. We remember God's love and compassion so that we will also be formed by that love and compassion. As we grow and that love shapes us, compassion and love become a larger part of our own lives.

Psalm 78 begins to shimmer and attract my attention when the psalmist deepens the invitation to remember the teachings and to pass on this wisdom to children "so that they should set their hope in God, and not forget the works of God." As one who once developed Sunday school and other religious curriculum resources for children, I tend to focus on the place of children in congregational ministry and mission. Every adult in every congregation teaches children. Some adults offer positive models of discipleship for children, while other adults may unconsciously model a faith that becomes more like that identified by the psalmist as "a stubborn and rebellious generation." All God's people need awareness that they model faith and discipleship for children. Our actions directly and indirectly show love and concern for children who are relatively innocent and powerless. Look for the children around you. They may not be visible in your congregation's Sunday gatherings, but children are in your community. How will you pass on traditions of faithful discipleship to the next generations? Be a faithful friend of God for the children.

Holy God, keep us faithful in mission and ministry for the sake of your love. Amen.

Multiplying Mercy in Many Forms

NOVEMBER 13–19, 2017 • DONNA CLAYCOMB SOKOL

SCRIPTURE OVERVIEW: In the book of Judges, we find a woman confidently leading a patriarchal nation as though it were an everyday occurrence. The psalm reminds us that the need for mercy reduces each and every one to a posture of outstretched hands and upturned eyes. To sing such a song on the way to worship, as was traditionally done, is to prepare the mind and heart for the possibility of whatever blessing may be given upon arrival. In First Thessalonians we overhear an apostle's exhortation to live openly and expectantly regarding God's future revelation—alert to the coming of Christ but also aware that Christ may come in sudden and unanticipated ways. Finally, a parable in Matthew runs counter to our instincts to safeguard that which we treasure, challenging us to consider the ways in which faithfulness involves a strange coupling of risk and reward.

QUESTIONS AND SUGGESTIONS FOR REFLECTION

- Read Judges 4:1-7. Reread the last paragraph of Monday's meditation and reflect on the writer's two questions.
- Read Psalm 123. How do you address God? Is God more "enthroned above" for you, or "right here in [your] midst"?
- Read 1 Thessalonians 5:1-11. The writer states, "We stay awake each time we practice acts of love and mercy." When have you felt divinely awakened by an act of love?
- Read Matthew 25:14-30. Identify ways you take risks in your life presently. Do any of these risks relate to living out your faith?

Pastor, Mount Vernon Place United Methodist Church, Washington, DC

"The Israelites again did what was evil in the sight of the LORD." How often have we read these words? The Israelites repeatedly worship other gods, receive punishment, call upon God for help, and wait for God to send a rescuer. And God always responds.

The Israelites have been in bondage to King Jabin of Canaan, suffering oppression for twenty years. He and his commander have a distinct advantage over the Israelites with a mighty army of nine hundred chariots. It would be tempting to accept a life of oppression. But the Israelites summon the courage and find the faith to request help. God responds by calling Deborah who calls for Barak who calls for ten thousand fighters from the tribes of Napthali and Zebulon. They help pave the path to deliverance.

Faith leads to prayer. Prayer leads to possibility. Possibility leads to action. Action leads to deliverance. Deborah knows the enemy. But Deborah also knows that something extraordinary happens when people listen for instruction and unite what they have with the power of God.

We may not know what it's like to be enslaved or have an army marching toward us, but we can seek to understand what it is like for God always to be on our side. The Israelites fail time and again, but they never let go of their belief in God who is always with them, on their side, ready to lead them through whatever opposition they face.

What challenges that you face make you feel hopeless? How might your circumstances change if you believed God is always with you, never leaving your side?

Mighty God, we do not always understand our circumstances, and we acknowledge our wayward actions. We believe you are with us. Increase our faith. Give us the capacity to follow your leading. We are ready for deliverance. Amen.

When did you last stand in the middle of a circle? If you've ever faced a challenging medical diagnosis, then you may know the power of people circling around you, placing hands on your shoulders, arms, or back before someone anoints your forehead with oil and prays for healing.

Or perhaps you know the pain that can come when you're in the middle of a circle. Some of us can recall moments on the playground when a group of children gathered around us and proceeded to call us derogatory names. Bullies used the circle as a tool to ensure that we could not escape without hearing their hurtful words.

Police encircle crime suspects. Family members circle around runaway pets that have been found. We circle around things that we don't want to get away.

But have you ever imagined your prayers forming a circle around God? How can we repeat our words of praise and petition in such a way that God feels our eyes fixed upon God and understands that we refuse to let go until God responds?

The psalmist teaches us to pray in such a way. He fixes his eyes on God, addresses God, affirms his trust in God, and then repeats the same request three times. The psalmist refuses to remove his gaze until God has not only heard his cries for mercy but actually has mercy on him and the gathered community.

"Have mercy upon us, O Lord, have mercy upon us."

We are tempted to believe that prayer is a language that requires an impressive repertoire of words. But what if prayer is as simple as following the psalmist's pattern of repeating words over and over again?

Can you circle God with these words?

Lord, Jesus Christ, have mercy on me, a sinner. Amen.

Psalm 123 is one of several "Songs of Ascents" that pilgrims would pray as they journeyed to Jerusalem. The psalm, while short in length, carries rich imagery and words that proclaim the fullness of God's nature.

The psalmist looks to God and describes God as a ruler, master, and mistress. Many of us address God as "mighty king" or "all powerful" or "ruler of heaven and earth." We desire God's control over all things.

But few of us address God as "my master," let alone "my mistress." These labels force us out of our comfort zone where we choose to remain until we seek to understand what the psalmist may have imagined.

At the time the psalmist penned these words, servants lived in the home of their master, who provided a job, a bed, food, and even community. Servants and maids received their livelihood from their master and mistress. Perhaps you can imagine television parallels like Alice, the beloved maid on *The Brady Bunch*, or Mrs. Hughes and Mr. Carson on *Downton Abbey*—characters who serve as an extension of the family and do everything to please and care for their employers.

The psalmist invites us to know and serve God in a similar way. God is one who rules all things, but God is also one on whom we can depend. God sits enthroned above, but is also right here in our midst. God desires to care for us, but we are also called to care for God's needs until God shows mercy.

How are we being invited to tend to God's needs this day? Where are we being led? How could we care for God as though mercy depended on it?

Thank you for caring for us, God, and enabling us to care for you. Amen.

The people living in Thessalonica expected Jesus' quick return. While it's only been two decades since his death and resurrection, the early followers do not expect to linger this long. They weary of waiting and grow more anxious as they ponder the possibility that one of their loved ones could die before Jesus returns. Paul tries to encourage the Thessalonians, providing instructions on how to wait faithfully for Christ's return.

The instructions sound simple: stay sober, wear faithfulness and love in such a way that it protects the body, place the hope of salvation on top of the head as though a helmet, and continue to encourage each other while building one another up.

Many of us wear a heavy coat while waiting for the bus in the winter. We wear paper glasses that never fit while waiting for our pupils to readjust after an optometrist exam. We wear a protective vest while waiting for the completion of an x-ray at the doctor's office. These articles of clothing, while often not so comfortable, nevertheless protect us from the cold, the sun, or harmful rays.

But what do you wear while waiting for Jesus? How are you wearing faithfulness, love, and the hope of salvation?

If faithfulness signifies unwavering loyalty in practice, then imagine starting the day by putting on a desire for loyalty to God just as you put on your pants and shirt. Then allow your devotion to God to cover your body as you seek to make Christ shine through all that you say and do. Next put on love, allowing it to penetrate your interactions with the people in your home, school, work, or play. Finally place hope on top of your head, assuring yourself that Christ loves you, forgives you, and will be with you always.

Dear Jesus, please help me get dressed and ready today. Amen.

Multiplying Mercy in Many Forms

"A re you awake?" our mother inquires while knocking on the bedroom door, making sure we are ready for school.

"Are you awake?" our spouse asks when our eyes close halfway through a movie.

"Are you awake?" we ask a friend who sounds as though she is asleep when she answers the phone in the middle of the afternoon.

Are you awake? It's a question we ask and respond to often.

Jesus had one request of the disciples while waiting in Gethsemane on the eve of his crucifixion: Can you stay awake? The disciples could not. Are we any different? Are we awake—ready for the day of the Lord? Paul encourages the Thessalonians to stay awake because no one knows when Jesus will return.

How awake are you?

Do you remember the first time you were awakened, roused to the place where you started to comprehend and accept Jesus' love and mercy? To be awakened is to see and sense Christ's presence at work in your life. But to stay awake requires that we respond to his grace with our whole being, allowing ourselves to be transformed into the image and likeness of Christ.

We all have tricks for how to stay awake: drink extra caffeine, stretch our legs, go outside. But do we know how to remain awake for Jesus?

We stay awake each time we repent of our sin, turning away from our ways and turning toward Christ's ways. From what do you need to turn away?

We stay awake each time we let go of old habits. Paul names drunkenness as an example. What do you need to let go of?

We stay awake each time we practice acts of love and mercy. How can you offer love or mercy to the people around you today?

> *Creating God, awaken us to your presence in our lives and help us stay awake always. Amen.*

Matthew goes to great lengths to prepare us for Jesus' return. There will be great suffering, changes in the sun and moon, the stars will fall, and Jesus will appear, accompanied by trumpet sounds. (See Matthew 25:29-30.) And while we may be tempted to sit back and wait for these signs, we have work to do to ensure our readiness. Fill lamps with oil. Purchase extra oil. Feed the hungry. Welcome the stranger. And invest wages in ways that will double their return.

We approach the end times with different emotions depending upon what we have been taught about God. Is God like a parent who punishes offspring by withholding play and food? Is God a scorekeeper with a large pad of paper on which are noted our sins and shortcomings? Or is God like a father who sits by the window waiting for a runaway child to come home? Is God one whose arms remain outstretched, eager to embrace whoever wants to receive love, mercy, and affection?

Who is God to you? Our answer to this question dictates how we speak, how we act—how we live. If we believe God is always more eager to punish than to forgive, then we are likely to walk a narrow line that provides a limited return, aligning ourselves more closely with the third slave in our story from Matthew 25. But if we believe God eagerly loves and affirms us, then we are more apt to do what we can to love, affirm, and serve others in similar ways, multiplying the gifts God has given to us like the first two slaves.

God's greatest desire is for us to celebrate, to enter into God's joy. This joy will come at the end, but we receive glimpses of it today. What can we do to double all God has given to us?

Gracious God, help us multiply your many gifts! Amen.

How risk averse are you? Do you let fear of the unknown dictate how you live? Or have you mastered the capacity of placing fear aside, learning to trust the unknown?

Fear paralyzes us more than any other emotion, making us play it safe in order to avoid danger or punishment. And fear can lead to our downfall, which is exactly what happens to the third slave. He fears his master, and this fear penetrates his ability to use the gift that has been given to him. The only option he can imagine is to hide his talent in the ground until the master returns, a decision that leads to his demise. How often does your fear prevent you from taking a risk?

The wisdom of Dietrich Bonhoeffer greets every visitor arriving at Philadelphia's National Liberty Museum. "Silence in the face of evil is itself evil. God will not hold us guiltless. Not to speak is to speak. Not to act is to act." Visitors are then encouraged to "live like a hero."

Heroes do not allow fear to dictate their lives. Rather, they trust that a fullness of joy awaits them when they love, advocate, and serve with reckless abandonment. Many courses in history would not have changed if people had always played it safe. We needed the risky behavior of people like Dr. Martin Luther King Jr. and Desmond Tutu to show us a different reality where justice and joy are doubled.

Jesus rarely invites us to play it safe. To love another person is risky because we do not know if we'll be loved in return. To forgive another person is risky because we do not know if we'll be hurt even more. But we will never know the fullness of joy without taking these risks. "Enter into the joy of your master."

Risk-taking God, may we be risky like you! Amen.

The God Who Searches for Us

NOVEMBER 20–26, 2017 • JOE E. PENNEL JR.

SCRIPTURE OVERVIEW: The universal rule of God, expressed in Christ the Shepherd-King, is a dominant theme in all the texts assigned for the week. Both Old Testament texts dwell on the nurturing, protecting role of the Shepherd-King, whose people we are. Ezekiel 34 gives the shepherd's guiding and defending role a political twist by condemning the succession of shepherd-kings who have neglected and exploited the flock. Both New Testament passages celebrate the victory of Christ: the enthroned Son of Man of Matthew 25 separates the flock, and the risen Christ of Ephesians 1 is seated by God "far above all rule and authority and power and dominion." Christ guarantees God's completed reign.

QUESTIONS AND SUGGESTIONS FOR REFLECTION

- Read Ezekiel 34:11-16, 20-24. How does it feel to be compared to sheep with God as the shepherd? What would the sheep expect from the shepherd? What would the shepherd expect from the sheep?
- Read Psalm 100. How would a total stranger know that your faith in God brings you joy?
- Read Ephesians 1:15-23. Would you say that you love God more with your mind or with your heart?
- Read Matthew 25:31-46. What is required for you to be so attuned to others that you would recognize the Christ in them? How will you ensure that Christ's kingdom comes on earth as it is in heaven?

Former bishop of The United Methodist Church; Professor of the Practice of Leadership, Vanderbilt Divinity School, Nashville, Tennessee

I was ordained as a United Methodist minister over fifty years ago. I now have file drawers and three-ring binders filled to overflowing with lessons taught and sermons preached. Today's reading has awakened me to the understanding that I have been guilty of telling one side of the story to the exclusion of the other.

Most of my preaching and teaching has focused on how to search for God. I have encouraged people to search for God by hearing the message of scripture, practicing deeds of mercy and kindness, being prayerful, being faithful to private and public worship, and sharing in Christian fellowship. I have admonished my congregants to be faithful and steadfast in this search for God.

Ezekiel points us to God's redemptive activity and personal involvement with the people. He also points me to the other side of the story. He believes that God also searches for us. He writes, "Thus says the Lord GOD: I myself will search for my sheep, and will seek them out." I now wish that I had given more attention to God's quest for us.

One way that God searches for us is through the love that others have for us. We experience God's reaching out to us when we, in humility, accept the love of family, friends, and strangers. In some moments God approaches us through music, liturgy, and sermon. It does not happen in every act of worship, but God is unveiled to us as we listen for the word behind all of the words that call our name.

God also meets us as we relate to the poor, the imprisoned, and to those who have been pushed aside. One of my favorite professors in divinity school would encourage us to meet Christ in the poor. I find it both disquieting and comforting to know that God is one who "search[es] for my sheep."

May we be open to God's search for us.

In June of 2015 I traveled to Scotland. I saw hundreds of sheep who were maintained in lush pastures surrounded by low stone walls. In our seven days of driving around the country, I did not see one shepherd.

In Bible times, shepherds tended the flocks. A relationship existed between the sheep and the shepherd. The prophet Ezekiel felt strongly convicted of Israel's need for a shepherd. Writing at the close of the Babylonian exile, Ezekiel addresses a disheartened people. And God moves from redemption to judgment: "I will save my flock, and they shall no longer be ravaged." The weak ones are experiencing deprivation. And Ezekiel looks for a person in the Davidic line to shepherd the people according to God's covenant.

Like the people in Ezekiel's day, we may feel the need for a shepherd. We may feel pushed and butted at. We may experience a division between the weak and the strong. Thankfully, Christ our Good Shepherd feeds his sheep.

Today I know I shall fail to follow the teachings of the Good Shepherd. I will not be open to the leading that Christ offers through the nudging of the Holy Spirit. I will turn in upon myself and allow my own concerns to preoccupy me.

As believers in Christ we not only follow him but take up our vocation as shepherds for the rich and the poor, the sick and the healthy, the poor and the marginalized, the friend and the foe—neither one to the exclusion of the other. I can be a better shepherd when I take seriously God's redemptive action that cares for the weak and downtrodden. I shall be intentional in my relationship with the Good Shepherd.

O God, guide me to those who need a shepherd. In the name of Christ, the Good Shepherd. Amen.

Most of the time I pray for those whom I know from personal experience. I keep a list of those persons in my journal and on a slip of paper that I attach to my pocket calendar. The listing contains the name of relatives, friends, and members of my congregation.

In Paul's prayer, as recorded in Ephesians, he is praying for believers whom he does not know and whom he has never met. He has "heard" about their faith and love, which causes him to give thanks for their witness. Paul reminds me to expand my prayer list to include persons in the church universal.

Although I do not have a personal relationship with people in other congregations, I am called to pray for them. This scripture lesson has quickened my heart to pray for those whom I have "heard of" because all of us belong to the church, which is "his body."

We can easily think of the church as just another institution with its many extensions and expressions. The local congregation is not a franchise of the denomination. Paul wants us to understand the importance of praying for the body of Christ in both its local and global expressions.

Several years ago I preached in a congregation in Angola located in an area of grinding poverty. The pastor prayed for his congregation, and he also prayed for the church in America. I have listened to hundreds of pastoral prayers, but I cannot recall a time when an American pastor prayed for the church in another country.

God gives us a "spirit of wisdom and revelation." We pray expressing confidence in God's "immeasurable greatness," acknowledging God's great power as the source of all we do.

Loving and listening God, I praise your immeasurable greatness. May your power help me widen my circle of prayer to include those whom I do not know. Amen.

THANKSGIVING DAY USA

I do not always enter worship in a joyful manner. At times I come to worship with a heavy heart or a broken spirit. Some Sundays I enter the church with sorrow because of the pain of the world or burdened by my sin.

On the Sunday after 9/11 my wife and I worshiped with a congregation located just a few blocks from the Pentagon. We brought feelings of fear and extreme anxiety. *What does this mean? How could this happen? Will attacks like this happen again?*

As we waited for the service to begin, a man seated near us uttered these words aloud, "I cannot say the Lord's Prayer today. It will be impossible for me to pray for forgiveness, and I hope we do not sing 'Joyful, Joyful, We Adore Thee' . . . I am not joyful and I do not have a forgiving spirit." On that day he did not agree with the psalmist. But we are not to confuse "joyful noise" with experiencing the pleasures of life or being entertained or being remembered by someone.

Yet in times like the one I cite above, we need the reminder of the psalmist who calls us to praise. We make a joyful noise and come with gladness and singing. Why? We belong to God.

In verse 4 the psalmist enjoins us to enter, offer praise, give thanks, and bless. And verse 5 offers the reason for our celebratory attitude: God is good, offering us an enduring steadfast love and faithfulness. God desires our well-being.

Those who come with this joy share the conviction that love will ultimately win. If we believe this affirmation, we can enter the sanctuary and make a joyful noise no matter what our life circumstances. We are the sheep of God's pasture.

God of wonder, help me to experience joy that is holy and everlasting. Amen.

In today's reading Paul pours out his soul with thanksgiving for the faith and love that is evident in those who belong to the church in Ephesus: "I do not cease to give thanks for you as I remember you in my prayers." Note that Paul prays for their hearts to be "enlightened." His words help me understand that my openness to God will enlighten my heart.

When I was a divinity school student, I focused on having an intellectual understanding of the Christian faith. I was intent on trying to comprehend God. I was eager and determined to reflect critically on life from the vantage point of faith. I wanted to love God with my mind, but I knew something was missing.

A young woman who was struggling to figure out God preached a sermon at my church in Brentwood, Tennessee. She recalled her early struggles to understand God. She said to God, "Why can't I fit you into a nice, neat, intellectual box—especially one that can help me feel like I am in control?" Perhaps that's what we all desire. She did not understand that God dwells just beyond the power to reason. Like that young woman, I had to come to the place where I could fully believe even when I could not completely understand. If I could not completely grasp God with my mind, I could grasp God with my heart.

With the passing of time I have come to learn that we can love God with our mind *and* our heart. I believe that Paul prayed for enlightened hearts because he knew that human reason could not contain all that there is to know about God. With our hearts enlightened we recognize the riches of our inheritance through Christ and acknowledge God's greatness. Then we continue to cultivate a spirit of wisdom and revelation.

Mysterious, yet ever-present God, enlighten my heart so that I may realize my richness in you. Amen.

Christ is present in those who are hungry, thirsty, naked, sick, and in those who are strangers. When I served as the United Methodist bishop in Virginia, I found myself preaching in many and varied congregations and settings. One Sunday I proclaimed the word in a large prison for women. The auditorium, turned into a chapel for worship, was filled to capacity with inmates, guards and some administrative staff. Everyone genuinely participated in worship, including the singing, the readings, and the prayers of the people.

While I preached, I noticed a well-dressed man and woman sitting on the last row near the aisle. After the service, we introduced ourselves, and I inquired about their presence in worship: "Why do you worship here on Sunday"? The woman replied, "We come every Sunday because we meet Christ here." Her response directed my thoughts to Matthew 25:36 where Jesus said, "I was in prison and you visited me."

We meet Christ in worship, in nature, in searching the scriptures in prayer and meditation, and in fellowship with other Christians. The Christ who comes as judge, as king, as the Son of Man, ultimately resides within the dispossessed, the poor, the marginalized, and those who have been pushed aside.

I am often tempted to stay in my comfort zone and allow "group think" to dominate the conversation. But Christ calls me and you to connect with those outside our immediate circle of friends and family. Where do you meet Christ?

Guide me, loving God, to where you are present, both in my personal relationships and beyond. Amen.

THE REIGN OF CHRIST SUNDAY

On the day that I was ordained as an elder in The United Methodist Church, a beloved older pastor gave me some well-intended advice: "Joe, as a pastor you are so very fortunate to be able to carry Christ to little children, to the sick, to the funeral home, to those in prison, to the lonely, and to all who are broken."

My pastor friend, while quite sincere, was wrong. As I shepherded the people in my community and in the congregation, as I tried to be present to the hurts and hopes of people, I learned that the living Christ was already present in their situations.

My opportunity came in witnessing to Christ's presence. The reign of Christ reminds me that I do not need to "carry Christ" anywhere; he is ever present with those who are cursed with overabundance and those who live in poverty. Our task is to bear witness to the One who is already present.

One way we show our love for God comes in loving others. God is incarnate in all people; all of us are God's children.

When I am honest with myself, I acknowledge that I can so easily get caught up in my own interests and concerns that I have no room for others. I pray that the faith of others will not be crushed or stifled because of my introspection.

Jesus clearly states what we are to do. He also tells us what we are *not* to do: "Truly I tell you, just as you did not do it to one of the least of these, you did not do it to me." When we turn from "the least of these," we turn from the Christ who reigns over all and in all.

Almighty God, help me to glorify your reign by loving all whom you love. In the name of him who reigns with you and the Holy Spirit, now and forever. Amen.

Longing for Hope

NOVEMBER 27–DECEMBER 3, 2017 • GINGER E. GAINES-CIRELLI

SCRIPTURE OVERVIEW: Advent begins not on a note of joy but of despair. Humankind has realized that people cannot save themselves; apart from God's intervention, we are totally lost. The prayer of Advent is that Christ will soon come again to rule over God's creation. The passages from Isaiah 64 and Psalm 80 express the longing of faithful people for God to break into their isolation and to shatter the gridlock of human sin. The New Testament texts anticipate with both awe and thanksgiving the coming of "the day of our Lord Jesus Christ."

QUESTIONS AND SUGGESTIONS FOR REFLECTION

- Read Isaiah 64:1-9. When have you found yourself in a disorienting setting? What was your cry to God? What response to your lament did you seek?

- Read Psalm 80:1-7, 17-19. What in you needs the restoration that only God can give?

- Read 1 Corinthians 1:3-9. How might you become a means of reconciliation in your family, your work setting, your city?

- Read Mark 13:24-37. What especially do you long for this Advent-Christmas? How can you participate in the transforming love of Christ to manifest a reconciling spirit?

Senior pastor, historic Foundry United Methodist Church, Washington, DC

A god from a machine"—that is the literal translation of *deus ex machina*. This Latin phrase refers to the ancient Greek and Roman dramatic device used to solve an unsolvable problem at the end of a play by using a crane ("machine") to lower a god onto the stage from above.

"O that you would tear open the heavens and come down." Imagine this as a *deus ex machina* moment, when God comes and sorts out all the discord, violence, and worry of our lives and world. Wouldn't it be wonderful for God to fix it all—especially when it seems God has abandoned us?

It is an ancient hope, this desire for God to swoop down from on high and tidy up the messes we make and to heal our brokenness, the woundedness of a loved one, or a world at war. These verses reflect that hope. Isaiah's people find themselves embroiled in conflict as they return to Jerusalem after a long exile. Power struggles, land disputes, and violence are pervasive. These words of lament long for God's divine power to bring change into what must seem a hopeless situation.

Some things in life do seem hopeless—things as simple as how to wrestle our schedule into a sustainable rhythm or as complex as the challenges of race relations in America or the deep distrust barring peace in the Middle East. Situations both personal and global threaten to steal our hope. And yet, even when all seems lost, we hope that in Jesus, God has torn open the heavens and come down, has come right into the midst of the violence and despair of the world. Jesus comes not to make the painful bits of life disappear but to assure us that God is with us through it all, mending, loving, saving.

Ever-present God, help me trust you more than I distrust everything else. Amen.

In the midst of the resettlement of Jerusalem following a long exile, conflicts arise among people who stayed in the land, foreigners who moved in, and those who return. Who has—or hasn't—remembered and honored God? Whose fault is it that things are so difficult?

The words of lament from today's passage are a sputtering, frustrated, angry accusation that God is at fault (Isa. 64:5); that God has "delivered us into the hand of our iniquity." The argument goes this way: because God "hid," the people seem incapable of doing what is right; failure to do right incurs suffering. God is to blame!

We depend upon God's grace for help to do what is right, but the argument breaks down after that. God's grace is always at work—even when we are unaware of it. Therefore, we cannot blame God's absence for our failures to love, to serve, to do what is right. Spiritual giants from Saint John of the Cross to Mother Teresa have experienced a sense of God's absence. But their witness testifies that even in that painful experience they persevered in prayer and service. Those who have traveled through a "dark night of the soul" look back and see God's presence inviting them into a more profound faith.

Sometimes we may need to hurl our accusations and anger at God to get those feelings out of our system. The Bible gives us permission to do just that! The Bible also reminds us that we are in the hands of a God who as Father loves us and as potter always labors to form us into our most faithful, loving shape.

Potter God, even when I can't feel your presence, help me trust that I am held in the palm of your hand. Amen.

Come to save us!" This is the hopeful cry of God's people throughout the scriptures. Unfortunately, in many circles—both within and outside the church—the word *saved* has a rather narrow or shallow meaning. It has become a code word for hypocrisy, intolerance, and even hateful judgments against other people. Surely, this isn't what the psalmist has in mind when praying for God to "save." So what does it mean to be saved? What are we saved *from*? And what are we saved *for*?

Psalm 80 was possibly written in a time of deep despair just prior to or following the Assyrian invasion of the Northern Kingdom of Israel. The people cry out to God to fight for them, to restore what has been lost. We may not experience a conquering army, but other things invade and threaten to steal or destroy life—our lives as well as the lives of others. What things come to mind? Slavery to schedules, prejudice, resentment, racism, selfishness, fear, addiction, greed—anything that keeps us from loving God and loving our neighbor as ourselves. Perhaps God can save us from some of these things.

But what are we saved *for*? The psalmist prays to God as the Shepherd, an image that evokes care, guidance, sacrifice, protection, watchfulness, awareness of the dangers afoot and of the path toward safety and good pasture. God, like a good shepherd, can lead us along paths of peace and restored relationship with self, others, and God.

As those who have been so lovingly cared for, we are then called to share that same loving-kindness with others. We are saved for the purpose of love, mercy, compassion, justice, and joy. We are saved for sharing the life and love that God shares with us. And being saved becomes a blessing after all.

God, our Shepherd, save me from harmful living; save me for good! Amen.

Restore us, O God of hosts; let your face shine, that we may be saved." This psalm of lament cries for God's presence in the midst of great distress. The people interpret God's seeming absence as anger, which fosters their great anxiety. In verse 5, the psalmist states that the people have been fed the "bread of tears." This stands in sharp contrast to the bread of the Presence (literally "bread of faces"), which is the bread offered to God in the Temple. (See Exodus 25:30.) The sacred bread of the Presence evokes the remembered experience of God's nearness and sustenance. The people hunger for God's "face," for God's presence. For God's face to shine metaphorically indicates that God has turned toward the people in loving concern.

Stories of people who seem to be given nothing but tears to consume fill the headlines. In the midst of violence, suffering, and loss in our neighborhoods and around the world, the refrain of this psalm seems perennially resonant. Where is God in the midst of suffering? Why does God seem so far away? If God loves us, why are things allowed to be as they are?

Though the psalm doesn't answer these deeply human questions, its words point to an equally human response: hope in the restoring, life-giving power of God's love. As we draw closer to the first Sunday of Advent, we remember that God, out of love, came into the world in the flesh. We remember that in Jesus we see God's love in a human face. We remember that in the midst of all the world's pain, God's love has drawn near to sustain, restore, and save.

Let your face shine on me, loving God. Grant me hope, that I may live. Amen.

Longing for Hope

In these opening lines of Paul's letter to the church at Corinth, we see the apostle's deep desire for that beloved community. Paul writes in order to encourage the church to live the way of Jesus, to be strengthened in its witness to the gospel of Jesus Christ, and to develop the spiritual gifts among the members. Evidently, the church is dealing with power struggles, judgmental attitudes, doctrinal disputes, and disparities of treatment between rich and poor members.

In a city like Corinth—a large, wealthy, diverse urban center—power, money, and knowledge are hot commodities. But Paul speaks of being enriched not by money and power but by Christ Jesus. The gospel of Jesus radically shifts the focus and invites the church to turn from "idols" (1 Cor. 12:2) and toward the Spirit of God who is both source and activator of what is worth the most: spiritual gifts (1 Cor. 12:4-5). In this letter Paul reminds the church of the great dignity and value of every gift and every person. The Corinthians find themselves in the time between Advents; they "wait for the revealing of our Lord Jesus Christ." Paul advises them that they have the gifts and grace necessary for this time of waiting, and he admonishes them to demonstrate unity in their fellowship while they wait.

As we enter into the Advent time of waiting, Paul's words remind us that Christ Jesus is already among us, gracing us with gifts to share for the common good. It is in the waiting time that we receive the opportunity to welcome the love of Christ to transform us; to free us from rancor, judgment, injustice, and conflict; and to make of us a community that offers the world a sign of the faith, hope, and love that is our true calling.

Generous Spirit, open my hands and heart to receive—and share—your love and compassion. Amen.

SATURDAY, DECEMBER 2 ～ *Read Mark 13:24-31*

"**B**ut in those days, after that suffering. . . . " The opening words of today's reading speak to the whole point of Advent and Christmas. The community for which Mark writes faces persecution because of their Christian faith. In our own day, suffering, injustice, and persecution remain. At this time of year, it isn't uncommon to hear the phrase, "Remember the reason for the season." The reason is, of course, the birth of Jesus. That is why we celebrate.

But a reason for the reason we celebrate also exists: The world and its people were suffering, living in darkness—ruled by blindness, fear, violence, and confusion. And God so loved the world that, in that great sacrificial mystery of Incarnation, Jesus was born to be the Light of the world. The reason for the "reason for the season" is that God loves us so much that God gives us what we need: God, light, hope. In Jesus we learn that our hope is not in vain. Jesus fulfills the prophecy of the ancients: "Behold, a virgin shall conceive, and bear a son, and shall call his name Immanuel (Isa. 7:14, KJV).

We, like Mark's faith community, anticipate Jesus' return. The signs noted here signal great change: a darkened sun and moon, stars falling from heaven. We are to watch for the signs because only God knows the time of the Son of Man's return. The world takes hope in the promise of our God who proclaims that just as Christ came into a world in need, Christ will come again and all things will be made righteous. God's word will not pass away. The Light shines in the darkness—even in whatever darkness threatens or overshadows our lives. The Light shines in the darkness and the darkness does not—will not—overcome it.

Loving God, thank you for fulfilling your promises and not abandoning me. Amen.

Longing for Hope   399

FIRST SUNDAY OF ADVENT

The word *advent* means "coming" or "beginning." It represents a new start. And so, with the beginning of Advent each year, we may find ourselves thinking about how things will be different this year. This year the stress of the season won't lead to arguments or unhealthy overindulgence; this Advent we will truly sense God's presence, be mindful of what it's about; this Advent and Christmas will be happy, peaceful, perfect.

This longing may be a holdover from childhood—or a residual feeling left from years of romantic holiday ads—but the season's temptations to stress and excess challenge our longing. Advent invites us to wait, slow down, and stay awake to look for the coming of Christ, to open ourselves to receive this perfect gift. The culture around us crams our bodies and senses so full that there's little room left for the holy family to dwell—no room in our calendars, no room in our minds, no room in our budgets, no room in our bodies. How often do you suppose we metaphorically turn Mary and Joseph away because there's "no room" in us for them to give birth to the Christ?

A flight attendant once misspoke in giving the standard directions for deplaning saying, "Be careful as you open the overhead bins, as your *longings* may have shifted during the flight." Journeys do tend to shift things, and the journey we begin today invites us to shift our longings away from anything that distracts us from what matters most of all. We are invited to be alert instead to the surprising inbreakings of hope, of gentleness, of peace—even in the midst of stress, failure, and struggle. The journey we begin today calls us to direct our longings toward God and the promises for transformation that we receive in Jesus Christ.

> *Surprising God, slow me down and open me up to receive the peace that is your love for me in Christ Jesus. Amen.*

Faithful Wilderness Waiting

DECEMBER 4–10, 2017 • FRANK ROGERS JR.

SCRIPTURE OVERVIEW: Hopeful anticipation characterizes this week's texts. God's people have come to terms with their inability to save themselves. Isaiah 40 states that Jerusalem has "served her term" in bondage to sin; a new era is about to dawn. Psalm 85 continues the theme of old sins forgiven, emphasizing an urgent need for some fresh outbreak of God's initiatives. Harmonious and responsible relationships are to dominate the hearts of the people. Thoughts of righteousness and peace also pervade the passage from 2 Peter 3. Yet the focus is clearly on Christ's Second Advent. His coming will be sudden and unannounced; the new creation will then appear. The Gospel text focuses on the earthly ministry of Jesus as John the baptizer comes to sensitize all hearts to the advent of the One promised long ago.

QUESTIONS AND SUGGESTIONS FOR REFLECTION

- Read Isaiah 40:1-11. God's word of comfort brings challenge as well: How are you preparing the way of the Lord?
- Read Psalm 85:1-2, 8-13. What glimpses of heaven in your daily life give you confidence in God's steadfast love?
- Read 2 Peter 3:8-15a. How are you using this time of Advent waiting to move toward more faithful living?
- Read Mark 1:1-8. John identified himself as "messenger." How would you identify your role in working toward the reign of Christ?

Muriel Bernice Roberts Professor of Spiritual Formation and Narrative Pedagogy and codirector of the Center for Engaged Compassion at Claremont School of Theology, Claremont, California

Wilderness: barren wasteland; scorching desert by day; bone-chilling badlands at night. Wilderness is the territory of danger and desolation. Jackals prey in the wild; marauders raid from the shadows; nothingness extends beyond the horizon in every God-forsaken direction. It is the province of the outcast, the exiled, the refugee fleeing from terror, the wanderer without a home or a safe place to rest.

In today's text, Jerusalem has fallen to Nebuchadnezzar's army. The Babylonians have destroyed the Temple and carried the leading citizens from their homeland into Babylonian captivity. They find themselves despised, oppressed, displaced, and dispossessed. They fear they have wrought God's wrath, that God has judged them and found them detestable, that God has abandoned them to the schemes and shackles of their captors.

And against all hope, God speaks to them with tenderness. Of all things, God says, "Comfort my people." God is with them. However deep the valley of despair, however high the mountain of oppression; however rough and uneven the barren ground of hunger and affliction, the compassionate God is with them. And God's compassion brings the balm of comfort.

We often find ourselves in the wilderness as well. Vast arid plains of grief; the endless glare of aloneness; sweltering canyons of persecution; swirling sandstorms of despair; the soul-stealing pillagers of violence and poverty, bigotry and injustice. Our hearts cry out. How long can we go on depleted and beaten down, banished and abandoned?

Isaiah reminds us that God hears our Advent cry and speaks a tender word. A word that will stand forever. "Comfort. Take comfort. I am with you. Even in the wilderness."

Within whatever wilderness I may wander, help me, God, to know you are with me. Like a healing spring in the desert, you comfort me. Amen.

My wife and I were driving through the desert on our way to the Grand Canyon. We navigated the two-lane highways crisscrossing the barren expanse when, seemingly out of nowhere, a sandstorm engulfed us. Gale-force winds pounded the car from the side as sand blew so hard the wiper blades, snapping at full speed, could barely clear a patch of windshield.

We inched along, hoping to drive through it, guessing our direction at each dust-shrouded intersection. The storm was too much. With visibility reduced to near zero, we pulled alongside the road, truly in the middle of nowhere. With sand drifting at our tires and windows, we waited. How long, O Lord? Will this monsoon of sand last forever? How long until you deliver us?

The Israelites are ensnared in the wilderness as well. The winds and sandstorms of Babylonian oppression threaten to rob them of their faith and hope. Yet, within the storm a voice cries out, "In the wilderness prepare the way of the LORD, make straight in the desert a highway for our God."

Isaiah is steadfast. He reassures the people that God will not abandon them; God will come down the desert highway, guiding them like a shepherd, leading them safely to freedom.

For my wife and me, a prophet did not appear on the highway; a shepherd did not lead us to safety. We simply sat the storm out. The winds died down. The dust stopped its raging. The wipers wiped the windshield clean. And before us, we saw it: a highway stretched out straight through the desert, pointing to the mountains where our destination awaited. We followed the highway to safety. Yet so much wasteland remains in our world. Isaiah invites us to hold fast to our hope. A highway will appear. God will hear us. Wait. Wait with hope.

Help us trust, O God, that within our wilderness your path will appear. Amen.

An elderly man at my church, a widower for a dozen years, endured chronic pains from aging, a drafty downsized apartment, a dwindling social security check, and several thousand miles between him and his adult children and grandchildren. Yet, his spirit was always buoyant. I asked him once, "What sustains your hope?"

The man told me a story. He and his missus, on their fortieth wedding anniversary, searched for a first-class restaurant. They found one that surpassed their imaginations—adorned with white tablecloths, fine china, and sculptures made of ice. Upon hearing about the anniversary, the entire staff, some thirty people—tuxedoed maître d's and aproned dishwashers alike—broke open bottles of champagne, on the house, and toasted the couple, total strangers, as if they were celebrities. My friend glowed just remembering. It was a peek at heaven, where persons from around the globe will break bread together at the feast of life. These moments keep him alive and going.

Today's psalm, written after the Israelites' return from Babylon, does not speak of triumphant homecoming. The Temple still lay in ruins; the land yielded few crops; the threat of war seemed ever present.

And yet, the people remember. Jacob had fallen on hard times, drought leading his people to exile in Egypt. God heard their plight and restored them into a twelve-tribe nation. Remembering God's faithfulness gave the Israelites hope. In the midst of decay and division, it kept their spirits alive.

Waiting faithfully within the wilderness includes remembering our hope—remembering our peeks at heaven in the past and remembering that the God who has restored before will restore God's people once more.

Remember a sacred moment in your life. Savor God's presence within it. Allow that moment's grace to nourish hope within your life today.

Raul Torres, a retired custodian, lived on a corner lot in south central Los Angeles. When his wife of forty-five years passed away, he transformed his yard into a memorial garden. Flowers, fruit trees, herbs, vegetables, and rows of roses, his beloved's favorite, flourished under his care.

One morning, he discovered several rosebushes butchered as if assaulted with a machete. Two days later, it happened again. Holding vigil another morning, he spied who did it. A young boy, walking with a cane after a gang bullet nicked his leg, pummeled yet another bush. When he saw Raul in the window, he spit with defiance and left.

Raul could see the boy's despair, and he felt mercy. Instead of turning him in, he found the boy later that day. He shared that he had a problem with his rosebushes. The boy swore innocence. That's not what Raul meant. Raul wanted to hire the boy to protect them. Raul would pay him, and teach him how to garden along the way. Though skeptical, the boy dropped by. He took to gardening and to Raul. From that day forward, the garden was never vandalized again.

When God restores God's reign, the psalmist declares, mercy and truth, justice and peace will embrace. The fruits of faith's fullness will rise from the ground, and the land's harvest will flourish. How do we wait for the coming of God's reign? We lay out a path for God's footsteps, a path of righteousness and compassion.

Raul makes a path for God. And God is faithful. The soil of Raul's mercy, laced with justice and the invitation to right relationship, takes root. Healing rises from the ground, as does new life. God's regenerative Spirit follows the path laid out, transforming despair's wilderness into a garden's abundance.

As we await your reign, O God, help us lay a path for your coming, a path of mercy and truth, justice and peace. Amen.

Faithful Wilderness Waiting

Though eighty years old, Mawanda held vigil each Friday at noon in front of the local police station. For years, she had endured Zimbabwe's brutal dictatorship without protest as farmlands withered, thugs confiscated whatever they chose, and dissenters disappeared into secret torture camps. Then her husband and son were arrested, driven away in hoods, and never seen again. Now, Mawanda stood in protest. Enduring beatings, tauntings, and public strip searches, she had held weekly vigils for over three years. Justice seemed an impossible dream.

One of the militia taunted her, "Why do you keep this up, old woman? You have no hope. We are too strong. We will beat you down until you can't get up and we will be here to stay."

Mawanda replied, "I hope because the power within me is stronger than the power of this world. God hears the cries of the oppressed and will raise the lowly up. You can beat me down, but I will rise up out of the grave if necessary. The power of justice, the power of God, does not die. Maybe today, maybe in a thousand years, tyranny will fall, and God's righteousness will reign across the land."

Today's text was written several generations after Jesus' death. His followers expected him to return and establish God's reign within a few months of his death. Now those months stretched into decades. Scoffers were rampant, chastising Christians for continuing to believe.

God will return. Oppression, in all forms, will be vanquished. Truth and justice will be secured. It will happen like a thief in the night, like the Berlin Wall crumbling in a moment. So wait steadfastly. And keep your hope unblemished. Stand up for righteousness with courage, for the impossible dream is God's guarantee.

Faithful God, as we wait for the coming of your reign on earth, help us be strong in the truth of our hope. Amen.

Can you imagine living in the segregated South of the 1950s where African Americans were banned from public facilities; where black schools, hospitals, and neighborhoods were under resourced; where dissent was silenced by lynchings, beatings, even bombings? And can you imagine, after decades of discrimination, somebody racing down the street shouting, "He's here! The one we have been waiting for! The one who's going to mobilize the masses to defy racism, end segregation, and restore the dignity of African Americans. His name is Martin Luther King. His weapons are love and compassion. He's mobilizing hope. I'm telling you, the time has come. The people are rising."

Can you imagine the people on the banks of the Jordan who first hear John the Baptist? For generations, the Israelites have proclaimed Isaiah's hope—in the wilderness, prepare the way of the Lord, for God is coming to restore God's people. And now, after centuries of suffering, the herald announces that the time of God's arrival has come! It is happening as he speaks. God, already, is coming down the highway.

John is the messenger Isaiah had promised centuries before. John embodies his role as a prophet. He dresses like Elijah, eats like Daniel, and experiences God's coming, not in the ecclesiastical and political centers but in the wilderness. And in the wilderness, John speaks Isaiah's electrifying words. The One we have been waiting for . . . our hope and salvation . . . is coming—*now*.

Within our contemporary wildernesses, prophets have arisen: ambassadors of hope, mobilizers of transformation. Their voices cry out in the desert, "It is happening. Gather with the faithful. Rise up from oppression. God is coming. Here. Now." Can you imagine?

O God, may we hear the voice of your prophets who assure
us that our cries have been heard; you are on the way. Amen.

Faithful Wilderness Waiting   407

SUNDAY, DECEMBER 10 ～ *Read Mark 1:1-8*

SECOND SUNDAY OF ADVENT

Mike hated the commercialism of Christmas. When forced to retire early, he checked out altogether. "Get me nothing," he grouched, "until people understand what Christmas is all about." That year, his wife, Nan, gave him a white envelope, which she nestled into the tree. Inside, Nan pledged to sew uniforms for an underprivileged wrestling team. Once she started, Mike decided to help. Together, they sized the children, cut the fabric, and befriended the school kids. By year's end, Mike was ready for another envelope. Nan left another that Christmas, and each year thereafter. The acts of kindness they shared together sprouted throughout their city: birdhouses for a refuge, a playground for a children's home, a community garden from a vacant lot. Those became the best years of their lives.

One year, Mike passed away three days before Christmas. Friends and family gathered to share Nan's grief. On Christmas Eve, Nan placed, for Mike, one last envelope into the tree. She awoke Christmas morning to squeals downstairs. As she came down, she surveyed her loved ones. Then she saw the tree. It was covered in white. Dozens of envelopes—from every child, grandchild, nephew, and niece—pledged acts of kindness in honor of Mike, the man who loved Christmas.

How do we wait faithfully for God in the wilderness? The prophet Isaiah says, "Prepare the way of the Lord; make his paths straight." We pave a straight path for God through acts of kindness, justice, generosity, and compassion. When we love, God will come. "The one who is more powerful than I is coming after me," John says. As sure as a baby's birth in a manger, as abundant as Christmas envelopes multiplying into the future, God will walk the path laid out. Love will encompass our world.

Baby of the manger, may each act of kindness be a straw in your crib, preparing the way for your coming. Amen.

The Shape of Advent Joy

DECEMBER 11–17, 2017 • BETH LUDLUM

SCRIPTURE OVERVIEW: In Isaiah 61, the Anointed One declares a message of liberation. Justice, righteousness, and praise will blossom as new shoots of growth in the garden of the Lord. Psalm 126 remembers a time in the past when God's mercy broke forth in an unparalleled manner. The character of the community and of the individual members will be transformed. The First Thessalonians text voices a yearning for the "coming of our Lord Jesus Christ," yet the promise of the Second Advent has kindled great hope and gladness in the heart of the Christian community. The reading from the Gospel of John also raises the issue of the mood of expectancy that characterizes the period of time between promise and fulfillment.

QUESTIONS AND SUGGESTIONS FOR REFLECTION

- Read Isaiah 61:1-4, 8-11. If "the spirit of the Lord GOD is upon" you, what does that mean for the way you live day by day?
- Read Psalm 126. Have you experienced joy in a time of brokenness? How do you understand the seeming contradictions?
- Read 1 Thessalonians 5:16-24. Which of the disciplines Paul speaks of in verses 16-22 do you faithfully practice? Which might you cultivate further?
- Read John 1:6-8, 19-28. John not only knows his role; he knows who he is not: the Messiah. In this time of Advent waiting, consider who you are not. How does that consideration simplify your life? What may you release?

Vice President for Strategic Initiatives at Wesley Theological Seminary, Washington, DC

Many Advent calendars refer to the third Sunday as Gaudete Sunday—the Sunday of joy. In many churches, congregants will light a candle and read words that remind us to lean into the season with joy. Beyond the church walls, generators of joy surround us as well—ribbons and bows, carols and classic movies, extravagant menus and time with those we love.

But we know the joy of Christmas rarely lasts long. The carols cease, and our indulgences perhaps lead to a gym membership. We pack away the nativity set even before the kings have arrived at Epiphany. Maybe that's why, before Christmas has even passed, stores stock shelves for Valentine's Day, the next shot of commercially available happiness.

This week's passages allow us to explore the nature of Christian joy. Paul's letter reminds us that joy is a core component of the Christian life, a quality of life we should recognize, practice, and cultivate continuously, not just in particular seasons or circumstances.

In the past several years, Christian and secular authors alike have brought a renewed focus to cultivating gratitude. A friend of mine adopted a daily discipline of posting on social media things for which she is grateful. As a result, she has found her outlook on life transformed. When we acknowledge the joy in our lives, we become more joyful.

Cultivating joy requires human effort alongside divine work, so perhaps this is the orientation for the week ahead: to begin by naming goodness wherever we see it and by giving thanks for ribbons and bows and sweet music and strong memories and a kind smile and, most of all, the ways the Christ child is revealed to us even now. Perhaps, as we practice joy, we will begin to enter into the joy of Advent, the joy of anticipation, the joy of the Christ whom we await.

What are three specific moments, people, or things for which you are thankful today?

The psalmist voices a joyful, hopeful poetic account of the community's life in God. But it's written in a curious structure. It's hard to tell what is past, what is present, and what is a hoped-for future. We can't really tell what's a proclamation of fact and what's a proclamation of faith. Throughout the passage, the author moves from recounting to petition to proclaiming the good news of what God will do. Remarkably, that's exactly what Advent does, as well.

The season of Advent reminds us that joy is tied up in longing, belief, waiting, and anticipation. Joy is born in the fullness of life's brokenness, as well as in the fullness of God's promise. We cry out for God even as we proclaim God's nearness; we acknowledge our pain even as we name our blessings and as we ask for more.

Psalm 126 reflects a beautiful movement from recollection to petition to anticipation, sometimes all in the same breath. And perhaps that's an appropriate characterization of a faithful life. Life is seldom stagnant and our minds are seldom still; we live in a swirl of memory and anticipation, anxiety and hope. The psalmist shows us that in the swirl of remembering, rejoicing, and praying for more, we can abandon ourselves to the hope and joy of God who stands beyond the constraints of time. And as we do so, we become bearers of the good news to the world—proclaiming simultaneously what God has done and what God will do, even as we cry out for God's presence and action to join our kingdom work here and now.

God, help me to step into the wonder of life in you. Help me see the places where I can faithfully tell of your goodness, proclaim your hope, and stand with others in prayer. May I learn to let go of my time line and expectations in order to step into your joy that knows no bounds. Amen.

"Know thyself." In my world, this is an oft-repeated maxim. Ancient wisdom and modern psychology have taught us that self-awareness is essential for any leader, any church, or any relationship to succeed.

But while most personality tests or spiritual-gifts assessments focus on who we *are*, some of the crucial self-discoveries are about who we're *not*.

The Gospel of John's introduction of John the Baptist exemplifies this reality, describing him almost entirely by who he's not. He's not the light. He's not the Messiah. He's not Elijah. He's not the prophet.

Taken out of context, we might wonder if John is having an identity crisis. And yet his message seems refreshing—a message we probably need to hear during this season: It's not about him.

How would repeated reminders of this message affect how we engage in Christmas preparations? Perhaps they would cause us to rethink what we do and how. Do the Christmas cards with the beautiful family photos show that our life is great, or do they point to the One who is coming? Are the exquisitely wrapped gifts an attempt to match our mental image of holiday perfection, or do they point toward the Christ child?

This realization is not meant to bring guilt or judgment but freedom. It's not about you. When the turkey doesn't turn out quite right or the gifts aren't wrapped on time, it's okay—because this is not about you. When the same family argument breaks out in spite of your attempt to appease everyone, it's not about you. When you're the preacher and you run out of words to comfort or transform, it's not about you. We have a part to play, but it's not about us. One who is greater is coming.

God, may all our Advent reflections and Christmas preparations be not about me but about pointing to your light, your joy that is to come. Amen.

My five-year-old godson dreams of things beyond any waking experiences: dragons and castles, flying trains and talking trucks, foreign lands and mighty wizards. When he wakes up, he's always on the lookout, certain that the dragon or talking truck will show up any time. My dreams—and my confidence in dreams—are pitiful by comparison.

I recently asked several friends if they've ever used the phrase, "it's a dream come true," as an adult. None could recollect a time. Like me, they could name many things they've hoped for, even wondrous and unexpected changes in the world that have come to pass; yet nothing reached beyond what could be imagined, planned for, and accomplished by human power.

I write this reflection during a troubled season. It's been a hard year, filled with racial unrest and injustice, civil war, abuses of power, and natural disasters. Whenever I tune in to the news, I find it difficult to stretch my imagination beyond simply hoping for less violence, less destruction, and some relief for those already caught up in tragic situations.

In contrast, both the psalmist and the prophet Isaiah testify to a different reality. Nations are restored. Cities are repaired. Sadness turns to joy. The oppressed are lifted up, justice reigns, and all people are free. These are not Band-Aid™ solutions. This is a God-sized vision, a faith proclamation that God will make all things right, will redeem and restore all of creation.

Can you imagine what might happen if we learned to dream again? These sorts of dreams can seem so improbable as to be foolish. They are beyond anything we can accomplish solely through human effort. Yet we know in our bones that such dignity, freedom, justice, and joy is meant to be. God's promise is nothing short of a dream come true.

God, grant me the ability to dream your salvation-sized, God-sized dreams that lead me into joy and praise. Amen.

The Shape of Advent Joy   413

The opening lines of this reading speak clearly to my heart. Jesus reads these verses aloud in the synagogue after his wilderness temptations; they set the tone for his ministry. They've been central to the mission of many faith communities of which I've been a part. The passage offers a vision of what God will do, but the words also proclaim that God has anointed the author to play a role too.

Once we have opened our minds to God's dream for the world—once we have refocused our dreams on what only God can do—then we discover that we also have a role. Isaiah reminds us that it's not one or the other, dreaming or doing. Joy comes from the deep belief and trust that God will restore everything, but joy also comes from knowing that we join in with our own efforts, resources, and prayers. Joy comes from the knowledge that we can sow seeds of transformation and that God's harvest will be more abundant than we can ever imagine.

Our engagement is essential even as we acknowledge that we cannot do it all. We may not be able to eradicate poverty any time soon, but we can ensure that more children feel loved and celebrated this Christmas. Although we cannot automatically end the preschool-to-prison pipeline that exists for young men of color, we can disrupt it by mentoring a boy or by advocating for educational access and quality in underserved communities. Although we cannot reverse the effects of decades of pollution on our earth, we can commit to recycling and walk instead of drive this week.

During this Advent, we are invited into the joy of the triune God by joining in the work of creation and restoration.

God, give me confidence in your promise of restoration, and help me see my role in your kingdom work of mending the world. Amen.

SATURDAY, DECEMBER 16 ～ *Read 1 Thessalonians 5:16-24*

I need goals and deadlines. Whether it's a work project, exercise habits, or writing these devotions, I do my best when I have a goal that stretches me and a plan to get there. That's one reason I love the new year, with its emphasis on new goals.

Yet psychologists report that in order for someone to reach a goal, it has to be explicit, achievable, and, best of all, be taken on with others. If the goal is simply to lose weight, you'll forget about it soon; if it's to lose one hundred pounds, you'll probably give up; but if you and your running partner set out to add one mile each week to your route, you're likely to succeed.

Paul offers explicit instructions to the Thessalonians about how to practice their faith, and he spells out essential disciplines to cultivate: prayer, discernment, thanksgiving, and listening both to the Spirit and to prophets.

I'm grateful for these tangible instructions for growth. But the best part comes in the final lines of this passage. It is not our efforts alone that will achieve our sanctification, Paul reminds us. God works with us and ultimately will accomplish this work in us. Throughout our moments of strength and of greatest weakness, God remains faithful to God's promises.

We are called to work, to pray, and to join the movement of the Spirit. We attend to the needs of the world and our own souls. But in the end, our confidence lies not in our own abilities but in God's. And for that, we rejoice always.

God, draw me nearer to you. Help me to pray, to rejoice, to discern, and to cling to what is good, that my soul and life may be shaped by you. But most of all, help me place my full confidence in your work in my life and in the world. Amen.

The Shape of Advent Joy   415

THIRD SUNDAY OF ADVENT

Afew years ago I went to a restaurant that had earned a wonderful reputation. Once seated, I learned that I had no decisions to make because the restaurant served one standard eight-course tasting menu. When the first appetizer courses arrived, one at a time, I was taken aback by the small portions.

Determined to enjoy the experience anyway, I slowly savored each course, grateful for each bite, as well as the good conversation and beautiful surroundings. When the server placed the final entrée before me—a gorgeous beef tenderloin grilled to perfection—I had to concede that the chef knew exactly what he was doing. The first four delectable but not fully satisfying courses had perfectly primed my palate to enjoy the centerpiece of the meal.

During the Christmas season, I find myself wanting everything to be perfect now—the presents wrapped just right, the cookies flawlessly arranged, the decorations warm and sparkling. For many people, the Christmas season brings out the highest and lowest human emotions, the simplest joys and the most complicated feelings. And while we need to be fully present to the love, the beauty, and the brokenness we may experience during the season, John reminds us that all of this is but an appetizer.

During long-anticipated family homecomings, John still whispers, "This is a foretaste of what is to come." When perfect facades no longer hold back the mounting stress, John reminds us, "There's more to the story." When we feel overwhelmed by the world's problems, the promise of Advent is simply, "This is not the end."

God, in the most beautiful and the most painful moments alike, help me find joy and peace in the promise of your kingdom and in the Prince of Peace who is coming to reign forever. Amen.

Imagine!

DECEMBER 18–24, 2017 • STEPHEN BAUMAN

SCRIPTURE OVERVIEW: Second Samuel 7 extols Yahweh's choice of the family of David as the extraordinary vehicle for divine salvation. God now plans to do a new and unparalleled thing in the life of humankind. Mary's song of wonder from Luke 1 serves as the psalm selection. It centers on her realization that human life will now never be the same. In the epistle reading, Paul rejoices that by the power of God the times are what they are. In the Gospel text, Gabriel announces to Mary that she will bear the "Son of God." Overwhelmed by both the holiness and the enormity of the moment, Mary nonetheless consents to the will of God as brought by God's messenger.

QUESTIONS AND SUGGESTIONS FOR REFLECTION

- Read 2 Samuel 7:1-11, 16. Respond to the author's question, "How shall we interpret good fortune or bad from the perspective of God's good care for us?"
- Read Luke 1:47-55. How do you learn to embrace the mystery of holy time in the commonplace events of your day?
- Read Romans 16:25-27. How has God's love shown through Jesus Christ proved to be an antidote to your fears?
- Read Luke 1:26-38. Where do you see the "lowly lifted up and the hungry filled with good things"? How can you participate in that gracious work of God? What fears can you name before God?

Senior Minister, Christ Church United Methodist, New York City; author of *Simple Truths: On Values, Civility, and Our Common Good* based on award-winning radio commentary

When God gave the law to Moses, God instructed him on how to build a tabernacle. Throughout Israel's history, from Mount Sinai to the reign of David, the tabernacle had functioned flawlessly. God remained with the chosen people as the ark sat sheltered in the tabernacle; when the people moved from one location to another, the tabernacle holding the ark went with them. God ultimately gave them victory over their enemies and possession of the promised land.

When David becomes king, he builds himself a beautiful palace. Admiring his good work and fortune, he notices the ark and decides that he will build an appropriate house for God. But through his counselor and prophet, Nathan, God informs David that it is God who will build a house for David, not the other way around.

God promises David an everlasting throne, continued rest from his enemies, a good name, and a house that will last forever. The descendants of David—his "house"—will enjoy a unique and privileged relationship with God, often described as a father-child relationship.

Yet, as is often the case with biblical revelation, the human actors think and behave one way, while God reveals another possibility. God's intended outcomes are vastly more expansive than the ones humans can conceive as they strive to place their own mark on history. How do we align our aspirations with God's? How are we to make sense of our relative place in the created order? And how shall we interpret good fortune or bad from the perspective of God's good care for us?

As the biblical story unfolds, David's own story finds an astonishing climax with the birth of a boy in a stable centuries later, "of the house and lineage of David." Imagine!

Holy One, break open our hearts and minds to the astonishing outcome you intend! Amen.

The young woman who came to see me one December was in her early twenties and obviously pregnant. As she spilled out her story, tears welled in her eyes. She had fallen in love, she said. The young man had spoken of commitment, but when he discovered they had conceived a child, he fled, leaving her alone. Some combination of instinct and "in-your-face" resolve led her to decide to keep the child.

Now, with about a month to go before delivery, she had fallen into a great depression. She had lost hope. Her job was precarious, and anyway, wasn't our culture hostile to children? Wasn't it an impossible task for a single woman of little means to raise an emotionally healthy child?

Because of the time of year, it came to me to remember the story of another young, single, pregnant woman who conceived an infant in dangerous days. And though difficult, wasn't the gift of life the harbinger of hope?

Did this young woman seated before me remember the story? I asked if I could share it with her. She nodded her approval, and I read Luke's account of Gabriel's dialogue with Mary. She stopped me when Gabriel said, "Do not be afraid, Mary," and we considered how frequently fear came stomping through our lives as the great enemy, the great interrupter.

We acknowledged that she had chosen to follow a potentially difficult path in the pattern of many women for millennia. Decisions and hard choices lay ahead. After forthrightly naming our fears, we prayed for strength, courage, love, and grace.

The young woman endured, then thrived, as did her child; and twenty-five years later I had the privilege of baptizing her grandchild.

Holy God, help me to name my fears with courage. Give me strength, love, and grace in the name of the child of Bethlehem who came that I might have and share abundant life. Amen.

Imagine!   419

At the time of Jesus' birth, Israel groaned under Roman oppression. The Israelites yearned for release from the harsh yoke, in part because an aspect of Jewish identity was bound up in understanding themselves as agents of God's redemption for the world. This understanding helps account for the confusion surrounding Jesus' actual identity. He definitely challenged the status quo political culture but never self-identified as a political liberator for Israel. This confounded the disciples as they attempted to understand the meaning of Jesus' life and mission.

Mary's Song reclaims God's redemptive intention established through Abraham who gave birth to a great nation. For followers of Jesus, Mary's prophetic idea exploded into a wondrous revelation of freedom for all people. In one sense the prophecy was "spiritualized," released from physical boundaries in the resurrection dynamic. In this way it became available to everyone in every time. But then, it only made sense when this spiritual truth took root in individual lives once again.

An energetic flow between the spiritual and physical realms is at play here. The timeless nature of Jesus' redemption is potently available in our own time. Jesus is God's commitment to a radical redefinition of those found acceptable to God. It's a topsy-turvy revelation straight from God's imagination that continues to confound contemporary disciples. Mary, God's handmaiden, poor, accused of breaching vows of engagement, breathes an electrifying call-to-arms for the sake of God's love and justice.

We may ask these questions: Where today does God scatter the proud in the imaginations of their hearts? Where are the lowly lifted up and the hungry filled with good things? And then, where is the evidence of God's intention in those who follow after the way blazed by Mary's child?

Holy God, help me to sing like Mary. Amen.

It has never been harder to encourage sustained spiritual behaviors among people who are attracted to The Way Jesus blazed. Your reading this devotional is a minority activity, probably even among the members and friends of your church and family—not that this series of reflections is the be-all and end-all of spiritual wisdom. They are an offering from your fellow sojourners on The Way, to help focus your attention on the small child of Bethlehem, the unknown young man of Nazareth, the rejected preacher, the naked man on the cross, and all that came before and after to the present moment of your reading.

Wow! Is it ever hard to cut through the clutter and noise and info bits and videos and pics and whatnot and hooha! We find it hard to sit still, quietly, intentionally, prayerfully, allowing ourselves the holy luxury of spiritual perplexity in the manner of Mary and a time for "pondering." It requires seemingly enormous energy to construct a spiritual discipline that returns us to the heart of life each and every day. Our time consumed by many trifles, we leave little in reserve for the things that matter most of all hiding in plain sight but lacking the snap-crackle of Instagram and Snapchat flicking across our consciousness like a stone skipping on water.

Is it my imagination or is there an epidemic of adult ADHD on the horizon? Enduring relationships require focus, energy, commitment, attention, time—including spiritual relationships with self, others, and God.

How can we ever find the wherewithal to leap into the realm of God's imagination, especially at this crazy-making time of year? I am relieved to read that for all our haphazard attempts at keeping our eye on the manger, Gabriel assures us that nothing will be impossible with God.

Sit quietly for five minutes in a state of spiritual perplexity, marveling at the incomprehensibility of Incarnation—Emmanuel, God with us.

I live in midtown Manhattan amid a forest of tall buildings—with many more under construction. Wandering among these massive structures, some with impressive cranes pricking the sky, can make a person feel insignificant by comparison—small, vulnerable.

I was present the dreadful day when two of the tallest buildings came crashing down in a deadly conflagration at the end of my island home on infamous 9/11. The magnificent city built from human ingenuity had become a target uncovering our formerly disguised vulnerability. Everyone felt it. In the days that followed, churches clogged with scores of those who had not set foot in one for a long while. This newfound *en masse* religious awakening did not last; but at the time, New Yorkers shared an experience of our fragile condition.

We all have occasions when circumstance underscores the precarious nature of our situation as creatures fashioned of frail flesh. And this was true for the early Christians. Paul found his way into prison and martyrdom; so too did many other followers of The Way. But in the meantime he rests confidently within God's imagination, telling his friends that God alone "is able to strengthen you according to my gospel and the proclamation of Jesus Christ."

We read this doxology in Advent to help ignite our own imaginations about the true nature of Bethlehem's child. We feel at risk when we consider our particular precarious situation, but this child will prove the antidote to our fear, for he will take on the burden of human weakness so that we can find strength to live with confident hope in the face of every adversity. This great truth calls us to embrace our better selves while kneeling in the straw cradle-side in Bethlehem.

Awesome God, you are my strength. You alone know the nature of my precarious situation. I will trust you as the child of Bethlehem takes on the burden of my weakness. Amen.

Every parent who has been present at their child's birth will tell a variation on the same experience: the most amazing thing ever! Words cannot contain the range of emotion. I well remember the birth of my firstborn who is now thirty-six years old. When a nurse handed Luke to me immediately after delivery, I said aloud, "Well, all right! Here you are! So be it! Whatever happens, you are mine and I am yours; you will be a gift for certain!" And we have had many adventures ever since that continue to unfold in ways that could never have been known or predicted, yet inevitably led to a wondrous gratitude.

Given my gender, I can only marvel at the experience of a child leaping in the womb; but the awesomeness of life begetting life is among the most spectacular facets of human self-awareness. Advent is all about this elemental aspect of existence—a celebration of life, the begetting of life, the promise of life, and the gift of life abundant for all!

Elizabeth and Mary, the mothers of John and Jesus, experience this wonderment, this promise of life ahead. They cannot know the paths their sons will travel, that their lives as well as their deaths will forever point to a future imbued with hope.

Death leading to hope points to the paradoxical nature of the season. We know the trajectory of the lives these men will lead, yet here's the thing: Though headed for brutal deaths they remain beacons of hope for life abundant. That is the mystery that holds the key to the door of faith—faith in our God of life that inevitably leads to a wondrous gratitude.

Holy One, surely you are the God of life, the one who makes things that are out of things that are not. What an awesome, grace-filled awareness we have been given! All praise to you! Amen.

FOURTH SUNDAY OF ADVENT, CHRISTMAS EVE

The stable has always intrigued me. Not the shepherds and wise men, so-called. Not Joseph and Mary. But the stable. The idea of it. The feel of it. The smell of it. The sounds within it. The earthiness and even vulgarity of such a setting for such a thing as we celebrate. I am taken with its fundamental humility. Holiness incarnate comes in a squealing child of questionable genetics born under unfortunate circumstance. God with us. God. With us. Deeply intimate with our humanity, exposure, vulnerability. Only a God such as this could have my allegiance—*does* have my allegiance.

Author Madeleine L'Engle refers to this strange occurrence in her book by the same title as "the Glorious Impossible." Sprung from God's holy imagination, human minds could not have conjured such a thing. It situates just beyond the limits of believability, beckoning our faith that this child holds the key to unlocking life's great mysteries.

Once again Mary has reason to ponder these matters in her heart. As the story is told, you recall she did the same following Gabriel's announcement; that is, she set to pondering. In the face of such an astonishing occurrence, pondering seems an appropriately humble posture. We can benefit from a lot more of it.

Among the things we might ponder includes the path this child will walk as he grows into adulthood. How it begins in humility and ends in humility. And in between those bookends, a revelation of love that was higher, wider, deeper than any humans had yet imagined. This love would prove larger than death and, looping back to this night's wonderment, how appropriate that this love begins in birth.

Glory to God in the highest heaven! All praise and thanksgiving to the One who comes clothed only in humility. Amen.

Love Is Born

DECEMBER 25–31, 2017 • BECCA STEVENS, DON WELCH

SCRIPTURE OVERVIEW: Ecstasy over the Christmas miracle binds these passages together with unrestrained joy over what God has done and over who God is. The God whom these texts celebrate is a God who reigns in strength and whose activity on behalf of humankind is timelessly ancient. As worshipers, we join in rejoicing over the coming of the messenger "who says to Zion, 'Your God reigns'" (Isa. 52:7). We also celebrate "the LORD, for he is coming to judge the earth . . . with righteousness, and . . . equity" (Ps. 98:9). Then a note of immediacy is struck by the focus on what God has done just now, in these "last days," in which "he has spoken to us by a Son" (Heb. 1:2). The One who was present at Creation, the eternal Word, "became flesh and lived among us" (John 1:14).

QUESTIONS AND SUGGESTIONS FOR REFLECTION

- Read Isaiah 52:7-10. Where do you see signs of God's peace amid the world's brokenness?
- Read Psalm 98. Where in your life has a new beginning come most startlingly from an ending?
- Read Hebrews 1:1-12. When you next celebrate the sacrament of Holy Communion, reflect on how God has brought healing to your life.
- Read Luke 2:22-40. When have you been surprised by an inbreaking of God's extraordinary love in an ordinary moment?

Becca Stevens, President & founder of Thistle Farms, Episcopal priest, author, and 2016 CNN Hero, Nashville, Tennessee; Don Welch, St. Augustine's Chapel, Nashville, Tennessee

CHRISTMAS DAY

"The Lord GOD will cause righteousness and praise to spring up." Every Christmas morning for the past twenty-five years I have sprung up out of my bed to celebrate with children the joy and wonder that we call Christmas. Because of them I can see the magic of how hope changes the ordinary life in our house to a wonderland of love. Christmas comes like a gift. It sweeps in during Advent to say simply, "Love is born"; you don't have to wait or watch. It has sprung up in the middle of night while you slept and has brought you good tidings of great joy.

Isaiah accurately reflects that such unbounded joy feels like "the robe of righteousness" covered with a garland and jewels, like we are going to a feast. We spend much time in our lives working hard, discerning the call, standing for justice, and loving our neighbors. Ah, but every now and then, the waters part and joy shines out like the dawn. This is that day! This is the day to see the sunrise as a miracle. This is the day to remember that in the midst of violence and oppression, life is full of freedom. This is the day to know that in the midst of hurt and fear, hope never dies!

I believe Christmas was created to remember that there is a space for the optimist. A place exists for those who want to live and work as a witness to the truth that in the end love is the most powerful force for change in the world. In this way, the true gift of Christmas comes—where each of us remembers we are "a crown of beauty in the hand of the LORD."

O God, you have caused this holy night to shine with the brightness of the true Light. Grant that we, who have known the mystery of that Light on earth, may also enjoy him perfectly in heaven; where with you and the Holy Spirit he lives and reigns, one God, in glory everlasting. Amen.

"G lory to God in the highest," proclaim the angels at Jesus' birth. Birth is always a miraculous event, a happening that evokes praise for our Creator and brings forth new life.

The angels' proclamation echoes an ancient Hebrew call to praise! In today's passage, the psalmist exhorts all of creation to "Praise the Lord!" This summons is directed to all rulers, all people, the sun, the moon, all stars, and all creatures on the earth. God is to be praised, the psalmist tells us, because God commanded and through God's proclamation all were created.

We are called to praise not only with our lips but through our lives, our words, and our deeds. We live in praise when we live in gratitude for all that we have received, with reverence for the sacredness of the whole of creation. We express our reverence for creation through stewardship of the gift from the One we praise. We acknowledge and respect each and every thing in the world that surrounds us. We are created to praise by giving ourselves to God's service and walking in holiness all the days of our lives.

These sentiments sound familiar to our ears. They form a constant, recurring refrain in our faith communities. Just as the language of the psalm, from hundreds of years earlier, echoes in the words of Luke, so did Francis of Assisi sound the theme hundreds of years after Luke. Today we continue the traditions and give them new life by singing his words of praise: "All creatures of our God and King, lift up your voice and with us sing, O praise ye! Alleluia!" (UMH, no. 62)

God, we praise your holy work. Help us bend our will in reverence to all creation, express gratitude for the life to which you have given birth, and remain dedicated to faithful stewardship in our life among all life. Amen.

Love Is Born

Even as the apostle Paul exhorts his readers in first-century Galatia to remember the adoption of God that envelops all hurts and abandonments, we bear witness to the truth that no one is alone, that all are beautiful children of God, worthy of being welcomed home. This passage proclaims that good news, and I have learned this lesson a hundred times through the community I founded called Thistle Farms, which serves women who are survivors of trafficking, violence, and addiction.

On one of my recent speaking engagements, Lori, a resident in our community, came with me. I love the joyous spirit she brings to new communities around this country as we strive to open housing for women who were traumatized as children and on average hit the streets between the ages of fourteen and sixteen. Recalling her place as a beautiful child of God was never more poignant than on the night she knocked on my hotel door late and asked if she could come in. I opened my door and asked her what had happened. She said, "You won't believe what happened. I looked in the mirror, and I saw something beautiful." As she told her story I imagined that as the scales fell from her eyes, she felt the arms of every person who loves and supports her healing, and she realized that she was an heir to an inheritance of grace.

Love showed this young woman that she was no longer in bondage to the chains of oppression and social evil that denied her humanity and made her feel that the only worth she could offer was the going price for her priceless body and soul.

As we sojourn through our lives, I pray that we remember with Lori that we don't have to remain in bondage to fear and cynicism. We are heirs apparent to childlike wonder, idealism, and hope.

God, thank you for your redemption and adoption. What a priceless gift! Amen.

 New beginnings fill our lives—some long-awaited, some-carefully planned. Others emerge from the routine of ordinary life like in today's reading.

A look at the calendar tells Mary and Joseph that the time has come for Mary's purification and for Jesus' presentation. Mary and Joseph follow the requirements of Mosaic law by journeying to Jerusalem and offering the prescribed sacrifice. This event is not exceptional. Other firstborn males have been designated as holy in this customary fashion.

But something extraordinary flows from this widely practiced ritual. Simeon and Anna testify to the birth of something new. They witness a departure from the usual presentation of a child. Simeon and Anna see a boy unlike other boys; they see a light for revelation, a redeemer. Two lessons follow from this story of good news. The first: Simeon's faithfulness provides the extraordinary moment of revelation. That signals a call to us to keep going to the sanctuary, to continue praying, to keep our eyes and ears open for divine moments of revelation. I have discovered that they usually come as a surprise even though I have been praying for them for years.

The second lesson: Beyond seeking the usual prescribed path and expecting nothing new, the extraordinary comes from the ordinary. We remember to keep praying for fresh insights, new understandings and a deepening of our faith. Simeon's song of praise that now he can depart in peace beautifully reassures those of us seeking new life in the old temples. It reminds us to keep searching for God's revelations and the truth that dwells in us.

Gracious and loving God, open us to your renewing work in our lives. May we relax the clenched fists that hold tight to what is known and comfortable and open welcoming arms to new revelations that come at unexpected times. Amen.

It is audacious and prophetic to declare peace in hard times. Like the feet of the messenger in this passage, we find that the miracle of the peace given to us is born in the brokenness around and in us. To a city and people in disarray, Isaiah speaks peace and salvation. The gospel we share with the world invites others to live into a hope that never dies and acknowledges a kingdom that will one day be revealed. The prophet proclaims it faithfully and poetically, "All the ends of the earth shall see."

Isaiah supports us in this season when we celebrate peace in the midst of a violent world. The Lord's approach encourages us and the sentinels to "sing for joy," for we see the promise of peace and hope even when mired in our troubles. God comes, comforts, redeems, and liberates.

Over ten years ago, I worked on building what is now the Magdalene home on Lena Street. Amidst dirt, dust, and the pain of giving life to a dream, a red ribbon appeared behind the broken stucco and drew my eyes to it. Inspired and moved to tears by my memories of Christmas and this humble sign of the season—the only sign the house had to offer—I took that ribbon with me in my spirit. The next day, the ribbon was gone, but I realized that it had a permanent home within me, as does every moment in which the kingdom of God breaks through.

If only for a moment, I take comfort. Then, moved to invite others to protest life's uncertainty with me, I take a deep breath and allow my body to be still. This is by no means a solution to every evil we confront as actively engaged people of faith in a fallen world, but God appearing in plain sight is not something I can ignore.

Love is the rule of the universe, sown in the seeds of creation and awakened time and time again by the presence of this season's joys. May these oracles reach a critical mass that results in the revelation of God's salvation to the ends of the earth.

Sing to the Lord a new song because of the marvelous things God has done. God has vindicated the people. The psalmist calls the whole earth to make a joyful noise in celebration of God's steadfast love and faithfulness.

I have been married to a songwriter for more than twenty-five years. One quality I honor in him more than any other is his faithfulness in creating. He never doubts a new song will come. Each morning, with a cup of coffee and the sun rising in pale lavender bands, he sits at his baby grand and begins creating melodies. Even as I write this piece, I can hear waves of music maybe never heard by another soul in this world as he composes in a different room.

The psalmist understands that God is coming to set matters right. God's ongoing work in creation, in you and me, is joyful. It opens up new possibilities for others, for communities, and for ourselves. We embrace these new beginnings, welcoming them as new revelations of God's steadfast love.

Every beginning in our lives has an ending. Each ending marks a new beginning. Always we begin anew with confidence that we will not be alone. There are countless new melodies and endless new mornings. We live in faith that God meets us in all of our futures. Wherever life leads us, God is with us

We sing a new song in praise of what has happened, what is happening, and in anticipation of what is yet to come. We embrace new songs for the transformations we witness in individuals and communities. We rejoice in each new day that God has made and the promise of renewal and rebirth that comes with those days.

God, our Creator and Sustainer, continue to be with us. We live in gratitude for and in reliance on your presence. Help us know that you are the Rock, the core of permanence when all else falls away. Amen.

FIRST SUNDAY AFTER CHRISTMAS

As a servant to a faith community, I have the privilege of presiding at the sacraments that commemorate events across the span of life. I am there for baptisms, confirmations, weddings, and funerals. As more time passes, it feels like these rites live closer and closer together. Years merge together, and memories grow crowded like the growing number of framed pictures on my mantel that try to hold all the moments in one place. Each of these moments maintains its place as both distinct and interconnected, yet this vision in Hebrews of the circle of all of life captures my imagination more. It reminds me that all the sacraments are part of one healing sacrament, born in the vision where God's throne is forever. All our journeys begin and end with God, and the sacraments remind us of the consummation of love's highest order to return to our Creator, who is eternal.

Long ago, on the first morning after God declared creation to be good, the beacon of humanity's redemption was a speck in the eye of the Creator. It was already formed and simply waiting to be brought forth. In God's timing, there is no beginning and no ending. There is only the eternal now. Jesus—both exalted one and atonement, heir of all and present at creation, the beginning and the end. Such an idea is prescient to us on the final day of December.

As we reach the end of another year, I can feel the pulse of a new year starting to beat. Such a rhythm resounds in the vein of God's hands, where the temporal and eternal meet in a holy kiss.

May God open our eyes to what lies before us, extend us the grace to bless what lies behind us, and then welcome us into the now of Christ's reign.

The Revised Common Lectionary* for 2017
Year A – Advent / Christmas Year B
(Disciplines Edition)

January 1
NEW YEAR'S DAY
Ecclesiastes 3:1-13
Psalm 8
Revelation 21:1-6a
Matthew 25:31-46

January 2–8
BAPTISM OF THE LORD
Isaiah 42:1-9
Psalm 29
Acts 10:34-43
Matthew 3:13-17

> **January 6**
> EPIPHANY
> *(may be used on January 8)*
> Isaiah 60:1-6
> Psalm 72:1-7, 10-14
> Ephesians 3:1-12
> Matthew 2:1-12

January 9–15
Isaiah 49:1-7
Psalm 40:1-11
1 Corinthians 1:1-9
John 1:29-42

January 16–22
Isaiah 9:1-4
Psalm 27:1, 4-9
1 Corinthians 1:10-18
Matthew 4:12-23

January 23–29
Micah 6:1-8
Psalm 15
1 Corinthians 1:18-31
Matthew 5:1-12

January 30–February 5
Isaiah 58:1-12
Psalm 112:1-10
1 Corinthians 2:1-16
Matthew 5:13-20

February 6–12
Deuteronomy 30:15-20
Psalm 119:1-8
1 Corinthians 3:1-9
Matthew 5:21-37

February 13–19
Leviticus 19:1-2, 9-18
Psalm 119:33-40
1 Corinthians 3:10-11, 16-23
Matthew 5:38-48

February 20–26
THE TRANSFIGURATION
Exodus 24:12-18
Psalm 99
2 Peter 1:16-21
Matthew 17:1-9

February 27–March 5
FIRST SUNDAY IN LENT
Genesis 2:15-17; 3:1-7
Psalm 32
Romans 5:12-19
Matthew 4:1-11

> **March 1**
> ASH WEDNESDAY
> Joel 2:1-2, 12-17
> Psalm 51:1-17
> 2 Corinthians 5:20b–6:10
> Matthew 6:1-6, 16-21

March 6–12
SECOND SUNDAY IN LENT
Genesis 12:1-4a
Psalm 121
Romans 4:1-5, 13-17
John 3:1-17 or Matthew 17:1-9

March 13–19
THIRD SUNDAY IN LENT
Exodus 17:1-7
Psalm 95
Romans 5:1-11
John 4:5-42

March 20–26
FOURTH SUNDAY IN LENT
1 Samuel 16:1-13
Psalm 23
Ephesians 5:8-14
John 9:1-41

March 27–April 2
FIFTH SUNDAY IN LENT
Ezekiel 37:1-14
Psalm 130
Romans 8:6-11
John 11:1-45

April 3–9
PALM SUNDAY
Liturgy of the Palms
Matthew 21:1-11
Psalm 118:1-2, 19-29
Liturgy of the Passion
Isaiah 50:4-9a
Psalm 31:9-16
Philippians 2:5-11
Matthew 26:14–27:66
   or Matthew 27:11-54

April 10–16
HOLY WEEK
Monday, April 10
Isaiah 42:1-9
Psalm 36:5-11
Hebrews 9:11-15
John 12:1-11
Tuesday, April 11
Isaiah 49:1-7
Psalm 71:1-14
1 Corinthians 1:18-31
John 12:20-36
Wednesday, April 12
Isaiah 50:4-9a
Psalm 70
Hebrews 12:1-3
John 13:21-32
Maundy Thursday, April 13
Exodus 12:1-14
Psalm 116:1-2, 12-19
1 Corinthians 11:23-26
John 13:1-17, 31b-35
Good Friday, April 14
Isaiah 52:13–53:12
Psalm 22
Hebrews 10:16-25 or Hebrews 4:14-16; 5:7-9
John 18:1–19:42
Holy Saturday, April 15
Job 14:1-14
   or Lamentations 3:1-9, 19-24
Psalm 31:1-4, 15-16
1 Peter 4:1-8
Matthew 27:57-66
   or John 19:38-42

EASTER DAY, APRIL 16
Acts 10:34-43
      or Jeremiah 31:1-6
Psalm 118:1-2, 14-24
Colossians 3:1-4
      or Acts 10:34-43
John 20:1-18
      or Matthew 28:1-10

April 17–23
Acts 2:14a, 22-32
Psalm 16
1 Peter 1:3-9
John 20:19-31

April 24–30
Acts 2:14a, 36-41
Psalm 116:1-4, 12-19
1 Peter 1:17-23
Luke 24:13-35

May 1–7
Acts 2:42-47
Psalm 23
1 Peter 2:19-25
John 10:1-10

May 8–14
Acts 7:55-60
Psalm 31:1-5, 15-16
1 Peter 2:2-10
John 14:1-14

May 15–21
Acts 17:22-31
Psalm 66:8-20
1 Peter 3:13-22
John 14:15-21

May 22–28
Acts 1:6-14
Psalm 68:1-10, 32-35
1 Peter 4:12-14; 5:6-11
John 17:1-11

ASCENSION DAY–MAY 25
(*may be used May 28*)
Acts 1:1-11
Psalm 47 or Psalm 93
Ephesians 1:15-23
Luke 24:44-53

May 29–June 4
PENTECOST
Psalm 104:24-34, 35b
Acts 2:1-21
      or Numbers 11:24-30
1 Corinthians 12:3b-13
John 20:19-23
      or John 7:37-39

June 5–11
TRINITY SUNDAY
Genesis 1:1–2:4a
Psalm 8
2 Corinthians 13:11-13
Matthew 28:16-20

June 12–18
Genesis 18:1-15; 21:1-7
Psalm 100
Romans 5:1-8
Matthew 9:35–10:23

June 19–25
Genesis 21:8-21
Psalm 86:1-10, 16-17
Romans 6:1b-11
Matthew 10:24-39

June 26–July 2
Genesis 22:1-14
Psalm 13
Romans 6:12-23
Matthew 10:40-42

July 3–9
Genesis 24:34-38, 42-49, 58-67
Psalm 45:10-17 or Song of Solomon 2:8-13
Romans 7:15-25a
Matthew 11:16-19, 25-30

July 10–16
Genesis 25:19-34
Psalm 119:105-112
        or Isaiah 55:10-13
Romans 8:1-11
Matthew 13:1-9, 18-23

July 17–23
Genesis 28:10-19a
Psalm 139:1-12, 23-24
Romans 8:12-25
Matthew 13:24-30, 36-43

July 24–30
Genesis 29:15-28
Psalm 105:1-11, 45b
Romans 8:26-39
Matthew 13:31-33, 44-52

July 3–August 6
Genesis 32:22-31
Psalm 17:1-7, 15
Romans 9:1-5
Matthew 14:13-21

August 7–13
Genesis 37:1-4, 12-28
Psalm 105:1-6, 16-22, 45b
Romans 10:5-15
Matthew 14:22-33

August 14–20
Genesis 45:1-15
Psalm 133
Romans 11:1-2a, 29-32
Matthew 15:10-28

August 21–27
Exodus 1:8-2:10
Psalm 124
Romans 12:1-8
Matthew 16:13-20

August 28–September 3
Exodus 3:1-15
Psalm 105:1-6, 23-26, 45c
Romans 12:9-21
Matthew 16:21-28

September 4–10
Exodus 12:1-14
Psalm 149
Romans 13:8-14
Matthew 18:15-20

September 11–17
Exodus 14:19-31
Psalm 114 or
        Exodus 15:1b-11, 20-21
Romans 14:1-12
Matthew 18:21-35

September 18–24
Exodus 16:2-15
Psalm 105:1-6, 37-45
Philippians 1:21-30
Matthew 20:1-16

September 25–October 1
Exodus 17:1-7
Psalm 78:1-4, 12-16
Philippians 2:1-13
Matthew 21:23-32

October 2–8
Exodus 20:1-4, 7-9, 12-20
Psalm 19
Philippians 3:4b-14
Matthew 21:33-46

October 9–15
Exodus 32:1-14
Psalm 106:1-6, 19-23
Philippians 4:1-9
Matthew 22:1-14

October 9
THANKSGIVING DAY CANADA
Deuteronomy 8:7-18
Psalm 65
2 Corinthians 9:6-15
Luke 17:11-19

October 16–22
Exodus 33:12-23
Psalm 99
1 Thessalonians 1:1-10
Matthew 22:15-22

October 23–29
Deuteronomy 34:1-12
Psalm 90:1-6, 13-17
1 Thessalonians 2:1-8
Matthew 22:34-46

October 30–November 5
Joshua 3:7-17
Psalm 107:1-7, 33-37
1 Thessalonians 2:9-13
Matthew 23:1-12

November 1
ALL SAINTS DAY
(*may be used November 5*)
Revelation 7:9-17
Psalm 34:1-10, 22
1 John 3:1-3
Matthew 5:1-12

November 6–12
Joshua 24:1-3a, 14-25
Psalm 78:1-7
1 Thessalonians 4:13-18
Matthew 25:1-13

November 13–19
Judges 4:1-7
Psalm 123 or Zephaniah 1:7, 12-18
1 Thessalonians 5:1-11
Matthew 25:14-30

November 17-23
REIGN OF CHRIST SUNDAY
Ezekiel 34:11-16, 20-24
Psalm 100
Ephesians 1:15-23
Matthew 25:31-46

November 23
THANKSGIVING DAY, USA
Deuteronomy 8:7-18
Psalm 65
2 Corinthians 9:6-15
Luke 17:11-19

November 27–December 3
FIRST SUNDAY OF ADVENT
Isaiah 64:1-9
Psalm 80:1-7, 17-19
1 Corinthians 1:3-9
Mark 13:24-37

December 4–10
SECOND SUNDAY OF ADVENT
Isaiah 40:1-11
Psalm 85:1-2, 8-13
2 Peter 3:8-15a
Mark 1:1-8

December 11–17
THIRD SUNDAY OF ADVENT
Isaiah 61:1-4, 8-11
Psalm 126
1 Thessalonians 5:16-24
John 1:6-8, 19-28

December 18–24
FOURTH SUNDAY OF ADVENT
2 Samuel 7:1-11, 16
Luke 1:47-55
Romans 16:25-27
Luke 1:26-38

December 24
CHRISTMAS EVE
Isaiah 9:2-7
Psalm 96
Titus 2:11-14
Luke 2:1-20

December 25–31
FIRST SUNDAY AFTER CHRISTMAS
(*Optional texts*)
Isaiah 61:10–62:3
Psalm 148
Galatians 4:4-7
Luke 2:22-40

December 25
CHRISTMAS DAY
Isaiah 52:7-10
Psalm 98
Hebrews 1:1-12
John 1:1-14

A Guide to Daily Prayer

These prayers imply worship time with a group; feel free to adapt the plural pronouns for personal use.

MORNING PRAYER

"In the morning, O LORD, you hear my voice;
   in the morning I lay my requests before you
   and wait in expectation."
                                    —Psalm 5:3

Gathering and Silence

Call to Praise and Prayer
   God said: Let there be light; and there was light.
   And God saw that the light was good.

Psalm 63:2-6

   God, my God, you I crave;
   my soul thirsts for you,
   my body aches for you
   like a dry and weary land.
      Let me gaze on you in your temple:
      a Vision of strength and glory
      Your love is better than life,
      my speech is full of praise.
      I give you a lifetime of worship,
      my hands raised in your name.
      I feast at a rich table
      my lips sing of your glory.

Prayer of Thanksgiving

We praise you with joy, loving God, for your grace is better than life itself. You have sustained us through the darkness: and you bless us with life in this new day. In the shadow of your wings we sing for joy and bless your holy name. Amen.

Scripture Reading

Silence

Prayers of the People

The Lord's Prayer (see Midday Prayer for text)

Blessing

May the light of your mercy shine brightly on all who walk in your presence today, O Lord.

MIDDAY PRAYER

"I will extol the LORD at all times;
God's praise will always be on my lips."
—Psalm 34:1

Gathering and Silence

Call to Praise and Prayer

O LORD, my Savior, teach me your ways.
My hope is in you all day long.

Prayer of Thanksgiving

God of mercy, we acknowledge this midday pause
of refreshment as one of your many generous gifts.
Look kindly upon our work this day; may it be made
perfect in your time. May our purpose and prayers
be pleasing to you. This we ask through Christ our
Lord. Amen.

Scripture Reading

Silence

Prayers of the People

The Lord's Prayer (ecumenical text)
Our Father in heaven,
hallowed be your name,
your kingdom come,
your will be done,
on earth as in heaven.
Give us today our daily bread.

Forgive us our sins as we forgive
    those who sin against us.
Save us from the time of trial,
    and deliver us from evil.
For the kingdom, the power, and the glory
    are yours, now and forever. Amen.

Blessing

Strong is the love embracing us, faithful the Lord from morning to night.

EVENING PRAYER

"My soul finds rest in God alone;
my salvation comes from God."
—Psalm 62:1

Gathering and Silence

Call to Praise and Prayer

From the rising of the sun to its setting,
let the name of the LORD be praised.

Psalm 134

Bless the Lord,
all who serve in God's house,
who stand watch
throughout the night.

Lift up your hands
in the holy place
and bless the Lord.

And may God,
the maker of earth and sky,
bless you from Zion.

Prayer of Thanksgiving

Sovereign God, You have been our help during the day and you promise to be with us at night. Receive this prayer as a sign of our trust in you. Save us from all evil, keep us from all harm, and guide us in your way. We belong to you, Lord. Protect us by the power of your name, in Jesus Christ we pray. Amen.

Scripture Reading

Silence

Prayers of the People

The Lord's Prayer (see Midday Prayer for text)

Blessing

> May your unfailing love rest upon us, O LORD,
> even as we hope in you.

This Guide to Daily Prayer was compiled from scripture and other resources by Rueben P. Job and then adapted by the Pathways Center for Spiritual Leadership while under the direction of Marjorie J. Thompson.